Marketing in Japan

About the author

Few Westerners have as thorough a background in different areas of Japanese trade as Ian Melville. In addition to several years of exporting to Japan, Melville teaches Japanese business to both foreigners and Japanese students. He lectures in Japanese business and the economy at Tokyo's Sophia University, he is completing a PhD in Japanese business at Tokyo University, and also lectures at MITI's Institute of Developing Economies – all extremely prestigious institutions. He has also taught Japanese business and history for Richmond College in Shizuoka, Japan.

Originally from New Zealand, Melville resides in Tokyo.

Marketing in Japan

Ian Melville

BUTTERWORTH
HEINEMANN

OXFORD AUCKLAND BOSTON JOHANNESBURG MELBOURNE NEW DELHI

Butterworth-Heinemann
Linacre House, Jordan Hill, Oxford OX2 8DP
225 Wildwood Avenue, Woburn, MA 01801-2041
A division of Reed Educational and Professional Publishing Ltd

℞ A member of the Reed Elsevier plc group

First published 1999
Reprinted 2000

© Ian Melville 1999

British Library Cataloguing in Publication Data
A catalogue record for this book is available from the British Library

ISBN 0 7506 4145 2

Composition by Genesis Typesetting, Rochester, Kent
Printed and bound in Great Britain by
Biddles Ltd, www.biddles.co.uk

FOR EVERY TITLE THAT WE PUBLISH, BUTTERWORTH-HEINEMANN
WILL PAY FOR BTCV TO PLANT AND CARE FOR A TREE.

Contents

Foreword

Over the past year or so I have given a talk whose main theme appears perfectly obvious to Japanese listeners but which somehow seems to shock Western business people. My point, simply put, is that there has never been a better time for foreign companies to set up a business in Japan than right now.

I can see how this might sound odd to some. The world media have been focusing on the problems in the Japanese economy, failures of big banks and brokers, the ongoing recession, and so on. Company failures always make good headlines. But this approach misses a key point: when the world's second biggest consumer market stumbles for the first time in a quarter of a century, it's time for hundreds of Western firms large and small to take advantage of it.

Instead of shaking their heads about the weakness of the economy, Western companies should be looking at the golden opportunities the recession presents. The problems in the banking sector mean that Japanese companies are short of funds. They can't maintain either their R&D or capital investment levels; not only can't they expand, but many big companies nationwide are contracting, laying off staff, trimming advertising expenses, and searching for ways to cut costs. More interesting to us, Japanese companies are tying up with foreign firms at an unprecedented pace. Why? Because they need new products, new ideas, and new approaches to do their business in a changing environment.

Part of that changing environment is the consumer, who now demands greater variety and lower prices, two things Japanese producers have never been famous for delivering. And part of that new environment is the government, which, due to pressures both from within and without, is starting to deconstruct some of its fortress of regulations.

In short, it is precisely because of the problems in the Japanese economy that the timing could not be better to stake a claim in this market. The reality is:

1 If you're going to be a world-class player in any big business, you've got to be in Japan.
2 If you're a smaller business and can only focus on a few markets with huge potential, you've got to be in Japan.
3 If you decide to get into the Japanese market, you have two choices: you can do it when your competitors are strong and when office start-up costs are high, or you can look for an opening when potential rivals are weak and rents and salaries are low. That means right now.

Do not misunderstand me: I am not saying that setting up your business in Japan will be easy or that making profits is a foregone conclusion. Every market requires a serious commitment of time, effort, and capital, and it's safe to say that Japan requires a greater commitment than other major markets. To those who ask, 'Is it worth that extra effort?' I can only answer: 'Look at the numbers.'

The Bank of Japan estimates that domestic personal financial assets amount to roughly ¥1200 trillion. Anyone thinking of doing business in Japan should write that number on the back of their hand and look at it every day . . . simply because it will remind you that Japan's personal savings is the biggest pot of gold in the world, and earning even a tiny fraction of it will repay your investment a dozen times over.

Since Japanese are habitual savers, you can assume that 99 per cent of those savings will continue to be held for long-term goals. I usually advise people to consider only one-quarter of 1 per cent as their mental target – that's a healthy foundation for a sales plan.

How much does that one-quarter of 1 per cent come to? About ¥3,000,000,000,000, or roughly US$22 billion. And remember, that means $22 billion of ready cash just sitting in banks, money not earmarked for retirement, health care, living expenses, etc. No one is saving that quarter of a per cent for a rainy day, and at less than 1 per cent bank interest per annum, no one thinks of it as an investment. Japanese people young and old would be willing to spend that money (and more) if the right opportunity were to come along. In fact, not only is the Japanese government priming consumption, but Japanese producers are under-exploiting several categories of consumer. This is your market – if you've got the right product, if you've got the right strategy, and most of all, if you've done your homework.

And there's the problem.

Every company that comes into Japan, big or small, American, British, German, Australian, or whatever, is convinced that it has something terrific to sell. Yet the majority of them go home a few years later, richer only in experience. Why do so many fail? Because they don't study this market. They don't learn the basics of how to survive and how to succeed in Japan. They don't learn the lessons of the past and they don't adapt to a changing environment.

Part of the problem lies in the lack of good material available about what really goes on inside the Japanese market. Yes, there have been several books in English to instruct foreign business people about how to get along with those inscrutable Japanese. Some of these have been worthwhile, but many are simply a waste of time (one of the most popular tomes a few years back was written by an 'expert' who had never set foot in Japan).

What has been needed for a long time is a clear, well-written book that explains in simple language what any intelligent person needs to know to do business here. And this is exactly what Ian Melville has given us. Melville is an all too rare writer on an important subject which he knows intimately. He began with a hands-on business background, not with some giant multinational (the kind of company that is already well established in Japan or can set up with relative ease if it wishes to); instead, Melville worked as an independent, learning first-hand the right ways to export to Japan, to set up a company, interact with the distribution system, and market his products. After many years he turned to academia (he lectures in the Economics Department of Tokyo's prestigious Sophia University, among other positions) to analyse and draw conclusions from all this experience. I doubt there is any other Westerner who understands trading with Japan from the inside out, who understands the perspective of the small-business executive, and who has had the time and desire to collect and explain his thoughts on the subject.

Melville is, to use a horribly over-taxed term, unique, and his insights will prove extremely useful to any serious reader. There is no doubt in my mind that this book will serve as a primary resource for thousands of business people in the coming years as they approach the world's most challenging, but potentially most rewarding market.

David W. Russell
Tokyo

Preface

Several years ago, while marketing New Zealand products in Japan, I came to the conclusion that it was quality – as the Japanese interpreted it – that was, or should be seen as, the main concern for foreigners selling here. When I discussed this, amongst other issues, with our trade experts, what I found was that they had a good knowledge of how trade *should* work but a rather surprising lack of knowledge of how Japan really does work. It struck me that if our trade 'experts' don't understand our second biggest export market, what does that imply for our economy? No retailer or wholesaler would know so little about the character and needs of its major customers: Japan is an important market, one we need to know a good deal more about.

I know now, if I couldn't have guessed then, that both the lack of knowledge and other problems that inevitably accompany dealing with Japan don't merely apply to New Zealand. That small country is more like a microcosm; in it can be seen the same difficulties that occur everywhere. In Japan I've not only seen exactly the same problems reappear amongst people trying to export from different parts of the globe, but I have taught foreigners from various areas about business and have come to realize that when they study international business outside of Japan they learn little or nothing about Japanese business. Not that this is anyone's fault as such. It is a result of Japanese business historically being drastically under-studied – both by the Japanese and by foreigners. It is also the result of Japanese business being sufficiently outside the imagination of most foreigners: we can draw upon our own general business sense to understand how to navigate through other Western business environments, but we need much more information to understand business in Japan.

Marketing Japanese-style poses its own problems. It involves few research or marketing rules, at least that you could write down in a list, and of the rules that exist, some run counter to intuition – such as the absence of market research. It makes a 'how to' book more interesting – and certainly more challenging.

The content of this book is a product of years of teaching foreigners in Japan (both formally and informally) about how to succeed in their business dealings with the Japanese. In addition, there are the years I spent dealing with both foreigners and Japanese in the process of actually exporting and importing products. Those experiences and knowledge have been brought together in the following pages in a form that for the first time clearly and fully explains Japanese business, and marketing in Japan.

This book is aimed at big business and small; it draws examples from a range of areas and comments on different types of business from different positions of power and size in the market. The one central and common feature is that it is targeted toward those who want to know how to enter and succeed in the Japanese market.

If you are already operating any kind of business venture either in Japan or with Japan, or if you hope to do so in the future, this book is for you.

Ian Melville
Tokyo

If this book doesn't answer your questions about Japanese business, or you have other comments please send them to me at: mktentry@venture.co.jp

Acknowledgements

Thanks to Ōmori Marie, through whom I was able to see and understand Japanese business.

Thanks also to Dr James Abegglen for his critical comments; Dr Hirose Kawaguchi Kazuko, of Sophia; Andō Masahiro, ex-Sanyō Securities, for his insights into the industry; Ōkawara Mami, of Sophia; Komori Keiko, author of *Direct Marketing in Japan*; Professor Robert Ballon, of Sophia; The Kichi-Do Kai; David Hughes and Stephen Walsh for a lot of input and feedback; and Simon Oliver and Hamish Ross for their resourcefulness.

Special thanks to David Russell both for his Japan expertise and for agreeing to edit and write the Foreword to this book.

I'm also grateful to those unsung contributors who gave me their time and information but couldn't – because of fear for their jobs and well-being – be identified. In addition, thanks to the many people who have simply given me their views and other information over the years.

Terminology

The words *foreigners* and *Westerners* are used, often interchangeably. Foreigners living in Japan use the word to describe themselves, often with tongue-in-cheek, since no matter how comfortable we are, it reminds us that we remain outsiders in Japan. Also, in cases where I've been unable to generalize to all non-Japanese I've used Westerners as a narrower term.

Japanese names are written family name first.

Currency conversions are based on the rate at the time cited, or are rounded where appropriate.

In accordance with the US and French system:

Billion (bn) = 1,000,000,000
Trillion (tn) = 1,000,000,000,000
mn; bn; tn = million; billion; trillion
All dollar ($) references refer to US dollars

This book uses non-sexist language.

Abbreviations

ACCJ	American Chamber of Commerce in Japan
BIS	Bank for International Settlements (Basel, Switzerland)
bn	Billion (1,000,000,000)
BOJ	Bank of Japan (also called *the central bank*)
DKB	Dai-Ichi Kangyō Bank
DM	Direct marketing
EU	European Union
FDI	Foreign direct investment (into or out of Japan, as specified)
FTC	Fair Trade Commission ('Watchdog' for the Antimonopoly Law)
GDP	Gross domestic product
GHQ	Post-World War II Occupation headquarters
IBJ	Industrial Bank of Japan
ISO	International Organization for Standardization
JADMA	The Japan Direct Marketing Association
JETRO	Japan External Trade Organization (marketing wing of MITI)
JV	Joint venture
KK	Kabushiki Kaisha (joint-stock company)
MITI	(pronounced *meaty*) Ministry of International Trade and Industry
mn	Million (1,000,000)
MO	Mail-order
MOF	(pronounced *mof*) Ministry of Finance
NHK	Japan Broadcasting Corporation (Nippon Hōsō Kyōkai)
ODA	Official Development Assistance (foreign aid)
PM	Prime Minister
POS	Point of sale, restocking system
QC	Quality control
SII	Structural Impediment Initiative Talks, trade talks held between the US–Japan from 1989
SMEs	Small and medium sized enterprises
tn	Trillion (1,000,000,000,000)
TOPIX	Tokyo Stock Price Index, Japan's second stock exchange index
TSE	Tokyo Stock Exchange
YK	Yūgen Gaisha (limited liability company)

Terms used

Amakudari   Descent from 'bureaucratic heaven' to work in the private sector.

Antimonopoly Law   Introduced by GHQ in 1947. It outlawed holding companies, cartels and trusts.

Bussan   Indicates trader, but used alone refers to Mitsui Bussan (trading company).

Dangō   Collusive activity in the construction industry with the purpose of pre-arranging (rigging) bids.

Dual economy   As used in Japan, the idea that there is a wealthy strata of companies that, at various points, and to various degrees in history, has been distinct from the majority of smaller firms. The division is accentuated, in Japan, by privileges available to large firms which allow the big to get bigger.

Edo (Edo period)   Edo period (also called Tokugawa period) from either (Battle of Sekigahara) 1600 or (initiation of Tokugawa shōgunate) 1603–1868. Edo was renamed Tokyo (*Tōkyō*), meaning East Capital (vs. Kyōto = Capital City) after the Meiji Emperor moved there.

Endaka (the crisis of) high yen.

Gyōsei shidō   'Administrative guidance'.

Japan Incorporated   The idea, or criticism that Japan is like a ship where public and private institutions function together to drive Japan rather than operate independently and competitively.

Jinmyaku   One's (*old boy*) network of associates, important in Japan for social and business relations.

Kabu   Stock or share.

Kabushiki Kaisha (KK)   Company registered on the stock market (the correct form is 'kabushiki gaisha').

Kaisha   Company.

Kaizen   Product improvement through 'nervous' attention to detail.

Kanji   Chinese written characters.

Keiretsu   A 'group' of cooperating companies.

Meiji period   1868–1912; representing the end of Tokugawa rule, and the restoration of the (Meiji) Emperor.

Meishi   Business card.

Nikkeiren   Japan Federation of Employers' Associations.

Nomination   Combination of nomi = to drink (alcohol) and communication, referring to the need for informal business communication after hours, at the pub.

Occupation, the   Post-World War II allied forces in Japan from 14 August 1945–28 April 1952.

Shōgunate   Government associated with rule under the shōgun; in Japanese it is called the bakfu.

Shōkai-sha   Person who introduces or mediates a relationship.

Shōji   Applied as a suffix to such companies as Mitsubishi and Sumitomo trading companies, it indicates trader. Used alone, it refers to Mitsubishi Shōji.

Sumishō   Shorthand for Sumitomo Shōji.

Sōgō shōsha   Literally general + trading (company). The name normally given to the large companies that grew as the trading arms of the zaibatsu, and continue to function as trading companies associated with keiretsu groups.

Tegata   Promissory note, for delayed payment in a business transaction.

Tokugawa   Family name of the third and final shōgunal dynasty, of 15 shōguns, lasting from 1603 until 1868.

Tonya   Wholesaler.

Yakuza   Japanese mafia.

Yoroshiku   Please 'take care of' or look after my interests, thank you.

Yūgen gaisha (YK)   Limited liability company.

Zaibatsu   Family-centred 'conglomerate' of companies, dissolved after World War II.

Introduction

Japan, a changing market

Virtually all of those who have tried to get into the Japanese market have found it extremely difficult to enter. Foreign complaints about dealing with a nation that was a prolific exporter but was reluctant to import had slow and limited effect. The most active change emerged in the 1990s as the recession-battered economy struggled to regain its footing. Trade barriers had always existed to guard against the risk of destabilizing a steadily growing economy. Accordingly, the pinch of an economy showing the wounds of recession gave support to calls for deregulation and internationalization, weakening the case of those who preferred to 'play it safe'. Amid some turbulence, the pace of change began to quicken.

A coveted economy

Throughout and despite the recession of the 1990s, Japan maintained the world's second highest GDP – equal to about two-thirds that of the US. And of all of Asia's combined GDP, about two-thirds has been generated by Japan alone. No nation outside the US has been able to, or will, catch Japan in the foreseeable future. Despite having to import its raw materials, Japan remained world leader in the production of cars, ships, robots and machine tools, and was the world's most generous donor of 'official development assistance' (ODA). Moreover, Japanese purchases of US bonds have continued to support the US economy, and thereby the international economy as well.

Japan's sōgō shōsha (general traders), entering an era of decline in demand for their traditional services, redefined themselves, pumping billions of dollars into economies within Asia, as well as making heavy investments in telecommunications. Japan maintains a strong international trade surplus which occasionally threatens to erupt. It has received a great deal of bad press for its failing economy – not least of all from the self-critical Japanese themselves – but it has remained an amazingly powerful economy despite a decade of stagnation.

Japan has been an attractive destination for foreign business, and progressive businesses are aware that they need a presence there. There has been a steady flow of familiar names into Japan; music retailers such as Tower Records, Virgin Megastores and HMV have successfully entered. In clothing/direct marketing, L.L. Bean, Eddie Bauer, Land's End, and in business supplies, Kinko's, Office Max and Office Depot have both entered and succeeded – and these represent just a few sectors. Furthermore, these are examples of firms that have jumped to the front of the queue in that they bring their products all the way to the Japanese consumer. This has traditionally been very difficult to accomplish: many businesses have had to work through a Japanese trader, being allowed only partial involvement in the sales chain.

But still, it is easy to cite companies that have successfully entered the Japanese market after the fact. The reality is much more complex. There have been failures amongst a lot of good firms. Success is not just based on perseverance and time – though these are of course factors. It is also important for foreign businesses to understand the Japanese business environment in detail. Entry into Japan should be based on a realistic understanding of business-related factors; it is outdated to rely on faith in one's products and determination.

Japanese business does have weak points and these in particular constitute areas that foreign businesses can take advantage of, especially in a deregulating environment. They are weaknesses that exist or are exaggerated by the fact that much of Japanese industry has been protected in one way or another from competition. Finance is a case in point. Since World War II the finance industry has been coddled and protected by the Ministry of Finance in order to maintain stability within the economy. The result was an inefficient financial system, which itself contributed to the financial mess that followed the collapse of the 'bubble economy' of the late 1980s. The system entered a period of deregulation in the latter 1990s. And as Japanese financial institutions tried to pick themselves up, foreign institutions poured in to take advantage of the opening market. Agriculture is another example. In 1991 quotas were relaxed on the import of beef and oranges. By 1993 imports resulted in the retail price of pure orange juice being halved.

In computer software, countries including the US, India and Singapore trade favourably with Japan, which imports about 20 times more than it exports. Traditionally, Japan has identified and tackled industries it considers important, but it has problems with computer software, as well as with other forms of creative development. These areas are providing niche entry opportunities, especially for small foreign companies.

Some of the walls that have protected Japan against foreign entry have been crumbling away – some faster than others. This has made Japan more accessible to foreign business. But there is still a long way to go. By 1998 only about 7 per cent of Japan's GDP was related to imports, one of the few countries with a figure in single digits and the lowest figure amongst industrialized nations. With such a high GDP and a deregulating economy, this constitutes a huge potential, which some foreign firms have seen materialize.

An appealing market

It is still difficult to sell in Japan. In the following pages we will look at how, at the dawn of the twenty-first century, it is possible to enter that market.

To quote an American Chamber of Commerce/Council of the European Business Community study on the reasons firms are entering Japan:

- 'More than any other factor, Japanese consumers are beginning to prise the market open to access competitively priced, high-quality goods regardless of country of origin.'
- 'The time frame to gain success in Japan will continue to decrease as the economy deregulates and otherwise liberalizes.'[1]

---

[1] *Japan in Revolution, An Assessment of Investment Performance by Foreign Firms in Japan*, ACCJ, The Council of the European Business Community and A. T. Kearney, Inc., 1995, p. 43.

Japanese firms are concerned about foreign companies coming into the market. Research by MITI found that 50 per cent of both large and small Japanese firms believe that their future international competition will not result from their efforts to set up shop overseas, or from their customers buying from overseas – these accounted for a relatively low share of their perceived threat – rather, they are concerned about competition from an influx of foreign companies coming into Japan.[2]

Maker of an economic miracle

Before looking at how to do business in Japan today it is important to understand the roots of the Japanese 'economic miracle', simply because Japan's economic, political and social background were important in setting the stage for the business activity that continues today. Though the post-World War II period is often cited as the phase in which Japan's economy flourished, it is important to understand that Japan's business success is not just a product of 'post-World War II democracy', but a product of more fundamental and enduring factors.

Even before World War II, in certain areas Japan's productivity accelerated beyond that of other nations. By the end of the 1890s it was producing three-quarters of the world's raw silk. Cotton fabric became the next major export and, aided by the invention of Toyoda's automatic loom, by 1932 Japan had become the world's leading cotton goods producer, decimating the British weaving trade in the process. Toyoda's loom-making company became the foundation of another machinery maker that emerged just a year later in 1933, a firm that came to be known as Toyota Motor Company.

Japan was also strong in shipping, steel production and shipbuilding. By the early 1880s, within just 30 years of resuming foreign trade, Japan had reclaimed surrounding Asian shipping routes at the expense of established US and British firms. By the mid-1930s it had matched Western shipbuilding and aircraft technology; and despite the immense destruction of the war, by 1956 it had picked itself up again to become the world's leading shipbuilder – a position it has held virtually uninterrupted ever since. Despite its lack of resources, by 1943 Japan was producing roughly the equivalent of 10 per cent of America's steel output, and after World War II it became both the world's largest steel exporter and second largest producer of crude steel.

My purpose is to demolish the myth that Japanese enthusiasm and the care Japan was given by the US after World War II was what made the Japanese miracle, and to get the reader to look more deeply at what makes Japan tick in the way it does. What Japan has is more historical and deeply ingrained. The logical conclusion is that Japan's ability to perform won't disappear simply by taking away those post-World War II conditions, and this is important for the foreign businessperson targeting the Japanese market for the long term.

Furthermore, it is necessary to look at Japan's business roots in order to more fully understand its current business behaviour – people routinely misunderstand Japan because they lack this breadth of knowledge.

The first two parts of the book deal with just that – an overview of important events and concepts in Japanese business. Then, in the third and largest section, we get fully into the Japanese market. There I have assumed that the reader is a seller – anyone can buy from the Japanese but foreigners come unstuck in trying to sell to them.

---

[2] *Small Business in Japan*, MITI, 1997, p. 110.

Part One

Essential background

Chapter 1

Business organizations old and new

Business background

From 1600–1868 Japan was governed by the third dynasty of *shōguns*, the Tokugawa family. Perhaps most significant here is that as a result of the threat of destabilization by Western missionaries the *shōgunate* (government) expelled or killed most of the foreigners and then sealed off the nation to virtually any transit in or out. Also significant is that the Japanese then developed their own unique types of social and business practices – the legacy of which remains evident in business today. The prohibition on entry to Japan was broken with the arrival of the American 'black ships' under Commander Matthew Perry in 1853. Perry, in a style that would become popular in America–Japan relations over the following century, delivered an ultimatum: he would give the Japanese one year to reconsider their no-trade policy; if they refused, America would use force to pry the country open. At gunpoint, the Japanese agreed to grant access to the foreigners, a situation that at the same time signified the end of *shōgunal* rule.

Once introduced to the idea of Western industrialization, progressive elements in the government began to invest in industries they thought were essential for national development. These included paper, textiles (silk and cotton), glass, munitions and cement. The new Meiji government also invested in developing Japan's infrastructure, including rail and other communications links, and shipping. But government investments proved largely unprofitable, and in 1880, facing financial hardship, the denationalization of state-owned enterprises began. In 1881 the Minister of Finance said that the government didn't have the skills required for business. The state, he said, should be involved with 'education, armament and the police', rather than with trade and industry, since it couldn't compete in 'shrewdness, foresight, and enterprise' with people who were motivated by immediate self-interest.[1] The abdication of the state from active pursuit of commerce set the stage for the rise of the huge, family-owned business combines called *zaibatsu*.

The zaibatsu

The *zai* in *zaibatsu* means finance, the *batsu* means clique. The term was given to the Japanese corporate groupings that emerged and played a dominant role in business following the opening of Japan in the Meiji period (1868–1912). They continued to play a leading role in the Japanese economy until their dissolution at the hands of the US Occupation forces following World War II. The groupings had shared features – notably unity, wealth and power.

The *zaibatsu* were business enterprises controlled by a single or extended family. The family-owned holding company held shares, or, prior to shareholding, owned firms, or was heavily involved in related firms. The businesses involved covered a wide range of fields, and the *zaibatsu* were typically large. The Japanese *zaibatsu* form was not unique, but the number and scale of such businesses that appeared in Japan constituted a distinct phenomenon.[2] They played a useful role in Japan's industrial expansion, providing it with business structures that were well financed and had, in many cases, skilled management. They were therefore able to break new ground better than either government bodies, which lacked business acumen, or smaller businesses, which lacked scale. The glue holding the firms together, and the source of much of their power, lay in the social bonds and loyalty that tied the satellite businesses to the founding and central entity.

After World War II the *zaibatsu* were dissolved because the American Occupation decided that they had played a part in war mobilization, and that they monopolized business. The Americans wanted political and economic democracy and believed that having a group of families dominating business worked against this.[3]

After the Occupation forces left, the constituent *zaibatsu* companies drew back together. These new entities, which had had to restructure around new antimonopoly restrictions, were given the name *keiretsu*.

First, a look at the origin of the four oldest and most well-known *zaibatsu* – Sumitomo, Mitsui, Mitsubishi and Yasuda – names still common in Japanese business today.

Sumitomo

Of these four, Sumitomo is the oldest; it was founded in the early seventeenth century around a printing shop and a pharmacy. The Sumitomo family was involved in metallurgy, and began exporting copper. They also became official copper suppliers to the Tokugawa *shōgunate*. In 1690 they bought the Besshi Copper Mine, which became the family's main source of income and which continued as an important earner for Sumitomo well into the twentieth century.[4]

Mitsui

Mitsui became the wealthiest of the Tokugawa period business houses, and the largest business group prior to World War II. It was founded in 1673, though had really begun much earlier.

The Mitsui family – originally *samurai* – began commercial operations by making soy sauce and *saké*, but were not successful. They moved into pawnbroking and money lending, and eventually opened a clothing and textiles business in central Edo (pronounced *aydoe*; now Tokyo). The store was the precursor to the Mitsukoshi store – one of Japan's most prestigious department stores, and the retail operation of the Mitsui group.

Mitsubishi

Iwasaki Yatarō was a former Tosa (now Kōchi prefecture) domain *samurai* who had worked and been successful in local government. In 1871 he was able to take over two steamships and other assets when samurai territories were repatriated to the new Meiji state, and the prefecture system began. The new Meiji administration prohibited domain-run enterprises so, encouraged by other Tosa officials, Iwasaki decided to take over some of the proceeds of the dissolution himself. In 1872 the company was named Mitsukawa (three rivers) after the common Chinese character (*kawa*) in the names of three of the directors. The next year Iwasaki changed the name to Mitsubishi (three diamonds), using a combined form of his own family crest of diamond-shaped water-chestnut leaves, in the triple-point structure of the original Tosa domain clan crest, creating a close form of Mitsubishi's now characteristic logo.

In 1874 the company became Mitsubishi Steamship Company (Jōkisen Kaisha). When in 1874 the government needed to ship troops to subdue locals in Taiwan – which became a Japanese colony in 1895 – the government called on Japan's National Steamship Company

(YJK). However, it was weak and poorly run, and balked at the request. But when asked, Mitsubishi jumped at the chance. It carried out the Taiwan expedition, thereby gaining government trust and future shipping privileges. Mitsubishi thrived under government patronage, granted in part so it could challenge the shipping firms P&O (of Britain) and Pacific Mail Steamship Co. (of the USA) which were dominating Japanese domestic and international routes – routes eventually won from them by Mitsubishi.

The privatization of government industries took several years, and the prices had to be reduced in order to dispose of them. Mitsubishi benefited well from the sale. It acquired Nagasaki Shipyard, now part of Mitsubishi Heavy Industries, and it absorbed two failing banks, which became the roots of today's Tokyo–Mitsubishi Bank.

Yasuda

The least famous of Japan's four 'old *zaibatsu*', Yasuda emerged from the money-changing business of its founder, Yasuda Zenjirō, who had entered banking in 1864. He formed the Third National Bank in 1876 – three years after Mitsui co-opened Japan's First National Bank. Zenjirō was assassinated in 1921 after he refused to make a financial donation to a nationalist. Unlike the other 'big three', Yasuda continued to specialize in finance rather than trade and industry. While it had diversified, most of its other enterprises didn't survive beyond World War I. Its name remains on a narrow range of financial and insurance institutions, including Japan's oldest life insurance firm, the Yasuda Mutual Life Insurance Co., dating from the 1880s. However, the old core of the *zaibatsu*, Yasuda Bank – like other *zaibatsu* banks – was forced by the US forces after World War II to change its name. Unlike others though, it chose not to return to its old *zaibatsu* name and is still known as Fuji Bank. Today, Yasuda group companies reside in the Fuyō *keiretsu*.

Pre-World War II industrial growth and the 'new zaibatsu'

The automobile industry was amongst Japan's new start-up businesses. Kuhara Fusano-suke bought and revitalized a copper mine in Hitachi in 1905, the beginning of what became the Kuhara Mining Company, and later the Kuhara *zaibatsu*. He diversified, but speculated, getting into financial trouble in the 1920s. He lost his *zaibatsu* trading company in 1924, and left business in 1927 to enter politics. In 1928 he handed over his mining business to his brother-in-law, Aikawa Yoshisuke. Aikawa had a casting works in Kyushu, and turned the combined businesses into a holding company called Nippon Sangyō (Japan Industries), which became the biggest of the 'new *zaibatsu*'.[5]

By the 1930s the military had come to dominate the Japanese government. In 1931 the army conquered Manchuria and began industrial development of the area, for which the army needed to work with Japanese companies.

The army brass disdained the old *zaibatsu*, partly because of a *samurai* view that mercantilism was a profane activity. Among the lower ranks, the Imperial Army was also a people's army, largely made up of the poorer peasantry, many of whom couldn't find better employment elsewhere. Many soldiers came from desperate families: some farmers and townspeople were so poor that they sold their daughters into prostitution. The impoverished circumstances of the soldiers impassioned younger officers, who held in contempt politicians and the wealthy *zaibatsu*, whom they saw as collectively responsible for the nation's weakness.

Though both parties profited from it, the relationship between the military and the old *zaibatsu* was an uneasy one. It was understandable then that 'new *zaibatsu*' were favoured by the army. Nippon Sangyō management had strong ties with key people in politics and the military administration. It was given favoured treatment in Manchuria, and after 1937 was granted control over the network of industrial operations there.

Overall, it was the newer *zaibatsu* that ventured into new industries, including electrical, heavy and other machinery, and automobiles. For example, in Japan, Nippon Sangyō had been involved in vehicles and engines and in 1933 established an automobile division that would one day become a famous post-World War II firm. It formed a joint venture with another firm that in the 1910s had produced a car named DAT (from the initials of the financiers of the project: Den, Aoyama and Takeuchi). DAT had been followed in 1918 by the 'son of DAT', called Datson. In order to connote the Japanese sun symbol, in 1932 this was changed to Dat*sun*. In 1934 the venture set up in Yokohama and in the same year the firm – now Japan's number two vehicle manufacturer – used the abbreviated form of Nippon Sangyō as the formal company name of Nissan Motor Co. Ltd. Nissan continued, in more recent times, to use Datsun as its overseas moniker, though it switched to Nissan in the early 1980s.

Aikawa had brought other related companies into the Nippon Sangyō (Nissan) *zaibatsu*. One of these had been a service company for the electric machinery at the Hitachi mines. It was established in 1910 and was later to become Japan's leading electric machinery manufacturer, Hitachi Ltd. The Nissan *zaibatsu* was broken up after World War II, and today Nissan Motor Co., Hitachi and related companies share a place with old Yasuda companies in the Fuyō *keiretsu*.

Even before World War II the old *zaibatsu* had grown quite conservative, continuing to focus on finance, commerce and trade. The family members, now two or more generations removed from the founders, had lost their original pioneering spirit, they were risk-averse, and wanted to preserve their position amongst the gentry. Their cautious approach ensured stability, but it also meant they couldn't adapt to changing economic conditions. While individual *zaibatsu* industries continued to flourish, the in-house financing system provided insufficient levels of investment for the emerging industrial environment. The closed single-family structure proved inadequate and began to break down.

By the 1920s the families had already begun to relinquish control to salaried managers.[6] In 1946, when the American Occupation ordered the families to divest their shares, rather than sounding the demise of the *zaibatsu*, the edict initiated the restructuring of the conglomerates.[7]

Zaibatsu dissolution

In April 1946 the American GHQ formed the Holding Company Liquidation Commission (HCLC) to handle the dissolution of the *zaibatsu* control centres. The HCLC gradually sold off the shares of *zaibatsu* member firms over a period of years to buyers apparently glad to buy into them. Many shares went to ex-employees, to other individuals, and to banks and other businesses, but interestingly, before the end of the Occupation in 1952, 70 per cent of the shares were in the hands of about 10 per cent of the shareholders.[8] Following the Occupation, individual share ownership was increasingly replaced with ownership by financial institutions and other companies, increasing what is known as cross-shareholding – amongst friendly (*keiretsu*) firms.

The matter of dissolution is complicated in that while commonly described as the break-up of the *zaibatsu*, the focus was not only on redistributing the shares of the central holding companies of each *zaibatsu* group. The Americans also targeted some of the trading and other large businesses which had themselves become holding companies. Amongst those were Mitsui Bussan and Mitsubishi Shōji, which were not *zaibatsu per se*, but trading companies with many smaller firms under their control.

Further, GHQ wanted other areas of economic control that restricted free competition destroyed. In addition to breaking up the conglomerates, GHQ also wanted to break up specific firms that held monopolistic power. The result was the eventual break-up of 18 additional companies. Among GHQ's efforts was the break-up of Nippon Steel into its pre-merger constituent parts: Yawata Steel and Fuji Steel. The two remerged in 1970 to form (New) Nippon Steel. Hitachi had 19 of its factories spun off. Marubeni, C. Itoh (later Itōchū) and others which had merged in 1944 (to form Daiken Sangyō) were separated again in 1949.[9]

GHQ would have broken up more companies but for the growth of the Communist threat in Asia. As Washington began to worry more about leftist influences than conservative business executives, MacArthur's mandate was changed. From 1947, the American overlords became concerned with helping Japan get back on its capitalist feet, in order that it stave off any challenges from the left. Also, it was considered that the dissolution of so many companies was too drastic a move. It would damage Japan's economy, and halt economic growth. As a result, only a relatively small number of the original businesses targeted were affected.

And get back on its capitalist feet Japan did. Still, despite the new antimonopoly provisions introduced into Japanese law by the Americans, the tendency to engage in cooperative business practices kicked in again after the Occupation forces left. Following that, breaches of anti-cartel provisions were often ignored, if not initiated by the controlling government bureaucracy. Exclusionary bodies took the form of trade organizations, of *dangō* or bid-rigging groups, but the most prominent bodies were the business conglomerates referred to as *keiretsu*. Indeed, the *keiretsu* remain an important feature of the Japanese business landscape; the sales of all the firms within the six largest *keiretsu* equate to a quarter of Japan's GNP, and within the different *keiretsu* are the nation's largest general traders, the *sōgō shōsha*, which over the last century and a half have handled much of Japan's foreign (as well as domestic) trade. It is essential for foreign business people to know something of these.

The modern business context

The keiretsu

The term *keiretsu* means lineage, or a line of connection. It originally referred to what are now called the horizontal *keiretsu* (the financial or *kin'yū keiretsu*); that is, the companies centred around a common bank. After World War II large-scale business in Japan – still only decades old at the time – had developed along characteristic Japanese patterns of association. A new term was needed for the revamped industrial groupings, to replace the now tainted term *zaibatsu*.

The word *keiretsu* also came to be used for what is known as the vertical *keiretsu*. These may be divided into two basic types: manufacturing (*sangyō*) and distribution (*ryūtsū*) *keiretsu* – that is, *keiretsu* in which components move up, and those in which goods move down, respectively.[10]

Corporate ties

By the time the Occupation ended in 1952, the *zaibatsu* and other monopolistic businesses had been dissolved. But Japanese business people soon re-established the corporate links that had existed before the end of the war.

The *keiretsu* groups involve a set of relationships between companies, loosely bound together by a continuation of both business and social obligations, as well as a desire to prosper by combining resources. The tangible obligations include mutual stock ownership, and responsibility for funds and goods exchanged within the group.

Considerable debate and disagreement surrounds the relationship, or lack thereof, between the *zaibatsu* and *keiretsu*. Many people are adamant that they are completely different entities, others that the *keiretsu* are a recent form of the *zaibatsu*. It is important to clarify their similarities and differences. As a social phenomenon the *keiretsu* pattern is the same as the *zaibatsu*: corporate members came together as interdependent units. But administratively the dominant *zaibatsu* families, also banned under the Occupation, had been replaced with professional management, and holding companies had been made illegal, which meant that centralized control was not allowed. Perhaps the real mistake that has been made is to assume that there is an insidious aspect to the *keiretsu*, and that this is a legacy of the *zaibatsu*, which are sometimes associated with military build-up prior to World War II – there is no foundation to this belief.

Horizontal and vertical keiretsu

It is not uncommon for those writing or talking about *keiretsu* to confuse or just fail to differentiate horizontal from vertical types (see Figure 1.1). There are some areas of overlap, but when speaking about the *keiretsu* it's necessary to identify which you are talking about.

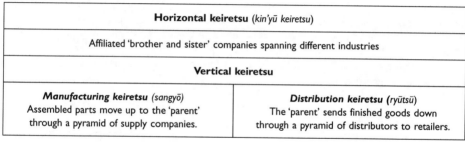

Horizontal keiretsu (*kin'yū keiretsu*)	
Affiliated 'brother and sister' companies spanning different industries	
Vertical keiretsu	
Manufacturing keiretsu (*sangyō*) Assembled parts move up to the 'parent' through a pyramid of supply companies.	**Distribution keiretsu** (*ryūtsū*) The 'parent' sends finished goods down through a pyramid of distributors to retailers.

Figure 1.1 Horizontal and vertical *keiretsu*

Horizontal keiretsu

While *keiretsu* come in all sizes and exist throughout Japanese industry, when we talk about horizontal *keiretsu* it is the 'big six' large bank-centred groups that people commonly think of. These *keiretsu* are 'horizontal' because in appearance they are comprised of a range of brother and sister firms, all providing a function for the group.

Following World War II, instead of the originating families, it was the banks that became the focus of the new groupings. This was facilitated by the shortage of finance that followed the war, and by the fact that the stock market was not taken seriously as a source of business finance. Both of these meant that emphasis was placed on banks as the centres of industrial funding. The Japanese administration encouraged this situation. It could indirectly influence the shape and direction of industry by administering control over that funding.

Three of the big six – Mitsui, Mitsubishi and Sumitomo – have direct *zaibatsu* origins. The others – Fuyō, Sanwa and DKB (Dai-Ichi Kangyō Bank) – pieced themselves together out of *zaibatsu* and other large firms after World War II.

The shachō-kai

While antimonopoly restrictions have meant that none of the *keiretsu* have been allowed to operate a central coordinating body, each has a *shachō-kai*, or presidents' club. These are

Table 1.1 The 'big six' horizontal *keiretsu*, plus two

Keiretsu	Bank	Other central members		Members
Mitsubishi	Tokyo–Mitsubishi	Mitsubishi Shōji	Mitsubishi Heavy Inds.	28
Mitsui	Sakura	Mitsui Bussan	Mitsui Fudosan	27
Sumitomo	Sumitomo	Sumitomo Chemical	Sumitomo Metal Mining	20
DKB	Dai-Ichi Kangyō	Itōchū		48
Fuyō	Fuji			29
Sanwa	Sanwa			44
Tōkai	Tōkai			32
IBJ	Industrial Bank of Japan			16

comprised of the heads of the main member firms, who meet periodically for informal get-togethers. For instance, in Mitsui's case there are 27 members in its Nimoku-kai or Second Thursday Club – which meets on the first Thursday of each month! Though they meet ostensibly for social purposes, what the councils of each *keiretsu* actually discuss is shrouded in much secrecy, with note-taking in the meetings of some groups prohibited.[11] There has naturally been speculation about what actually happens in secret meetings, at which it is claimed that nothing important takes place. The concern is that these business people are coordinating their business activities and, in doing so, fostering monopolistic behaviour rather than a competitive business environment.

Are they just social gatherings or are they business-orientated? The reality lies between the two. Suspicion of what takes place occurs in part because to Westerners business is business and things outside of that are social. But in Japan 'the social' is the foundation of virtually any business, at least of business with any integrity. A further problem is the inability of Japanese to articulate this point.

The leaders of their respective industrial sectors need to establish positive and constructive relations with each other in order to be able to engage smoothly in future business. Western business relations are normally based on cut-and-dried rational, pragmatic grounds, but Japanese people want to feel there is a trusted 'old friend' calling to see them to ask for a favour. It is through these meetings that this relationship is able to be established and reinforced amongst otherwise very busy people, operating in different arenas. The matter is summed up well by Makihara Minoru, Mitsubishi Shōji president from 1992. He said that before becoming head of Shōji he only knew a third of the other presidents, but through the Friday Club meetings got to know all of them: that is useful if he needs to contact them, it enables a 'quick meeting of minds'.[12]

Keiretsu participants
Within each *keiretsu* there are a range of companies, servicing different fields. This gives the group the chance to compete in each sector, though there is doubling up of industrial representatives in some groups, and some *keiretsu* don't have representation in some industries.

It has been in the group's interest to encourage a balance of companies to join in order that fellow members, too, may profit from the successes of others. And good backing can lead to success: manufacturers can get good long-term financing without having to satisfy the short-term needs of shareholders, and a firm with a strong *shōsha* can expect good market penetration for its products. For instance, Hino, top truck maker and also manufacturer for Toyota, formed a joint venture with Mitsui Bussan when, in 1985, it wanted to establish a sales subsidiary in the US. The powerful Bussan gave Hino quick market penetration, and Bussan, too, profited from the part-time membership Toyota (Hino) has in the Mitsui *keiretsu*.

Vertical keiretsu

The vertical *keiretsu* are so called because of their hierarchical structure, normally centring around a manufacturer or distributor at the top. The lower layers, which expand in number as in the form of a pyramid, act as suppliers to a manufacturer, or as second- and third-level wholesalers, in the case of a distributor. These are also hierarchical because there are status and power relationships running down from the top of a vertical *keiretsu*.

The manufacturing *keiretsu*'s upper members draw parts or semi-finished items from lower-level subcontractors, and these suppliers in turn have smaller, component suppliers providing them with parts.

The distribution *keiretsu* begin with products supplied at the top of the pyramid, initially to first-level buyers, and on through other levels of wholesalers until the items reach stores at the retail level.

Toyota

Let's look at Toyota as an example. Toyota Motors captures between 40 and 50 per cent of the Japanese automotive market. Its production in vehicles is twice that of Nissan at number two. As a grouping, outside the 'big six' the Toyota *keiretsu* is the most powerful in Japan.[13]

Not only does Toyota have supply and distribution *keiretsu*, but it even has its own horizontal *keiretsu*. Horizontally, Toyota has ties with Daihatsu, Hino, Tōwa Real Estate, Chiyoda Fire & Marine Insurance and Toyota Tsūshō, which is the Toyota group's sole trader.

In terms of Toyota's vertical supply *keiretsu*, its ten first-level subcontractors are all big companies in their own right; all are listed on the First Section of the Tokyo Stock Exchange. One of these is Toyoda Automatic Loom Works, the company from which Toyota Motor Corporation emerged in 1933. Toyoda is a strong company in its own right. In addition to being a major supplier to Toyota, it is a strong forklift manufacturer as well as a supplier of textile machinery. Beneath these ten firms are another 250 middle-level suppliers, and below them are more levels containing thousands of small-scale sub-subcontractors.

Many smaller business owners are also in the process of carving out their own vertical and/or horizontal *keiretsu*. Essentially, *keiretsu* are an expression of people's desire to cooperate in order to compete more efficiently and more safely. This is much more possible in Japan, where fellow business people spend time creating trust and are willing, able and feel it necessary to cooperate. A businessperson might think about expanding, and put it to an acquaintance that they should join in a business venture by having their companies work together, or by one party putting up cash and providing facilities to start a new enterprise, using the other's skills. This is the start of part of a *keiretsu* centred on the original firm. How big it becomes depends on the founder's skill and the viability of the enterprise.

Criticism of the keiretsu

Criticism levelled at the *keiretsu* normally centres on their exclusionary nature. Most criticism has been directed at the vertical type, but because all *keiretsu* are social units they can all be accused of blocking entry to outsiders. For foreign parts suppliers, the vertical supply *keiretsu* have been the problem. The car parts talks between the US and Japan that were concluded in mid-1995 took place because of the frustration felt by foreign parts makers whose products weren't getting an equal shot at the lucrative Japanese auto industry. Kodak's failure to gain equal access to Japan's photographic retailers is related to the bonding the Japanese retailers feel toward Fuji Film and their place in its distribution *keiretsu*. As for the horizontal *keiretsu*, it is common knowledge that Mitsubishi companies prefer to serve only Kirin beer (Kirin is part of the Mitsubishi *keiretsu*), which of course means that other beers don't get equal access to Mitsubishi patrons.

Figures are often cited nowadays showing that there is much less *intra-keiretsu* trading. Since this implies that the market is more open, it is used against foreign criticism that Japan's *keiretsu* continue to block entry by foreign firms. *Intra-keiretsu* trade may have decreased, but this is not for the benefit of foreigners. It was when Japan's firms were weak and struggling to export that *intra-keiretsu* help was needed. Buying at a lower price outside the group was short-sighted in that it starved emerging fellow members of income at a time when they were too weak to survive a free market. Now it's in the interests of firms to become competitive, which means buying from the most economic source. *Intra-keiretsu* links still exist, but have simply decreased in importance.[14]

Under the direction of a bank, fellow members may still support neophyte or weakened firms. For instance, a Mitsubishi Heavy Industries (MHI) plant that supplied military tanks faced a decrease in demand following the end of the Cold War. Mitsubishi Motors, which had been supplying dump trucks to Shin Caterpillar Mitsubishi, terminated its supply and handed the business over to MHI.[15] In another example, in late 1997 a number of Mitsui companies agreed to pitch in to help Mitsui Construction, which had, along with other construction firms, suffered in the recession. Financial firms, including Sakura Bank (a descendent of Mitsui Bank), offered Mitsui Construction credit and other firms offered it preferential orders.

Essentially, *keiretsu* firms have good reason to buy from fellow members. If related group firms are healthy and the price of goods or services is better outside the group, then a *keiretsu* member might choose to purchase outside the group. But since trust and reliability are important business assets in Japan, being trusted means a supplier has a 'cost advantage'. Supplies from firms without established relations entail an element of risk that in effect makes them more expensive than those from a known buyer. On top of this, loyalty to patronize existing suppliers also keeps newcomers out.

The exclusionary nature of the *keiretsu* became an issue at the US–Japan Structural Impediments Initiative talks that began in 1989. At that time it was formally decided by the US that the *keiretsu* were a non-tariff barrier to trade. They were interpreted as Japanese firms closing ranks, conspiring in order to block out foreigners. There is not a great deal wrong with this assumption, except that it is not a matter of picking on 'foreigners' as much as the *keiretsu* protecting members from any outside threat.

Furthermore, a few foreigners have begun to appreciate that the tendency for Japanese firms to function together runs deep. The logical conclusion that some foreigners have hit upon is that those protesting are wasting their time trying to dissolve that structure in a hurry. If the behaviour of the *keiretsu* were a post-World War II aberration within a basically Western market system, then some anti-cartel, legal hand-slapping and knocking into line would bring the recalcitrants around. But it is clearly more deep-rooted than that.

That there has been increased understanding of the system was indicated by US Under-secretary of State Joan Spero when she acknowledged, in mid-1995, that the *keiretsu* system is not without its benefits. She said there needed to be a way of not overthrowing the system, but of encouraging foreigners to work with it.[16] Furthermore, there's a strong case for the idea that the natural state is for people to cooperate with those familiar to them, just as Japanese companies and other Japanese business people do. On this matter, James

Abegglen suggests that family-based and *keiretsu* groupings are common not only in Asia but in several Western countries. It is Americans, rather than Asians, who appear out of step. Perhaps, he says, Americans should re-examine their laws to improve competitiveness.[17]

Cross-shareholding

Cross-shareholding between Japanese firms that do business with each other is not uncommon; it is the tangible affirmation of essentially social and historical links. It means that shares are in the hands of associated businesses rather than individual investors. Businesses that trade with a firm are more interested in its long-term business performance, whereas individuals tend to be more interested in short-term capital gain. The tendency for Japanese firms to have strong cross-holdings has therefore allowed those firms to focus on long-term goals without needing to worry about the more immediate profit requirements of other shareholders.

A major factor influencing cross-holding came during Japan's period of industrial growth after World War II. When, in the late 1960s, foreign investment restrictions had begun to be liberalized, there was an increasing threat of foreign takeover. With a company's shares loose on the market, and hungry foreign firms looking to buy into low-priced but up-and-coming Japanese businesses, the natural reaction for Japanese firms was to make sure their shares were safe in friendly hands. The government was also concerned about 'too much' foreign involvement in Japanese industry. When GM bought 34.2 per cent of Isuzu in 1971, MITI intervened and GM had to guarantee that it wouldn't attempt to control Isuzu. Japanese shareholders, too, were asked by MITI to hold onto their shares, and especially not to allow them to go to GM.[18] GM now owns 37.4 per cent of Isuzu.

With, in many cases, up to 70 per cent of a firm's shares held by fellow *keiretsu* firms, only about 30 per cent has been traded, making it difficult for a raider to accrue enough shares to have an impact on a company; though this hasn't been impossible.[19] Isetan, a large department store, was drawn closer into the Mitsubishi *keiretsu* when Isetan faced a takeover threat from Shūwa, a Tokyo real estate speculator. Eight Mitsubishi companies protected Isetan by buying its shares. Shūwa also threatened a clothing chain store called Nagasakiya. Nagasakiya asked DKB to help, and three DKB *keiretsu* real estate firms bought back nearly all of the Nagasakiya shares held by Shūwa.[20]

Slim Pickens

In a 1988–89 deal, an American investor became embroiled in a nasty mess involving the Toyota *keiretsu*. The entire drama seems to have been engineered by a clever Japanese businessman who used an equally notorious Texas investor by the name of T. Boone Pickens as his foil.

The story revolves around Koito Manufacturing, a specialist in the production of lighting equipment. Toyota happens to be the head of the *keiretsu* in which Koito is a leading member – Koito is one of the top ten first-level supply firms in Toyota's *keiretsu*; about half of Koito's sales go to Toyota. A large block of Koito's shares were acquired by a certain Watanabe Kitarō, known as a successful property and foreign car dealer during the 'bubble' years, and also as a successful greenmailer (someone who buys stock in a firm and then forces the company to buy back the shares). After accruing Koito stock, Watanabe approached Toyota through a third party, suggesting Toyota might like to buy the stock back.

Watanabe mentioned to Toyota that should it not take the stock, he would sell it to an overseas buyer. That 'buyer' was internationally known corporate raider T. Boone Pickens.

Pickens' own Boone Co. suddenly became Koito's single largest shareholder, with about 26 per cent of the outstanding shares. Although Pickens later admitted that Watanabe had 'loaned' him the money (about $1 billion at the time) to buy the stock, the American insisted that he was a legitimate, long-term investor who now wanted to exercise his right to put three members on Koito's board, exactly as Toyota had done with its (lower) 19 per cent shareholding. Pickens went on to complain about the *keiretsu* structure, saying that Toyota was dominating Koito and obstructing the rights of the other shareholders. He asserted that shareholders are the real company owners and management are their employees. This, of course, is the antithesis of Japanese thinking on the operation of a company.

While some (Japanese) might complain about the oppressive nature of a parent firm, it is inappropriate to assume that, fundamentally, there is a 'conflict' relation between such companies as Toyota and Koito. The reality is that Japanese companies have done very well being driven by workers, and watched over by administrative bodies such as banks and the government, while their shareholders have taken a back seat. No one who was Japanese was too concerned about Pickens' call, and workers and management blocked the efforts of Pickens, who they saw as disruptive and a threat to the stability of their organization. Pickens failed to get a director on Koito's board, and over the next three years the economic collapse more than sliced the value of his shares in half.

The way the T. Boone Pickens story was represented in the foreign press and interpreted amongst foreign observers was also unfortunate. Westerners tend to react in support of the 'little guy' who is thwarted, especially if it's by a big company breaching the rules of the free market. But that that's what people thought simply illustrates the rigidity of the Westernized mindset, and at least those planning on dealing with Japan must break out of exactly that way of thinking. The Japanese didn't see him as defending anyone's freedom; virtually all saw him as a destabilizing element, disrupting a very productive business.

The subcontractor[21]

Between 70 and 80 per cent of the production costs of Japan's manufactured goods are supplied by outside subcontractors. In cars, the ratio is 70 per cent subcontracted to 30 per cent internal, which is just the reverse of the ratio at the big Detroit auto makers. Much of this supply originates from small subcontractors, who feed parts into the *keiretsu* system, and who also act as an economic cushion for the system in tough times. Many subcontractor owners chose to work in a small firm, about two-thirds of them having been in related positions as salary workers, but who left because they preferred the freedom of operating their own business, and the chance to be creative. While many are satisfied with their lot, many suffer because as small businesses their fortunes are more closely tied to the swings of the economy.[22]

Historically, much of Japan's production was cottage industry-based, and much involved cotton and textiles.[23] After Japan opened to the West (1868), industries began to grow in scale, yet even today small-scale firms are plentiful. Until World War II small-scale production had been seen to be of low quality, so firms preferred to manufacture in-house. But during World War II increased demand forced manufacturers to turn to small firms for supplies, and this in turn allowed these small firms to hone and improve their skills.[24] Then, with heightened demand in the post-World War II, rapid growth period, the number of small enterprises increased.

It is useful to get an idea of the type of businesses involved. While Koito Mfg. (mentioned above) has 4600 employees, others are small-factory operations of the type Westerners might associate with parts manufacture. Tokyo's Ōta ward is, for instance, the most famous centre of small factory production. There are also smaller-scale operations. A small engineering firm might occupy the garage of a house, and turn out a small range of electronic parts with a few staff; these businesses are still very common. Historically, much unskilled work, such as TV parts assembly, assembling toys, dolls or fireworks, or sewing, has been done at home. In 1977, 4 per cent of all households had at least one member doing this type of work on a subcontracting basis. Of this work, 93 per cent was handled by women, for a fifth of a full-time manufacturing wage.[25]

Following the 1973 and 1979 oil shocks, as the shock absorbers of the system, subcontractors faced a chequered career that followed the dips in the economy. When Japan wasn't recoiling from the oil shocks, in both the mid-1970s and mid-1980s it faced a spiralling yen which lessened the saleability of exports, affecting the price assemblers could pay subcontractors. Following that came the economic collapse of the 1990s, which led to parts sourcing from cheaper Asian locations.

About two-thirds of Japan's small and medium-sized enterprises (SMEs) are subcontractors for larger firms – that's a lot, considering that over 98 per cent of all Japan's firms are SMEs. Technically these are part of the *keiretsu* pyramid, but in a Japanese sense they're not really part of *the group*. These small firms, and individuals, in an in-group-orientated society, are not insiders. Lower-level subcontractors should either be seen as partial *keiretsu* insiders or, even better, as outsiders.

Many subcontractors are often only marginally profitable. When times get tough, these firms have no option but to lay off staff, and a percentage will go bankrupt. They often work long hours, with heavy and immediate demands placed on them by buyers. They conform to demands which they cannot realistically refuse because to do so would mean the buyer would source from another firm next time.

Subcontractors are subject to 'economically rational' demands from their buyers, who try to drive down the price in tough times. There have also been objectively less than fair demands. Prices have been driven down to unreasonable levels – a characteristic normally not found in Japanese business, where it's normally accepted that everyone needs a reasonable profit. It hasn't been uncommon for buyers to refuse unwanted orders on the pretext of poor quality, to delay payment or impose unreasonable delivery time limits on orders.[26] A 1991 government SME Agency survey found that 41 per cent of 40,000 subcontractors surveyed frequently received orders just prior to holidays for delivery immediately after, and nearly one fifth got orders after work hours for delivery the next morning.[27]

Government has faced complaints about the poor treatment of subcontractors since World War II. After the post-Korean War slump, in 1956 the Law to Assure Prompt Payment to Subcontractors was passed. The Fair Trade Commission has occasionally felt obliged to request that buyers not pressure subcontractors with such things as arbitrary refusals of orders or unreasonable price cuts.

Many suppliers have felt obliged to remain loyal to their one patron, lest they lose their rights as supplier. But as the 1990s moved into recession, orders from assemblers were so poor that subcontractors couldn't maintain old loyalties, nor could assemblers enforce loyalty by shutting off orders, and suppliers began supplying different buyers.

The sōgō shōsha

An important part of the *keiretsu* are the *sōgō shōsha* – literally, general trading companies. Since World War I these have been important and central features, helping drive the economy.

Table 1.2 The nine sōgō shōsha in order of sales

Sales	Sōgō shōsha	Income *	Established	Keiretsu	Zaibatsu	Ancestry
1	Itōchū (C. Itoh)	1	1918	DKB	–	Itoh family
2	Mitsui Bussan	2	1876	Mitsui	Mitsui	Mitsui *zaibatsu*
3	Marubeni	4	1921	Fuyō	–	Itoh family
4	Mitsubishi Shōji	3	1918	Mitsubishi	Mitsubishi	Mitsubishi *zaibatsu*
5	Sumitomo Shōji	5	1919	Sumitomo	Sumitomo	Sumitomo *zaibatsu*
6	Nisshō Iwai	6	1928	Sanwa & DKB	–	Suzuki *zaibatsu* + Iwai
7	Tōmen	8	1920	Tōkai & Mitsui	(Mitsui)	Mitsui Bussan
8	Nichimen	7	1892	Sanwa	–	Cotton spinners & merchants
9	Kanematsu	9	1918	DKB	–	Kanematsu + Gōshō

DKB = centred around the Dai-Ichi Kangyō Bank.
* Current (pre-tax) profit ranking.
Tōmen has weak ties with the Mitsui keiretsu. Tōmen was an offshoot of Bussan, not the Mitsui zaibatsu.

There are now nine large Japanese companies that are commonly referred to as the *sōgō shōsha*, though some other smaller firms are described as such. And of those nine, the top five (see Table 1.2) stand above the rest as a distinct high income earning and trading group. It will be these nine companies that are referred to as *sōgō shōsha* here.

What constitutes a *sōgō shōsha* has been subject to interpretation, but there are some prerequisites. In order to be referred to as a *sōgō shōsha* a company must:

● handle a diverse product range
● handle a large share of the nation's trade
● have an international network.

The *sōgō shōsha* are perhaps best known for handling Japan's international trade. However, it's worth noting that on average just under half the sales of the nine *sōgō shōsha* are domestic, and just over half are international transactions.[28] And while they did grow with Japan's economy, as their trade shifted from heavy industry, in which they excelled, to consumer products, the *sōgō shōsha* experienced problems. They began to suffer through the 1980s and were affected by the recession of the 1990s, though they did to some extent bounce back with a shift in focus, taking the opportunity to invest in both communications technology and in the Asian economies. In many ways the *sōgō shōsha* are a microcosm of the Japanese economy, and in many ways they continue to follow its fortunes.

Unfortunately, people often confuse the names of the *sōgō shōsha* with those of the *keiretsu* to which they belong. In the press the *shōsha* Mitsui Bussan and Mitsubishi Shōji are often abbreviated simply as 'Mitsui' and 'Mitsubishi' respectively, meaning they aren't differentiated from their *keiretsu* or from other *keiretsu* firms that carry the same name. Instead, it's much better to refer to them as the Japanese do, either in full, or as Bussan or Shōji – unprefixed, these refer to Mitsui Bussan and Mitsubishi Shōji, respectively. And as for Sumitomo Shōji, in Japan it is shortened to Sumishō.

While the different *sōgō shōsha* claim specialization in certain fields, with the possible exception of some large business areas, most will perform much the same marketing function and will be able to handle any business that you're likely to approach them with. What's more, because of changes in the economy they're all searching for innovative new business. And while they have been criticized for cutting into new-business profits, they have tremendous access to distribution in Japan; they can give you better distribution in a shorter period of time than any other route. So if you get a contact with a *sōgō shōsha*, it's a good idea to follow it up.

Functions of the sōgō shōsha

When trade re-opened in the Meiji era, Japanese manufacturers were limited in their ability to access foreign markets. Japanese lacked foreign language ability as well as knowledge of business protocol, and they simply weren't as outgoing as many foreign business people. This apparent handicap of Japanese manufacturers ironically became an advantage. Whereas Westerners have often felt confident to market products themselves, most Japanese have instead preferred to specialize in their own domain of business, and have been prepared to share the pie with a trader. One reason why the *sōgō shōsha* emerged was to fill the marketing gap, and in doing so they provided related benefits which Western businesses haven't had available. Accordingly, the *sōgō shōsha* were able to export the products of many of Japan's small firms. This was most important when the country opened during the Meiji era, and after World War II – times when small firms had no other vehicle to do so.

Information brokers

Able to provide basic communication and negotiation skills, the *sōgō shōsha* then went further. They became an information resource providing not only physical links in the form of transportation, but communication links through their offices around the world. They were able to keep abreast of, and pass on, information to companies they represented. The *sōgō shōsha* network has become a highly complex database through which information is instantaneously exchanged on such matters as consumer trends, weather trends, commodity prices and political factors.

The *sōgō shōsha* also introduced technology, either via physical imports, or by acting as brokers to facilitate patent contracts. As importers, they exposed Japanese manufacturers to technology they would have had difficulty gaining access to by themselves. When their own manufacturers began production, they typically ceased import and then benefited as traders of the locally made product.

The introduction and manufacture in Japan of synthetic materials and textiles and of high-technology goods, including computer components, involved the *sōgō shōsha*. For instance, in 1938 DuPont filed a patent in the US for a product called Nylon 66. Mitsui Bussan in New York collected and sent patent information and a sample of the fibre to its subsidiary, Tōyō Rayon (now Tōray Industries) in Japan. Tōyō Rayon examined the product and then developed its own, called Amiran (or Nylon 6) – which was determined by a 1946 Occupation Commission to be significantly different from DuPont's product. Amiran became widely used in such things as fishing nets and ropes.[29]

Following the appearance of such new technologies, rival Japanese manufacturers also soon began production. In addition to establishing a domestic market for their group manufacturers, each *sōgō shōsha* also provided them with the best assurance of an overseas market.

Trading partners

Japanese companies have often been criticized for maintaining favoured trading relationships, rather than relationships based on free and competitive purchasing arrangements. The *keiretsu* have often been the target of such criticism. However, this view fails to appreciate that without the assurance of intra-group purchasing, and marketing support, in such cases as these Japanese manufacturers would have been foolish to risk entering new business fields. Furthermore, without such strong relationships, *sōgō shōsha* would have been foolish to provide manufacturers with technology and funds. That is, a lot of the investment and development responsible for Japan's early growth wouldn't have been prudent if market forces dictated that a manufacturer should change to deal with other traders or buyers every time someone offered a lower price. The interdependent trading structure, originally based on *zaibatsu*, and later on *keiretsu* companies, provided manufacturers with the confidence that they could rely on a *sōgō shōsha* to dispense their finished products.

By having good market information *sōgō shōsha* have been able to link foreign exporters to Japanese buyers. They have also been able to locate foreign buyers for Japanese products where individual Japanese manufacturers would have found doing so too difficult. *Sōgō shōsha* have also been able to locate raw materials and foods at the best price where it would have been impractical for their clients to do so.

They have even gone one step further by developing economical sources of supply, sometimes also creating new markets. One example is mining. In 1996 Itōchū became involved in a coal mining venture in Australia. This provided Itōchū with a stable supply of high-quality, low-priced product. What's more, Itōchū intended to expand the mine's output – in other words, going beyond its role as a 'trading company'. Also in 1996 Itōchū formed a partnership with Sumishō and Sumitomo Metal Mining to rebuild and expand a copper refinery in China. Another example is the rather complex broiler chicken processing business, which in Japan is dominated by *sōgō shōsha*. Kentucky Fried Chicken (KFC) entered Japan in 1970 via a joint venture – still operating – with Mitsubishi Shōji. To supply the KFC operation Shōji originally imported chickens from the US, and contributed know-how, construction materials and machinery to establish breeding and processing locally. It continues to import and supply grain and arrange processed chicken distribution. In 1996 Marubeni made a $3.2mn (40 per cent) investment in a broiler venture in China, with the capacity to handle 44 million chickens annually, with the intention of initially supplying China, and later Japan.

Whereas the *sōgō shōsha* have been able to commit resources to gaining information, doing so has been bothersome for smaller businesses committed to the production process. Investment in information involves economies of scale. While costly for one manufacturer, the *sōgō shōsha* can spread its investment across all of its clients in the same business field.

Trust and finance brokers

Despite their role as agents – anathema to much of Western business practice – the *sōgō shōsha* have been able to engender the trust of both buyers and sellers, globally as well as domestically.

For those selling to buyers with questionable credit standing, the *sōgō shōsha* are in a position to ask for collateral or a guarantor. Manufacturers themselves are, however, generally too small to do so, and the bounds of their operation don't give them access to information on the performance, reliability and creditworthiness of customers, especially those abroad.

And as large organizations with a strong international presence, the *sōgō shōsha* have also been seen as good credit risks by banks extending finance. While investment opportunities after World War II enticed companies to venture into business, the Ministry of Finance (MOF) didn't want bankruptcies of firms such as had occurred before the war. Therefore MOF advised banks to limit lending to smaller firms. By contrast, the *sōgō shōsha* were seen as more stable and better risks than such firms, and were able to borrow up to more than ten times their equity. With hands-on access to what was happening in the various markets, as well as information about individual company performance, and information as to the prospects of an industry expanding, they could in turn lend money without facing the same risk as the banks. In this way they took over the lending role, but they were much better positioned than banks to do so.

There have been problems, of course. Though the *sōgō shōsha* lost less through bad loans than banks,[30] they haven't been infallible. In addition to various mergers that rescued *shōsha* that were experiencing difficulties, in the mid-1970s a major *sōgō shōsha*, Ataka, overextended itself in an oil venture and went bankrupt. It was absorbed by Itōchū in 1977.

How big is big?

Since they get finance from banks at good rates, and their risk assessment abilities translate into an economic advantage, the *sōgō shōsha* don't need to charge a high levy on the funds they advance to those firms they deal with. This translates into an advantage for small borrowers, who get both the services of a *sōgō shōsha* plus finance at relatively good rates. It also means that the *sōgō shōsha* don't make their money on loans. Instead, they normally make their profit by taking a commission on the goods they trade. *Shōsha* commissions depend on the product and service, but are normally between 0.5 and 5 per cent. This is a narrow margin; their prosperity has instead generally come from processing high volume.

Measured by income (current, or pre-tax profit[31]) the *sōgō shōsha* don't rank highly. There are normally only two or three *sōgō shōsha* amongst Japan's top 100 earning companies. We can get a glimpse of the performance of the *sōgō shōsha* by comparing them with Toyota, which often ranks as Japan's highest earning company:

- Toyota's income is eight times that of Itōchū, the top *shōsha* income earner.
- In total assets Toyota (with ¥6.9tn) – often referred to informally as Toyota Bank because of its strong holdings – is followed by Mitsubishi Shōji, top asset holder of the *shōsha*, with ¥5.5tn. Nomura Securities, also known for its strong reserves, is ahead of both, at ¥11tn.
- Itōchū, the top *shōsha* in sales, actually sells almost twice as much as Toyota. Sales of the top five *shōsha* are in double figures (in ¥ tn) while sales of Toyota and the other four (of the top nine) *shōsha* are in single figures.
- It is on this measure of sales that the *sōgō shōsha* rank impressively internationally. Until the mid-1990s *sōgō shōsha* held the top four positions in Fortune's 500 largest corporations in the world. Five are still in the top ten. Toyota is number 11.[32]

Risk and cost reduction

Risk is a cost that the Japanese will often go to extremes to avoid while they get on with their real business. By providing financial backing, market information and in many cases customers, the *sōgō shōsha* have removed risk for their clients. Because the *sōgō shōsha* are large as well as informed organizations, investment risk has been spread or hedged. An investment that may bankrupt a small firm might therefore be unacceptable to it, but for a large *sōgō shōsha* might simply be a risk able to be calculated against profits.

A common feature of Japanese business is interdependence among related members, whereby 'everyone performs a function, everyone gets a reasonable cut'. Everyone is reasonably satisfied and there's good opportunity for expansion. On the other hand, having an intermediary in trade is something that many Westerners do their best to avoid because it appears to come at a cost.

In many ways, because of what they provide and their economies of scale, the *sōgō shosha* save either manifest or latent costs. According to Mitsui Bussan, in most cases costs to the client are lower if they use a *sōgō shosha* than if clients undertake intermediary tasks themselves.[33] No doubt other *shosha* would make the same claim.

A change of tack

The *sōgō shosha* have excelled when the economy has been in flux. When markets were developing or changing, they were able to compensate for, in particular, the lack of expertise and organization of manufacturers. But as businesses became more sophisticated and wealthier, they became more self-reliant. Both suppliers and buyers grew to understand markets as they stabilized, and so were able to negotiate and arrange details themselves, leaving less of a role for the *shosha*. Bussan and Shōji, respectively, tried to market Toyota and Mitsubishi cars overseas but failed. The manufacturers had become capable of doing it themselves.[34]

Also, when the nature of trade shifted from such heavy products as minerals and machinery to consumer and other high-tech goods, the *sōgō shosha* found it more difficult to maintain a competitive advantage. While suited to large-scale business, it has been awkward for them to handle small-lot orders and deal with customer service. Still, the *sōgō shosha* have tried to incorporate or retain small-lot sensitivity in their large-scale operations. Bussan, for instance, has maintained trade not only in finished textile goods, but also in high-fashion items imported from Europe.

In the latter 1980s and 1990s many Japanese companies began to set up business overseas, reducing their need for the *sōgō shosha* to export their goods or handle their imported materials. Of Japan's total imports in 1987, 67 per cent were handled by 22 major Japanese *shosha*. By 1990, while the dollar amount imported had increased, the proportion of Japan's imports handled had dropped to 57 per cent.[35] In other words, the value of imports increased, but *shosha* were handling proportionately less of them.

During the recession, which kicked in around 1992, there was a drive to streamline supply channels combined with a shift to larger retail outlets as well as computerization of ordering, warehousing and distribution. This meant individual firms became even less dependent on such service providers as the *sōgō shosha*. The discount chain Daiei, for instance, set out to cut costs by simplifying its domestic distribution and its sourcing channels. Daiei has a subsidiary called Emmac with offices worldwide, devoted solely to sourcing imports.[36]

In the midst of the recession the *sōgō shosha* were accused of being 'dinosaurs'. Asked if they would die out, the managing director of Marubeni said, 'yes, they will if they maintain their traditional course; but that won't happen'.[37]

While continuing many of their traditional activities and functions, by the mid-1990s the *sōgō shosha* had shifted focus. Two domains of business were of particular significance: investment in telecommunications, and investment in Asia.

In the latter 1980s it was wealth that drove Japan's companies to establish operations abroad, in the 1990s it was the threat of poverty that drove them to do it. The hollowing out of Japan's manufacturing sector in the mid-1990s, whereby firms set up in ostensibly cheaper Asian pastures, further lessened demand for the *sōgō shosha*'s services in Japan and encouraged them to also shift the focus of much of their activity offshore. In the developing Asian economies too, they could provide their traditional services, including finance, information and coordination. Intending to increase its role as a supplier of capital, in July 1995 Mitsubishi Shōji started Mitsubishi Corp. Capital Asia Pte., a Singapore-based firm capitalized at $80mn, created to fund investments in Asia. Similarly, that November, Sumishō started Sumitomo Capital Asia Pte., and in

December Mitsui Bussan established Mitsui & Co. Asia Investment Pte., both also in Singapore.

In large-scale overseas projects the *sōgō shōsha* have typically offered their services within the framework of a joint venture with a local government, or other specialist parties, and perhaps also with another Japanese *shōsha*. In the mid-1990s Itōchū, for instance, joined Mitsubishi Shōji in a project backed by Indonesia's state-run highway corporation, to build a 5.4km bridge connecting Java's Surabaya with Madura Island. The deal was that the consortium of interests generate a profit through collecting bridge tolls, and in the year 2025 hand the bridge back to the Indonesian government. Such operations, in which *sōgō shōsha* build, operate and then transfer the project, became popular amongst the *sōgō shōsha* at this time. The *shōsha* bring to the table all those assets already mentioned, such as funds and knowledge, many of which are unavailable in developing economies. The risk for the *shōsha* is exposure to economic and political factors over their period of stay.[38]

The telecommunications industry represented a new area. In addition to financial investment, it needed coordination of materials, of information, and of other parties. The digital satellite TV broadcaster PerfecTV, after a merger in April 1998, included, amongst others, Rupert Murdoch, Son Masayoshi and four *sōgō shōsha*: Itōchū, Sumishō, Mitsui Bussan and Nisshō Iwai.

In 1996 Sumishō joined with the US firm Telecommunications Inc. to form a joint venture called Jupiter Programming to supply documentaries, news, sports, films, TV shopping and other programmes to Japanese cable TV operators.

Sometimes these two new investment domains – Asia and telecommunications – have overlapped. Sumishō led a consortium, including Supernet (Hong Kong), Pacific Internet (Singapore) and Internet Initiative Japan Inc. (Japan), which, together with additional backing from Toyota, Matsushita Electric, Itōchū and other Japanese companies, invested in the development of the Asian Internet route called A-Bone (Asian Internet Backbone). Using the Internet within Asia had been expensive and slow. Information had to go through privately leased networks and much of the traffic had to go via the US.

Setting up such a project is extremely difficult, and in such cases the *sōgō shōsha* offer considerable resources. For instance, they supply staff on loan from their own organization, including legal and accounting expertise, they provide information and investment finance.[39]

Energy

Energy development has been a logical investment for the *sōgō shōsha*. It's long-term and speculative, requires a lot of capital and is often either offshore or requires international links. In 1969 Mitsubishi Shōji became involved in importing Liquefied Natural Gas (LNG) from Alaska to supply energy utilities in Japan. In Asia, the richest LNG resource was in Brunei, where Royal Dutch Shell held the rights. Shell approached Mitsui Bussan in order that Bussan could market the product in Japan, but, despite Shōji having already moved into Alaska, Bussan was too cautious to seize the opportunity and this, too, went to Shōji.

The gas came on stream in 1973, the time of the first oil crisis, and the revenue accounted for a third of Shōji's total company profits at the time. Shōji built on its success in other projects, even teaming up later with Mitsui Bussan in an LNG project in Australia.

Energy development is not without huge risks, though. In 1973 Mitsui Bussan and the Iran Chemical Development Co. Ltd created the Iran–Japan Petrochemical Company (IJPC), and began building a petrochemical plant in Iran. The project had excellent potential; Iran had oil and Bussan had the resources to exploit it. Estimated completion for the mammoth task was 1979. Unfortunately, in 1979 there was a revolt in the country. The

Shah of Iran made a speedy departure and Ayatollah Khomeini established an Islamic republic there. Project construction work was halted. Then in the following year the Iran–Iraq War (1980–88) began, and the plant became an Iraqi target. The IJPC parties anticipated restarting work, but continued Iraqi attacks over the following years demolished that hope, and in 1990 both groups agreed to abandon the venture due to the effects of the war. Bussan only finished writing off an approximate ¥200bn ($1.5bn) loss from the project in 1992.

Until 1996, importing refined fuel into Japan had been virtually prohibited. However, pressure from within Japan resulted in deregulation that came into effect on 1 April that year, allowing anyone with 'adequate facilities' to import gasoline. It opened the way for investors representing a range of industries to enter the gasoline market. Naturally, amongst these were the *sōgō shōsha*. On 1 April 1996 Itōchū became the first *sōgō shōsha* to take delivery of imported gasoline. Discounter Jusco, Japan's third largest retailer in sales, joined Shōji to retail low-price gasoline to Jusco customers. Shōji was to provide research and contribute know-how in areas such as design, construction and quality control.

Still, the deregulated gasoline market was not the godsend that free-marketeers had hoped for. An increase in the price of crude oil and 'excessive competition' – what had inspired trade and industry ministry bureaucrats to maintain a regulated pricing system – cut into anticipated profits and kept erstwhile players out of the market. Itōchū ended up selling off its supply as soon as it arrived.

Notes

1 Cited in Beasley, 1990, p. 107.
2 Morikawa, 1992, p. xvii; also see Morikawa's definition, 1992, pp. xvii–xviii. Although the *zaibatsu* form developed in the 1880s, it wasn't until at least the 1920s that the term gained currency.
3 Eleanor Hadley ('Catching Up', *Nippon, Japan Since 1945*, BBC TV series, 1990).
4 See Sakudō, in Nakane and Ōishi, 1990, pp. 152–55.
5 According to Morikawa's definition, the new *zaibatsu* weren't *zaibatsu*, as they lacked exclusive family control. (1992, pp. xviii and 226).
6 Beasley, 1990, p. 189; Morikawa, 1992, pp. 223–24.
7 See Uchino, who comments that GHQ functioned to rid the *zaibatsu* of pre-modern management (1978, p. 22).
8 Nakamura, 1981, p. 24; Morikawa, 1992, p. 237–38; Roberts, 1973, p. 395.
9 Nakamura, 1981, pp. 24–25; Nakamura, 1994, pp. 138–40; Bisson, 1954, p. 291.
10 Other terms, some overlapping one another, are used to describe *keiretsu*. For instance, a firm heading a *kigyō keiretsu* is supplied by its subcontractors; in a *shihon keiretsu*, a common parent owns over 50 per cent of its subsidiaries' stock.
11 Miyashita and Russell, 1994, p. 62.
12 Rafferty, 1995, p. 95.
13 Ohsono, 1995, p. 17.
14 In 1991 *Tokyo Business Today* cited research that showed that 85 and 94 per cent of *keiretsu* firms would refuse to buy consumer goods and capital goods, respectively, from inside their group if prices were lower outside (February 1991, p. 30).
15 Dodwell, *Industrial Groupings in Japan 1994/95*, p. 46.
16 'US to target "keiretsu" next', *The Japan Times*, 22 July 1995.
17 Abegglen, 1994, p. 206.
18 Miyashita and Russell, 1994, pp. 66–67; Johnson, 1982, p. 288.
19 Hsu, 1994, p. 81.

20 Dodwell, *Industrial Groupings in Japan 1994/95*, pp. 46 and 93.
21 Few Westerners have sought the opinions of subcontractors. For a rare and excellent account of their hard times, read the first-hand interview material in *Keiretsu*, by Miyashita and Russell, 1994.
22 'Japan's Subcontractors: The buck stops here', *Focus Japan*, JETRO, September 1978; *Small Business in Japan*, MITI, 1996, pp. 77 and 220.
23 Nakamura, S., 'The Development of Rural Industry', in Nakane and Ōishi, 1990, pp. 81–96.
24 Nakamura, 1981, p. 15.
25 'Japan's Subcontractors: The buck stops here', *Focus Japan*, JETRO, September 1978.
26 Nakamura, 1981, pp. 175–76; *The Japan Economic Journal*, 30 March 1991, pp. 1 and 15.
27 *The Nikkei Weekly*, 14 March 1992, p. 4.
28 In 1998 the trade (to total sales) ratio was: Mitsui 65 per cent (were international transactions); Mitsubishi 61 per cent; Itōchū 47 per cent; Sumitomo 42 per cent; Nichimen 71 per cent; both Marubeni and Nisshō Iwai 56 per cent; and Tōmen and Kanematsu 66 per cent (*Japan Company Handbook*).
29 Tsurumi, 1978, p. 62.
30 Yoshihara, 1982, p. 216.
31 Japanese normally use pre-tax profit as a measure of income, whereas net profit (before tax and extraordinary items) is used in other countries. The government fiscal year and the closure of most Japanese company accounts is as of 31 March.
32 *Japan Company Handbook* figures for 1998; *Fortune*, August 1998.
33 'Analysing the sōgō shōsha', *Mitsui in Action*, January/February 1995, Vol. 36, p. 9.
34 Yoshino and Lifson, 1986, p. 72.
35 *The Japan Economic Journal*, 16 March 1991, p. 14, measured in dollars.
36 *Tradescope*, JETRO, April 1994, pp. 3–4.
37 *Tokyo Business Today*, February 1995, p. 22.
38 *The Nikkei Weekly*, 29 April 1996, p. 18.
39 Source: Itōchū.

Chapter 2

Financial markets in the throes of transformation

Finance is the area of the Japanese economy that has, in recent years, undergone the most change. In addition, opportunities have become increasingly available for foreign financial organizations to take advantage of the deregulating environment, and offer services that Japanese organizations are neither familiar with nor skilled at providing.

Banking

In the 1980s, Japan's banks were viewed by many as the strongest in the world. Their strength was, however, based on a high throughput of funds serving a very strong Japanese manufacturing sector. In a flourishing economy, an appreciating currency fuelled inflation that served to fan the value of assets. This encouraged a growing entrepreneurial group which, in turn, called on banks to supply them with more money. The administration's eventual attempt to curb the inflation by increasing the discount rate and limiting bank loans for property development collapsed the nation's entrepreneurial base, taking the strength of the financial sector with it. That the government had shielded the banks from market forces for so long only exacerbated the crisis that followed. The result was an empty shell of banks riddled with unrecoverable debts.

By the mid-1990s it was decided that in order to profit in the international financial market Japanese financial institutions needed to learn to cope with competition, and in late 1996 a plan proposed by Prime Minister (PM) Hashimoto, and dubbed Japan's 'Big Bang', after Britain's financial deregulation of a decade earlier, was set in place. Meanwhile, as Japan's financial market was trying to prise itself open, foreign financial institutions began scrambling to take the opportunity to fill the breach left by the weakened Japanese banks, before those Japanese institutions could re-establish themselves and attempt to win back a place in the new market.

Money in the bank

From the end of World War II until at least the early 1990s there was a widespread belief that 'no bank will ever go under'. The Ministry of Finance (MOF) bureaucrats had been careful to avoid instability in the financial sector, and accordingly the activities of Japanese banks had been heavily regulated. And when the banks acted, they acted in concert under the guidance of MOF. This system of all-encompassing government regulation earned the epithet the 'convoy system', in which MOF steered the entire banking community, controlling competition, and ensuring that even the smallest banks stayed together in the group. The strongest players were allowed to grow to gargantuan size, but none was allowed to outperform the others in any real competitive sense.

The system involved reciprocity such that those banks that conformed to the plans of MOF were supported by MOF, and the whole structure thereby remained stable. Where there were problems that institutions couldn't work out for themselves, MOF would engineer a resolution, which of course meant drawing on the cooperative spirit (including the financial resources) of others in the system, or MOF might arrange a 'merger' or send business the way of an ailing organization.

But the system hadn't always operated as smoothly as that. In the 1920s Japan experienced a run of bank collapses. And what's more, bank failure had at the time been considered fairly routine – as were the poor banking practices that underscored the failures. The failures were attributed to loose management and liberal lending policies. It wasn't uncommon for inadequate security to be taken on loans, nor was it uncommon for loans to be disproportionately directed toward the interests of the bank directors.

City banks

After World War II the government wanted to hasten industrial development, and following the departure of GHQ it directed the finance that was available into the particular business areas it decided should be nurtured. In doing so it focused on, and increased the role of, the city banks (Japan's largest commercial banks) as intermediaries (see Figure 2.1). From around 1950–51 the Bank of Japan (the central bank) began a process of overloaning – of printing (more) money and loaning it to the banks. This indebted the major banks to the central bank, deepening both MOF's and the central bank's influence

City banks (Toshi Ginkō)

Nine city banks	'Original' 13 city banks	Origin
Tokyo – Mitsubishi Bank (1996 merger: Tokyo + Mitsubishi Banks)	Bank of Tokyo (1946)	Yokohama Specie* Bank (1880)
	Mitsubishi Bank (1919)	Mitsubishi *zaibatsu*
Asahi (1991 merger: Kyōwa + Saitama Banks)	Kyōwa Bank (1948)	Nippon Savings Bank
	Saitama Bank (1943)	85th + Oshi + Bushū + Hannō Banks (Saitama region)
Fuji Bank	Fuji Bank (1948 name change)	Yasuda *zaibatsu*; Yasuda Bank (1864)
Sumitomo Bank	Sumitomo Bank (1895)	Sumitomo *zaibatsu*
Dai-Ichi Kangyō Bank (DKB)	Dai-Ichi Kangyō Bank (1971)	Dai-Ichi (1873) + Nippon Kangyō (1896) Banks
Sakura Bank (1990 merger: Taiyō Kōbe + Mitsui Banks)	Mitsui Bank (1876)	Mitsui *zaibatsu*
	Taiyō Kōbe Bank (1973)	Taiyō (1940) + Kōbe (1936) Banks
Tōkai Bank (Nagoya area)	Tōkai Bank (1941)	Aichi + Nagoya + Itō Banks (Tōkai region)
Daiwa Bank (Osaka area)	Daiwa Bank (1948 name change)	Nomura *zaibatsu*; Nomura Bank (1918)
Sanwa Bank	Sanwa Bank (1933)	Kōnoike + Yamaguchi + 34th Banks: 3 Wa's
(Bankrupt 1997)	Hokkaidō Takushoku Bank (*Takugin*)	Hokkaidō Takushoku (1900)

* Specie = silver, gold, foreign exchange; (date) = date established or changed.

Figure 2.1 On 1 October 1948 Mitsubishi, Sumitomo, Yasuda and Nomura Banks were required by GHQ to change from their *zaibatsu* names. The former changed to Chiyoda and Osaka Banks, respectively, but were changed back in 1952.

over the economy. That influence was translated via government policy along the chain, finally into requests for guidance on how businesses should act in the market. Through these financial routes government exerted leverage over the business community while undertaking its industrial objectives.

But even in the absence of heavy loaning or of strong bank shareholding in firms, banks and financial authorities have wielded influence over Japanese industry. This is related to the historical acceptance or 'tolerance' in Japan of control from above. In contrast to Westerners, who often seek independence – business and personal – many Japanese are comfortable with, or at least accustomed to, working beneath authority. Using the financial system as a vehicle, government has exerted its influence over business, which has meant a very controlled and stable financial–business structure. And banks have played their part by exerting a degree of control – much greater than that experienced in the West – over those they have loaned to.

This is a fundamental part of what is still sometimes referred to as 'Japan Incorporated'; it is a typical example of the influence those in authority in Japan feel obliged to maintain over those systems under their jurisdiction.

As a direct result of the 1947 Antimonopoly Law, the banks were allowed limited *explicit* control: financial institutions were limited to a ceiling of 5 per cent shareholding in any one company. The ceiling was raised to 10 per cent in 1953. But following that, with the exception of life insurance companies, the limit was again lowered to 5 per cent in 1977. Then, with the virtual removal in 1997/98 of the law banning holding companies, the ceiling was all but scrapped, as restricting firms to a 5–10 per cent limit was incompatible with owning (holding) other firms. The changed law is discussed in more detail later in this chapter.

The main bank

Not to be confused with the big six *keiretsu* banks is what firms refer to as their *main bank*, though for many firms they are the same institution. While firms may borrow from several lending institutions, their main bank is normally that from which they borrow the most. The main bank is also normally one of the firm's main shareholders, and will likely hold more shares than any other bank.[1] Further, even when the bank was limited to holding up to 5 per cent of the shares of other firms, other members of the group held shares at the request of the bank – so indirectly representing the bank's and the *keiretsu*'s interests.

There is an implicit agreement between a firm and its main bank that it is the bank that has control and responsibility. The main bank undertakes performance and credit assessments, and in doing so becomes more informed than any other organization about the firm. It takes on the responsibility of offering management guidance. In doing this it may place a member of the bank on the board or place a staff member in the firm in a supervisory or advisory capacity. At a broader level, it will take the lead in a crisis and will often take the role of *de facto* guarantor of a firm's activities. In return for providing this role, the bank is then entitled to manage problems by calling on group member support, where a group (*keiretsu*) exists. In this way the *keiretsu* (big or small), with the bank at its head, functions to maintain stability amongst its members.

A firm that talks about its main bank, and Japanese firms normally indicate their main bank as part of their business resumé, is saying it has been checked out by the bank. The firm is implicitly stating that by providing loans and holding its shares the bank has placed its trust in the firm and, should there be trouble, the firm has the bank behind it. Therefore naturally, the bigger the main bank, the better.

Bubble trouble

In the mid-1980s a period known, largely in retrospect, as the bubble economy began. The word *bubble* symbolizes the price increases, in particular of land and securities in Japan, during the latter 1980s. Prices escalated to an unsustainable level, and in the early 1990s the economic bubble burst, bringing about a recessionary situation.

It is natural to look for a single cause, but the roots of the bubble extend into several areas. Underpinning the bubble was the strong growth of Japan's economy. In 1985 there was the Plaza Accord, an international agreement which resulted in an increase in the value and the supply of the yen. This ultimately served to further kindle the fiery Japanese asset markets. It is well believed that Japan's administrative officials then intentionally triggered inflation in order to counter the effects of the Plaza Accord and to invigorate the asset base of Japan's big companies by (artificially) boosting their worth and availing them of cheap financing.[2] Later, starting in 1989, the Bank of Japan, in an effort to quell the inflationary trend, placed restrictions on the amount of money available to property investors. This restricted cash flowing through the economy, depressing business activity.

In part, the boom was a result of the confidence the business community had come to have in the strength of the Japanese economy. This over-confidence prompted risky investments, and among the biggest risk-takers were banks. This was partly the result of operating in a cosy, regulated and stable environment, in which banks could feel secure following MOF's lead. To put it another way: 'what's happening must be OK, because if it's happening it must be condoned by MOF' – and some pretty strange things happened.

Also, many long-standing Japanese firms, and so the banks that loaned to them, had strong hidden assets. Assets including stocks and land declared on Japanese corporate balance sheets have not been listed at current market value but at their acquisition price. This is still the case at the time of writing, though the system is targeted for revision. We will look at this in more detail soon. For companies with long-standing cross-holdings of *intra-keiretsu* shares, or that have owned land, particularly in such expensive areas as Tokyo, that purchase price had little bearing on the peak value of those assets in 1989–91.

For instance, when, in March 1890, Mitsubishi settled the land in the Marunouchi area of central Tokyo, it paid less than one yen per square foot, and this is the value at which it remained on the company books even when, by the late 1980s, it had become one of the world's most expensive pieces of real estate. Exactly 100 years after Mitsubishi's purchase, it was often jested that the sale of the Imperial Palace grounds just down the road could buy Canada, or the sale of all of Tokyo could buy all of the US.

While land owned by city banks as a whole was on the books at a value of ¥2.6tn, even when prices were declining in 1992 it was worth over ¥10tn ($80bn).[3] It is understandable that both Japanese banks and businesses using land as collateral for loans were confident that what looked like a high leveraging, of a lot of cash on loan, backed with low land value, actually involved high asset value.

Large Japanese companies tied into a *keiretsu* were in an economically more stable position than comparable foreign companies. The mutual interests of *keiretsu* members meant that they would have the backing of the *keiretsu* bank, and they would otherwise help each other when in trouble. This teamwork approach created a much more stable and safer Japanese business environment than exists in the climate of individual responsibility in the West, where it is normal for related companies to take their money and run when one firm appears to have financial problems.

This system of mutual assistance availed support most of the time, but failed on the one occasion – when there was a blanket recession – when virtually all Japanese companies faced problems and needed to help each other, but therefore couldn't.

BIS

Banks need a level of cash in reserve, but what is an acceptable level is a matter of judgement. In 1988 an accord was reached under the auspices of the Bank for International Settlements (BIS), based in Basel, Switzerland, establishing new capital adequacy requirements for banks trading internationally. It was done with the intention of putting rationality and stability into international banking, but specifically it was a move by other major economic powers to bring Japan's banks into line. They had become the top banks in the world in terms of assets and deposits, but all built upon unrealistically slim profit margins. Since their assets were ultimately unstable, this made them banks with large liabilities and low profitability. After the bubble collapsed and many of their loans defaulted, they were hard pressed to re-establish financial stability, partly because of their low profit margins.

The BIS stipulated that banks should have capital equal to at least 7.25 per cent of their assets by the end of March 1991, and 8 per cent by the end of March 1993. But Japan claimed that its banks were supported by those huge hidden assets not reflected on their balance sheets, so in a compromise the BIS allowed the Japanese banks to count some of their huge but unrealized stock portfolio gains as capital.

In good times, this means the availability of a lot of money. It also means, however, that the security of the Japanese banking system rests on assets that will, in bad times, lose value at the time they are most needed, that is, as soon as the economy thinks about collapsing.

Many commercial banks had felt confident in meeting the BIS requirements. But the decline in the stock market eroded the unrealized value of their assets. This meant banks had to find other ways of meeting the BIS criteria. Should the banks not achieve the BIS requirement, their international credit rating would be downgraded, and this would mean an increase to them of the cost of capital on the international market.

Subordinated debt was one option. This involves other financial institutions (mainly life insurers) lending cash to the banks or buying bonds sold by the banks. The priority for banks to repay this debt in the event of business failure is subordinate, or secondary to other debts. But these funds were relatively expensive, and interest on subordinated debt began choking bank profits.[4]

By October 1990 those banks affected, mainly city banks, had established a policy of reviewing their outstanding loans, and declining the reissue of loans to poor performers and/or those who refused to accept higher interest rates and fees. One way of trying to meet the criteria was for the banks themselves to off-load assets such as stocks, but this served to depress the market further. Still, by March 1991, large banks which had held the shares of fellow companies as a matter of traditional Japanese business practice, without expecting significant returns on them, were trying to sell some of them.

Bursting the bubble

The government decided to stop the runaway price increases, reversing the policy of relaxing the availability of money in the economy. The bubble was intentionally burst. In May 1989 the official discount rate was raised in order to increase the cost of credit, and it was raised four more times over the following 15 months, peaking at 6 per cent on 30 August 1990. From 1 April 1990 MOF also imposed a restriction on the credit available for property-backed loans. Bank real estate lending was restricted to no more than the rate of increase in overall loans.[5] This edict was later extended to non-bank and leasing institutions.

Symbolic of the frenzied decade, at its close on the last day of trading for 1989, Friday 29 December, the Nikkei Stock Average peaked at an all-time high of 38,915. It began to drop seriously at the beginning of 1990, and in the following 12 months until December 1990 the stocks on the First Section of the Tokyo Stock Exchange dropped in value by well over half. But stock markets go up and down, and its drop was seen as an aberration – interpreted with typical stock market optimism, it was seen as due to various short-term influences, such as the Gulf War, which would soon disappear. But things didn't work out that way.

Copy-cat investment

Despite their prowess as manufacturers and marketers, Japanese abilities when it came to dealing in real estate were somewhat haphazard. Popular markets that were assailed by Japanese investors were Hawaii, Guam and Los Angeles. Many purchases in these areas seemed irrational, and were based on copy-cat behaviour.

On top of this, Japan also faced bad luck. In 1990 California entered the worst real estate slump since the 1930s. Japanese had not only made heavy property investments in California but had become heavily involved in the banking organizations which provided finance there. Japanese-owned banks included Union Bank, owned by the Bank of Tokyo; the Bank of California, owned by Mitsubishi Bank; and Sanwa Bank of California, owned by Sanwa Bank.

Of the top 20 banks in the world in terms of assets, in 1991 and 1992 13 were Japanese, and Japanese banks held the top eight positions. By 1991 Japanese owned over 12 per cent of American banking assets, and accounted for a quarter of Californian banking assets.[6] Unfortunately, Japanese banks bought into much of the US at top-of-the-market prices, and at the beginning of the 1990s California went into recession, nicely coinciding with the banks' troubles at home. By the end of 1991 office buildings in California had dropped by up to one third of their late 1980s value – which gives an indication of the problems the Japanese faced.[7]

Japanese investors were having their candle burnt at both ends; companies, including banks, that were having to support their foreign interests were doing so to the detriment of their home market, where they needed money. Banks needed to meet the BIS standard, and were starting to need money to respond to the effects of the bursting of the bubble. It was time for Japanese to retrench and sell off assets abroad that were not performing – but those assets were, by definition, unsaleable.

Land of opportunity

Land was a very important player in the bubble drama: with over 70 per cent of land in Japan mountainous, much of its population, equal to about half that of the US, is packed along a belt which includes six of the seven largest cities, spanning from Tokyo to Kōbe. And within this area about 44 per cent of Japan's population is further concentrated to within 50km of each of three of the major centres.[8] Understandably, land prices in these built-up areas, especially in the bubble period, increased along with continued pressure for urban space. For instance, 1985 prices of *commercial* land tripled during 1986, then almost doubled again in 1987, and 1986 prices of *residential* land almost tripled in 1987.[9] This led to a belief amongst Japanese people that the land would never drop in value.

Faith in land was reflected in bubble era corporate policies. In the latter 1980s the management of Cosmo Credit Corp., Tokyo's largest credit union, had a policy of making any loan that was backed by Tokyo real estate. Its progressive attitude also enabled a policy, unusual for a credit union, of not bothering to solicit small depositor savings accounts of under ¥30,000 ($300).

But with the credit crunch, city real estate prices did fall. One reason was that there is a fundamental difference between residential and business space – despite the occasional use of apartments as offices. As business declined, so did demand for office space. Pressured by tight incomes, some central-city businesses relocated to less expensive areas. It's interesting that by the time the Big Bang began in 1998, foreign financial institutions were choosing the popular Chiyoda, Chūō and Minato wards – the central business areas of Tokyo – that had a few years earlier been abandoned. Prices had by then declined to more 'reasonable' levels and there had been a reshuffling of tenants. For office space within the whole of central Tokyo (its 23 wards), the total vacancy rate had, over the three years to 1998, fallen from 10 per cent to 5 per cent.

Meanwhile, other aspects of the Japanese economy also went through adjustment. Merchants had to shed their excess of high-priced stock and regear their operations such that there were lower inventory levels in the system. Demand by consumers to pay less meant that new stock coming into the system came in cheaper and travelled through cheaper, establishing a new price equilibrium. New traders importing and selling cheaply attracted good custom, taking part in a type of lean operation more suitable for so much of the post-bubble buying habits. All this happened while established businesses struggled or went bankrupt under the pressure of trying to operate within an existing expensive and weighty marketing system.

Market adjustment

Financial pressure quickly worked its way through the system. It moved from those who had borrowed money, and began to affect those who had lent it. Japanese financial institutions were harbouring a lot of undeclared debt. Instead of writing off the debts, enabling dead assets to be sold and brought back into productive use, thus also allowing creditors to quickly recover what they could, the banks' reaction was to wait until the stock and real estate markets rebounded, which would clear some of the debt and raise the value of their collateral. This is rather like driving around feeling car-sick, but not wanting to stop and get out, hoping it will go away naturally. It didn't.

Banks began by disguising their losses, keeping them from the current year's balance sheet in order that it too would look healthy, so they would maintain confidence amongst the public. The inevitable result was that it would appear on next year's balance sheet; but hopefully things would be better by then.

Holding one's breath until things improve assumes that the cost of the extrapolated debt will be less than going bankrupt. In Japan, where social factors are often more important than elsewhere, the cost of bankruptcy is perceived to be high. It's seen as responsible to look after workers, and it's embarrassing for workers to have belonged to a failed company. Further, the lifetime employment system has made it virtually impossible for a career employee to gain an equivalent position in another Japanese company. And of course – on the positive side – for companies that do 'hang in there', the possibility is greater in Japan that those firms around it will eventually help pull the company out of trouble. Though with all of them facing the same difficulty, mutual help within corporate Japan became more thinly spread.

Tight lending

By 1997 Japan's banks, yet to clear their bad debts, remained in poor health; a situation exaggerated by impending deregulation and competition with foreign banks, for which they were ill prepared. In order to maintain the BIS 8 per cent requirement they began selling their loans, some at discount rates, to foreign banks entering or already in Japan. Unlike Japanese banks, foreign banks could afford to buy, and the loans provided them with income in the form of interest payments. Foreign banks had been lending to their own securities affiliates, but loans to domestic Japanese concerns, while steadily increasing, had remained low. Alternately, ailing Japanese banks were retrenching, and this did give foreign banks a first-time golden opportunity to secure the business of some large Japanese companies.

The 8 per cent BIS rule had applied only to banks operating internationally. But MOF decided that it wanted to improve the stability of all other banks, and announced that as of 1 April 1998 Japan's remaining banks would have to meet a (less stringent) capital to asset ratio of 4 per cent. Failure to do so could lead MOF to restrict dividend payments and the opening of branches, in addition to being required to buoy up capital. The result of this, however, was even tighter lending policies amongst those banks trying to increase their internal reserves, which by late 1997 included more than 90 per cent of Japan's regional banks.[10] This meant a shortage of capital for Japanese business, and at the same time an opportunity for foreign financial institutions to continue to fill that void in lending.

The shortage was accentuated by other factors inherent in the Japanese financial system. As mentioned above, much of the risk-lending has been in the hands of *sōgō shōsha*. Japanese banks have had a policy of not lending without collateral. Those wanting to borrow have typically had to produce assets or a guarantor to cover any loss. Clearly, this dampened venture business, and put companies wanting to expand into a dependency relationship with such firms as the *shōsha* or other backers.

One consequence is that Japanese bankers have not been skilled credit analysts, and according to some, during the free lending–free spending bubble era of the late 1980s, as a group their appraisal abilities further degenerated. (Nearing the end of the 1990s, amid a growing number of small business bankruptcies, foreign software makers did well supplying Japanese financial institutions with credit-risk-assessment software.)

Banks in a bind

Under the tight financial situation, exaggerated by the demands to meet the BIS standards, banks turned to life insurers, the traditional suppliers of subordinated debt, for funds. However, insurers became less willing to lend because of the increased risk in the changed Japanese financial environment; an environment that had, in the 1990s, seen financial institutions go bust for the first time in the memory of most Japanese people.

Japanese banks had, by this stage, come to terms with the idea of declaring and writing off bad loans as losses. This had been spurred by a MOF decision to introduce, on 1 April 1998, new harsher definitional categories for (bad) loans. The new standards also gave MOF the prerogative to order banks to undertake corrective action or to close or merge. Doing this put further pressure on banks to tighten lending.

The market was further shocked when the *Nikkei Shimbun*, Japan's business news-paper, ran an article on 7 November 1997 saying that the Bank of Yokohama, Japan's largest regional bank, planned to sell off 'almost all of its stockholdings'. This news not only sliced away almost a quarter of the value of Bank of Yokohama shares, but also took almost 10 per cent off the value of bank shares as a whole, and it caused a severe drop in the value of the stock market in the week that followed.

The *Nikkei Shimbun* was roundly criticized for announcing what had, in a low-key way, been taking place for some time anyway. Banks had been quietly reducing their cross-shareholdings, particularly in poorly performing firms, in order to shore up their own finances. Furthermore, there was a type of morality to holding 'friendly' shares – banks were playing their part in the business community – so to ditch them wouldn't be seen in a positive light. But now that one bank had been seen, in a sense, to have taken the first step, it was feared that it would be easier for others to follow, and this would lead to a flood of shares that would further depress the market.

By this time, the government was in a quandary as to how to resolve the bind: they felt it necessary to pressure banks to shore up their liquidity, but doing so forced banks to tighten lending, which starved industry of finance. Ironically, while all this was happening, money, for those who could get it, was virtually free. The official discount rate – at which government loans money to banks – had, since 1995, remained at a rock bottom 0.5 per cent.

Options available

In order to ease the situation, several measures were undertaken. At the end of 1997 MOF announced a one-year moratorium on the 4 per cent capital adequacy requirement for banks operating (only) within Japan. Banks were also given the 'opportunity' to revise their assets to current market value rather than purchase value. This gave them the chance to include the gains achieved through revaluation of their land as part of their (Tier-2) capital. While these gains were only on paper, doing so would help boost their capital–asset ratios, making them appear more liquid, and so would allow them to lend more.

Another means of dealing with the problem was through stock options. Stock options were first permitted in Japan in 1995, initially as part of an effort by MITI to spur the growth of a few small businesses. Options, which allowed employees to buy company shares at a set price in the future, were seen by workers as a morale booster, plus holders of the options were given favourable tax treatment. The options are not taxed, that is, until they have been realized as shares and a capital gain is made on their subsequent sale. And options allowed companies to expand while keeping employee wage costs low.

The system was further liberalized on 1 June 1997. Previously, Japan's Commercial Code only allowed firms to hold up to 3 per cent of their own shares at a time, and they could only do that for up to six months. The new regulations allowed a firm to hold 10 per cent of its own shares for up to ten years, and required firms to hold enough shares to cover demand at maturity of the options.

Given lacklustre stock trading and that banks were selling off 'permanent' share-holdings in related companies, further flooding an already depressed market, the government decided that if firms were able to buy their own shares this would soak up some of that excess and help prop up the stock market.

For instance, trouble struck the 65-year-old machinery parts-making business of an old friend of mine. While his firm's real estate earnings were high, manufacturing, the company's main business, was doing poorly. Three major banks, IBJ, Sakura and Tokyo–Mitsubishi, each held between 3.5 and 5 per cent of its shares. But because of the firm's performance, the banks were beginning to treat their loans to the company with trepidation.

They began shortening the loan terms, and then in 1997 IBJ announced that it would sell off its shares in the firm. This was interpreted with anxiety: on the one hand, it raised the possibility, in my friend's mind, even with this small number of shares, that control might slip into unfriendly hands – this is a fairly standard Japanese reaction. On the other hand, if there were no buyers it would devalue his firm's shares. Until 1997 the situation wouldn't have occurred – the banks wouldn't have traded in his shares – but now he had to worry about those shares going onto the market. The change in the Commercial Code, on the pretext of granting stock options, allowed such firms to pull their own shares off the stock market. Since the wheels of a 65-year-old company don't move very fast, nothing has happened in his case to date, but at least his firm has that route available. Incidentally, his response to his banks' pulling back was to try to establish a borrowing relationship with a smaller regional bank.

Why had the stock options system been prevented in the past? Essentially, Japan has loose disclosure rules, and it was decided that if company management could directly profit from changes in their share values, that would encourage share price manipulation. Indeed, in an environment in which, even amongst the nation's lawmakers, inside information is seen as a privilege rather than a crime, allowing companies to keep their own stocks without beefing up the disclosure laws is to invite trouble.

Foreign financial institutions in Japan: a case study

Retail banking

The Dutch bank ABN AMRO has a longer history in Japan than any other foreign financial institution (its roots go back into the Tokugawa era, well before the 'birth' (in 1868) of modern Japan). ABN AMRO was keen to establish itself in retail banking in Japan, but foreign banks were not always shown the red carpet. According to one of the firm's executives,

> 'previously, whether there were regulations or not, if MOF didn't want a bank operating in a particular field – and this applied particularly to foreign banks – they made it difficult for it to enter. For example, a few years ago when Citibank of the US wanted to enter retail banking, MOF in effect prevented it from doing so. But such things are possible now.'

From a practical point of view, as a foreign bank, ABN AMRO faced the problem of needing a network of branches in Japan. In lieu of creating its own customer base it had the option of merging with or taking over a bank with an established network. ABN AMRO decided to buy a controlling interest in an existing Japanese bank. By 1997 there were two possibilities: take over a bank with a strong regional network, or take over one of Japan's city banks. This would involve the surprise buy-up of a sufficient number of shares to gain control.

ABN AMRO Japan, in concert with headquarters in Holland, decided to get the Japan division of one of the world's largest consultant firms to survey the market in order to clarify their position regarding their take-over bid. This turned out to be a mistake. The result of the research was that, in the view of the consultancy, ABN AMRO should not expand into the market, at least not at this point. Head office in Holland took this as gospel and called off the move. This wasn't, however, how ABN AMRO in Tokyo saw or assessed the situation. Staff in Tokyo continued to see the buyout as judicious and well timed. Having read the report they considered that the consultancy lacked an appropriate grasp of the financial and cultural realities of the Japanese situation. So this set ABN AMRO Tokyo and head office at odds with each other, with Tokyo trying to convince Holland that it should ignore the report and continue with the expansion.

Then, in late 1997 came the economic crisis that badly affected several of the economies in Asia. Since Holland has a history of strong investment in the region, this side-tracked head office from further decisions on the buyout, which was at least put on hold.

Stock trading

In 1987 AMRO Bank (part of what would become ABN AMRO) became a fully licensed broker in Japan, though without a seat on the exchange it was only able to purchase stocks and bonds through brokers with exchange membership. It initially traded primarily on behalf of Dutch investors while also creating its own local client base. However, the collapse of the bubble economy in the 1990s meant that was severely cut back. The business had only just begun to generate a return, but its profits were slashed, resulting in staff layoffs.

In countries other than Japan, like other financial organizations, ABN AMRO's banking and securities functions operated together; but regulations prevented them from doing so in Japan. The two divisions had operated literally within a thin wall of each other but, as in the case of other banks that did the same, in Japan they were prevented from sharing such resources as client details, information on rates, office equipment and clerical staff – when MOF was watching.

The reality was that not sharing resources was impractical, or practically impossible. According to an executive at another large foreign broker, 'In 1992 a couple of our staff visited MOF and inadvertently mentioned the access that the broking and banking divisions had to each other. One or two weeks later MOF phoned us and ordered us to submit a layout and photos of the office and wall.' The regulation governing this matter is known 'affectionately' in the industry as 'Article 65', and although it has been weakened, allowing more interplay between broking–banking, there are no firm plans for complete removal of the 'fire-wall'. Still, MOF does grant flexibility in administering the regulation. Asked if he thought MOF was losing power to enforce this type of rule, this executive said: 'MOF isn't losing power. They will never lose power.' And the basic reason, he says, is because of the control they have available through *amakudari* (post-retirement placing) connections.

On 1 November 1997 ABN AMRO furthered its commitment to Japan's finance industry by buying seats on both the Tokyo and Osaka exchanges. It bought the TSE seat from a small Tokyo-based securities firm for over ¥1bn (about $10mn). This represented the first sale of an exchange membership by a Japanese firm that was not the result of a merger between two existing exchange members. This reflected the problems Japanese brokers were having in the market as a result of both residual debt from the collapsed bubble and the threat to their stable and protected environment due to the approaching Big Bang.

ABN AMRO's advance is representative of the general tenor of both entry into and the expansion of foreign business in Japan's finance industry. Their activities also reflect the general breakdown of restrictions in other areas of Japanese business, which is increasingly allowing greater entry into Japan of foreign business.

The stock market

At least until the latter 1980s Japanese people had never seen the stock market as the source of business finance that it was in the West. Instead, it had often been seen as a type of investment entertainment, and treated with some derision.[11] Furthermore, Japanese shareholders were, and still are, not given the same authority or the return on dividends that Western shareholders get; instead, stocks have typically been bought in order to make capital gains at the time of their sale.

That began to change during the period of the bubble economy, during the latter 1980s, when fortunes were made through stock and property investment. After the bubble collapsed, all forms of investment slowed, and while banks continued their existing role of providing finance for business, in the reshuffling there emerged a larger role for the stock market.

Background

The Tokyo Stock Exchange (TSE), Japan's largest exchange, was established on 15 May 1878 as the Tokyo Stock Exchange Co. Ltd. The stock exchange began by trading *samurai* bonds. We've all heard of *'samurai* bonds' ... but these were the real thing. As Japan Westernized it paid off its *samurai* – who had been allocated a regular gratuity – with lump sum government bonds, and these were handled by the TSE.

In addition to the TSE, Japan has eight other exchanges. In total there are six exchanges in the main island, Honshū (Tokyo, Osaka, Nagoya, Kyōto, Hiroshima and Niigata), one in the southern island, Kyūshū (Fukuoka), and one in the northern island of Hokkaidō (Sapporo). The TSE handles 80–90 per cent of Japan's traded share volume, Osaka is the next largest, followed by Nagoya.

Actually it is Osaka rather than Tokyo that can claim to have had Japan's first exchange. Residents of Osaka are still proud of being Japan's historical centre of trade, and historically commerce centred around rice. In 1697 the Dōjima rice market was established on a narrow island delta between the Shijimi and Dōjima rivers west of Osaka Castle. *Daimyō* (regional lords), at times notoriously hard-up, would sell the rights to rice in storage or rice not yet harvested. These rights, in the form of rice certificates, in turn became tradable items – merchants buying them were speculating on the future harvest price – and this made Dōjima one of the world's first futures markets.

Osaka formally established a modern exchange in June 1878, one month after Tokyo did. Originally called the Osaka Stock Exchange Co. Ltd, following World War II, when trading started again in 1949, it took its present name, Osaka Securities Exchange.

The remaining five regional exchanges combined handle just 1 per cent of Japan's trading volume. The smaller exchanges were originally set in place to help promising ventures go public in order for them to secure working capital, and thereby contribute to economic development and employment in local regions. But in the 1990s, in an increasingly competitive environment, and with companies having greater access to Japan's over-the-counter national pool of finance, the smaller exchanges began finding business difficult. Suggested remedies included that these local exchanges improve efficiency by merging, or operate as branches of the larger exchanges. Alternately, in 1997, in Sendai in the north of Japan's main island, Tōhoku University and other local institutions began discussing the possibility of creating Sendaq, a regional over-the-counter market. If they could offer creative investment products and trading methods the regional exchanges would be able to differentiate themselves from the major exchanges, providing specialized services to venture business.

Internationally, the TSE is second only to New York's exchange in market value, and it's generally considered the world's second largest exchange. However, both London and New York exceed the TSE in number of listed companies and in trading value. These relative rankings have remained the same since before and throughout Japan's 1990s recession.

Table 2.1 Major foreign brokers[12]

Company	Branches	Employees	Japan office established
Merrill Lynch*	Tokyo, Osaka, Nagoya	589	1972
Morgan Stanley	Tokyo, Osaka	679	1984
Goldman Sachs	Tokyo	524	1983
Salomon Smith Barney	Tokyo	382	1982
Lehman Brothers	Tokyo, Osaka	323	1986
UBS	Tokyo, Osaka	284	1987
SBC Warburg	Tokyo, Osaka	223	1986
Credit Suisse First Boston	Tokyo, Osaka	334	1985
Deutsche Morgan Grenfell	Tokyo	432	1986

* In 1998 Merrill Lynch Japan Securities, a separate company from Merrill Lynch, above, set up a retail network of, by 1999, 33 branches.

Foreign brokers

In 1973 the TSE was opened to foreign stocks, for which a foreign section was added, and amid Japan's flourishing economy accusations of a closed market led the TSE to grant membership to foreign brokers (see Table 2.1). Beginning in 1986, it increased the number of foreign seats on the exchange in stages. In 1986 the total number of exchange seats rose from 82 to 92, six of which were allocated to foreign brokers. In 1988 another 16, and in 1990 another three foreign brokers joined the TSE.

Japan has several stock indexes. The traditional indicator of stock movement is the Nikkei Stock Average, named after Japan's Nikkei business newspaper company. While the original Nikkei 225 today remains the standard, since it relies on a sample of 225 of the top shares from the First Section of the Exchange, it has a clear bias. Because of this, in 1969 TOPIX (Tokyo Stock Price Index) was started. It gives a weighted average of all stocks on the First Section of the TSE. Then in 1982 the Nikkei 500, and in 1993 the Nikkei 300 were introduced. In addition, Nikkei introduced specialized indexes, including the Nikkei Over-the-Counter Stock Average, in 1985, and the Nikkei All Stock Index for all of the stocks listed on Japan's eight stock exchanges, in 1991, calculated retrospectively to January 1980.

The Tokyo Stock Exchange is also available on the Internet. It provides current TOPIX listings and other market data, and it can link users to information on listed companies and to financial institutions. It also provides information on exchange rules, listing requirements and fees for prospective members, all in English[13] (TSE: www.tse.or.jp/eindex.html).

Market players

In the latter part of 1997 those observing Japan's finance industry were treated to what could have been interpreted, by the way the media handled it, as a kind of team event. Japanese securities firms that had long held dominance were having their position shaken by foreign securities firms that were gaining ground in the Japanese market. In August 1997 the combined share volume handled by the 21 foreign brokers on the Tokyo Stock Exchange exceeded that handled by Japan's big four: Nomura, Daiwa, Nikkō and Yamaichi. And by October the top individual traders in terms of volume were foreign; first Merrill Lynch, followed by Morgan Stanley. A weak Japanese economy had played a part, but what had capped that off was the revelation, and then punishment, of Japan's major brokers plus one of Japan's largest banks, the Dai-Ichi Kangyō Bank, for involvement in corporate extortion.[14]

Nomura, by far Japan's largest brokerage, has been no stranger to both corruption and scandal. In 1991 it had been punished for compensating the trading losses of favoured investors. In addition to all the big four, including Nomura, having to halt sales activities with corporate clients for four days in October 1991, Nomura's penalties included a suspension of broking in 87 of its 153 branches for up to six weeks; stock trading at Nomura's headquarters was stopped for a month; and the World Bank excluded Nomura and Nikkō from underwriting activities from September–November 1991. The scandal brought down then MOF minister Hashimoto Ryūtarō, as well as Nomura Chair Tabuchi Setsuya and President Tabuchi Yoshihisa (unrelated), all of whom resigned to take responsibility for the mess. And yet, within a few years, both of the (supposedly disgraced) Tabuchis returned to the upper echelons of Nomura's management and Hashimoto went on to become Prime Minister.

Nomura was also found to be involved in share price manipulation on behalf of Ishii Susumu, the boss of Japan's second largest *yakuza* (Mafia) gang, the Inagawa-kai. The *yakuza* had become interested in upmarket financial investment, spurred on by the burgeoning stock market. They, however, wanted the speculative aspects removed from their dealings, hoping the stock market would instead function as more of a straight-out, no-risk, investment. Nomura, with input from Nikkō, was able to help Ishii corner the shares (gain a monopoly of shares in the market). Nomura then promoted the shares through its branches, which drove up the price, with Ishii benefiting from their increase in value.

Its public chastising left a feeling that Nomura would then atone. However, in 1997 it was revealed that Nomura had been making loss compensation payments to a *sōkaiya* ex-gangster. *Sōkaiya* buy enough shares in a firm to attend shareholder meetings and are paid either for ensuring they go quickly, unhampered by difficult questions from shareholders, or for threatening to disrupt the meetings by asking difficult questions. Nomura disguised the payments by compensating the trading losses of a firm owned by the *sōkaiya*'s brother. In 1995 alone, the *sōkaiya* received an illegal ¥320mn in cash and ¥50mn from stock trades ($3.9mn total).[15]

'One woe doth tread upon another's heels, how fast they follow. . .'

By this stage, observers were simply waiting for the other major securities brokerages to also be implicated, and sure enough, one by one it emerged that they too were embroiled in payoffs. It's not actually surprising that they were all involved in what was in effect 'corporate-culture Japan'. Covering risk by paying money for favours has been going on in Japan since the year dot – this is common knowledge – what was interesting was that these big institutions were all paying a *lot* of money to this one very influential *sōkaiya*.

And then there were three

The 'big four' had become a part of the Japanese business vernacular, as familiar as Detroit's 'big three'. So despite recent business closures in Japan, what was broadcast from a press conference on 24 November 1997 sent a particular shiver down the spine. Japan was to be treated to what was the third of eventually four financial collapses that month. The Hokkaidō Takushoku Bank had collapsed a week before, Sanyō Securities filed for protection on 3 November, and later, on 26 November, the Tokuyō City Bank collapsed. But what rocked the nation was the announcement that Yamaichi, a mainstay of Japan's financial structure, was to close down. There was a sense of fireworks in the air that month, as financial firms were going off as if at random one after another.

Unbeknownst to most people outside of Yamaichi, and its main bank (Fuji Bank) and, though they denied it, MOF, Yamaichi had been strapped with debts. Its immediate difficulties traced back to its failure to recover from the collapse of the bubble in the early 1990s. And in addition to that, it was caught up in the loss compensation débâcle which resulted in it losing corporate sales. Since Yamaichi gained 90 per cent of its profits on sales commissions, not only was this a heavy blow, but it made it difficult for Yamaichi to diversify to other revenue-generating operations.

Yamaichi had chosen to hide the losses in one form or another. Traditional methods of doing so – and those also adopted by Yamaichi – include flipping debts between related firms with different accounting periods and sending debts to dummy companies, and in Yamaichi's case it also sent debts offshore. According to former Yamaichi executives, a president of Yamaichi visited MOF's securities bureau twice over the period December 1991–January 1992. When asked how it should handle the losses, the MOF official reportedly suggested that Yamaichi deal with them offshore, otherwise MOF would have to investigate. This fits in with the standard pattern of informal 'administrative guidance' issued by officials. Still, the MOF official denied having made the suggestion.[16] Anyway, ultimately Yamaichi declared off-the-books losses of ¥264.8bn ($2.12bn), two-fifths of which was offshore.

Getting staffed

One of the most challenging problems for foreign firms trying to establish a beach-head in Japan is the difficulty of securing good staff and of opening local offices. Now, with even big-name Japanese companies going to the wall, there is an unprecedented opportunity for foreign firms (assuming they have the capital resources, the negotiating savvy and the corporate resolve to succeed in Japan) to acquire two of the most important assets of any well-established Japanese firm: experienced staff and their aggregate *jinmyaku* (personal networks).

For example, in the case of the Yamaichi collapse, many of Yamaichi's employees were quickly scooped up by both Japanese and foreign firms. Amongst the foreign firms, American Family Life Assurance Co., in line with its expansion within Japan, decided to hire about 600 Yamaichi employees, mostly sales agents, plus some executives. Whole Yamaichi units were purchased by other foreign firms wanting to buy in Yamaichi expertise. The French bank, Société Générale, announced that it would buy 85 per cent of Yamaichi International Capital Asset Management Co., retaining its 130 employees, while installing some Société Générale directors.

Also, top foreign broker Merrill Lynch took advantage of the Yamaichi collapse to build the foundations for a retail brokerage network of the type that would normally take a decade to put together. Using about 30 of Yamaichi's branches and 2000 Yamaichi workers, Merrill Lynch launched the first attempt by a foreign firm to target individual investors – adding to the problems of Japanese brokers, which up until that time hadn't had to worry about foreign competition in the retail area. Of a total of 8200 Yamaichi staff to look for new jobs, by April 1998, three months after the collapse, 70 per cent had found placements, a large number with foreign firms.

Financing SMEs: problems of Japan's over-the-counter (OTC) market

Japan's stock exchanges comprise two sections, a Second Section having been added to the Tokyo Exchange in 1961, with other exchanges following suit. In addition, stocks of some smaller firms not on the exchange are traded over-the-counter. OTC stocks are traded by securities dealers and their price is negotiated between buyer and seller at the time of sale. The OTC market was patterned after America's NASDAQ, as a mechanism to assist smaller firms to get finance in order for them to develop, and while many people in Japan also see that as a mission of their OTC market, this is not how it has functioned.

The matter has its roots in the way large and small businesses are perceived in Japan. There is an inherent bias toward large firms – this is part of what is referred to as Japan's dual economy, whereby large, established firms remain at the top. In Japan this dominant group of big businesses has ready access to capital, top employees, good *jinmyaku*, and they command high status amongst the public. Each of these assets serves to facilitate and strengthen the existence of the others.

Amongst small businesses, the absence of each of these assets in turn weakens the others. A perception of small businesses as unstable and weak keeps away good employees and limits other opportunities, and this helps keep them weak. This social structure functions to ensure a polarization between large and small firms – one which works to the disadvantage of the small and medium-sized enterprises (SMEs). Still, since SMEs are of growing importance to Japan's economy, these characteristics of Japan's business environment stifle not only SME growth, but the considerable benefits they could in turn bring to the rest of the economy.

Access to finance

Fundamental to the matter is SME dependency on, but inability to access, finance. Indeed, as there are regulations that stifle business activity in other areas, access to Japan's OTC market is no exception. Regulations have made it expensive and otherwise difficult to achieve OTC registration in Japan. In addition to other regulations, unwritten rules have required firms to have net assets of ¥1bn ($10mn) and pre-tax profits of ¥300mn ($3mn) – this is a very high ceiling. As a result, it has taken OTC companies on average upward of 25 years to be listed. The result is that the OTC market has not hosted innovative new start-ups; listing on it has rather been a form of status, an acknowledgement of the achievement, or coming of age, of mature firms.

Illustrative of the matter is the Japanese software firm Dynaware. Dynaware was formed in 1984 by some graduates of Osaka University who were involved in innovative work with 3-D graphics software. This gradually spread to the development of other software systems. A decade later, Dynaware had ¥2.8bn ($25mn) in sales, it had secured some very large Japanese customers and was engaged in joint development with Apple Computer. Furthermore, according to Dynaware President Fujii Nobuyuki, Dynaware had developed operating software that had paralleled Microsoft's, before Microsoft had released theirs, but Dynaware couldn't get access to the necessary development finance that would, in the opinion of Fujii, have made Dynaware a world leader in software development.[17]

In reality, SMEs have found it particularly difficult to get any funding, not only from the capital market but also from banks. Rather than assess firms on their potential, banks make – or don't make – loans based on a client's access to collateral, or their current financial disposition. And what actually happens is that, ultimately, if firms don't have assets or a guarantor, they simply don't bother trying.

In the mid-1990s Japan's administrators came to appreciate the situation which began to show up as a clear problem in such areas as Japanese computer software production. The case of Dynaware is reflected in the statistics. A 1994 survey showed that computer software trade ran at approximately (imports) 19:1 (exports).[18] The following year, the Japanese government came up with the Temporary Law Concerning Measures for the Promotion of the Creative Business Activities of Small and Medium Enterprises – the

'Creativity Law'. This was designed to foster the type of inventive business processes that, it was decided, were lacking in Japan – that is, to actively foster the development and utilization of entirely new technology and to foster the involvement of 'creative' businesses in new markets. But attempts to encourage small business growth still faced tough barriers, not the least of which were finance-related.

In order to give SMEs a boost, MITI, on its own and together with the Fair Trade Commission and MOF, undertook measures to ease access to capital, expertise and training for venture businesses. MITI and MOF also negotiated the easing of OTC registration restrictions. This led in 1996 to a second, more flexible OTC market intended to foster innovative firms.[19] However, SME earnings declined and investments in both the OTC markets stagnated. This meant that it was somewhat redundant that, as of 1 July 1997, securities firms were allowed to broker shares of companies not on the exchange or OTC market, providing a market approximating the 'pink sheets' market in the US.

Administrative caution

The Ministry of Finance was at this point wedged between the need to progress and its instinctive desire to move with caution (the *'kanryō's* paradox'); MOF's cautious approach was not without some foundation.

Post-World War II industrial growth led to a flurry of companies wanting their stocks traded on the (at the time) very loose 'over-the-counter market'. Establishing the Second Section in 1961 represented an attempt by MOF to bring order to the situation. The money that flowed into the market in response further stimulated stock values. However, the cycle soon began to reverse and the Bank of Japan and MOF spent the next four years trying to offset panic and collapse.

When, in 1997, the fourth of the big four collapsed, strapped with debt, many people failed to realize that 35 years before, as Japan's then largest securities firm, it had experienced almost the same thing. Yamaichi Securities Co. was, at the time, at the fore in fostering new listings. It had invested heavily and profited well from the rapid growth of new stocks. Yamaichi had not only undertaken the function of underwriter but in many cases had borrowed to speculate in the new listings itself.

But when trouble struck and weaker firms departed, Yamaichi was left with a body of worthless paper and overwhelming interest payments. The 'panic of 1965' put Yamaichi, and Nikkō, on the verge of collapse, requiring financial intervention by the central bank, and while both survived, Yamaichi fell from first place amongst Japan's brokers. In 1965 the Securities and Exchange Law was modified to reduce the chance of future problems. The percentage of their own assets that brokerages could commit to stockholdings was limited, and the authorities wanted supervision of the accounts of companies whose shares were being formally traded.

In the 1990s too, there were many bankruptcies amongst highly capitalized firms that had grown during the bubble period. For instance, in a historical first, in the first half of 1991 six firms with debts of over ¥100bn ($769mn) went under in just six months. In that period the increase in number of bankruptcies over the previous year was more than 60 per cent, but, even more astounding, the *total debt* for that six months increased by almost 400 per cent.[20] Aoyama Building Development is a good example. It operated from 1987–91, when it found itself unable to off-load ¥40bn ($307mn) of Tokyo real estate. This $3\frac{1}{2}$ year-old company had only 14 employees, but took with it ¥110bn ($846mn) of debt. In the same period golf club membership fees had skyrocketed, reaching into millions of yen. They became popularly traded items in a market of their own by brokers who, after the market collapsed, admitted that there should have been more regulation. Many clubs used a system of ten-year redeemable investor deposits. When these began to come due in the late

1990s, it was estimated that demands on the weakened clubs for refunds could bankrupt a fifth of Japan's golf clubs and cause a drag on the whole economy. It would cause job losses and drag down the stock market, before impacting on consumer spending. Accordingly, authorities have reacted cautiously toward the marketing of shares of what may turn out to be weak firms.

Conclusion

The finance system is set up to fund established firms. Traditionally, funding has trickled through large businesses (e.g. the *sōgō shōsha*) which have acted as credit assessors. Smaller enterprises have generally been able to entitle themselves to financial and other assistance by presenting themselves as reliable entities to, and in the service of, such larger firms. But Japan lacks the authoritative structures to deal with smaller operations and Japan's banks lack the risk assessment skills; they lack a culture of funding small firms, and more recently the money to support small business.

On the one hand, this has restricted new business start-ups. However, on the other hand, it is providing opportunities for foreign financial institutions that have entered Japan. Because of their attitudes toward lending and their financial strength, in Japan's deregulating environment these foreign firms will increasingly gain both large and smaller Japanese firms as customers.

Notes

1. Miyashita and Russell cite research which shows that, of the 873 non-financial firms on the First Section of the Tokyo Stock Exchange, the main bank was the number one shareholder for over 16 per cent, and number two for over 22 per cent. The main bank was the prime source of loans for over two-thirds of those firms (1994, pp. 48–49 and 214).
2. Murphy, 1996, p. 199.
3. Kanō, in Kanō *et al.*, 1993, p. 14.
4. Interest on subordinated debt for Japan's 11 city banks and three long-term credit banks had, by April 1991, reached an estimated (per annum) ¥350 bn ($2.6 bn) (*The Japan Times*, 1 June 1991, p. 9).
5. These restrictions were 'administrative guidance' rather than law. In full, they said that financial institutions can't allow the growth in their financing to real estate, non-bank and construction industries to be greater than growth in their overall lending.
6. *The Economist*, 18 January 1992, pp. 70 and 72; Wood, 1982, p. 31; *Tokyo Business Today*, November 1991, p. 43.
7. Wood, 1982, p. 34.
8. *Statistical Handbook of Japan*, 1993, p. 22.
9. *US and Japan in Figures IV*, JETRO, 1994, p. 22.
10. Survey by Nikkei Shimbun, in *The Nikkei Weekly*, 22 September 1997, p. 10.
11. Alletzhauser (1990, p. 33) refers to the low status of the stock market. Tamaki (1995, p. 205) notes that in the high-speed growth period of the 1950s–1960s over 80 per cent of financing came from financial institutions, under 20 per cent came from equities and debentures.
12. Source: *Nihon Keizai Shimbun*.

13 Nikkei also publishes a weekly newspaper in English, *The Nikkei Weekly*, which is a must for non-Japanese-speaking business operators in Japan, and should also be read by those with interests in Japan, living outside. Selections from the paper, including stock figures and subscription details, are available on the Internet: www.nikkei.co.jp/enews/TNW/page/index.html.

14 It was discovered that 300,000 shares in Nomura owned by *sōkaiya* Koike Ryūichi had been bought in 1989 with money from a ¥30bn ($217mn) loan made to Koike's brother's company (Kojin Building) by Dai-Ichi Kangyō Bank (DKB).

15 One of the reasons given for the payments was that the *sōkaiya*, Koike Ryūichi, would otherwise raise questions at Nomura's general meeting about Nomura's relations with the *yakuza* (Mafia) and Nomura's loss compensation payments. There was also the question of why in 1995, after an honorary period on the bench, both the Tabuchis (mentioned above) had been able to get back on Nomura's board.

16 *The Nikkei Weekly*, 2 February 1998, p. 3.

17 *Far Eastern Economic Review*, 30 June 1994, p. 48; *The Nikkei Weekly*, 1 August 1994, p. 1.

18 Figures for 1994, industry survey. In 1997 the Science and Technology Agency expressed concern at Japan's growing software royalty payments abroad; these typically indicate the strength/weakness of an industry (in *The Nikkei Weekly*, 14 April 1997, p. 3).

19 Whittaker, 1997, p. 210.

20 *The Japan Times*, 16 July 1991, p. 10.

Part Two

Four analyses of structure and strategy

Chapter 3

Setting up your business in Japan

The objective of many foreign firms is to get their product, or their company, into Japan – this section deals with the latter; foreign investment used to set up an operation in Japan. For this there are different options available, depending on the foreign company's financial and technical resources and the type of industry.

Starting with the broad picture of what is happening in terms of FDI going into Japan, we'll move through to the problems and to advice related to operating in the Japanese market.

Foreign Direct Investment (FDI)

FDI cuts both ways, or does it?

Historically, Japan has invested much more elsewhere than other nations have invested in Japan. In 1996 Japan invested $23,400mn abroad, while just $200mn came in. The ratio of incoming to outgoing investment is about 1 per cent, and while FDI amounts vary from year to year, this ratio is not necessarily unusual.

Investments made by different nations follow not only the fortunes of the donor economy, but also what investors think of the health of the recipient economy. US investor ideas about the merits of investing in Japan vs. elsewhere are reflected in the following: US outgoing FDI to *all* countries actually increased by 60 per cent between 1994/95, but that going to Japan dropped by over half in the same period, as can be seen in Tables 3.1 and 3.2. And in the mid-1990s, as the US economy improved, Japanese investors put money into the US as they pulled it from the EU.

The 1990s represented both a turbulent period for the Japanese economy, and a respite from the excesses of the 1980s. Japan's 1991 investment of $12,051mn into the US represented a tailing off of Japan's maniacal investments into the US during the latter

Table 3.1 FDI between Japan and the US ($ million)

	1991	1992	1993	1994	1995	1996
(a) US FDI into Japan	2,804	1,188	4,504	5,429	1,882	1,187
(b) Japan's FDI into US	12,051	2,627	2,952	2,278	4,934	10,183
(a) as a % of (b)	23	45	153	238	38	12

Source: JETRO

Table 3.2 FDI between Japan and the EU ($ million)

	1991	1992	1993	1994	1995	1996
(a) EU FDI into Japan	423	561	−1,424	318	−734	1,905
(b) Japan's FDI into EU	2,084	2,369	1,874	1,589	1,492	−230
(a) as a % of (b)	20	24	−	20	−	−

Source: JETRO
N.B. A negative figure indicates that more (existing) FDI was withdrawn than was invested.
EU = 12 countries, except 1996 = 15 countries

1980s, which peaked in 1988 at $16,700mn. Such amounts were not invested into Europe by Japan; Europe was not as popular, and the EU–Japan relationship has continued to be weaker than that between Japan and the US. According to Nagai Shin, Vice President of Treasury at Holland's ABN AMRO Bank (Japan),

'Europeans are sometimes hesitant when it comes to investing in Japan, Americans have had a closer relationship with Japan, they get more information about what is happening in the market and so are less reluctant to invest there.'

Despite the lacklustre FDI flows between the EU and Japan in many of the above figures, according to the Delegation of the European Commission the EU has achieved a lot in its methods of negotiating with the Japanese. While this is reflected in such positive figures as the very strong $1905mn of EU money invested into Japan in 1996, business figures are still not stable and are too contingent on such variables as the value of the yen. This means that European parts and finished products are in demand primarily when the yen is strong. There need to be factors that cause demand to be more stable and enduring, of the type that, for example, make European fashion items popular, at any price.

The upshot is that the patterns of FDI are not fixed, but change quite readily with the winds of the market. However, there are broad overall parameters, included in which is the fact that Japan's outgoing FDI is stronger than that coming in, and that the investment link between the EU and Japan has been weak. There is, however, no enduring reason for this and, clearly, given recent efforts by the EU, these conditions can change with the right administrative or other push.

The narrow picture

FDI gives a very broad picture of what foreign investments are actually taking place in Japan, but in order to understand what's happening in the market it's necessary to look beyond the gross figures, at the actual companies that are coming into or are in Japan. Knowing the amount of incoming FDI simply doesn't tell you how well small, or even large, firms are doing. But business people 'worth their salt' will of course want to know what the competition has done and what problems were faced by competitors who failed. While the field isn't well researched, a combination of examples and research information will enable readers to get a picture of the investment environment in Japan.

Market entry options

Options regarding market entry

The options for foreign firms wishing to enter the Japanese market are as follows:

100 per cent ownership	Establish a new plant or office (wholly owned subsidiary).
	100 per cent buyout of a Japanese firm (takeover).
Partial ownership	Establish a joint venture (subsidiary) with a Japanese firm.
	Purchase a controlling stockholding in a Japanese firm.
	Purchase a minority stockholding in a Japanese firm.
No ownership	Establish a supply relationship with a Japanese firm(s) (exporter).
	Enter into a licensing arrangement.

The dominant form of ownership amongst American and European business operations located in Japan is, by far, 100 per cent ownership.

In order to test the waters or because funding doesn't allow greater penetration, some foreigners initially get their product into Japan by exporting it through a foreign or Japanese trading company, by licensing its manufacture to a Japanese firm, or by entering into a joint venture with a firm. There is then a very strong tendency for firms to strengthen control over their businesses in Japan. About half of the firms in one survey had changed their business form, moving toward 100 per cent or at least majority ownership. That means a strengthening of position. Also, given that businesses move toward full ownership over time, it may indicate that, for planning purposes, more thought might be given by those planning on entering to the best form of initial ownership.[1]

Joint venture (JV)

Many companies still opt for a joint venture (JV) as a vehicle to entry. Survey data shows that, of both long-term and short-term American companies resident in Japan, just under one-fifth entered via a JV – as a category this was exceeded only by those who began by exporting.[2]

Following World War II, Japan's trade and investment laws and foreign exchange laws set limits on the establishment of foreign firms in Japan. This included the prohibition of 100 per cent foreign company ownership. And much of what was set up was at the discretion of, and done under the guidance of, MITI. Changes did gradually take place but, even as 'free market in principle' policies were adopted, respective ministries (though mainly MITI) retained the formal or informal prerogative to step in where it was felt necessary. This meant that in many cases written restrictions on investment activity were replaced with restrictions in the form of *gyōsei shidō* ('administrative guidance') or simply with intentional foot-dragging on the part of bureaucrats.

Through the 1990s a combination of foreign pressure and a troubled economy did result in government bureaucrats actually allowing much freer access in a number of areas, with fewer strings attached. This made it more possible for foreign firms to enter the market without needing to rely on a Japanese firm to facilitate business. Still, while restrictions on setting up wholly owned operations in Japan have greatly diminished, a JV does provide help in unknown territory, and means that firms can bypass many of the regulations that remain in Japan. A foreign firm can benefit from a JV by taking advantage of a Japanese partner's facilities and staff, and of less tangible assets, such as the network of business relations that a potential partner might have spent a lifetime developing – a part of which includes gaining access to the 'goodwill' inherent in a Japanese firm's distribution network.

There are still a variety of informal, semi-formal and formal restrictions remaining in Japan, but nowadays foreign capital is penetrating further and further along the sales chain to where majority as well as wholly owned operations such as Toys 'R' Us and Tower Records have control of goods right up to the customer.

Alive and kicking

Indeed, JVs in Japan are alive and kicking. Companies including Virgin Megastores (set up in 1990), Time Warner (1991) and Starbucks Coffee (1996) have entered Japan on the basis of a 50–50 JV. Eddie Bauer, in 1993, teamed up with an existing JV between the German mail-order firm Otto Versand and the trading firm Sumitomo Corp. (Sumishō). Otto–Sumishō, with a 70 per cent stake, provided Eddie Bauer (at 30 per cent) with distribution in the form of its existing mail-order structure.

Office Depot Inc., the largest office superstore chain in North America, and another top stationery retailer, Office Max Inc., both entered Japan by way of JVs (with the electronics chain Deodeo Corp. and discount chain Jusco, respectively) and opened outlets in Japan through 1996/97.

Stationery outlets had characteristically been the standard Japanese two- or three-person operations, which had been protected from competition by Japan's Large Scale Retail Store Law. These small shops had been tied to a rigid manufacturer-driven pricing system, which had contributed to high product prices. This state of affairs had led to an increasing shift in patronage to larger discount stores that offered a limited range of stationery products at lower prices. Office Depot and Office Max provided a combination of benefits by offering a comprehensive range of products at low prices. And both stores offered a 110 per cent refund of the difference in price of any product that could be found cheaper elsewhere.

Anticipating the arrival of such foreign stationery retailers, domestic suppliers began to try to streamline their supply routes in order to compete. The fate of many such small businesses was, however, imminent.

Kinko's: 'Bringing in success from home'

Kinko's is a seven-day, 24-hour business convenience store. In Japan it provides office support services; including self-service colour copying, on-demand printing, binding, layout and design consultation, film processing and (international) faxing. It also provides rental computers at ¥250 ($1.90) per 15 minutes, all in ample in-store work space.

Kinko's entered Japan in 1992, holding the majority share of a 51–49 per cent JV with Sumitomo Metal Mining. Sumitomo Metal, in a sluggish economy, had been looking for other investments, and one of its junior employees who had been sent to study in the US presented to top management his graduation report, written on how he envisaged kinko's could be brought to Japan. Duly inspired, Sumitomo Metal then contacted kinko's with a JV proposal, ultimately resulting in the formation of Kinko's Japan Co. Ltd.

Kinko's Japan initially set up shop in the suburbs of Nagoya, Japan's fourth largest city. Nagoya was badly hit during World War II, but was rebuilt with wider roads and a much more spacious layout than other Japanese cities. Thinking that Nagoya's landscape was similar to that of their location in the US, the firm expected that it could duplicate its US success by duplicating these circumstances. But in residential Nagoya, for two years kinko's experienced moderate performance – though it did turn a profit in the third year.

In retrospect, kinko's concluded that this was because small businesses in Nagoya were unfamiliar with both kinko's and the concept of a convenience business service. When kinko's established a store in Nagoya's central business district, business improved. Then in 1995 it set up in central Tokyo and within six months started to turn a profit there.

Helping the company's success is that about 30 per cent of kinko's customers have been foreign firms, either familiar with or at least prepared to use kinko's service. Also helping it become established was the Japanese recession, which forced Japanese companies to become conscious of their overheads, including labour. This encouraged them to look outside for services. Copying in-house is not free, nor is it necessarily efficient. Kinko's demonstrated that it was cheaper for companies to use them than to do copy work in-house. According to kinko's, they can, for instance, handle volume copying in one hour that would normally take three, and their copies are better quality. Demand has also increased for small-lot printing, which they can handle better than existing printers.

Neither does kinko's think that existing Japanese stationery service providers can adapt to match kinko's new services. According to the President of kinko's Japan, Nishida Ryōzō, the business structure of established print firms can't easily be changed. Their existing labour agreements, for instance, would make it difficult to move from a standard work day to 24-hour operation. Kinko's operating hours constitute a customer-service advantage, not only from the point of view of any-time access, but whereas a traditional store might take three days to complete an order, kinko's, with machines operating 'round the clock', might complete it overnight.[3]

Kinko's also faces competition from other US and Japanese entrants into the business convenience market, including Office Max and Office Depot, also of the US, as well as Fuji Xerox. But kinko's feels that its early lead gives it advantages. According to Mr Nishida:

'Our business style is quite unique, and if people associate this unique style with us, then the name kinko's will attain a sort of brand value. This is one reason why it is important for us to expand quickly.'

There is an interesting relationship between kinko's and one of those competitors, Fuji Xerox:

'Kinko's is the largest customer of Xerox in the world. This makes, or could make, for a slightly awkward situation if, for instance, Fuji Xerox decided to set up a store very near a kinko's outlet. Of course it's a free market, they can do anything they want to, but it would create an uneasy situation.'

Kinko's has the 'brand image' that comes with being both first and dominant within an industry. If kinko's remains innovative it should be able to stay ahead of the competition, setting new standards, as 7-Eleven did in the convenience food market.

Kinko's has other advantages. The twentieth century saw Japanese manufacturing firms excel in harnessing worker motivation and output. But Japanese tertiary sector firms are not as strong at extracting top performance from workers. Mr Nishida claims kinko's has a competitive advantage in business know-how, worker training and motivation – details of which kinko's is unwilling to disclose. Furthermore, this is know-how, he says, that is not Japanese or American but unique to kinko's.

Interestingly, according to Mr Nishida, the JV didn't bring with it any specific problems. The fact that Sumitomo Metal Mining had no knowledge of, or experience in, retailing presented advantages for the JV. Having a parent in the industry normally means a firm can draw upon the parent's resources; in many cases this means its clients. But kinko's competition, where it existed, was amongst disparate small service firms, not amongst firms with a fixed group of customers, so kinko's was in effect a pioneer, having to carve out a new customer base anyway. What it meant was that the parent didn't interfere in kinko's business. On the other hand, Sumitomo's name was still very useful. Kinko's was unknown in Japan and therefore had no influence, but Sumitomo is one of the biggest names in Japanese business, and that created instant trust amongst, for instance, landlords, and meant money could be borrowed 'from any bank'.

Unlike many Japanese JVs, kinko's was not a dumping ground for retiring personnel sent from the Japanese parent. Mr Nishida, as President, is one of the few who previously worked for Sumitomo. A common problem with JVs is that since many Japanese employees spend their whole working lives in one company, when, as seniors, they are transferred to a subsidiary, many can't shrug off the philosophy of the parent. Another problem is that many don't want to undertake action that works against the interests of the parent. This can cause problems for an otherwise innovative business, as it might have for kinko's.

JV with a keiretsu firm

Kinko's joined with Sumitomo Metal Mining, which is part of the Sumitomo *keiretsu* group of firms. Because these large *keiretsu* companies (there are many minor '*keiretsu*' groupings) have historically used their close 'family-member' nature as a basis for trade, a foreign firm that joins one in a JV might expect to be able to tap into other *keiretsu* supply and distribution channels. This is preferable to the outsider status, which has normally meant that such firms have been blocked out of *intra-keiretsu* trade which dominates some areas of industry.

However, firms thinking of tying up with a *keiretsu* company should check out the potential for trade with other *keiretsu* firms, without making the assumption that there is an inherent benefit in a *keiretsu* tie-up. Survey research found that of 29 foreign companies in Japan with *keiretsu* ties, only four claimed that they benefited from the *keiretsu* affiliation.[4]

Large *keiretsu* firms tend to be more traditional and staid – set in their ways – than firms without the established history, or the support of the *keiretsu* structure. Therefore the long-standing *keiretsu* have been less flexible and less able to change where needed in a changing business environment. The more flexible of the *keiretsu* brethren – at least because they, more than the other members, have international experience – are the *sōgō shōsha* trading firms, which have been responsible for many tie-ups, with a range of foreign businesses. Kentucky Fried Chicken's entry into Japan was through its joint venture with Mitsubishi Shōji. KFC reaped from the deal Shōji's skills at importing chickens and feed, their ability to organize the construction of facilities, and to distribute the chickens. Shōji holds 30.5 per cent of KFC Japan. Calvin Klein Japan Co. and Max Mara Japan Co. are separate JVs, both involving Mitsui Bussan as a minority shareholder. Giorgio Armani Japan Co. Ltd is a JV involving Armani of Italy and Itōchū (at 40 per cent).

Problems with JVs

JVs are not without problems, and many break up because the parties involved can't see eye to eye. While joint ventures share the common aim of putting product in the hands of customers and of making money, as can be seen by Figure 3.1, to a large extent they involve a conflict of interests, about which the parties must compromise if the venture is to be successful. Furthermore, differing perspectives about business held by each side puts them to a large extent (culturally) at odds with each other. While differences in *goals* are relatively easy to identify, the differences in *business perspectives* are more problematic because people don't realize they exist until it's too late.

One of the problems most identified with JVs is that while the foreign firm needs continued reliance on the Japanese partner's resources – distribution network, *jinmyaku* (contacts), factory, or simply navigating within Japan – in many cases the Japanese side has

Foreign	Japanese
Differing goals	
Wants access to distribution structure Wants its product to be the focus of the JV firm	Wants technology/know-how Wants product to supplement its existing range
Differing business perspectives	
Seeking profit ● Expects to demonstrate strong profitability	Seeking business growth ● Will plough money back into the business
Expects loyalty from all staff	Staff seconded from Japanese parent will be loyal (also) to interests of that parent
High quality ● is contingent on the cost of quality	Ensuring quality ● is a fundamental policy
Accepts turnover of management ● which brings changes in firm's policies	Expects stable management ● which results in stable company policies

Figure 3.1 Foreign conflicts with Japanese joint venture goals

entered the partnership to access technology, and once it has this its incentive to maintain the relationship greatly decreases.

Another problem is that in tying up with a Japanese retail operation, a foreign firm will want priority given to its product. A local JV partner, however, might be looking at the product only to supplement its range. It may therefore be necessary to build into a contract such details as amount of shelf space and location within a store to be committed to the project, or, if the project is large enough, to establish separate, dedicated outlet(s).

Quality

The problem of quality recurs throughout different areas of Japanese business. In a JV it can mean a head-on clash where both parties have control over production but have conflicting ideas about what's important in creating the product.

Hamada Tomoko provides a good example of the problem in her extensive study of American enterprise in Japan. She outlines two tie-ups between a single Japanese company and two (unrelated) US firms, each of which produced a JV subsidiary. The first JV made synthetic resins and polymer products, the other made a plastic wrapping material. Both JV firms used a manufacturing plant in Japan and US technology to make product for the Japanese market.

In both cases the Japanese noted aesthetic quality problems. In the first there was a slight odour that received complaints from Japanese customers. In the second the product lacked consistency in appearance, it contained a few air bubbles and the edges of the material were shabby.

In both cases the problems were dismissed by the American parents on the basis that the issue was one of aesthetics and didn't affect the function of the product. The products were successful and commanded a strong market share in the US and in other foreign markets, and they didn't consider it worth spending time and money addressing the matter. In the second case the foreign firm said that the aesthetic 'problems' were actually a product of the (unreasonable) demands of the Japanese market and that the Japanese marketing division should re-educate their customers accordingly. One of the American executives complained that the Japanese should be convincing the Japanese market that appearance has nothing to do with product quality. Instead, he said, the Japanese have 'placed an unreasonable burden on the production facility to produce products which suit the user's taste.'[5] This idea is incredible: in Japan the user's taste 'is everything' – as Japanese people say, 'the customer is god.'

In the first JV, after asking the American side to help resolve the problem, the Japanese finally decided to re-engineer the product themselves. By the time of the second JV, appreciating that they had previously wasted a lot of time negotiating the issue, the Japanese quickly took it upon themselves to again rework the product at their own expense.

This kind of activity naturally has implications for the concept of a 'joint venture'. We know that quality, in the terms that the Japanese define it, is a real problem for foreign firms in the Japanese market – the target market in this case. The situation might, as it did in this case, lead the Japanese to wonder if they wouldn't have been better off simply licensing the technology, since they couldn't get the foreigners to understand the problem, and because they did the additional work anyway. It is worth knowing that JVs are commonly seen by Japanese as a lesser alternative to licensing or buying the technology, as doing so avoids conflict – conflict which is exaggerated when dealing across cultures.

Finances

One of the biggest problems with JVs in Japan is conflicting expectations over finance. In Western firms, both shareholders and decision-making executives push for profitability more so than they do in Japan. Shareholders in Japan have little influence over company policy, and since jobs in Japan are held for longer there is an incentive to reinvest company profit in new product development in order to strengthen the long-term performance of the company. Where a foreign and a Japanese company work together, these goals quite clearly clash.[6]

The matter raises the importance in Japan of the employees. That it is the shareholders who own a business is a modern, Western idea – a response to a scarcity of capital which in turn led to a separation of the ownership of capital from labour. The idea of a business as a mutual concern, with the family head in overall control, is still at the root of Japanese corporate thinking. Western employees (in many cases begrudgingly) accept that control is in the hands of an abstract entity: a board of directors and a group of shareholders that the worker may have never seen. This is, however, anathema to business thinking in Japan, where directors are often derived from the company, and management has in many cases come up from union ranks.[7] And while Japan has of course adopted Western corporate practices, the dominant perception amongst those in Japanese companies is that the company belongs to those in the company, not the shareholders. What this means in practice is that while little attention is paid to what shareholders think in Japan, people believe that a lot of consideration should be given to the workers.

Acquisitions

Reassuring employees

This also means that buying, or buying into, a company is not just a matter of gaining the agreement of the shareholders, but also of winning the consent of the workers.

In its process of expansion, the electronics company Canon has, over the years, carried out its share of acquisitions, and, having undertaken many of them himself, Canon's Takikawa Seiichi comments, 'Businesspeople should forget about attempting American-style mergers and acquisitions in Japan.'[8]

Canon took over Copyer Co., a 60-year-old firm that had become successful in making photo-sensitive-paper copiers, but these had become dated with advances in plain paper technology. Copyer's president had come to Takikawa for assistance, and the two had decided on acquisition. They kept this quiet while details were settled, but news of the plan broke through the press, causing concern amongst the workers. Takikawa met the union leaders because, he says, 'I wanted to understand the worries and anxieties of Copyer's employees.' He adds,

> 'After the takeover, there was still much uneasiness, so I decided to go around the country and meet all the 1200 employees. . . . I spent the equivalent of two years visiting all the facilities, talking to just about every individual in the organization and trying to convince them that I . . . just wanted to make the company successful.'[9]

Misawa Homes is a major Japanese pre-fabricated house builder. It heads a group of Misawa companies, presided over by the very charismatic Misawa Chiyoji. Misawa made several acquisitions, based on the president's policy of diversification as the company moved into the twenty-first century. According to M&A analyst Ishizumi Kanji, Misawa has been successful, and has avoided criticism over its acquisitiveness, firstly because Misawa's target companies were 'either in financial distress or bothered by rigging attempts by groups of speculative investors, or both. In other words, as far as they were concerned, Misawa Homes came to their rescue as a "White Knight" in shining armour.'[10] And secondly, Misawa cared for the target company employees. In the words of President Misawa Chiyoji,

> 'Though corporations are owned by their shareholders . . ., in Japan, traditionally management, as well as the general public, consider that the employees are more important than the shareholders. . . . If you want to be really successful in making mergers and acquisitions in Japan, the first thing you must do above all is to persuade and get the support of the employees of the target companies.'[11]

Misawa's first acquisition in 1983 produced Misawa VAN Corp., from an ironworking and engineering firm called Suzuki Iron Works. Misawa VAN is now a data retrieval and information equipment business, as well as a real estate developer. While negotiating the takeover, Mr Misawa spent two days personally meeting Suzuki's 100 employees, a demonstration of sincerity which helped win them over.[12]

If you intend a friendly takeover, many of Japan's millions of small-to-medium-sized companies would be prime targets, particularly those in the manufacturing sector. A lot of these firms began after World War II, and in many cases their founders are today having difficulty finding replacements to head their firms as they retire. Many of the founders would prefer a descendant to take over the business, but this is very often not possible. If, in negotiations, consideration is given to the future of the company and the well-being of the employees, it might be possible to undertake a successful acquisition.

Head to head

One of the advantages of dealing with smaller companies is the ability to work directly with a founder–owner, who in most cases can expedite negotiations. However, small companies and small-company owners present other problems, which a culturally savvy foreign buyer would do well to keep in mind. Consider, for example, the case of a foreign semiconductor manufacturer who tried to acquire a local Japanese company.

The foreign firm, wanting to expand sales in Japan, contacted a local Japanese branch of its home bank to see if the bank could assist in finding a suitable Japanese company for it to purchase. The bank then contacted and confidentially met the president of a troubled Japanese firm. Initially, the bank simply discussed ways of improving the small firm's business performance. After a number of meetings, the bank gently introduced the idea of selling the business to a suitable local or perhaps even a foreign buyer. The president confided that as he had no heir to the business, and with poor business performance, he would be willing to sell an initial stake; if the relationship continued well, after a period of a few years he would be willing to sell his remaining interest. However, he was most concerned that this idea should not leak out, as he thought it would cause chaos amongst the management of his firm. He made it clear that while he was willing to discuss a sale in private, at this stage he would only tell others in management that he was entertaining the possibility of a business tie-up.

This situation was made clear to the foreign side prior to a meeting between representatives of the two companies. However, in his opening remarks, the lawyer for the foreign side used the term 'acquisition' to describe the relationship. The Japanese president stood up, announced that he was not here to sell his company, and left the room. Negotiations ended before they began.[13]

Hostile takeovers

You need friends in most areas of Japanese business; economic considerations are just one part of a balanced equation. Since a hostile takeover won't win you friends, inside or outside the company, it's likely that it will work to your disadvantage. This has changed in some areas of the Japanese economy due to Japan's prolonged recession. Economic instability has meant that Japanese companies have become more open to the idea of acquisition by a foreign firm, and even uninvited takeover in certain heady areas of the economy is seen as unavoidable; but it's still not typical and not normally accepted. If you intend to acquire a Japanese company, try to find out the climate of opinion amongst those that will be involved, and make 'public relations' a priority.

Communication

'Get to know your opposite numbers at all levels socially. Friends take longer to fall out.'[14]

Good communication is essential, as it leads to understanding, which enables compromise and trust. In order to facilitate communication, establish relationships with different people inside the partner firm. Relationships created through good communication are insurance against a complete breakdown of business in the event of problems – and problems are common, and to some degree inevitable. There is a need for communication, preferably involving someone familiar with both sides. If you were introduced by a third party, consult the third party about difficulties and they may 'have a discreet word' with your partner to try to iron things out. Consult your Japanese bank about the matter, and in particular, if you share your bank with your JV partner, it may function as an interlocutor. But you, too, must be prepared to listen to the third party which, in Japan, often undertakes the role of a sort of wise and benevolent mediator.

Acquiring a Japanese company

- Hostile takeovers create ill will.
- Focus on people as well as profit.
- Consult and gain the help of your bank and the firm's main bank.

Contracts

Flexible agreements

When mapping out an agreement, while it's impossible to foresee all eventualities, foreigners do their best by trying to cover all bases and make a contract foolproof.

Japanese, largely unaccustomed to contracts, use flexible agreements that will be negotiable if conditions warrant it. Japanese assume that both sides will attempt to resolve problems when they arise. Under these circumstances, when the two meet, difficulties occur because what is considered by the Japanese to be the 'most sensible option' might appear to the foreigners to be in breach of the agreement.

While Japanese may expect to deviate from an agreement, as a rule they will want nothing more than they would give if the situation were reversed. In this way it is a continuation of the flexibility, or leeway, and help Japanese companies accord each other. Japanese themselves come unstuck when they expect flexibility but have engaged in a contract with a foreign company accustomed to defending itself to the letter of the agreement.

Cooperation, not conflict

Japanese will readily override a contract, even when it's to the benefit of the other party. Rather than abandon commitments to ship grain from the Midwest down the Mississippi river when it was frozen over in 1978, four *sōgō shōsha* – Mitsui Bussan, Mitsubishi Shōji, Nichimen and Tōmen – unbeknown to each other, all went to the much greater expense of buying new supplies and freighting them overland by rail to San Francisco in order to meet their supply commitments.[15] They could have legally escaped their contractual obligations by claiming that the situation was out of their control (under *force majeure*), but instead responded to the demands of the situation.

Since Japanese see themselves as involved in long-term relationships, they can expect that an extra contribution made now will be reciprocated when they need a favour in the future. And of course a policy of making mutual contributions will eventually create an environment of greater productivity than will policies of defensive action. Many Japanese and Westerners, amongst friends and family, are helpful and fair, and operate in a 'help out when you can' manner. But Western business has dictated that it's often foolish to do this in business. Those who offer freely will sooner or later be taken advantage of.

Japanese take it for granted that fellow Japanese parties won't exploit a situation, at least because they are usually so deeply enmeshed in business relationships that there's no realistic way out of problems but to cooperate. Therefore, once Japanese decide they can trust another party, any contract that is required need only outline the functions and responsibilities of those involved. Because they rarely, if ever, look for a technical 'way out', Japanese don't need a watertight agreement.

But Japanese are not blameless. There are examples of joint ventures that have ended in disaster for the foreign party because the Japanese side has used the relationship to extract the foreign know-how. And between Japanese companies, where problems arise that can't be resolved, in many cases the weaker party accepts that their side must put in the extra effort to maintain relations with the larger, more desirable party – they simply concede and accept that that's their lot. At the national and international levels too, agreements lack specifics, allowing Japanese authorities to either not carry out the measures implied or to make changes based on an interpretation that suits them, at a later time.

There are other situations in which Japanese *appear* to be only looking out for themselves, and exploiting the foreign party. This may occur when the Japanese are trying to 'balance the books' in a relationship gone sour. In such situations the foreign party may be failing to appreciate breaches of protocol made by themselves prior to what was actually defensive action undertaken by the Japanese side. Such things as dictatorial management, continued late delivery and supplying inferior goods are matters dear to the heart of Japanese, but may be overlooked by foreigners. Subtle or implied dissatisfaction may also go unnoticed by foreigners accustomed to explicit complaint. Foreigners may then come away oblivious to any problems experienced by the other side, and so may feel shocked when the Japanese suddenly do something which seems to have no justification.

This began to happen in Hamada's JV example above (pages 55–56). The Japanese started to take matters into their own hands. But their actions were largely based on the need to satisfy their customers, and their conclusion that their American partners couldn't understand what needed to be done to achieve this.

If you can function along Japanese lines – being prepared to be flexible, and accommodating to changed demands yourself – then you might not be concerned about adhering to the letter of the contract, and your cooperation at that time will likely be appreciated and reciprocated in future. But, on the other hand, you might come to feel short-changed by this type of arrangement. In order to lessen the possibility of contract problems, be wary of such terms that lack definition as: 'utmost effort', 'endeavour to', 'within reasonable time', and 'as far as is practical'.

> Put your faith in a good business partner, not in a written contract.

Lawyers

Can't live with them … can live without them

Essentially, Japanese see the Western preoccupation with which party is technically right in a particular case as better replaced with common sense. They see the reliance on lawyers, and legal disputes in business, as a typical example of foreigners taking matters to an excessive point of logical reduction, *ad absurdum*. In this context, they see Westerners as we earthlings see Mr Spock.

Indeed, when entering a new territory an important part of the Western investment artillery is legal expertise. While Japanese would prefer to compromise, to discuss their way out of problem areas, or, better still, to avoid trouble altogether, as a result of an (albeit yet limited) legalistic assault, many have had to learn to cope with lawyers and contracts when dealing with foreigners.

During the 1990s the legal system did undergo changes that made legal action more available in Japan. Still, it should be remembered that most Japanese business ticks along as it always did. Existing values are still dominant. A foreign marketer shouldn't go into the Japanese business environment thinking that the legal system has been 'Westernized'.

Too few lawyers?

In 1998 Japan had one lawyer for every 6600 people, the lowest *per capita* figure amongst major industrialized nations. In the US at the time there was one lawyer for every 300, and one for every 650 people in the UK. Japan's relatively low number of lawyers and judges does slow the processing of court cases. However, this functions to minimize litigation. People in Japan are instead encouraged to come to a solution between themselves.

Furthermore, in contrast to the idea that the person who is 'right' should triumph against those who are wrong, Japanese tend to see *any* conflict as bad, and a negative reflection on both parties. Whether you're right or not is less important than the fact that you've sullied yourself by being involved in a dispute.

Avoid conflict of any type.

Japanese disdain what they see as a wanton level of legal activity in the West. Sony's former president, Morita Akio, observed that in the US many company executives have law degrees, whereas in Japan many top executives are engineering graduates. He points out the relative destructiveness of a society in which business is dominated by legal activity.[16]

Still, one problem with the Japanese system is that many deserving cases do not reach court, often to the advantage of big interests treading on the 'little person'. Another disadvantage is qualitative; a 1997 survey found that a quarter of Japanese manufacturers were 'dissatisfied' with, and many others had complaints about, their lawyers.

Changes in place

The problem most cited – by over a third of all the respondents in the survey – was that lawyers were expensive and gave a poor breakdown of charges. Closely following this grievance were complaints that lawyers worked too slowly, and that they lacked adequate practical business knowledge. Many respondents (30 per cent) also complained that Japanese law firms were too small to properly handle big cases that required a lot of resources. But changes are happening in Japan. The aversion to settling disputes through the courts is decreasing. This is a result of at least three factors.

One is the experience of Japanese business people dealing with legal issues in foreign courts. For example, MIZWA Motors (discussed in detail in Chapter 13) took the car maker Porsche to court in Germany when Porsche terminated its distribution contract – MIZWA was neither adept at handling contracts, nor the legal system. But Japanese firms are gaining more of this type of exposure as they are forced to cope with such foreign agreements.

The second factor is associated with the increase in dissatisfaction felt by investors during the 1990s as the economic bubble burst. Shareholders and other investors lost a lot of money, much of which was associated with duplicity or mismanagement on the part of those in control of investors' funds. This is coupled with the third factor, a 1993 change in Japan's Commercial Code that made it cheaper to sue. For those wishing to take legal action the cost had been contingent on the amount sought, but this was changed to a flat fee of ¥8300 ($65).

One Japanese lawyer told me:

> 'The amendment had a great impact on corporations and on lawyers. Corporations revised their internal codes in order to protect themselves against possible lawsuits, and lawyers initiated some lawsuits to try out the new laws. Since then there have been many leading cases that have resulted from this amendment. Before the amendment, litigation by shareholders was not common, but this amendment opened the door to low-cost court action. Now the idea of bringing a case against directors for improper management is more common amongst shareholders, even amongst minority shareholders.'[17]

Amongst those leading cases was court action related to Sumitomo Shōji's loss in 1996 of $1.8bn (later revised to over $2.6bn) because of illicit copper trading. Within the 12 months following the revelation, there had been six lawsuits seeking damages. In order to avoid interrogation by angry shareholders Sumishō held the general meeting that followed in two rooms, one supplied with closed-circuit TV. This sort of trick might have worked a few years earlier, but one of the suits was filed by a shareholder who claimed that Sumishō had breached the Commercial Code because shareholders couldn't ask questions. This thereby invalidated decisions made at the meeting. Directors of both the department store Takashimaya and of Nomura were sued because of the large sums of company money they paid to *sōkaiya* (corporate extortionists).

Some Japanese business people want to be more equipped to deal with both Japan's business internationalization, and with the possibility of lawsuits arising from such shareholder claims over mismanagement. In accordance with the changing demands, in late 1997 Japan's Federation of Bar Associations, with the Ministry of Justice and the Supreme Court, agreed to increase the number of candidates that pass the bar exam by over a third, from 746 in 1997 to 1000 in 1999. In addition to this, they agreed to shorten the period of legal training from two years to 18 months.

It's also getting easier for foreign lawyers to operate in Japan. Their activities in Japan are controlled by the Law Governing Foreign Attorneys (*Gaikokuhō Jimu Bengoshi*). It used to require lawyers to have had five years' minimum legal practice in their place of registration before conducting legal work in Japan. However, that has now been reduced to three years abroad, with the remaining two years able to be spent doing legal work in Japan, though not yet as a practising lawyer. Following that, a lawyer may apply to the Ministry of Justice to be registered as a qualified 'foreign lawyer' by submitting relevant documentation. In Japan they are then eligible to arbitrate, and advise on law – where they are qualified – but not engage in court litigation.

The rules are very detailed. Japanese lawyers, fearful for their small-business legal operations, have, understandably, relied on a body of obstructive regulations to protect them from an invasion by Western legal 'superstores'. However, American lawyers have had strong official-level lobbying power, and due to pressure from the US, the requirements to operate in Japan are now less stringent than before, with continued deregulation expected.

Market entry barriers

What those in foreign firms say about the Japanese market

Occasionally surveys are taken in Japan to find out how foreigners actually operating in Japan rate the market. Below are summaries of their reactions.[18]

Rank   Market entry barriers

1	Official and unofficial rules and regulations
2	High land prices
3	High cost of permanent staff
4	Difficulty hiring permanent staff

Both high labour costs and the difficulty of hiring people have been cited as major problems in operating in Japan. The severe shortage of employees faced by all companies in Japan during the bubble years of the 1980s diminished during the early 1990s but, particularly as more foreign firms have come into Japan, demand for suitable staff has remained greater than supply.

However, the biggest problems firms experience in gaining entry to the market include a body of both official and unofficial rules and regulations. The extent and nature of these depend to some degree on the industry. There are still many government regulations, both in the form of documented regulations (such as those that make it awkward to import food or cosmetic ingredients) and undocumented requirements expressed in the form of 'administrative guidance'.

Problems with official and unofficial rules and regulations

Rank	Government regulations	Rank	Unofficial rules
1	Lack of transparency	1	Vertical *keiretsu*
2	Too many regulations	2	Distribution system
3	Approval time takes too long	3	Trade associations

Trade associations

Japan's industrial organizations, or trade associations, comprise one of the non-official vehicles through which the government administration expresses its (unofficial) policy requests, and disseminates administrative information. In this sense, the administration uses these organizations as a vehicle to enact policy goals.[19]

On the one hand, trade associations are an expression of cooperation amongst a community of firms in the same industry. On the other, associations in Japan are a reflection of the collusive nature of Japanese business, and in this sense they may obstruct foreign business activity. Overall, many foreign companies make good use of these associations and a relatively small number have problems.

Because the Fair Trade Commission (FTC) has the task of policing the Antimonopoly Law, which forbids in principle industrial collusion, price setting and other anti-free-market activity, trade associations are of particular interest to it. This interest by the FTC has provided some useful information about these associations.

According to FTC research, foreign firms join trade associations for the following reasons:[20]

Reasons why foreign firms join Japanese trade associations	% of firms
Can get information about other (companies, clients . . .) in my industry	79%
Can get to know other companies in my industry on a friendly basis	54%
Easy access to notifications from administrative bodies	55%
Many of the companies in my industry are members	33%
Membership allows participation in research and surveys	22%

(Multiple replies possible)

About 80 per cent of firms surveyed didn't see any disadvantages in belonging to an association. But there were some difficulties. The main reasons for withdrawing given by those companies that pulled out of a trade association were:

- Membership fees, obligatory fees and levies are high.
- The association does not conduct useful functions.
- There's a heavy burden in supplying personnel for association activities.

In addition to the financial and human resource burden, and that, for some, associations were simply not useful, other specific disadvantages were noted. Foreigners, for no defensible reason, have been kicked out of or refused entry to industry associations. According to the FTC, out of 213 foreign firms that had applied for membership, five (2 per cent) had been turned down. And, of those that had joined, a similar percentage felt there were restrictions. These included exclusion from (non-public) meetings and from important decision making – in other words, exclusion from some of the most important association activities. Japanese people like to share information and ideas amongst those they know and feel comfortable with, which does not include outsiders. These figures indicate the closed-group character that these associations can maintain.

Foreigners are in an unusual position since on the one hand they are often seen by Japanese as interesting people who may provide, or have available, novel opportunities. But foreigners can just as easily be seen as a troublesome, destabilizing threat.

Restrictions on participation to foreign association-member firms	No. of firms
Not allowed participation in decision making for issues important to the assn.	5
Approvals and authorization rights are negotiated within the assn. rather than being open to competition	5
There are restrictions on full membership and on rights and privileges	4
Not allowed participation in non-public meetings	3
Access to important (e.g. administrative) information restricted	3

(Multiple replies possible)

The key to overcoming barriers in Japan is to become an insider, be part of the group, rather than to operate from the outside. As part of this process, identify the industry association(s) related to your business. Don't shun them as a waste of time, but become a member and attend association meetings or any social activity where you can show yourself as a pleasant, involved and interested and interesting person. Once accepted as a member of an industry association, as with inclusion in other groups or relationships in Japan, you may benefit from the advantages that the group has secured for itself, including lobbying power or simply right of passage, plus the trust of fellow members.

A list of Tokyo trade associations is available in a bilingual book published by the Tokyo Chamber of Commerce, called the *Shōkai keizai dantai meibo*, subtitled in English as 'Economic and Industrial Organizations'. The book is available at foreign Chambers of Commerce and at JETRO. Chambers of Commerce in other areas of Japan will, on a case-by-case basis, list their trade associations.[21]

Opinions from those in the know

As a continuation of our review of foreign reactions to the Japanese business environment, the following is a summary of advice from those with experience in the Japanese market.

- **Preparation:** Be patient. Ensure that you have adequate capital; establishment time and costs will be greater than you expect.
- **Management:** *In Japan*: Ensure that the Japan office has decision-making authority. Leave management to the Japanese, as they know how to operate in their business environment. At

home: Don't let management changes at home result in policy changes in Japan – the Japan office needs a stable course.

- **Personnel:** *Japanese*: Hire the services of a retired executive as an adviser. When hiring staff don't be swayed by English ability alone.
  Foreign: Expect that foreign executives should stay in Japan for upward of five years.
- **Product:** You need a unique or differentiated product. Customize the product to Japan. Quality, quality, quality.
- **About Japan:** Being in the Japanese market is important. Japan is different: realize that, appreciate it, live with it, learn about it, don't fight it; but be innovative.
- **Expectations:** Many of those firms who responded said that they were performing moderately well or better – while some firms admitted to doing poorly, overall during the 1990s there was a positive air.[22]

Notes

1 *Japan in Revolution, An Assessment of Investment Performance by Foreign Firms in Japan*, ACCJ, The Council of the European Business Community and A. T. Kearney, Inc., 1995, pp. 32–3.
2 *Attributes of Success of American Companies in Japan*, ACCJ, 1997, p. 16.
3 Interview with Nishida Ryōzō of kinko's, 1997.
4 *Japan in Revolution, An Assessment of Investment Performance by Foreign Firms in Japan*, ACCJ, The Council of the European Business Community and A. T. Kearney, Inc., 1995, p. 29.
5 Hamada, 1991, p. 178.
6 'Market share' and 'expansion of new products and new business' topped a survey of important business targets for Japanese firms. Top for US firms was ROI, then financial gain for stockholders. Top for EU businesses was ROI; gains for stockholders ranked low but ahead of Japan. All economies wanted market share; the highest was the EU, then the US. But there were strong contrasts between Japan vs. US/EU on the other factors mentioned. It's commonly said that Japanese firms want market share whereas Westerners want financial return. A better contrast is: Japanese firms want market/ business growth whereas Western firms want financial return (Economic Survey of Japan 1991–1992, Economic Planning Agency White Paper, 1992, p. 171, data for 1985).
7 In fiscal year 1990, Japanese listed firms had had a 'stable' 24.4 per cent of their directors drawn from outside the company vs. 56 per cent for US firms. The amount will certainly be far less for non-listed Japanese firms (Economic Survey of Japan 1991–1992, Economic Planning Agency White Paper, 1992, p. 177).
8 Kraar and Takikawa, 1994, p. 129.
9 Kraar and Takikawa, 1994, pp. 131–2.
10 Ishizumi, 1988, p. 42.
11 Ishizumi, 1988, p. 43.
12 Ishizumi, 1988, p. 43.
13 Ishizumi, 1988, pp. 48–50.
14 Ohmae Kenichi on business collaborations (1990, p. 150).
15 Hasegawa, 1986, p. 97.
16 Morita, 1986.
17 Yamada Miwa, LLB.

18 The information comes from sources including Nikkei Shimbun surveys; JETRO White Papers on Foreign Direct Investment; *Attributes of Success of American Companies in Japan*, ACCJ, 1997; *Survey Report on Foreign Affiliated Companies*, LBS, 1997; Robert March, 1990.

19 'Report concerning the Activities of Japanese Trade Associations from the Perspective of Foreign-owned Enterprises', *FTC/Japan Views*, No. 27, April 1997, p. 7.

20 FTC Survey on Trade Associations, 1996, 278 valid replies (= response rate of 55.6 per cent) from foreign capitalized (50 per cent +) firms. In *FTC/Japan Views*, No. 27, April 1997.

21 The *Shōkai keizai dantai meibo* is also on sale at the Tokyo Chamber of Commerce book store for ¥4000 ($30), in Marunouchi 3-2-2, central Tokyo (from Nijubashimae subway station). If asking directions to the Tokyo Chamber of Commerce, use its Japanese name: Tokyo Shōkō Kaigisho. For other regions, there is also a book (in Japanese) covering all associations in Japan called the *Zen koku kakushu dantai meikan*, available in the JETRO library.

22 Remember that such surveys cover firms already established and 'successful' – that's how they get to be survey respondents. For instance, in the Attributes of Success of American Companies in Japan survey, six of the 120 target firms 'did not wish to participate, some noting that they were not doing well in the market and had closed their office in Japan'. This is despite the same survey later mentioning 'a key finding' that none of the 'respondents' would withdraw from the market (*Attributes of Success of American Companies in Japan*, ACCJ, 1997, pp. 13 and 25).

Chapter 4

Guaranteeing quality in everything you do

Undoubtedly one of the most important – probably *the* most important issue in selling to Japan – is quality. But it's the area that foreigners almost always fail to get right; furthermore, they fail to realize they don't get it right. As a result, Japanese importers of foreign-made goods routinely face problems with quality.

Quality is also the issue that tops surveys in Japan, across the product spectrum, on questions of what is important to consumers in a product. In December 1993, at the trough of Japan's recession, product quality was, more than any other, the feature cited by Japanese retailers as important to consumers. Low price was second.[1] And despite the 'low price revolution' that followed, by 1996 price had actually dropped in importance relative to quality, which remained the top consumer consideration in making a purchase.[2]

To be successful in Japan, you need to put resources into quality. Foreigners typically don't handle quality well; and the reality is that it's likely that your company will not provide goods that meet the quality demands of your Japanese customers. If you are selling to that market (and really if you are selling to any market), you need to pay careful attention to quality.

On the matter of quality, it's important to remember two points:

- In product quality Japan routinely leads the world.
- Learn how to satisfy the Japanese consumer and you will have a product or service suitable for sale anywhere else in the world.

Is it difficult to embed quality into production?

Generally not. Adopting 'quality' is largely a matter of attitude, which can be easy, or it can be impossible, depending on one's willingness to do it.

Still, exactly because it's a matter of attitude it has been difficult to educate foreigners in methods of instituting 'quality', which often fall short of their target outside of Japan. The Japanese approach has served Japan very well, such that Western companies began trying to adopt Japanese methods. This has been in part successful; it forced Western firms to make changes, some of which have borne fruit (witness the Detroit auto makers' revival in the 1980s). Some Japanese ingredients have been able to be transferred abroad; however, certain concepts that are less tangible, and *kaizen* is the outstanding example, simply have not been understood.

This chapter draws out some of these hard to understand ideas, and makes them palatable. It also explains the rationale behind the different Japanese and Western approaches to the concept of quality.

Defining the limits to quality

What is 'quality'?

The Japanese approach to quality differs from that often found abroad. Very many Westerners focus on function and durability. But this approach is redundant, at least for goods that must compete with Japanese products on the world market.

> There are two fundamental characteristics important to Japanese quality:
>
> - Quality permeates every aspect of a product.
> - Quality involves continuous attention to improvement, or *kaizen*.

These two aspects, though to some extent treated separately, go to make up the same thing: quality.

Improvement and quality

To Japanese, quality means the product has been raised to a top standard. As this implies, in a competitive market there is no resting place where a product has finally reached a point of *quality*. For Japanese companies, this means a constant battle to develop better goods.

Furthermore, in the traditional Western sense improvement or development is often seen to involve technological advance and falls under the research and development areas of a company, away from the hands-on workforce. In Japan, those same people involved at the hands-on level of production use improvement as a means to maintain quality; improvement and quality are two aspects that make up a single package.

Kaizen

Understanding kaizen and quality

The literal translation of *kaizen* is 'improvement'; however, there is no adequate rendition of the meaning in English. To those involved in it, *kaizen* entails a feeling toward a product that Westerners seldom experience, at least in the situations and on the scale that Japanese do. Because it is so foreign, and difficult to fathom, *kaizen* is normally not dealt with at all in the West, or else an approximation is made of the meaning.

One of the ways Westerners have dealt with the matter of quality has been to adopt Japanese quality mechanisms. Ironically, it was an American, W. Edwards Deming (1900–93), who initially brought the concept of quality control (QC) to Japan, in 1950. Deming introduced a systematized, statistical approach to quality control, initially to ensure export production standards in steel and other industries. The Japanese readily took his ideas, and in their own context developed them into various other mechanisms to improve quality. These mechanisms include quality assurance, total productive maintenance (aimed at equipment maintenance), total quality control (TQC; also called company-wide quality control), and others. In Japan, quality control and *kaizen* meet at TQC. TQC embodies in action much of what *kaizen* is in spirit.

While Deming was (and still is) idolized in Japan, he was given little hearing in the US. It wasn't until the 1980s and 1990s that Westerners, puzzled over Japan's business success, wanted to try to do what the Japanese had been doing. But the Western interpretation of QC has largely been bereft of the human element that became a fundamental part of the Japanese approach. Instead, Western QC efforts have often remained at a technical level. Without the *spirit* of the workforce as a part of the drive toward quality, the process has remained remedial rather than progressive. Some Western companies have ventured beyond the statistical basics, but few have been able to achieve the total approach to quality that Japanese companies have. Over the following pages we'll see the way in which that remedial system can become a system of proactive quality development.

An example of the foreign effort toward attaining higher quality levels is the International Organization for Standardization (ISO) quality approval series. ISO is a worldwide federation of national standards bodies, originating in Europe. Its thrust is international standardization of technological specifications. A division of ISO, the ISO 9000 series, is concerned with quality, and many Western firms apply for it, hoping to be granted ISO standards certification. Somewhat ironically, ISO 9000 certification also became the pursuit of Japanese companies. This was not necessarily because they needed to improve, but because in an international market, where Japanese products were becoming more expensive, ISO certification was increasingly expected of suppliers by downstream buyers. Japanese companies wanted ISO certification to ensure access to the market.[3]

I went to an (overseas) presentation put on by an ISO approval organization and run by one of their approval staff. Essentially it was to promote the ISO idea to companies, encouraging them to become ISO 9000 certified. The presentation was held in a room the layout of which made it difficult for many people to see what was going on. You might think, 'well, that's simply bad luck'. But the whole point of this programme was to promote the idea of thorough attention to quality. What's more, the term *kaizen* was pronounced kaiz*a*n, and the word was explained as incorporating the *Zen* of Zen Buddhism – which is simply incorrect.[4]

The point is that the whole attitude of *kaizen* – a constant and eager effort to improve one's business – is missing in the West, even amongst those who should be most aware of its importance.[5] The irony is that there's a drive in the West to finally change the way products are made, a fundamental shift in thinking, led by a few people who are attempting to spread the word. Look at it from the Japanese point of view: Westerners, who have been so good at creative development, have always been poor at controlling quality; now they've caught on, and they're making an effort. But even the people who are spreading the word don't understand fundamental concepts of quality – what can we expect from their manufacturers?

It should be becoming clear that what is meant by *kaizen* isn't just an academic or a routine mechanical process. It is, rather, a psychological process. It's for this reason that *kaizen* can't be reduced to technical study. While Westerners have been able to get to grips with certain aspects of quality control, which can be a routinized, and sometimes little more than a statistical process, it has been difficult for them to understand the idea of improving product standard by a type of institutionalized conscientiousness. *Kaizen* is a way of looking at your work, and one which doesn't go away just because you're putting on a seminar.

Kaizen means continuous, even anxious, attention to improvement. Commentator Imai Masaaki says it applies not only to the workplace, but may also be applied in personal, home and social life. In the workplace it means the involvement of everyone – managers and workers – in continual improvement.[6] Included in the *kaizen* process is a constant vigilance, looking out for quality opportunities, looking out for how you can improve. *Kaizen* involves not just improvement, but also looking for it.

Definition of a quality product

'If it ain't broke, don't fix it. . .' Spend a few seconds thinking about how that applies to the Japanese industrial context.

For many situations this might be a useful adage, but in the international market, in order to keep ahead of your competitors you need to constantly come up with something of better quality or with new features. The way to do this is through *kaizen*.

I have referred to ISO, and it is indeed a very useful organization. Still, where ISO's mandate stops, *kaizen* takes up. The ISO defines a *quality* company as one which supplies what the consumer wants.[7] Is there anything lacking in that definition?

Many Japanese companies have routinely gone one step further. They have captured market share both at home and abroad by supplying consumers with what they don't yet know they want. After all, it's the manufacturers who are the 'experts' in development – who spend time and money looking at the needs and potential needs of consumers. The customer, be it a downstream company or an end consumer, is comparatively ignorant.

Secondly, if we assume it to be the job of the company to engage in *kaizen*, then it is almost certain that improvement will take place, and that they will produce goods beyond the performance of those currently on the market. Manufacturers can engage in product development, customers cannot.

> It is up to the company to produce what customers don't yet know they want.

Let's imagine a simple illustration of this concept. Consider the lowly clothes peg. A manufacturer who thinks in terms of 'if it ain't broke, don't fix it', or of supplying what the customer expects, will supply pegs which *meet* the consumer's expectations of a quality peg.

Those who've hung out washing will know that pegs have an expected life span, after which they break. Who is to define that life span, until they break? Who is to say that achieving that span is what we call quality? I personally think they break too quickly, and wouldn't it be just like the Japanese to invent a new type of peg using a new type of plastic which doesn't break? Thereby the Japanese, under their definition of how to approach quality, would, as they have done repeatedly, extend the boundaries of quality, while Westerners, with their definition of quality, will remain at the *status quo* by producing quality as defined by the expectations of the customer. That expectation is limited to their understanding of what is technologically possible. The Japanese will tend to develop quality while foreign companies will be either catching up or producing the same products as Japan. Foreigners will do so for as long as they can sustain market share from this secondary position.

The origins of kaizen

The important point about *kaizen* is that it is not a set of standards or rules or measurements; it is not a process but an *attitude*. If it took the form of a book of QC standards, *kaizen* could be easily copied and implemented anywhere. The problem is that *kaizen* is an attitude which must pervade a company from the CEO's office down to the shipping room. As a company boss, you can demand as much action as you see fit, but unless the attitude of striving for quality is there, it will at best be superficial behaviour. To effect *kaizen*, an executive must engender a shift in attitude. A shift in behaviour will then follow, and the ongoing pursuit of quality will become second nature.

There are places where this attitude does exist in the West: in small business, for example, and in sports competition. In these situations often a person will think, eat and sleep improvement. In contrast, workers at large foreign companies don't see their jobs as part of their lifestyle, but just as a source of income.

Unlike big corporations, many workers in small businesses don't feel alienated from their work. They feel close enough to the boss to empathize with the disposition and the needs of the company. Rather than alienation there is a feeling of understanding, which is the precursor to pulling together as a team.

And speaking of teams, nowhere is the concept of *kaizen* in the West as clearly visible as in sports. Serious athletes pour all their attention and energies into even small details in order to generate improvement at every possible point. Even amateur sports clubs have been motivated enough to adopt sophisticated training methods, including advanced technology to analyse detailed movements of team member performance, in order to extract more, and hone that performance. Think of any Olympic event. A very small improvement in a person's performance can mean the difference between a gold medal and being an also-ran. The nervous anticipation building up to competition can draw on all the available energies of those involved. No one has to demand that attitude; it's part of the competitive process. That's *kaizen*.

If Westerners could apply this to the work situation, then clearly the products that resulted would have features that were far better than those produced in a traditional environment. And this, in many cases, is how the Japanese work; it is part of achieving *kaizen* in the workplace.

Fundamental to the concept of *kaizen* is the notion of commitment to the task. Without commitment, people only come up with ideas and act when they have to – when, for instance, there is a manifest problem. Yet a system with well-functioning *kaizen* involves process or product upgrading prior to crisis. This allows problems to be nipped in the bud, and it provides for innovation which leads to improvement. To be truly effective, improvement must come not from overt pressure, but from within – it must be of one's own volition.

The intangible nature of kaizen

Quality control circles and statistical QC analysis are some of the physical manifestations of quality initiatives. The foundations of *kaizen*, on the other hand, cannot be seen or experienced. To use another analogy, if QC circles are the 'hardware', the easily visible or manifest activities, *kaizen* involves something like 'software'. Just as the software program of a computer is the way a computer *thinks*, *kaizen* involves motivational aspects of achieving improvement.

Kaizen involves ways of thinking about a product. But these are almost impossible to analyse or summarize without reverting to the hardware manifestation of improvement as a means of description. Consequently, descriptions that have made their way out of Japan have hardly touched upon (or, worse yet, badly explained) the intangible aspects of *kaizen*. They have instead focused on manifest practices such as QC circles and statistical quality control. This has left foreign quality programmes largely absent of *kaizen*; that is, absent of the social and psychological foundations upon which *kaizen* exists. It has meant that QC circles outside of Japan have been left empty of the substance necessary to actually generate quality improvement.

In its traditional form, QC involves the use of statistics and other information as feedback with which to better locate the source of, then rectify, a product problem area. For example, observing the reject rate is an obvious step in QC. This information draws our attention to problem areas, and may lead to system adjustments. The *kaizen* process is different. It includes the inspirational genius that innovates and redesigns a part in the system so that those rejects are no longer produced, or, one step better, anticipates that there will be a problem, and conceives of, initiates and executes a plan before the trouble appears.

This is an important aspect of *kaizen* – it means workers are always 'on the ball', anticipating problems before they become problems, constantly vigilant to improve present conditions and prevent trouble.

In a *kaizen*-driven environment the idea may come from a worker who sees the opportunity to improve things, even a little. Ideas can be simple, but the important point is that the 'we can do better' attitude is there. In one of Matsushita's plants, a QC circle organized by the cafeteria waitresses won the president's gold medal for the year by studying tea usage patterns, as a result of which they were able to reduce tea leaf consumption by half.

'Crisis management'

An important aspect of *kaizen* is that a properly motivated organization can often anticipate a crisis and thus save time and money in the long term. This may be referred to as the 'stitch in time saves nine' phenomenon.

The non-*kaizen* system does not subscribe to 'stitch in time'. Instead of deploying a stitch at an early stage, otherwise normal wear and tear in the system leads to costs later on. Whereas in a traditional system this wear and tear is seen as natural, in a *kaizen* system there are constantly people with needles and thread on the look-out for a place to put a preventative stitch. The problem may not be visible to the naked eye, but under *kaizen* conscientiousness these potential trouble spots are hunted out.

A hallmark of the non-*kaizen* system is therefore a tendency to allow 'crisis management' to dominate. Crisis management is a situation whereby inefficiencies in the system build upon themselves. Resources such as money or time are sufficiently scarce that they are necessarily directed to the cause most in need at a particular time – money is spent putting out fires. Resources are never available to put preventative stitches in place. When a particular crisis is over, the resulting drain on resources has allowed a crisis in another area. It is obviously inefficient since it doesn't allow judicious allocation of resources. Instead, resource allocation is out of management's control.

Quality is not expensive

In order to be efficient, there needs to be a constant allocation of resources to mechanisms or systems which act as preventative ('stitch in time') maintenance. Ultimately, if these resources are expended wisely and early there will be long-term savings, and those savings will eventually be returned to the system. This investment involves a combination of resources, including human resources, the potential value or impact of which is often underrated. Ironically, many Western businesses short of finance, or simply in the name of efficiency, cut back on labour and on other investment. This not only results in delays and other costs, but cutting back on staff reduces motivation and the staff's capacity to institute innovations, thereby stifling development. It's mind-boggling to think of how many good projects have been dropped by Western firms because there was nobody available to run with the idea. Video technology was invented in the US in the 1950s. How many employees in Western firms thought, 'Hey, that would be great in the home', but couldn't follow through with the idea, long before Sony came out with the home VCR in the 1970s?

Indeed, the suggestion system is one example of human resource utilization. Western companies typically can't muster the energy or resources to get a suggestion system (really) operating, but the Japanese have commonly utilized these to good advantage. Canon, for instance, in one year made an outlay of ¥250mn ($1.1mn) to institute 390,000 employee suggestions, but for this it got an estimated return of ¥19bn ($84mn), meaning a 77-fold payback.[8] Toyota workers produce 1.5 million suggestions a year, and 95 per cent of these are put to good use.[9] Here there is *kaizen* on both sides of the fence. Management is concerned enough to treat the system seriously, and the workers, appreciating this, are prepared to contribute. Suggestion systems require the follow-up of management. This is not only to implement the ideas, but because the commitment of management to incorporate worker suggestions reinforces morale. Making workers feel positive lays the foundation for them to care about the business and therefore care to improve it.[10] Also, their response, again, is the software. The suggestion system is one of the hardware mechanisms.

Still, many Western companies would balk at such a large financial outlay as Canon's, above. Indeed, most business systems start off resource-poor. However, the belief that high quality, in both human and tangible resources, will mean high cost is part myth; a keenly motivated workforce can instead compensate for a lack of capital. Costs often involve the cost of an idea, some materials and time, often all of which are tolerable.

The Japanese economy after World War II provides good examples. Notable is Toyota's just in time (JIT) system. After World War II Toyota was a small firm lacking good economies of scale. Toyota's Ōno Taiichi believed that the company could improve efficiency by streamlining the change-over time of tools used to work on different cars. His success is legendary. In the 1970s Toyota was able to set up and replace 800-ton body panel presses in 12 minutes, whereas the same task took its US competitor six hours. Toyota needed this advantage because it was operating manufacturing runs of just one day and couldn't spend half the day setting up.[11]

One of the simplest and least costly product improvements is the little notch pre-cut into plastic bags used for food products, which make the packets easy to tear open. Both the idea, and building the feature into manufacturing equipment, involves a relatively small cost. This is especially so if compared to the energy expended by customers to each time track down a pair of scissors to open the packet. The Japanese view on the value of this upgrade is clear: any such packets found in Japan without a tear notch are probably not made in Japan – according to Japanese confectionery maker Glico, adding such user-friendly features is a matter of course.[12]

Glico also makes a product called 'Putchin Pudding'. It incorporates a break-off stalk-tab on the bottom of its plastic container, which involved only a slight design change to the plastic moulding equipment. The small pudding is difficult to dig out with a spoon, but turning it upside down over a plate and breaking off the tab leaves a hole in the bottom of the container which allows air in. *Putchin* is onomatopoeia for the sound of breaking the tab, and the air rushing into the vacuum, which then lets the jelly-like pudding neatly slip out. The materials cost of the Putchin Pudding innovation is that of a 4mm piece of plastic, which is part of the moulded container anyway. The cost of a plastic key holder which was added into the pocket of a lifejacket we exported to Japan was 40c, but the value of the improvement to the product was far greater and became a main product feature.

The human element – the root of kaizen

It may appear that I have taken for granted that the harnessing of worker input is possible, but the reality is that it is a major problem faced by many foreign firms. How do the Japanese secure cooperation from workers?

Responsibility for quality

In the West, management has often viewed production from a desk in an office, sometimes in a fortress-like manner, detached from the work process. In many cases, those wishing to see a manager have to make an appointment. Western management often seems to do its best to isolate itself from its workers. The difference between the managerial suit-and-tie environment and the work floor is stark. Different uniforms for different ranks of employees, and such separate facilities as dining areas and toilets, are characteristic of 'well set up' Western business environments. But these are absent in similar Japanese contexts.

In Sony, employees work in close physical proximity to management, and management works in physical surroundings less plush than those of the production floor, and Sony staff – management and labour – are proud to wear the same uniform.[13] Rodney Clark, in his study of a Japanese company, observed the same point: that despite a hierarchy in the company, there wasn't the sharp status split that exists in the West.[14]

Divisions serve only to accentuate the distinction between management and workers, and even though people may at times like to be seen as different ... to be seen as individuals, essentially, nobody wants to be seen as inferior to others. This makes those in the 'second class' category find solace with others in the same situation, and ultimately, if they find enough power, disrupt the upper group. This has strong implications for quality since, as we have seen in a competitive environment, management needs not just to control, but to elicit cooperation from that group – management needs their goodwill.

It is also important for management to assume responsibility for the products manufactured by the company. Western management often sees the responsibility for quality maintenance, and for performance in general, to be in the domain of the workers. Good performance or slackness is in the hands of those doing the job. If there is a drop in quality, it tends to be seen as the fault of those in the front lines of the production process.

But it doesn't take long for a worker doing a boring job to figure out management's contribution to production. After all, it is the management that employed all the workers – good or bad – who trained them, who provides the tools – good or bad – for them to make products with, who has conceived the designs, and of how things should fit together. Management should be considered at least partly responsible for bad products. If workers see management as accepting that responsibility, then they will be more inclined to feel empathy with the boss, and they will take responsibility for their contribution to the quality – an attitude that will have a positive effect on quality.

In Japanese industry, management can often be seen to accept accountability when things go wrong. When business is poor, Japanese management takes pay cuts ahead of their staff. Company heads resign to take the blame for scandals or incidents associated with a firm, even where they are not directly involved. In July 1996 the president of Takashimaya department store resigned in order to apologize to its customers, staff and shareholders after company executives had been arrested for the firm's involvement in protection payments. Some take accountability very seriously. In 1991 poor management was seen to be the reason why an agricultural cooperative became saddled with bad loans. The president committed suicide to 'take responsibility'.

If one person in authority accepts the blame for products that leave the plant, that feeling of responsibility is more likely to then permeate through to those making the goods. Rather than being at odds with the boss, workers are more likely to support and cooperate with the boss. Western management expects commitment from workers, but too often management itself lacks a sense of commitment to the workers.

If the boss isn't sacrificing anything, then why should we, goes the logic. The Japanese-type approach isn't completely unknown in the West – this is why Lee Iacocca paid himself just one dollar in salary the year he took over a troubled Chrysler. He showed that he was making a greater commitment than anyone else, thus opening the way for his workers to follow his effort. In this type of situation the soil is ready for *kaizen* to take root.[15]

The Japanese have traditionally worked out of a sense of obligation and commitment. This is a productive form of motivation within which there is an additional human factor which translates into quality. Further, only if such attitudes are in place amongst the workers will they be interested in maintaining quality, and will it be at all possible to generate *kaizen*. It is otherwise pointless expecting results from *kaizen*, and of limited value initiating other QC programmes.

As will be clear by now, *kaizen* needs an attitude of commitment and concern in order to work. Part of *kaizen* is to be alert enough to look for trouble before it occurs; to be able to worry just enough about something that you can see that it could be changed for the better.

This anxiety can be seen as *soft* anxiety, since it contrasts with the bitter anxiety of management in a crisis. There is no comparison between the two; there are many advantages in the tension associated with *kaizen* which, instead of 'repair mode', involves 'challenge mode'. As examples of the anxiety involved in Japanese business, Japan's convenience store check-out staff (7-Eleven and the like) rush to serve customers as quickly as possible.

And foreigners are generally surprised that petrol station attendants in Japan, in a similar way, run to serve fuel and service customers. It's common for customers to drive into a gas station, surrounded by two, three or sometimes more attendants who wave the car in with calls of 'all right, all right' before descending onto the vehicle – one to ask what you want in the tank, others to check the oil, clean the windscreen, and one who will dive inside the car and empty the ashtray. At the most disciplined stations, their actions are coordinated, they call out in unison and stand in a line and bow as the car enters and bow again when it leaves, until it disappears. Now that's service. There are no alarm bells ringing and there is no emergency, but workers are keyed up and keen to add that extra bit to the service. This shows what a *kaizen* mindset can do to add value to such a basic task as pumping gas.

Notes

1 *Small Business in Japan*, MITI, 1994, p. 95. The trough of the recession – the point at which various 'production' indices began to turn – was around October 1993 (*Small Business in Japan*, MITI, 1995, p. 11).

2 In 1991 price was the primary factor for 20 per cent of buyers, in 1996 it was 13 per cent – while consumers cited quality as the most important factor in making a purchase. (Research by Hakuhodo, in *The Nikkei Weekly*, 13 May 1996, p. 23; 'National Survey on

Lifestyle Preferences, Fiscal Year 1995', The Economic Planning Agency, 1996, pp. 75–76.)

3 By 1997 3 per cent of Japanese SMEs had applied for or received ISO 9000 certification, over a quarter were considering or intending to apply, 62 per cent of Japan's SMEs had no intention of applying. Of large businesses, 36 per cent had or were seeking ISO 9000, 47 per cent planned to get it, and 17 per cent had no intention of doing so (*Small Business in Japan*, MITI, 1997, p. 151).

4 It should also be pointed out that it is not the job of the ISO to promote *kaizen per se*.

5 I'm grateful to Terry Hoskins, General Manager, Telarc New Zealand, for his correspondence and assistance in this (19 June 1996) – truly a response of the type one would expect from an (ISO) organization dealing in quality.

6 Imai, 1986.

7 While this is how ISO 'quality' was once described to me, in using it I take the liberty of abbreviating the ISO definition, which is actually multifaceted and complex.

8 Imai, 1986, p. 120.

9 Imai, 1986, pp. 20 and 15.

10 See Imai, 1986, p. 112. Not all workers in Japan take the suggestion system seriously. In many firms, token rewards such as cigarettes are given to workers who submit a high number, or submit very good suggestions. Some workers are only interested in getting these rewards.

11 Schonberger, 1982, p. 20.

12 Communication with Glico.

13 Morita, 1986, pp. 182–84.

14 Clark, 1979, pp. 109–10.

15 Yet this approach is unpopular among most Western companies. Primarily, this is because Western managers have come to see themselves (and this delusion is reinforced by the business press) as an extremely skilled group of professionals, in effect the chosen élite upon whose shoulders the fate of each nation's economy ultimately rests. The common understanding is that a company can be pushed to the wall but the president should receive a multi-million-dollar bonus upon retirement. Needless to say, this is not how the Japanese interpret affairs.

Chapter 5

Hiring and keeping local staff

Companies entering Japan must deal with the hiring of staff, but in doing so they face an employment environment substantially different from what they are accustomed to at home. Japanese attitudes toward the company imply a bond between the company and its employees. Among other things, this has led to difficulties in mid-career hiring because Japanese have been unwilling to leave secure corporate jobs, and because the system shuns laying off staff. In addition, Japanese have been reluctant to work for foreign firms in Japan due to the prevailing image of 'cold', Western-style management in which employees are fired 'anytime there is a downturn in business'. On the other hand, many foreign firms in Japan have learned how to function within the local system and thus have been able to attract and hold Japanese staff – to their mutual satisfaction.

What is this 'bond' within the Japanese company, and why are Japanese workers reluctant to work for foreign companies? This chapter provides an overview of the employment environment, practices and attitudes in Japan.

Employment practices

Think about companies in Japan, and one thing that springs to mind is the lifetime employment system. It's also fairly well known that lifetime employment is actually more myth than reality: companies offering lifetime employment, seniority-based pay and the various other formal and semi-formal worker benefits neither constitute the bulk of Japanese firms, nor do they hire the bulk of Japanese workers. Instead, estimates typically suggest that lifetime employment involves less than 20 per cent of Japan's working population. Weak companies or industries have – understandably – never been able to provide the same advantages to their staff.

There are differences of opinion about the origin of these practices. Some observers claim that lifetime employment and other benefits are only a product of twentieth-century industrial demands. Lifetime employment and seniority-based pay systems did have their immediate origins in industrialization, early in the twentieth century. By the beginning of that century, in an attempt to tie down a mobile labour force, companies were beginning to give workers incentives to stay in their jobs, including housing and other welfare benefits. The situation was accentuated by the end of World War I as industry became more skill-based. With the adoption of more sophisticated industrial machinery and work processes, an itinerant workforce was inappropriate; companies needed to hold on to their skilled workers, and companies responded by offering employee benefits, including improved job security, pay for seniority and low housing rentals.

After World War II the employment situation was reversed and there was a surplus of labour. The Occupation forces initially promoted workers' unions. The unions, in an attempt to secure tenure for their members, also pushed for lifetime employment.

Lifetime employment and other typical big-company practices fitted hand-in-glove with deeper-seated Japanese expectations about the master–subordinate, 'familial' relationship.[1] These basic values didn't need to be continuously apparent; they were instead subject to economic currents and attitudes. They were overruled in the context of opportunism and the exploitation of labour (which always was, and still is to some degree, apparent in Japan) that accompanied early Meiji period (1868–1912) industrialization.[2] This opportunism flourished in such new industries as mining and textiles that demanded not experience, but cheap unskilled labour; many such workers were women, and were exploited. But the 'familial' values were easily able to re-emerge, and fitted in well when a cooperative business environment (again) became important.

Nowadays these practices are criticized by foreigners and many Japanese for blocking a free labour market, and encouraging a stagnation of workers and their ideas. In some areas the pressures of a changing economy are forcing changes in Japan's typical employment practices, and they are being replaced, allowing greater labour mobility. This suits foreign companies because they can compete more easily to secure workers.

Industrial relations

The family–company

While much of the West suffers labour unrest, Japanese companies have had very little. How is it that in Japan there are harmonious management–worker relations?

One reason is that much of the unrest that does exist is quelled, often by simply not being given support in the broader social context.

Still, there is also a high degree of management–worker cooperation in even large businesses in Japan. The relationship is perplexing to foreigners in part because Westerners look on the Japanese worker as an 'employee'. We naturally tend to see the situation in the image of our own experience. However, traditionally the status of workers in Japan was quite different, and that traditional role has not yet disappeared.

Consider that the family, in the Western sense, historically didn't exist in Japan – though a pattern more familiar to Westerners has been emerging. The traditional family, the *ie*, which dates back hundreds of years, was based on pragmatic concerns. The idea of *kazoku*, the Japanese term closest in meaning to the word 'family', is only relatively modern,[3] and even now the Japanese *kazoku* is clearly different in character from at least the Western family. The husband and wife relationship is still in many cases surprisingly contractual and pragmatic.

When the *ie* needed to supplement membership, or when bereft of a suitable heir, one was adopted. Since a person brought into the *ie* was, fundamentally, not expected to fit into a genetic, but rather into a functional or practical position, it was easier to conscript an adopted person into the *ie* than it would have been into a Western-type family. Japanese staffing practices are still conceptually closer to adoption than to the simple act of hiring a new employee. Even now the Japanese company – an outgrowth of the *ie* – lies conceptually between the Western family and the Western enterprise. As such it retains a combination of not only pragmatic, but also emotional features.[4]

It is also interesting that there is a stark difference between those included in the enterprise and outsiders. It means that while large Japanese companies support their own staff, they can be ruthless toward their supplier subcontractors, part-time workers and, in some situations, competitors. In recent times those in large companies have still been treated as part of the 'family', but many of those outside are treated like workers anywhere.

Attitudes to employment

University students and new employees are often polled as to which is more important – the company or the family. They routinely say they will devote more time to their family and less to work. But in reality, when they go on to enter a company, their work gains precedence over their family life. Things are starting to change, however, as a number of factors, including a reduction of hours at work plus an emphasis on leisure, encouraged by both government deregulation and the general impact of Westernization, weaken these traditional mores of Japanese life. Younger people, more influenced by Western behaviour than the desire to pull together felt immediately after World War II, are becoming part of a body reluctant just to conform and sacrifice.

There are a growing number of seniors who think Japan should change, too. However, attempts to change create a Catch 22 situation. In an environment that shuns standing out, it's been almost impossible for lower rank employees to appear less committed by deciding to take more time off than their colleagues, and it is hard for any seniors to lead the way in reducing work time, since they are expected to set an example of commitment.

Creating at least the perception of being committed is important. It is typical for employees to wait around after hours at work, doing nothing until everyone has finished before returning home, and common for staff not to take paid leave. It's not that they would be needed at work, or that they don't want a holiday, but the fear of standing out – of being the only one on holiday. There would be a feeling – amongst their colleagues, or in their own minds – that they'd absconded, abandoning their fellows and their work. The risk is that others might think they were not pulling their weight, or that they lacked commitment.

Commitment to one's company is a mix of two factors, fear and genuine loyalty, and the ratio of this mixture has changed, in particular, through recent history. Much of the loyalty amongst the post-World War II generation was part of an effort to put Japan back on track, but as this generation has been replaced by young people who have only experienced relative luxury, the feeling of loyalty to Japan has diminished. However, a high degree of commitment in the workplace has remained because in a society which prioritizes group opinion – where the dominant view carries weight – as long as the dominant theme is to work hard for the company, workers must demonstrate commitment. Thus more recently, fear of not meeting the expectations of others has kicked in where loyalty has faded.

Most Japanese can't afford to deviate – they would risk being defined as 'strange'. Japanese must conform to conventional standards. To demonstrate the point: a young male Japanese company employee who used to leave work at 5.00pm because – he maintained – that was all his contract obliged him to do, found himself posted to Libya. This sends a message to all the other people in the office that, yes, it's all right to go home while everyone else is still working – but there are consequences associated with not following established procedure.

Employee as beneficiary

Historically, large businesses in Japan stressed the importance of the 'family–company', of seniority, and of long-term employment. Mitsui, for example, dating back to the early 1700s, preferred that employees be brought into the house and raised there from infancy. A long-serving employee was considered part of the family, and after a long term of service, of about 30 years, it was not uncommon for the 'family–company' or '*ie*' to supply such a person with some money as a gift, and other assistance to set up business alone. In the case of large enterprises, the person would, depending on the status he had generated within the *ie*, be allowed to use the company logo.[5]

The practice of giving one's help and good wishes to a long-serving ex-employee who is starting a business is carried on in Japan today. Of small and medium-sized business start-ups, roughly one-fifth are of this type.[6] This contrasts with the situation in the West, where an employee setting up shop is, in many cases, seen as a threat. Nor is it uncommon even for Japanese executives to openly have and promote their own companies, while working at their original job. (On the other hand, it's not uncommon for lower-level employees to be forbidden to have any extra employment, even in their own time, outside their job.)

There are two important reasons favouring the practice of allowing workers to set up their own shop. Rather than the fear Westerners have of competition and conflict damaging their business, Japanese see it as an opportunity to cooperate and expand. Again, this is not unlike the way one would feel about a family member in a similar situation; if possible, it would be best to give one's good blessings to a family member branching out alone, and create mutual benefit where possible. One way of turning any negative aspects of such a move, such as the possibility of competition, into positive, is for the old firm to get a piece of the action of the new firm. Therefore an ex-employer will more likely help in such a start-up, prompting a climate of mutual assistance, or, if possible, invest in the new business as a shareholder, thereby making the success of the new business also directly in the interests of the former employer.

Another reason why the formation of a company by an ex-employee is acceptable, is the higher concentration of customers in Japan. Since Japan's cities have always been highly populated – Japan is one of the world's most densely populated countries, with Edo (now Tokyo) thought to have been the world's first city to reach one million[7] – it has been possible for parallel companies to exist, specializing in slightly different fields, or operating in a different location, without competing directly for clients. Compare this with a business in a sparsely populated district in the West, where the appearance of a competitor may mean a serious drop in sales.

Career employment

Hiring

Perhaps the most fundamental difference between Western and Japanese company expectations about employment is that, in accordance with lifetime employment, Japanese hire employees young, train them and keep them. Westerners, on the other hand, generally expect a turnover of staff and, in the process, expect to hire mid-career employees who will bring experience to the job. Hiring experienced workers means the company doesn't need to invest so much in training, and can begin to extract a contribution from the employee immediately. It also means the ideas new workers introduce are available to mix with those already in the company. Why doesn't the Japanese company want to hire experienced workers, and lay off its excess?

At a practical level, life employment means quick results aren't as important as the long-term cultivation of staff. Companies have time to train employees who will bring forward their skills and knowledge later. The company also has the use of a cheap (young) workforce into which it is, at the same time, instilling the ideals of the company. Furthermore, the long-term worker is part of the structural jigsaw. Workers create, on the one hand, a community-like atmosphere that provides unity and drive for the company. On the other hand, the body of lifetime workers accumulates shared knowledge which they bring to the development and production processes. The short-term worker is a (Western) aberration who brings some degree of negative impact or trauma into business.

Westerners use change to advantage, so disruption isn't defined as being so problematic, but Japanese value stability and predictability and they will tolerate costs associated with maintaining that. Westerners focus on – and overestimate – the value of (apparent) economic efficiency in business: efficiency means removing or replacing all the unnecessary pieces. Furthermore, Westerners underestimate the value of long-term consistency and stability.

The employee hiring system

In Japan the employment by large companies of new recruits originally took place once a year, but a change in 1997 opened the door to year-round hiring. The annual hiring system goes back to 1953, amid the industrial boom spurred by the Korean War, when an informal (but not legal) arrangement was made between universities and the Japan Federation of Employers' Associations (Nikkeiren). The agreement said that major Japanese companies would not approach students before a set date each year. The purpose was to allow students to study until a set time, following which employers could all compete for students. The original contact date was 1 October for students who would graduate the following March, though over the years the date was moved, and the scheme was even abandoned for ten years from 1962.

Of course, many firms breached the date and real hiring began months earlier, albeit under the pretence of a fixed date. Some students, especially those from prized universities, were contacted well in advance for a secret interview. At its height, before the bubble burst, Nomura Securities, for instance, would start recruiting in May, and at interview time would whisk élite university candidates to Hawaii, where they couldn't negotiate with other companies.[8]

Nikkeiren announced that as of 1997 the system would be permanently scrapped. This was to the disgruntlement of universities, and also to small businesses, since it removed any possibility of them competing for students equally with big firms.

It has been standard practice for companies to recruit from universities with which they have links. Professors and companies linked by *jinmyaku* ties circumvent the hiring structure by arranging to have bright students placed in good company positions. But others are left to pound the pavements, submit hundreds of applications, and undergo extensive interviewing. My own experience is that the process – under either system – is a nuisance. Because the system hinges on them securing their 'job for life', for an immediate start after graduation, many students have no choice but to devote much of their final university year to serious job hunting, a by-product of which is that they effectively stop what little studying they might have been doing.

In the mid-1990s, when profits dropped as the bubble economy deflated, white-collar efficiency became the target of criticism. In order to redress the problem, a trend then emerged amongst some companies toward selecting recruits for their individuality. While many firms stuck to existing selection criteria, others maintained that they would seek employees with characteristics that would help differentiate their company.

Universities advise graduates on what the market is looking for in an applicant and applicants can buy publications attuned to the pulse of the times on how to present themselves well in interviews. There has always been a standard interview 'uniform': dark suits for both men and women. In 1998 these publications advocated wearing navy blue, black or grey. Demeanour is (naturally) important, and so now is English ability, in addition to which students should demonstrate creativity and imagination. And they had something in the order of two minutes (in the first screening) to convey this. The reality is that with so many job seekers applying at the same time, distinguishing them was impossible. Students instead had little choice but to present a certain interview persona in order to be accepted, in what was a factory-like selection process. The Internet did constitute one breakthrough whereby job seekers could find out more about the company at their own pace, and enter into a level of dialogue with the firm with the mutual objective of employment.

Company orientations

Learning the company ropes

Large companies instil their ideology in new recruits, starting with their initiation, shortly after entry. In this process recruits, who come in *tabula rasa*, are relatively easy to indoctrinate, and are exposed to high doses of group comradeship with fellow employees of the same year.

The nature of such indoctrination or initiation varies from company to company, but there are common themes. In many cases the recruits are taken on a camp for a week or a few weeks, during which time they engage in morning runs and other endurance activities, and are given instruction in the company business itself. It is a moulding process in which bright young employees who have proved that they can passively memorize facts in the Japanese education system come into a company 'empty' (of experience and business knowledge), but ready to absorb the company ideology and the business information that they must know in their jobs. That students gain little business knowledge at university is not a problem for companies keen to instil in their employees their own ways of working.

It has been said that when Japanese employees first begin work they know nothing, not even how to answer the telephone. They can go to the toilet by themselves, and perhaps eat lunch, if they're told that it's lunchtime. Such comments are, in many cases, sad but true. Japanese are so accustomed to form that, when formally doing anything, they first learn a process, perfectly, so they can repeat it correctly thereafter.

Through school, their life involves rehearsing the answers so they can repeat them perfectly in tests. In business, assembly-line work is incredibly accurate because it is rehearsed. And white-collar roles are so well defined that each worker provides information from his/her jurisdiction, meaning that in many cases nothing new is created.

When interacting with others, employees are expected to exhibit a set range of behaviours. Firstly, there are behaviours consistent with Japanese etiquette – there is typically one action or phrase for one occasion. Secondly, individual companies supplement these by specifying their own behaviours. This reduces ambiguity, it contributes to a consistency in the service, while also eliminating individuality. Nomura staff, for instance, must answer the phone on the first ring, they must smile, and customarily still say 'Sorry to keep you waiting'.[9] Essentially, for every situation there is a corresponding response that can be rehearsed. Thus by acting properly, the correct result can always be achieved, and errors will be avoided. If company protocol is not demonstrated or taught, employees, who are accustomed to being passive recipients in learning information, will be at a loss as to how to act – they can't even answer the phone.

As mentioned, Japanese at work fear making mistakes. It is often said that in Western business points are added for achievements. Japanese, however, start with a number of points which are subtracted for mistakes. Westerners achieve high marks by bold and creative moves. Bold achievements are not rewarded in Japan; instead, the greatest risk is of making an error. The *status quo* is, however, quite acceptable. There is no need, instead, there is a risk, in doing something different from company policy.

New company employees are expected to absorb the doctrine and spirit of the company. Some companies inculcate their initiates with sessions of a more spiritual nature, that spirit, of course, being appropriately linked to the needs of the company. And all this is done with their fellow employee initiates in order that they get a feeling of common experience, and perhaps common hardship, which are the fundamentals, if not the backbone, of empathy and friendship.

The nature and duration of new recruit orientations varies quite a lot, and depends on the company's resources and president's belief in its usefulness. Some companies are able to go out of town for up to three weeks – about the longest orientation time period – and in that time employees engage in formal seminars and instruction about the job, as well as go through some degree of physical training, or hardship, depending on one's perspective. Some companies skip the training altogether, deciding it is sufficient, and more practical, to spend a week in some degree of isolation somewhere in Tokyo learning the technical aspects of business. Some take their new workers on a tour of other branches, and of Japan.

Creating bonds

There are a number of ways Japanese companies instil a sense of unity into their workers. There are the regular morning briefings (*chōrei*) in which company goals, current projects and other announcements are brought up by management – thereby helping employees feel part of a team. And also, the orientation into the company is laced with mechanisms to make new recruits feel part of the group and allow the group to get to know and feel at home with the new workers. One of these is the company circular, which functions as a vehicle for interaction amongst staff. The example below, from a company that markets and sells goods produced by a major electronics manufacturer, contains a summary and selections from a special 'meet the new recruits' edition, in which the company's 11 new recruits for the year are introduced.

Company pamphlet – orientation issue

The first section features the answers of each new employee to seven questions, including:

1 Date of birth.
2 Place of birth.
3 'My PR' – self-introduction/promotion.
   Answers include: personal interests, achievements, interesting personality features, and blood type (widely assumed in Japan to reflect personality).
4 Current topics of personal interest, including sports and hobbies.
5 What I hope to do in or for the company, and what I hope to get from the company.
6 What is my favourite word?
   Answers include: 'play hard, work hard', 'progress', 'kindness', 'try hard', 'morality', 'love'.
7 What I hate.
   Answers include: 'university students', 'rough people', 'moths', 'bugs', 'vinegar', '*natto*' (fermented soy bean), 'shellfish', 'raw egg', 'coconut milk', 'dark places'.

The speech of the new recruit representative:

> 'We have just graduated from university and so far we've just been supported by our parents and our teachers; however, from now on, we're responsible for ourselves as

workers. We are going to work for this company, as well as work to contribute to society in general, and also work in order to help ourselves.

'We don't yet have any experience in life or society, so we should learn from our seniors in the company, and we will work hard in the company.'

The company president's address to the new recruits:

'Now in Japan the political and economic situation is changeable, and not stable. Under these circumstances, you should take advantage of this situation in order to learn from it, you should learn to cope with any such unstable situation as it arises.'

There are also six addresses from heads of each section of the company, giving variations on the theme of advice to workers. For example, 'Work should be creative, and you should make a strong effort in your work.' 'Learn and think and act.' 'You are young, use a young mind, and don't be afraid if you risk failure.' The head of the sales department said, 'When you meet a customer, employ honesty, sincerity, and work hard.'

The Japanese employee

Ties that bind

Not only do companies like to see employees as long-term members of the same firm but the employees also like to remain with a firm. In general, at least where the company has status and stability, Japanese workers prefer the security of an existing job under the aegis of lifetime employment. This might be hard to understand when – as is typically the case – the financial rewards and conditions would be better if the employee were to jump ship and work with a foreign firm, and when an employee may be fundamentally unhappy with his/her job, as many undoubtedly are. But beneath the surface there is a lot of good-will between the company and the employee.

There is a feeling that the company acts as a patron, looking after the employee – and from the company point of view there are many benefits in looking after and keeping the worker happy in this way. There is at least an economic payoff in terms of improved productivity gained through greater worker commitment. But these relations between worker and company are not only based on tangible benefits, including remuneration and a welfare system. At least Japan's larger and/or more traditional companies get involved in all aspects of the worker's life. They arrange social trips, and provide other leisure activities. Seniors in the company take on the role of patron, they advise on and arrange marriage partners and may mediate subsequent marriage disputes. In some cases the company may even provide a common company grave site. Workers respond by spending a lot of their time under the wing of the company. This constitutes a reciprocal relationship of dependency in which, in that archetypical situation, the company has adopted a parental-figure role, and workers have been able to relax and have the company arrange what would otherwise be their personal lives.

Indeed, individuality is not big in Japan, and the company environment certainly doesn't help individuality develop. The company presents an environment of extremely strong and supportive group consciousness; indeed, Japanese salary workers often have few or no friends outside the company.

Furthermore, at the individual level there are other factors constraining individual activity, including a shortage of creative expression and the practical concern of a shortage of time. Some Japanese people are at a loss in enjoying periods of leisure time. Organized events are not a problem. There are many organized parties which Japanese have no trouble participating in, in which they drink, sing and enjoy themselves; essentially, Japanese people have, from the year dot, been taught how to fit into an organized or group situation. But there is an inability to creatively break out, and it is the company that compensates by providing the social opportunities mentioned above.

In the 1980s the Japanese government responded to international pressure to limit average working hours in order that Japan reduce production. In 1982, for instance, civil servants started to have one Saturday off every four weeks, then from 1983 banks did the same. Over the decade, public and private institutions reduced their official work time, and this was followed by a reduction in hours at school in the 1990s. But despite this edict, many Japanese people continue to cheekily slip in extra holiday or other time at the office. The increase in leisure time, combined with government policies since the late 1980s to stimulate imports, did begin to result in an increase in leisure participation and an influx of foreign leisure products that produced a thriving market through the 1990s. However, such indulgences remain an awkward or uneasy option for many. Essentially Japanese can put up with the drudgery of the workplace, but many still don't know how to let go and enjoy themselves, and many look with anxiety at the trend toward longer holidays. Surveys carried out through the 1970s to 1990 showed that work remained the greatest source of satisfaction for Japanese workers, though leisure was becoming more popular.[10] In 1992 over 40 per cent of Japanese people said they would be at a loss to know what to do with a month-long vacation.[11]

Importantly, workers feel a lot of security in an established Japanese firm. This was illustrated somewhat ironically in the early 1990s when, as the recession hit, resulting in layoffs, the reaction of many affected workers was a feeling of betrayal and shock that their companies lacked compassion. But actually, of course, economic factors had exhausted other options and companies had to fire some of their workers. On the whole, however, permanent workers at large companies were not laid off, at least not in great numbers. Many firms coped with the situation by calling for early retirement in exchange for which retirees were offered severance pay-outs or by dispatching workers to subsidiaries or by redeploying them within the company.

Redeployment is relatively common in Japan, and is seen to be preferable to laying off workers. According to Takikawa Seiichi of Canon, in slow periods they assign employees from one department, such as administration, to sales in order to deal with new product releases.[12] The car maker Mazda has had its tough times. In the 1970s, when it faced trouble selling its rotary engine, it had its assembly-line workers knock on doors trying to sell cars – because there was nothing else for them to do. In April 1996, when Ford bought a controlling share of Mazda and put a foreigner at the helm – the first case of foreign control of a Japanese auto maker – one of the fears amongst the Japanese public was that Ford would 'rationalize' the business and lay off Japanese workers in the process. Perhaps wisely, Ford didn't take this approach.

Stories about Japanese company owners making crucial decisions about their company's future based on the best interests of the employees are legion. One reason why small firms 'hung in there' during the recession of the early 1990s was the responsibility felt by the owners to their employees and the employees' families: 'I have twenty employees. That means eighty mouths depending on me', was the attitude of one company owner.[13] In late 1997, when the supermarket chain Yaohan went bankrupt, company Chair Wada Kazuo, who 'took responsibility', expressed his gratitude to the head of Jusco, the supermarket chain that helped take over the company's Japan operations, that at least jobs would be secure. Wada also said that he hoped his company's overseas units would also be able to continue for the sake of the employees.[14]

Cynics will say that employers in Japan are out for themselves and not the workers, and indeed this is true of some people. However, in very many cases there is a real concern amongst employers for their workers. Staff concerns are central to the thinking of many business leaders, and accordingly workers perceive their companies to be looking out for worker interests.

This was also the case when the securities company, Yamaichi, collapsed in November 1997. Many TV viewers in Japan and abroad were exposed to a burst of emotion by the president of Yamaichi at the press meeting when the announcement to cease operating was made. But foreign viewers didn't realize that what they saw was Yamaichi's president crying apologetically that 'we, the management, are bad, not the employees', as he expressed deep concern that Yamaichi's workers would lose their jobs.

How about a foreign company?

In the early 1990s, forced by the recession, Japanese companies started undergoing *restora* (restructuring), which in reality meant retiring a lot of people they couldn't afford to pay, plus cutting various other costs. This loosened attitudes amongst workers toward staying with one firm for life, as some workers concluded that they couldn't rely on their existing firms, which were retiring or relocating permanent staff. Japanese workers became more responsive to the idea of mid-career recruitment, though in reality still only a small number were willing to switch jobs. On the one hand, Japanese workers have a feeling of security, if not commitment, toward their existing company. On the other hand, they have had reservations about working for a foreign firm.

So what *is* the perception of foreign firms amongst Japanese people? Historically, it's not been very favourable at all. Foreign firms have not been seen by Japanese people to provide stability – they have instead been perceived as unknown and unpredictable. The general perception is that foreign firms readily lay off staff, or may withdraw from the market when things get tough – pulling the plug on the various relationships that their Japanese business associates have begun to depend on. Indeed, this belief remains true in many cases. Foreign firms do lay off staff, and not only is this counter to what workers expect of a firm but it frightens Japanese workers.

Still, according to research there are many foreign firms in Japan that operate very much according to Japanese protocol. Staff in many foreign-affiliated companies are predominantly Japanese, and daily matters are executed along Japanese lines. In one survey of 133 foreign firms, two-thirds were found to be headed by a Japanese national. And regarding the mix of Japanese-to-foreign staff, a survey of US companies in Japan showed that the bulk of staff in most were Japanese – over half the US firms had a workforce in which more than 90 per cent of workers were Japanese. Most US companies in Japan, the survey found, have very few foreign employees – the majority have a workforce of fewer than 5 per cent non-Japanese, and only 1 per cent of US companies in Japan have a workforce in which over 50 per cent are non-Japanese. Furthermore, of these companies there is also a tendency for long-established and large firms to have a high ratio of local Japanese employees – relatively speaking, it is firms newer to Japan that have a lot of foreign workers.[15]

Concerning job evaluation, foreign-affiliated firms in Japan conform with the Japanese emphasis on seniority, added to which they use 'job performance' as a basis for deciding pay and promotion. As of the latter 1990s, 90 per cent of the US-affiliated firms in Japan that responded to the survey linked base pay to performance, and nearly half linked pay to seniority; the overlap indicates varying degrees of both systems being used. Again, it's newly established firms that tend to rely on performance as the prime measure, while longer-stay and larger firms are 'more Japanese', with a greater tendency to incorporate

Table 5.1 Starting salaries (monthly)[16]

Graduate of	Male	Female
High school	¥153,000 ($1180)	¥144,000 ($1100)
Two-year college	¥167,000 ($1280)	¥160,000 ($1230)
University	¥193,000 ($1480)	¥187,000 ($1440)

seniority as a measure. Also, in many cases Japan-based foreign operations offered benefits including housing, annual bonuses and tenure-based retirement bonuses where the foreign parent at home didn't.[17] In other words, foreign-affiliated firms have, overall, increasingly adapted to the Japanese context. (It should be remembered that this information is based on answers gained from the relatively few firms that responded or were contacted. Very many foreign firms aren't represented, and the data doesn't show what is going on inside them.)[18]

Commissions

An issue related to performance-based pay is sales commissions, which have not been a popular form of payment in Japan. Work in Japan tends to be done in groups, and normally groups, not individuals, have been rewarded. A weak group member may be tolerated, covered for or supported by other members. While performance-based pay is becoming more common, 100 per cent commission payment is seen as both too competitive and unreliable as a source of income, and accordingly is rare in Japan.

As early as the 1960s Canon became a pioneer in introducing Western-style performance-based pay, and the company still offers a portion of remuneration based on performance. But, says Canon, it experimented with commissions and finally abandoned the system. Canon concluded that its Japanese salespeople prefer at least 90 per cent of their salary to be fixed. It claims there are other ways of motivating staff; for instance, Canon salespeople each get their own desk, which it says constitutes a form of status and gives self-confidence.[19]

The 'thinking' Japanese company

While some Japanese firms are increasing the responsibility placed on their workers to perform, they're still not getting rid of workers, nor taking on mid-career outsiders, as is often believed in Japan.

A member of the shipbuilding division of Sumitomo Heavy Industries told me that in his firm the fixed portion of salaries for managerial level and up had been reduced and that a greater share was granted on the basis of achievement, though pay below management remained fixed. When I asked, 'Nowadays there's a lot of talk of scrapping the lifetime employment system, is that happening in your company?' his response was: 'No, no, absolutely not.'

While visiting Mitsubishi Heavy Industries I also asked whether they were following the (reputed) shift away from lifetime employment, and was told: 'We're a traditional company. . . . If we laid off workers it would take 15 years for us to replace the knowledge that has accumulated amongst our staff.' When I put the same question to an established medium to large-sized manufacturer, struggling in the economic downturn, I was also told:

'We're a traditional company. . .'. This company had tried to juggle the accounting figures in order to refrain from making changes, including staff cuts, and, despite having said they would have to, they ultimately managed to avoid any layoffs.

Research by the Ministry of Labour has turned up similar results. While many companies had de-emphasized the seniority portion of their pay system, there was a tendency, across industries and company size, toward more rather than less tenure. According to MITI, in the decade to the mid-1990s there had been an increase from about 30–50 per cent in the number of small and medium-sized enterprises coming up with ways to boost tenure; providing, for example, improved health and welfare schemes, improved retirement schemes, and seniority-related benefit packages. Amongst large firms too, almost 80 per cent were implementing policies to increase long-term tenure amongst workers, and very many of those large firms were actively increasing the scale of existing measures. Reasons given for this include the need to build up a store of in-house technology and know-how to cope with intensified competition.[20]

This was exactly the reason given to me by Mitsubishi Heavy Industries, and ties in with an interesting point made by Berkley professor Nonaka Ikujirō about the different ways information is processed in foreign and Japanese companies. Essentially, foreigners are better at developing (explicit) logical explanations and other communication. Japanese instead rely on contextual (tacit) communication.[21] This means that while foreign workers hired mid-career into a foreign company can efficiently exchange ('download') information with existing staff, since Japanese can't do this so easily it is important in Japanese companies to maintain a body of staff who have a shared basic understanding or 'knowledge' associated with their industry and, more specifically, with their particular company.[22] With this, Japanese employees can exchange and negotiate ideas, and upon this shared understanding they can build new ideas. Remove or replace those employees, and that common grounding between individuals communicating with each other disappears and this tacit level of communication becomes impossible.

So when a company like Mitsubishi Heavy Industries says they would lose 15 years of knowledge, they don't necessarily mean explicit information (that you could document in a book), but the intangible body of shared knowledge that allows employees to communicate, and which acts as a springboard for idea development. In computer terms, it's the rough equivalent of a language protocol exclusive to one company with a number of terminals (staff) familiar with that language.

This little-appreciated concept bites into the conceptual mechanics of how Japanese firms 'think', how they make decisions and create. It also cuts through the Western conventional wisdom that Japanese firms should streamline, get rid of unproductive labour and hire the most skilled employees the labour market can offer. Instead, Japanese firms don't want to change or shed their staff. It's not a matter of a lack of modernization – though they might believe they are behind the times in not getting 'with it' and getting rid of a few non-productive workers – these firms have a resource that they quite sensibly, albeit perhaps intuitively, don't want to ditch. The result is that, apart from a 'progressive' segment of industry – most specifically the finance, as well as other tertiary areas – Japan has yet to envisage a time in which companies get around to replacing a lot of 'permanent' mid-career workers.

Skill-building in finance

'We need specialists in investment banking and private banking. . . . Especially in investment banking, we need a flexible organization to beat the competition because we are dealing with overseas competitors. I don't think the seniority system would bring us victory.'[23]

These were the words of the managing director of a large Japanese bank, three months before the onset of Japan's Big Bang financial deregulation.

During the 50 years following World War II, Japanese financial institutions had operated as functional components locked within the rigid structure of 'Japan Incorporated'. In this system, where increasing the productivity and market share of Japan's manufacturing sector was considered vital, banks were required to be stable suppliers of finance, operating as functional utilities of the administration, rather than service creators themselves. However, in the context of the increasing reliance on and international competition in the tertiary sector it became important for financial institutions, too, to become creative suppliers and marketers.

It was a demonstration of insight, then, that just as the bubble was bursting in the very early 1990s, writer Christopher Wood noted: 'There are now about 150,000 people working in [Japan's securities] business, of whom at least 50,000 do not have the knowledge and sophistication to handle a deregulated financial world where they have to come up with their own ideas and not simply obey head office orders.'[24] By 1998 Japan was between a rock and a hard place. With financial organizations collapsing, it was decided that there was a drastic need to either overhaul or overthrow systems that were dysfunctional in a deregulating financial world.

One of the systems that fitted in well with Japan's communal and stability-orientated society was the seniority–lifetime employment structure. But in reality this didn't fit with the proactive, quick decision-making environment of modern finance. Policy decisions in both Japanese finance and manufacturing had been based on conference between politico-economic actors; 'who you knew' was at least as important as 'what you knew'. However, this focus caused drag within a fast-moving, performance-based modern finance system. In other words, the advantages of lifetime employment, the seniority, and other 'human'-orientated systems to tertiary areas including finance were largely outweighed by the inflexibility they brought with them.

As Japan's Big Bang deregulation measures approached, indicative of efforts to change, several of Japan's major banks had plans to scrap the system of *jinmyaku*-based recruiting – that is, where new recruits are located by existing employees or professors who search their *alma maters*. Stopping this practice would imply a subsequent breaking down of the loyalty structure upon which many of Japan's business decisions are based, replacing them with pragmatic market-driven decisions.

Foreign companies should, however, use this method to secure staff if they have such strong contacts as existing workers or professors from a 'good university'. This is both because it's one means of finding staff and because employees from strong universities, with strong connections, will be useful in Japan for some time yet. One Japanese executive of a major foreign securities firm told me:

'We need specialists who can perform. And they need to speak English well. If they can't speak English we don't want them, unless they come from a good university; we still need some contacts to other major organizations in order to do business with them. We are "fortunate" to have about ten Tokyo University graduates. We have to use their connections; if we don't have connections we can't meet new people.'

By 1998, in an environment of bank failures and an opening up of the market, some Japanese banks had decided they needed to fast-track staff to build specialists rather than company 'team workers'. Banks felt ill-equipped to handle new financial products that had, actually, never mattered to them before.

These banks also began to take on mid-career workers – some head-hunted workers from foreign banks in an effort to bring in necessary foreign skills. This represented a major shift in behaviour, and reflected how inadequate the banks felt about their in-house skills.

In the process, banks were having to restructure their pay systems. Until 1998 mid-career hires had generally held the status of non-permanent staff because they couldn't otherwise slot in alongside regular staff on the seniority pay–promotion track. But as it became more important to welcome these hires on-board, this system became untenable. And for their own talented regular workers, Japanese financial institutions had to start providing incentives so they wouldn't be lured away to foreign firms. Both of these factors gave more reason for financial firms to introduce a general policy of performance-based pay.

Head hunters

In spite of the changes in the personnel policies of Japanese companies, it will be a long time before there is anything like a pool of top Japanese workers on the labour market. Indeed, one of the main problems identified by foreign firms operating in Japan is hiring good local staff.

Head hunters in Japan have become increasingly active, as more foreign firms enter the Japanese market, trying to persuade Japanese workers that they can reap better rewards in a foreign company.

According to Japan's biggest domestic executive search firm, East West Consulting, demand for permanent staff has been booming. Foreign firms appreciate that they need a position in the Japanese market, and they need competent staff. Industry-wise, demand is across the board, though there are growth areas such as semiconductors, software and finance, albeit with fluctuations and cyclical changes in demand in some categories over time. As for workers, there is a considerable under-supply, with particularly high demand for engineers. In order to fill the gap, other foreign engineers, in particular from India and China, are being recruited.[25]

There is criticism of head hunters, especially in stable-employment-orientated Japan. Still, while people normally have the impression that it's the head hunters who initiate the messy business of luring workers from their companies, some Japanese firms, in an effort to avoid the painful task of making a worker redundant, slip the names of their excess staff to head hunters in the hope that they will be pulled, rather than have to be pushed out of the company. And accordingly some employees called up by head hunters wonder, or even ask the head hunter, where they got their name from: did their existing employer give it to them?

For foreign firms, hiring problems are heightened in Japan because it's so much more difficult for a foreign boss to check the suitability of Japanese staff sent by head hunters. Therefore, those going to the expense of using a head hunter should have an experienced Japanese staff member or acquaintance take part in the interviewing and listen to his or her evaluation. Or, in the opinion of one Japanese management consultant: '. . . get a trusted Japanese manager or two to interview the candidates separately and then talk over their reactions thoroughly before you make a decision.'[26]

There's also criticism that there's a lack of follow-up after hiring. Muromatsu Nobuko, who heads East West, says:

'We always follow up to see that everything is going well, or to see if there are any problems; we follow up on "problems and progress" . . . for about 3 to 6 months. . . . Candidates who work for a foreign firm are in a different culture. Some people are not flexible enough to adjust, and many have problems. We have to try to help; we have to counsel, we have to tell the candidate or client what needs to be done.'

On the value of using head hunters, two Japanese executives from different foreign securities brokers said virtually the same thing; according to one: 'We use head hunters to get our staff, they're useful because different head hunters deal in different, quite specific job classifications; for example, we can request an analyst or a dealer or a particular office worker. . .'. And on candidate selection: 'It is possible that a head hunter would choose a person who wasn't suitable, but the head hunter wouldn't last very long. And anyway there's a trial period in which we can reject an employee, and this dissuades head hunters from not offering good candidates.'

He did add, 'But head hunters are very expensive'. Payment for the services of a head hunter is normally on a placement basis, though some work on an up-front 'retainer' basis – the latter get paid to search rather than to place. Standard remuneration for the services of a head hunter in Japan is 35 per cent of the worker's first year annual salary. In the US, it's a third of the annual salary. The (small) difference is justified by the extra work involved in placing staff in Japan.

Somewhat less expensive is classified advertising, and the most commonly used English language newspaper for employers to seek employees is the Monday edition of *The Japan Times*. Foreign job hunters read this, and so do Japanese people who think their English is good enough to apply for a job in a foreign company. It's therefore a fairly easy medium to find staff – it means you don't have to translate the ad, and the applicants you will get will be fairly good English speakers. The cost for one entry of a basic advert in *The Japan Times* is about ¥35,000 ($270).

A very intelligent, 33-year-old, single Japanese woman explains job hunting like this:

> 'When we look for a job, firstly we buy newspapers or recruitment information magazines like B–ing, or *Recruit* or *Salida* [Japanese-language job magazines], and *The Japan Times*. The Japan Times has the most ads in English, so we can find some interesting jobs in it. Secondly we send a résumé to a head hunter. Thirdly we might go to a public employment office, but they don't have much information, especially about foreign companies. I send my résumé to a head hunter – but I don't think they introduce candidates to companies so often. So it's better to use newspapers or magazines – most candidates use this method to find a job.'

Hiring Japanese

There are some provisos to remember when hiring Japanese managerial staff. Since mainstream Japanese managers have been hard to recruit from the lifetime employment system, some of those available are on the job market because they can't fit into the Japanese system. That they aren't conventional is good, or appears good to the foreign company since the Japanese and foreign personalities are compatible – the foreign employers think they have someone they can communicate with, and who operates like them. However, the risk is that the Japanese staff member may be unable to fit well into Japanese business circles.

Even those with good English who claim to have good contacts may not be what is wanted. While most Japanese are reserved (and some of these well connected), there are extroverts who communicate strongly and confidently, but because they're unconventional they would not be trusted by those they 'know'. Someone who comes across as being much more than just pleasant may be seen as odd by other Japanese, who will want to keep well away from the person.

Amongst Japanese who have their feet placed solidly on the ground, those who have been educated abroad or have spent a long time out of the Japanese system may also not fit well into Japan. Remember, one of the assets foreign firms need in Japan is a *jinmyaku*, and that means you need people who know other useful people. Someone whose university life was spent abroad may not have those connections or may have fewer of them. It depends what your firm requires; whether you need someone to market your product and business, or you only need someone who is bilingual.

For a foreign company to do well, it may be better to forego the more comfortable relationship a Westernized Japanese manager may provide, and if possible recruit, understand and work with a mainstream Japanese manager. Strategically, you may be better off with one who fits in with other mainstream Japanese, on your side.

This, however, may mean language becomes an issue. For chief executive officer (CEO) positions, it may be more important to forego English ability if it means the person you are securing mixes well with other Japanese. The language problem can be covered by hiring twin CEOs, one English speaker to handle foreign-related issues, the other a Japanese executive to establish and maintain contacts within the local community. Or alternatively, hire a Japanese CEO on the basis of the skill s/he brings, and employ an interpreter/ personal secretary to handle language. Kishi and Russell recommend the idea of twin CEOs and suggest making the Japanese head the President, and the foreign head the Chair, as the title 'President' in Japan carries more weight – this is important, as it is the Japanese CEO who must parley with and be seen by other Japanese to carry influence.[27]

There's one important point to consider about employing a permanent interpreter. As mentioned above, one of the problems many foreigners confront is that Japanese people do not break down their world logically. The matter is trouble enough in a one-off interpretation session, but it is vital not to have this problem where the employee is the permanent bridge between the firm's foreign contingent and the Japanese CEO or other management. The foreign staff don't want to be tearing their collective hair out trying to understand what the CEO is actually thinking when what they are getting is simply what the CEO has 'literally' said. You need someone who can, in different ways where necessary, ask the CEO and then convey to you what the CEO is getting at.

Being able to do this is a valuable asset – something that becomes apparent when you realize that it's rare amongst Japanese people. When employing, how do you examine this ability? Firstly, in order to check their English ability, ask an 'or' question. The structure of Japanese language means those poor at English aren't used to listening for the 'or' between the two options, so such a question as: 'Would you like tea or coffee?' is often answered: 'Ah. Yes!' To check on their logical ability while talking to the person, expect a logical answer or some reasoned observations about business, Japan, or whatever the person is interested in, or whatever the topic at hand is. Ask, and evaluate answers to, a couple of 'why?' questions. 'Why?' to very many Japanese people is like 'garlic to the vampire'.

Remuneration

Japanese business perquisites

As indicated, Japanese pay has traditionally increased with age rather than performance, and there is less of a range between upper and lower salaries in Japanese companies than, for instance, the pay range in the US. As part of mutual Japanese–American criticism, Japanese commentators have said that American business leaders get paid too much, while expecting American workers to cut back in hard times. In 1980 salaries of American CEOs were, on average, 42 times greater than their employees. By 1991 the salary difference had reached 104 times, and by 1995 CEOs were earning 141 times more than employees averaged. In Lee Iacocca's case, his $20mn income for 1989 while he was at Chrysler was about a thousand times that of a Chrysler factory worker. Compare this with CEOs in

Japan, who earn six to ten times that of the *lowest paid* factory worker.[28] Americans have countered by saying that apparently selfless Japanese business management actually receives a lot in perquisites.

There are a lot of perquisites embedded in the lives of Japanese workers. Post-World War II tax laws helped institute a system of payment through company perquisites, since granting them was more practical than increasing wages. And though their tax deductibility has decreased, the perquisites have continued.[29] This is in part because of, or is accentuated by, the 'benevolent' approach of Japanese company owners inclined to provide such extras as part of the general concept of looking after the worker. In turn, this serves to bond the workers to the company. In a country that thrives on the proceeds of accumulated mutual obligations, being benevolent is a much more vague, and therefore better, way to secure a return of favour than is giving a clear-cut contractual payment. People like, and will be loyal to, a company that looks after its workers.[30]

Housing, or assistance with mortgage costs, is a perquisite that has been used to attract new employees. Also, in Japan senior executives in many cases have a company car and chauffeur. This and other commuting expenses are normally all paid for by the company, and a wealthy enough company will have facilities such as a holiday villa for its staff.

Accentuated by the importance of ties between business people, a lot of money is spent on entertainment – a lot of which is paid for by the company. Since golf is an excellent medium to informally develop relationships with business people, it attracts a lot of business patronage. The shortage of land, and its high price, especially in the 1980s, made it an important industry. Golf memberships reach into millions of yen – for instance, in the late 1980s Koganei Golf Club in Tokyo commanded the highest membership fee at ¥340mn ($2.4mn) – and those memberships became popularly traded by brokers within a market of their own. There is even a Nikkei Golf Membership price index, and in the latter 1980s it outperformed and even appeared to lead the stock market.[31] It is also very common for business people to take clients out to bars; the more expensive, the more status. 'The wealthy' used to frequent *geisha* houses – an innocent and high-quality entertainment service – but the hostess bar or *karaoke* bar are the common business person's version.[32] Both formal and informal company-funded 'entertainment' has been a characteristic of Japanese business for generations. Business entertainment expenses peaked in 1992, at which time they were 1.5 per cent of Japan's GDP. Following that, both a downturn in the economy and increasing concern about the illicit solicitation of favours paid for in the name of 'entertainment' sent such expenses into gradual decline.

The bonus system

The bonus system represents twice-yearly lump sum income payments which, since both payouts occur at Japanese gift-giving times (see *Ochūgen* and *Oseib*, page 182), in turn have an impact on retail sales. At the two bonus times manufacturers put on special sales programmes and customers buy not only consumer items but also special gifts and gift packs. Accordingly, rubbish truck workloads increase dramatically as TVs and other appliances are put out, as owners update to new models.

The bonus was originally given in appreciation of the efforts of the employee, in the spirit of the family-like company, but it has become institutionalized and, where unions exist, the bonus amount may be negotiated along with pay. From the point of view of the individual, it is a lump sum that may be locked away and targeted for special purpose spending, rather than disappear as part of the monthly budget, and in this way it has contributed to Japan's very high savings rate. From a company point of view, the bonus system also has advantages.

● It is another incentive for workers to produce, since the bonus directly reflects company and in some cases, more recently, individual performance.

- Since the bonus is adjustable, instead of laying off staff the bonus can be (legitimately) reduced when corporate income drops. (Essentially, though, it should remain fixed and be reduced only in real emergencies.)
- Unlike monthly wages, since the bonus is deferred, and paid at the end of a six-month period, the company can use this money as working capital.
- Overall, bonus increases or decreases are shared by all employees, and this reinforces the feeling of the team – workers and management – moving together.
- Even if the bonus is increased, this doesn't oblige the company to increase related payments, such as retirement pay, which are linked to the salary.

The bonus amount paid by employers in Japan varies quite a lot; however, the average has been equivalent to between two and four months' salary at each of the two payouts, though one of the immediate consequences of the recession was a drop in bonus amounts. In addition to private-sector workers, bonuses are paid to government workers and those in public corporations, and on some occasions a smaller payment may be made to part-time workers.

During the 1990s' recession when, in an effort to encourage greater worker productivity, some companies reviewed their seniority-pay systems, bonus portions in some cases became pooled and reissued on the basis of small group or individual payments for strong achievers.

Stock options

A more recent addition to the system of remuneration is stock options, mentioned earlier. These allow employees the option of buying shares in their firm at a set price. As a firm's share price rises, employees can reap capital gains on the eventual sale of the stocks. While elsewhere stock options have been a common part of the remuneration package, until 1995 the system of offering stock options to workers had not been allowed in Japan. From a labour point of view, they aim to encourage greater output from workers, who feel more enthused because they are working to boost their own profit. (The only problem with this part of the theory is that Japanese workers have always felt that they are working for their team, and that doing so will in turn provide a payoff for themselves.) From the point of view of the companies, they can afford to employ better staff because instead of having to pay high salaries they can offer a deferred reward in the form of stocks. There are other implications of the stock option system, as it relates to Japan, that are discussed above, in the finance section.

Unions

Labour disputes do happen in Japan. However, while some Japanese people are strongly supportive of workers' rights most people are not interested, and there are few militants. That there is not much labour unrest in Japan is reflected in the low number of days lost due to disputes compared to Western nations; see Table 5.2.

Rather than engage in conflict with the company, even in times of hardship there is a willingness amongst workers to support the company. Workers may accept a cut in wages, a delay in wage payment, putting in extra time, or even cancelling holiday plans if needed. And these, to varying degrees, apply to all levels of personnel in large and small companies. Whereas such measures could be expected to meet with opposition in the West, the idea of workers sacrificing for the good of the company is largely accepted amongst Japanese people. When the economy places demands on the company, workers don't question requests, and though they mightn't necessarily like it, they pitch in. The result is

Table 5.2 Days lost through labour disputes ($\times$ 1000)

Japan	US	UK	Germany	France	Italy
73	5711	415	247	784	909

Source: Keizai Kōhō Centre. Figures for 1995.

that even in an economic downturn Japan's productivity remains high; its domestic consumption drops and the nation's trade surplus increases. But helping out is a two-way thing – workers expect to be looked after by the company; hence, as mentioned above, there was a feeling of betrayal amongst those laid off when the recession hit in the early 1990s.

In spite of the lack of unrest, it's common for workers in larger Japanese companies to belong to a union. They automatically join on entry into the company and have their union fees deducted from their pay.

There are characteristics of Japanese unions that distinguish them from those in the West. Almost all unions in Japan are company 'house' unions (enterprise unions), rather than national trade unions. This means wages and other matters are negotiated within the company. It can also mean that negotiations are splintered amongst different companies that focus on their firm rather than the broad economy. There is unified action in the form of Japan's annual spring wage offensive (*shuntō*), where federations of unions coordinate wage demands. The situation is ritualized: everyone expects the 'protest', minimal damage occurs, and harmony is maintained. Still, this annual event does function to set the standard for wage increases, serving as a guide for other negotiations.

It's also interesting that many companies have two unions: one that everyone belongs to, and another, radical body, which is the original union. This is because a common way of dealing with antagonistic unions in Japan is for a company to form another, docile union. The company then sweetens the pot so it becomes more attractive to, and thus draws to it the bulk of, the employees. Amongst those companies that have had the experience of dealing with labour disputes by forming such a second union are both Sony (1961) and Nissan (following World War II).

Notes

1 Even through changed circumstances, such values can exist. Enduring over time, they surface when external factors such as the industrial climate permit them to become important ingredients in social-economic events. Such practices now considered typical of Japanese companies had applied to such business houses as Mitsui, but weren't widely observable until industrialization gave them the chance to develop into the large-scale business institutions that emerged in the early twentieth century. These concepts and practices applied squarely to, for instance, both the *zaibatsu* and then the *keiretsu*; these two were not 'constructed' economic edifices, but, along with industrial expansion, appeared out of the essential material of Japan's hierarchical society.

2 Beasley (1990, pp. 123–26) notes that factory-ization occurred with the beginning of export trade (p. 109).

3 Nakane, in Nakane and Ōishi, 1990, p. 221.

4 Nakane says that the *ie* might be better classed as an ongoing enterprise than a family. She also points out that the *ie* appeared before the Tokugawa era, and, though it was more common amongst Japan's 'higher strata', it existed amongst 'common people' (in Nakane and Ōishi, 1990, pp. 216–19).

5 Sakudō Yōtarō, pp. 159, 163–64; Nakane, p. 221, both in Ōishi and Nakane, 1990.

6 *Small Business in Japan*, MITI, 1997, p. 126.

7 Edo, at the time the world's largest city, seems to have reached 1 million early in the eighteenth century (Nakamura, S., in Nakane and Ōishi, 1990, p. 84). In population density, amongst nations of over six million people, Japan follows Bangladesh, South Korea and The Netherlands, in that order (*Statistical Handbook of Japan 1993*, pp. 15–16).

8 Alletzhauser, 1990, p. 184.

9 Alletzhauser, 1990, p. 190.

10 Surveys carried out through the 1970s and 1980s by both Japan's Ministry of Labour and the Leisure Development Centre. By 1990 those favouring leisure were 32.7 per cent (1.2 per cent up on 1989), those favouring work were 37.9 per cent (0.9 per cent down on 1989). The largest sub-category was of the latter, favouring work – they (33.5 per cent of the total) placed their main emphasis on work as a source of satisfaction, and spent some time pursuing leisure (from 'White Paper on Leisure' 1991, in *Japanese Corporate Personnel Management*, JETRO, 1992, p. 22).

11 The Leisure Development Centre's 'White Paper on Leisure' 1992 says that many Japanese don't know what to do with their spare time (in *Leisure and Recreational Activities*, Foreign Press Centre, 1993, p. 37).

12 Kraar and Takikawa, 1994, p. 92.

13 Whittaker, 1997, p. 153.

14 Nikkei Shimbun interview, in *The Nikkei Weekly*, 20 October 1997, p. 8.

15 *People Management Issues of American Companies in Japan*, ACCJ, 1977, p. 25; Nikkei Shimbun survey in *The Nikkei Weekly*, 3 November 1997, p. 8.

16 Source: *Setting Up a Business in Japan*, JETRO, 1996, p. 39, Ministry of Labour figures for 1995.

17 *People Management Issues of American Companies in Japan*, ACCJ, 1977, p. 20.

18 Response rates for surveys of foreign businesses in Japan range from about 20–80 per cent, with numbers of firms responding typically between 100 and 130. We should conclude from these surveys simply that the behaviours reported 'exist'. We can't conclude that they are dominant; there are simply too many firms that we don't hear from.

19 Kraar and Takikawa, 1994, p. 85.

20 *Small Business in Japan*, MITI, 1996, pp. 57 and 219.

21 The idea is developed in Nonaka and Takeuchi, 1995. This book is a rare example of work that starts to, and has significantly, cut through to the essential worker processes that make Japanese firms the 'creating companies' that they are, but still work in this area is incomplete.

22 A contrast often made between Japanese and foreign companies is that foreign firms have a lot of instruction manuals (by means of which they 'download' information) whereas Japanese firms don't (they rely on tacit, existing 'knowledge' inherent in the workforce).

23 Tanaka Kazuyoshi, Tokai Bank's managing director in charge of corporate planning (in *The Nikkei Weekly*, 15 December 1997, p. 12).

24 Wood, 1992, p. 109.

25 Interviews with Todd Miller and Muromatsu Nobuko of East West Consulting, November 1997–March 1998.

26 Kishi Nagami, in Kishi and Russell, 1996, p. 343.

27 p. 344.

28 'Who's Getting Rich and Why Aren't You?', CBS, 60 Minutes, 1996; Ohmae, 1990, p. 69. Ishihara Shintarō (1991, p. 91) criticizes Lee Iacocca for receiving huge bonuses while Chrysler employees had sacrificed their pay.

29 For instance, since the 1970s, the tax deductibility of entertainment expenses for companies with capital over 50 million yen had been gradually reduced and is now gone. Income taxes were lowered in 1988, while capital gains for individuals from stocks, etc., which had been virtually free of tax, from April 1989 were taxed at a flat rate of 26 per cent.

30 Being obliged in Japan, for kindness received, puts the receiver in the kind of awkward situation in which we would say 'I can't thank you enough'. When a wallet is found and handed to police, a figure of 10 per cent of the contents, as a gift to the finder, is standard. This makes life easy, since it ends the matter there. But a 'paranoid' feeling of indebtedness often weighs heavily on the recipient of kindness; the account cannot be cleared. Benedict talks about this point, suggesting that it can become a ploy, to have someone in your debt (1946, p. 104–05). This obligation is a tradition, and may be the expectation of many companies – expecting unmitigated commitment for their generosity – but is exactly the thing that is weakening in the modern worker's relationship with the company; commitment more and more being exchanged for tangible reward.

31 Ziemba and Schwartz, 1992, p. 137.

32 In order to address the most common myth about *geisha*; essentially, the occupation was not sexual, but could become so 'with the right person'. *Geisha* were quality house entertainers as well as servants. They would come to serve particular regular patrons, and in certain cases a strong and intimate relationship would develop between a patron and a *geisha*. The patron might sponsor the *geisha*, taking over financial responsibility for her, perhaps even taking her as concubine or wife. Originally *geisha* were male.

Chapter 6

Networking and other interpersonal business strategies

Business operations targeting Japan have often gone awry because foreigners haven't appreciated the importance of the interpersonal aspects of Japanese business. Western business people with a background in management or economics have come to Japan expecting that that will be sufficient to conduct business in Japan. However, the skills they bring don't equip them to understand the *social* aspects, which are fundamental to Japanese business.

Jinmyaku – it's who you know

A basic difference between Japanese and Westerners in business is the separation between work and leisure. In the West there is a clear line between business and personal life. However, in Japan the distinction is blurred: social life in many cases is part of business and vice versa. Friends and recreation are commonly company-related, which helps to further obfuscate the division between work time and private time.

At a party, a person hearing of what you do may offer to introduce you to 'my friend', who may be able to do business with you. This doesn't make the mediator business-hungry, but a helpful friend, who is also strengthening his/her relations – it increases the possibility for the mediator of reciprocity in future, potentially improving the mediator's lot.

This raises the issue of the value of 'who you know' in Japan. Amongst foreigners in Japan the term probably most commonly used in this context is 'contacts'; amongst Japanese the term is *jinmyaku*. More fully, however, *jinmyaku* means one's personal connections or one's network. It would be inappropriate to say that a *jinmyaku* is essential – some people have been able to sell 'cold' in Japan. And perhaps for a firm with a lot of power – good financial backing and a good product – pure popular demand might pull the product through the marketing system. But this is the exception rather than the rule. Products need some form of competitive advantage over and above their 'inherent value' in order to survive or pass through each point in the sales chain. While in the West a product is judged at each point in terms of price and quality–performance, often just as important in Japan is the established relationship between the buyer and the seller.

These business relationships were, for instance, exactly the target of accusations made by Kodak against Fuji Film. Kodak maintained that its product was cheaper and the quality just as good as Fuji's, but that it had been unable to get the market share it would expect because of the close relations between participants in Fuji's distribution *keiretsu*.

The reality is that it's very difficult to do business of any substance in Japan without a good *jinmyaku*. In some ways it is the *sine qua non* of business achievement in Japan – without a strong *jinmyaku* it is virtually impossible for Japanese or foreign firms to become successful. Indeed, the reason it takes a painfully long time to establish successful business in Japan is that it takes so long to establish a *jinmyaku*, or at least to build trust amongst your personal associates – which is, in effect, the same thing.

Networking starts at school

According to economist and former Tokyo University professor Kumon Shumpei, Japanese universities are places for 'making friends'. 'At university, the human network you develop is far more important than the education you receive.'[1]

For many children (in urban areas at least), their first educational challenge is gaining access to a good kindergarten. This may involve an IQ-like test to see if they're made of the right stuff. Some attend kindergarten prep-schools to ensure they acquire the right stuff. A good kindergarten provides entry to subsequent prestigious schools, which means access to a good *jinmyaku*. From there on, the educational process involves two main features, neither of which result in what Westerners normally term *education*. One is to expose the child to a quality of teaching that will enable the child to pass with good grades in order to advance into another good school. The other is to expose the child to the people, the peer group that – typically he – will be associated with in his working life. For women, a good education (traditionally) provides access to a good marriage partner.

Jinmyaku is more important than erudition. The motive for study is less for students to get a good academic education than to get a good job and get to know people who will also be in strong business positions. Having attended a good school will enable a person to construct relationships with ex-classmates in companies that can provide good business opportunities.

The epitome of *jinmyaku* activity exists amongst graduates of Tōdai – an abbreviation of Tōkyō Daigaku (University) – Japan's most prestigious university. Most students who pass the Tōdai entrance exam – itself the pinnacle of educational achievement – have by then committed a large portion of their life to study. And when they graduate, many enter top companies or the government bureaucracy; MITI, for instance, takes up to 30 recruits a year, most from the Tōdai Economics and Law faculties. These are the people you may meet if your work takes you to a government ministry in Kasumigaseki, Tokyo's bureaucratic centre, to discuss business policy. A Tōdai graduate might be employed by a top company in order to form links with ex-classmates from Tōdai who are now in the bureaucracy. In doing so the graduate may be able to help his/her company cut through red tape, gain useful information or get access to business deals.

Become a social climber

And foreigners can have a piece of this action too, though it is not necessarily easy. I met a foreign marketing student who was studying at Tokyo University on an exchange programme. He told me how he'd regularly be invited to go drinking with some fairly influential people, including a number of bureaucrats, and that he had a stack of *meishi* (business cards) that he, in effect, didn't know what to do with. I told him that in terms of how the system operates he is constructing potentially good links with people in the system who could be very useful if he were here operating a business.

But the irony is that at that time, as a student he couldn't take advantage of what he had. In five years, after being employed by a foreign company and coming to Japan with specific marketing goals, he would know exactly which of those links would be useful. But without that knowledge it is impossible to know which bureaucrats and business cards might be useful, in order to know who to maintain contact or to develop a stronger relationship with. And without maintaining some sort of contact, the relationship would have faded in five years anyway.

At the root of the matter is that if you are, for whatever reason, associated with Tokyo University – or, to lesser degrees, with other universities – you are immediately attractive as someone to know. Important people want to go drinking with you, at least because they know you're going drinking with other important people. So it's a good medium to make useful friends. But ironically, whereas most foreign students can't use these contacts, most foreigners in business need, but have no opportunity, to make that sort of contact.

It would be useful to combine these two. Take, for instance, the European Delegation's ETP programme (detailed later on pages 124–25). It deals in 'students' already in business, who have existing market goals. It would be useful to link such students into a top Japanese university – this doesn't have to be Tokyo University (but that would help). Students with a good capacity for socializing, over the 18 months that these students spend in Japan, may be able to develop good social relationships with some interesting Japanese people.

A reminder: these are social relationships first, then business opportunities. This is reiterated by the following advice, by way of example, from a mid-level bureaucrat: 'I used to spend all my money on drinks – I would shout everybody, until I had no money left for myself, and everybody thought I was a great guy. . .'

Legwork

Given the importance of 'who you know', clearly most foreigners are disadvantaged because they don't have a strong *jinmyaku*. The most basic way of dealing with the situation is to work your way up from the bottom, building your own *jinmyaku*. For many business people this means spending a long time building friendly, informal relationships with relevant others. This allows those people to build trust in you – exactly what you want.

As part of this process, identify the trade associations related to your business (discussed earlier). Become a member of trade associations and other organizations. Join meetings or other activities where you can show yourself as a pleasant, involved and interested person. Get in their photos, and become known amongst the other participants.

This idea of building your social environment is repeated in different examples throughout the book. While looking at these examples you should try to gain an idea of what it means to mix business with your personal relations in Japan, in order that the process becomes natural.

Amakudari

For those who can afford to do so, *jinmyaku* can be bought. Or perhaps it is better to say that one's *jinmyaku* can be supplemented or strengthened with money. Amongst those who can afford it the buying happens in various ways. The most basic process, and one that many foreign firms undertake, is securing the employment of an *amakudari* bureaucrat: an ex-government official who brings (typically his) contacts with him to your company.

Amakudari literally means 'descent from (bureaucratic) heaven', into the private sector, typically to work as an 'adviser'. Bureaucrats normally retire in their 50s, which means they still have a lot of working life left in them. Furthermore, their pay as a bureaucrat is not high, so a 'post-retirement' slot is, finally, their chance to have their status, as a member of Japan's élite, pay real dividends.

Needing to navigate through official regulations has been a main reason for employing an *amakudari*. While a combination of bureaucrat-related scandals and deregulation in

Japan has weakened the importance of 'discretionary' decision making amongst officials, its importance has by no means vanished yet. Partly because the phenomenon of *jinmyaku* is fundamental in Japanese society, it will disappear from business neither easily nor quickly.

For the employing company, an *amakudari* officer serves the function of securing lines of communication between business and the bureaucracy. This is done by using the ex-bureaucrat's connections back in the bureaucracy to clear a path for the requests of the new employer company. Understandably, the particular rank s/he held within government will affect the bureaucrat's influence as a private sector *amakudari*. Accordingly, top officials are taken on by top companies – it is, after all, a market economy!

This can mean mediating some very big deals, and, understandably, good pay. Those ex-bureaucrats with good connections may get over double their previous earnings, plus perquisites. According to one Japanese executive of a foreign securities firm, their *amakudari* gets a salary of over ¥20mn ($150,000) a year plus a secretary and a car. In Japan, where multi-million-dollar salaries are extremely rare, that's a very comfortable package for someone who is already on a substantial pension from a former post. What's more, an *amakudari* can collect additional retirement money from the present employing company, or from each company, for the many who move through several post-retirement jobs.

It may be useful to remember, though, that the *amakudari*, once employed, has loyalties to two organizations, the new employer and former subordinates at the donor ministry. It's not surprising, then, that those in *amakudari* positions act as in-the-field informants, feeding back information to the bureaucracy on the activities of the business sector.

A continuation of the discussion of the means by which money can enhance one's *jinmyaku* leads into the murky business of cash for favours, or the fine line between generosity and bribery. And exactly because of the tight link between 'the social' and business, the Japanese have established a reputation for liberally moving back and forward across that line.

To foreigners, the construction industry has been one of the most troublesome areas in this respect. A friend of mine, Hiroshi, is currently an executive in DKK Industrial Ltd., a construction machinery sales company, and he has also had considerable experience in other construction industry firms. When I asked him if the links between the bureaucracy and business were still strong after much of the Japanese business environment had undergone restructuring, he said: 'If my boss needs a customer, he phones a politician, the politician's secretary phones the relevant ministry, and an official there then asks a construction company to purchase from DKK. A construction firm in that position would be wise to take the opportunity ... DKK would then feel obliged to reimburse the politician – but not so that it was obvious.' This, according to Hiroshi, could be done in several ways: 'A common form is by DKK buying expensive tickets to functions put on by the politician. In this way money could be transferred to the politician. If the politician had a company, a transfer of money could be made to appear legitimate by DKK becoming a paying customer of the company, but of course DKK would pay above-market rates ... One politician had a real estate company, and DKK was in the market to buy some land. So DKK bought the land from the politician, and paid top price – of course this was much, much more than the politician's firm had paid for it.'[2]

Hiroshi had decided to set up on his own and wasn't happy about the need to have *jinmyaku* links in order to get anywhere in business, so he was quite happy to herald the deficiencies of the system. When I asked him about the existence of *dangō* (negotiations for construction bid rigging), he said of course it continues, and gave me the name of the region's official construction industry organization that, he says, is responsible for (illegally) coordinating bid prices and successful bids.

Leadership material

Given that *jinmyaku* is relied on to the extent that it dictates business activity, it is not surprising that leaders in Japan, in many cases, are more skilled at social relations than they are competent at business. This applies equally in Japan to bureaucrats, business people and politicians, including the odd Prime Minister. One well-reputed publication politely (euphemistically) notes Suzuki Zenkō (PM 1980–1982), for instance, as 'known more for his skill in mediating differences than for strong leadership'. The foreign business person may notice this phenomenon in meeting Japanese company heads, especially in second-generation or later businesses. Presidents and company chairs are often figure-heads who speak at meetings, rally the group, and spend a lot of time meeting others – bolstering their *jinmyaku*. But they don't seem to have that sharp business acumen that Westerners identify with, feel reassured by, and in many cases like to enter into dialogue with.

One business consultant, on surviving in the Japanese business–social environment, advises:

'Identify all the participants and map the relationships among them. . . . Only with map in hand can you identify potential allies and enemies. You will soon discover it is not simply "us" the foreigners versus "them" the Japanese. Enjoy the insecurity of abandoning your favourite rhetorical tools. For example, scrap terms such as "fair" that have no pragmatic definition in English and no equivalent in Japanese. Accept the intellectual challenge of defining your own interests from the perspective of the interests of your customers.'[3]

The myth about getting an introduction

A common theme of explanations about 'doing business in Japan' relates to the importance of getting an introduction to those you need to do business with, rather than trying to meet them cold. Implicit is the availability of an introduction and of a subsequent business association. But a basic problem is the failure to appreciate that an introduction in Japan is also fundamentally a social matter. It is performed by a mutual friend who can give the parties confidence in each other. This means quite simply that introductions amongst people who don't know each other well, where the mediator therefore can't pass on his/ her confidence in the integrity of each party to the other, are of limited or no value. Hence the need for a *jinmyaku*, which constitutes a body of people personally linked to each other, comprised of those with the confidence to make recommendations to one another.

The shōkai-sha

The mediator, or introducing party, in Japan is called a *shōkai-sha* (introduction-person), and associated with this title there are two distinct, but overlapping functions. One function is the above, which involves introducing two parties wanting to do business. It involves brokering trust, that is, passing on the *shōkai-sha*'s confidence to each party that the other is dependable. And it is this 'guarantee' that is important for and needed by the majority of companies who are unknown and trying to do business in Japan.

The other function applies where trust is not a factor, for instance in cases where two parties are well known to each other by size or reputation, but need someone to broker the negotiations. Japanese don't like awkward or confrontational situations. Broaching the matter of starting business may meet with rejection or raise difficult negotiation terms which would be awkward for the two parties in a face-to-face situation. This second form of *shōkai-sha* is used to absorb the discomfort of awkward requests or problems, to smooth over the formality between parties who are not on familiar terms. Accordingly, the same *shōkai-sha* may be used again to mediate later problems which arise between the parties.

When GM teamed up with Isuzu in 1971, Sony's Morita Akio acted as an intermediary, assisting with problems. Later, when GM tied up with Toyota, a Japanese trading company representative who had previously worked with both companies contacted GM as a first step, initiating and facilitating negotiations. Unlike the case of smaller companies, GM didn't need to supply a 'good character' guarantee to Isuzu. Its requirements were quite different from that of a smaller unknown company new to Japan needing to establish trust in its abilities.

Misunderstanding by operators of smaller businesses entering Japan occurs because writers about business feel obliged to mention the importance of getting a *shōkai-sha*. However, they draw upon examples of this latter type of relationship where the *shōkai-sha* successfully facilitates negotiations between larger companies that are already well known and in a sense can trust each other. Or writers explain how the *shōkai-sha* are vital mediators of Japanese firms, without pointing out that friendly links already exist between the *shōkai-sha* and the respective other parties. These examples don't address the sticky problem of a small or otherwise unknown foreign firm needing to create trust amongst those in a Japanese firm. Hearing about successful *shōkai*-matches between such firms leads smaller foreign companies to feel baffled when they find that introductions, which they understand to be essential, aren't freely available.

It's often expected that JETRO (Japan External Trade Organization) will function as a mediator, but JETRO doesn't really know you, so it can't truly act as an introducing body. JETRO has an extensive database that in the West would function as a good source of contacts for those wanting to do business – as has been JETRO's intention. JETRO gets a phenomenal annual budget from MITI – it got ¥26bn ($246mn) in 1996 – plus JETRO itself generates another ¥10bn. This money is spent assisting foreign and Japanese companies to move their goods and services across their respective borders, and on facilitating business tie-ups between Japanese and foreign companies. But despite their effort and the money JETRO consumes, it hasn't overcome the problem of how to engineer the (social) links needed between Japanese and foreign firms that are unfamiliar to each other.

Responsibilities of a mediator

The responsibilities of those in a relationship in Japan are different than in the West. In the West, if a person introduces a friend to a company, and suggests that they do business, the person who arranged the introduction may be able to expect some thanks, and a beer if things turn out well. Generally the person making the introduction has little or no obligation, and no responsibility. The success of the relationship is completely in the hands of those involved.

In Japan the situation is different; says business consultant T. W. Kang:

'There, the friend not only matches up the two parties but is also considered responsible for what happens later. If a commitment is broken, the person in the middle will be put under pressure. In addition, the party who was introduced is considered to have signed up to a commitment with the acquaintance who introduced him or her. And the salesperson will owe the acquaintance a favour, usually in a tangible form.'[4]

In the event of a successful transaction, the two parties have an obligation to the mediator. At least, the party that made the first approach – depending on the nature of the tie-up – should give that mediator priority in any future business opportunity. This obligation to return the favour creates an ongoing bond of reciprocal business involvement.

The opportunity to be involved in productive business tie-ups is one of the reasons why Japanese devote energy throughout their life to establishing good relations with influential people. Then, when an opportunity ultimately presents itself, they will be able to call on their 'friend', or their friend will call on them to do business or introduce them to a business associate. Alternatively, it's unnatural to orchestrate relationships in Japanese business. It's the equivalent of an arranged marriage in the West – it's possible, but goes against the grain of tradition.

A new reality

It's been a luxury for firms to trade only amongst those they know, either directly or through known contacts. Traditionally they've been prepared to pay for this in the higher prices associated with such closed market trade, even when cheaper alternatives have been available from foreign or other Japanese suppliers. However, the years of harsh economic battering experienced by companies through the 1990s fostered an acceptance of change. The new reality for many Japanese firms is that in order to survive they need cheaper supplies. And particularly when the yen has been strong, the only realistic supply for many has been from overseas. This has created an opportunity for foreign suppliers to link with Japanese manufacturers.

Japanese companies needing foreign input do, however, face the problem of not knowing anyone who can introduce them to a dependable foreign firm, so they have to risk working with an unknown firm. A foreign company that has something unique and valuable to offer – a good product, or software, or other knowledge – may be able to win a supply agreement under these circumstances. In addition to JETRO's company database, there are other sources, such as the embassies, Chambers of Commerce and the European Delegation, that are able to provide names of firms wanting to find a foreign joint venture or trading partner. For larger businesses, private consulting firms may help, and banks may introduce firms to their client companies.

Despite the risk foreigners present due to their lack of familiarity with (or acceptance of) Japanese business practices, as mentioned, they are good potential sources of new business. Still, a Japanese person will feel much more comfortable if a foreigner has good *jinmyaku* credentials. That engenders confidence because it implies that s/he has gained the trust of others in Japan. What's more, that status in turn breeds status: the more *jinmyaku* credibility you have, the more you can get . . ., and that credibility enables you to get even more.

Japanese business concepts

In our own country, most of us could probably start up and operate a business, one of the main tools being our intuition. We all have an in-built general sense of the buyer–seller relation. We've seen other people engage in sales transactions, both in life and in the media. We use these situations as models to develop our own conventional knowledge, and sense of business protocol. Those who've grown up around merchandising will have been exposed to business concepts simply by having been around people discussing, worrying about and making business decisions. Such people are more likely than others to be familiar with business methods and have a 'head for business'.

But a common mistake made by foreigners trading in Japan is to assume that all business concepts are transferable, and will therefore apply in a Japanese context. Ironically, our notion of appropriate business practices restricts our openness, or ability to accommodate new methods. In the process of doing business, that conventional wisdom can make a foreigner react to situations in a 'conventional' manner.

Westerners use the concept of fairness, their understanding of how much trust they can put in people they deal with, including their understanding of a verbal agreement and a written agreement. They use and understand the concept of obligation to pay, obligation to supply, of back-up service, the concept of ownership, and, proverbially, their concept of quality. Look at this brief list once more. All are examples of concepts which can be and are interpreted differently in Japan than in the West. By logical extension, they are examples of areas where many foreigners fail to concur with the expectations of people they do business with in Japan.

Trust

Western business relationships often continue only as long as it suits one participant. If opportunity is better somewhere else, or an existing business relationship encounters some sort of trouble, that participant will be inclined to look after his/her interests at the expense of others. Grey areas of disagreement involving damage or loss are more likely than they are in Japan to be resolved in court or by other forms of dispute.

In Japan the high value placed on relationships normally means that preserving the relationship has top priority; thus disputes are avoided. The reason is that while to Japanese the cost of a compromise might be high in the short term, it will be small considering the potential gains of preserving and continuing the relationship. Therefore, this and other examples of yielding (which normally advantage the buyer) simply represent an investment. In the West, often there can be no such assumption of future business. Business relationships are often based on suppliers competing for and displacing each other on price, resulting in much more transitory relationships.

The situation also means Westerners can trade with almost anyone, but they must constantly be alert. In contrast, Japanese let their defences down, and because of this they have to be careful about who they start doing business with. Once Japanese start interacting at a business level, the stability of the relationship is rarely maintained by the legal system. Rather, it is social forces, similar to those governing financial obligations between friends or relatives in the West, that maintain stability. In this type of situation a Japanese company can be severely damaged by anyone who decides to ignore the validity of those informal forces.

Cooperation and conflict

There is often a *conflict* relationship, explicit or implicit, between foreign buyers and sellers, where each is trying to extract as much as possible for his/her side. The matter over which this conflict is most evident is price.

Often in Japan, however, buyer and seller have a more cooperative relationship. Many Japanese employees of a company or group see themselves as working for the mutual goal of 'moving the goods' to get to the customer. The enemy is failure to sell, or (sometimes an abstract) opposition firm.

Cooperation is, however, to some extent influenced by institutional pressure. Many Japanese would rather not conform to the expectations of their boss or with what their supplier wants, but they are servants of buyers with more power than them, or they are in a system where they can't afford to stand out by not toeing the party line. Nevertheless, whatever the reason, the result tends to be that there is a unified rather than a conflict-orientated force.

Since they can trust and work with their counterpart, such things as a supplier providing labour to help the buyer promote the product, or a buyer advancing finance in order that the supplier can purchase goods, are not unknown in Japanese business. When I began exporting to Japan I was advanced tens of thousands of dollars, unsecured, with no contract, and I hardly knew the benefactor. We did have a reliable middle person, and through him trust existed. Japanese are accustomed to thinking that those they understand to be of good character feel an incentive to fulfil their obligations, which all adds up to strong long-term business.

Concepts of ownership and liability

Japanese business relationships transcend Western concepts of boundaries of ownership. The rule in foreign business is that once you have the money, it is yours, and the product is theirs, unless a guarantee, or a fair trading or liability law regarding the quality of the item, dictates otherwise. Possession is nine-tenths of the law. Both parties understand that this is how the game is played, and if pressured the seller may well be prepared to sever the relationship rather than refund any money.

In Japan the fact that a product has been sold, and is *owned* by the buyer, may mean little. In the event of the buyer being unsatisfied, or the product being in the hands of a downstream vendor and simply not selling, the supplier may again sacrifice short-term profit for the long-term gains of the relationship by, for instance, taking back the product.

The parties in Japanese business see it as a mutual problem if a product can't sell down the line, so both may cooperate to get saleable products on the shelves. Leaving an unsatisfactory product in the merchant's hands will only reduce turnover, when it is in the interests of both to promote turnover.

In this context, the market changed to some extent during the 1990s. Many products in Japan are now discounted, and in exchange for accepting less in payment suppliers are not expected to provide the same level of after-sales support. But for many goods, and foreign products are no exception, a traditional form of service is still expected. At least you should go into the Japanese market expecting to provide traditional Japanese-type service – foreigners have had problems when assuming they don't need to do so. If you find that price cutting has meant that the demands for service in your industry have become relaxed, then that may be a bonus.

Communication in business

There are many situations in Japanese business where information is tailored so as not to offend the listener. Japanese appear to be in agreement with everything proposed in a business meeting, but ultimately they either don't reply, or come back with a refusal: why didn't they bring up any problems at the time?

One reason is that they normally need group agreement before making decisions. But the other is that they are unwilling to be confrontational, so they say little about problems or difficult issues. While this system functions amongst Japanese, it perplexes and frustrates foreigners. In this section we look at a deeper, more subtle level of Japanese communication in order to see how Japanese people convey meaning and interpret each other.

At the root of a lot of Japanese communication is a desire to avoid uncomfortable, confrontational situations. Since life, and in particular the business world, is full of conflicts of interest, the Japanese employ a variety of mechanisms to avoid them. These include tailoring behaviour and information to make it clear that you in no way want to challenge, but, rather, are in overall agreement with the other party.

Where both sides in a negotiation are Japanese, there is no problem; it is expected that the listener will be sensitive to dissatisfaction or other difficulties. Listeners know that problems are expressed subtly and must then be reinterpreted, re-magnified back to their true value. They know that their counterpart won't be explicit in complaining; indeed, Japanese who do loudly voice complaint are seen as 'strange'.

Where there is a problem, a Japanese speaker may say something like '*cho . . . tto muzukashii*' (it's a little bit difficult), from which the listener should understand that there is in fact an insurmountable problem. In other words, it isn't 'a little bit difficult'; the problem is being understated to avoid unpleasantness.

In this situation it is up to the listener to identify and clarify any problematic aspects of the discussion and, depending on the situation, possibly offer alternatives. This is especially true when speaking to a customer. Indeed, regardless of who is responsible for the problem, it is typically up to the seller (other power relationships being roughly equal) to interpret problems and provide a way out, without distressing, embarrassing or taxing the buyer.

How Japanese communicate

Conveying meaning is made awkward in Japan because much of the communication is presented in a formal manner – no one can take you aside in a business context and say, 'hey, this is what's actually going on'.

Alternately, Westerners not only don't mind doing this, they like to bring into business an element of informality. It helps communicate exactly those things that are too awkward to convey formally. Problems with one of the senior staff, if expressed formally, may have to be presented as a formal complaint, but the situation might not really warrant that – it might just warrant a quiet word in the boss's ear. But it's virtually impossible to be informal in a Japanese business relationship, and the stiff atmosphere makes it difficult, if not impossible, for good ideas, cautions or suspicions to be channelled to those in authority, unless they travel as part of a formal route. A personal view or interpretation of matters may contain valuable information but in a formal business context these cannot be 'tossed around', so many Japanese people exist in an office environment unable to express what they really want to say. However, there are two ways in which some of that information can be conveyed.

One way is via the relaxed environment of the pub after office hours. Part of the vast amount spent on entertainment in Japan is devoted to buttering-up clients by giving them an expensive night out, but this process also has the function of getting clients, or staff members, into a more relaxed mood than is possible in the office. It allows for the breakdown of the strictly formal business-communication structure of the office, enabling the transfer of important information that is unable to flow in a formal medium. This is referred to as *nominication*, derived from *nomi* – to drink – plus *communication*.

This information exchange applies between members of the same company, and to communication between suppliers and customers of different companies. But there is a cost. Not only is it at great financial expense, but at the cost of what would be the health and leisure time of sales employees who must go drinking to fulfil business obligations, for some, several nights of the week.

The second method of communicating is indirect, and draws upon implied meaning. For instance, the word *chotto*, mentioned above, is a mechanism used to add emotional depth to otherwise stiff, very structured speech. *Chotto deki-nai* (a little + cannot) means '. . .very sorry but at present we can't do . . .', whereas *deki-nai* (cannot) alone would be too blunt, as it often is in English. At a physical level, turning the head to one side and audibly sucking through clenched teeth can also indicate that something is near impossible.

Still, these are relatively clear indicators. Japanese explanations are often not very explicit, and Japanese listeners have to be able to infer meaning not only from what others are saying, but also what others are not saying.

I once arranged a homestay abroad for two Japanese people. Afterwards I asked their Japanese supervisor about one particular place the couple stayed at, and was told that the place was perhaps not satisfactory. I asked him why, what did they say? 'Nothing', was the answer. In other words, they would not be blatant enough to say what they didn't like. But amid their discussion, it was up to their supervisor to infer this from their lack of comment. Japanese are so sensitive and specific that they can convey and interpret displeasure by a lack of any other positive statement. You can imagine the type of unresolved communication problems Japanese tourists – unaccustomed to complaining bluntly – have overseas. And since Japanese tourism continues to grow, and remains a lucrative market, if you are in that market there is a clear advantage in having people on your staff who are capable of understanding such nuances.

For the purpose of communicating with Japanese in business, it is essential that foreigners, if they want to function in a Japanese environment, have their ears to the ground. This analogy is very useful since, in the same way that Japanese people lower themselves in bowing, their general posture is to look up to the person with whom they are communicating; to cast aside their own self, their skills, abilities, pride and confidence, in order to listen to the other. This has made the Japanese very good listeners, and because of that particular stance it has enabled them to take in a lot of knowledge and adopt a lot of technology from the West. The sometimes arrogant stance of Westerners has done the reverse; by not looking up at their counterparts, i.e. by not listening to what they are saying, it has been impossible for many of them to learn from the Japanese.

Confusion compounded

In addition to their aversion to confrontation – which reduces their clarity – Japanese are disposed to vagueness. This is in part because they are not good at breaking matters down logically in order to explain them. It is also associated with them belonging to a close-knit and shared culture with shared meanings, such that amongst themselves there is little need to be clear.

The situation is exemplified in the lifetime employment system, where the same group of people spend their working life together in the one company. For a Japanese person who has spent a long time sharing the same values and objectives in such a work environment, interpreting what another person from that environment means is not so difficult and requires little explicit information. After years of living together, a husband making coffee for his wife doesn't have to ask each day whether she wants milk, one or two spoons of sugar, strong or weak? A single nod is sufficient.

This tendency not to rely on detail fuels the non-explicit communication that the Japanese are famed for, it makes meaning sometimes illusive, it's often confusing, and it frustrates foreigners. But by listening and being sensitive to them, the motives and behaviour of Japanese can, in many situations, become clear. The following excerpt by writer Richard Halloran is an example, as true today as when it was written, of an office scenario which sums up much of the subtlety of Japanese interpersonal communication and deference. It's a very good illustration of the Japanese being effective listeners, being aware of communication that is indirect, and being non-confrontational.

'One day in the office, a man who works near me went to the desk of the section chief and talked to him for a long time. I could not hear what they were saying, but I noticed that the section chief looked in my direction several times. After they finished talking, the man went back to his desk without saying anything to me. But the next day, when we met in the washroom (I think he deliberately followed me in there), we discussed our work and he made a slight reference to one of my accounts, saying he hoped it was as accurate as the last time the auditors looked at it. Right away, I was sure he had seen something wrong, and I was not surprised when the section chief called me over. He discussed something else but mentioned briefly that particular account and said he knew the auditors would find it in order whenever they checked it. That night I stayed late in the office to go over the account and found a bad mistake, which I corrected. Nothing else was ever said about it.'[5]

Notes

1 'Learning to Think', *Far Eastern Economic Review*, 30 June 1994, p. 50.
2 Interview, early 1998.
3 James Rudy advises global corporations about PR and investor relations strategies. His company, Pacific Associates, can be contacted by e-mail: jrudy@typhoon.co.jp or home page: pacdata.typhoon.co.jp (quoted in *Gaishi*, October 1995, p. 62).
4 Kang, 1990, pp. 58–59.
5 Halloran, 1969, p. 218. Written in 1969, this piece, as does the book it came from, remains very relevant today.

Part Three

Inside the Japanese market

Chapter 7

Entering the Japanese market

Factors important to market entry

According to the hard-earned wisdom of the electronics maker Canon, once a company is active in the Japanese market, it is three times harder to fail in business there than in the US.

On the other hand, as many a foreign firm will tell you, it's three times harder to become successful in Japan in the first place.[1] The reason: the American market is much more receptive to a 'good product', which can become a hit based on its merits alone. In Japan success is based on a number of other factors, which act as barriers at the beginning, but which support those who are already doing business in Japan.

Since Japanese business generally centres on close-knit groups or relationships that make access difficult for outsiders, the marketing of products in Japan is best handled by those with the patience and resources to establish long-term relations and become insiders there. Those dealing with Japan need to be sensitive toward the Japanese at a personal level, understand Japanese protocol, the Japanese interpretation of quality, and have staff able to handle the language. These factors, and others important to market entry in Japan, will be discussed below.

What it takes

People typically assess their ability to crack the Japanese market by evaluating their own product in terms of the two or three qualities that will make it important to the market in Japan. For instance, for machinery, performance, function and possibly price; for gifts, packaging and quality might be seen as important. And these are factors that you either have or you don't have; you have good packaging, good performance and good price, and if you don't, then you can't expect to succeed. If you do have what is required, then, logically, you can compete with existing products in Japan.

But the 'either have it or not' model doesn't work in Japan; the 'logic' has repeatedly failed. There are a lot of products that foreigners have introduced which are better quality than those on sale in Japan, but they can't seem to sell there. Kodak has, for instance, complained that 'it isn't getting the market that it would expect'. This model doesn't explain why this is.

It is inappropriate to look to any single factor, such as good quality or low price, as an entry ticket to the Japanese market. What happens in reality is that successful market entry depends on a combination of important factors. Neither a high nor a low rating on any one means success or failure; success is based on a 'high aggregate score' over a number of them. There are a range of assets which, to varying degrees, each marketer brings to Japan. A strong combination of these is essential.

Product features		Company features		Personal features	
Price		Capital		*Jinmyaku* (network)	
Product quality		Reliability/punctuality		Japanese language	
Product uniqueness		Corporate recognition		Personality	
Brand recognition					

Figure 7.1 Factors important to success in Japan

The assets mentioned above in Figure 7.1 are of particular importance when dealing with Japan. If each of these had a maximum possible score of ten, and successful market entry required gaining an aggregate score of 80 or 85, poor performance on one factor may be acceptable, assuming the loss can be made up in other areas. Add up your own score. . .

Of course this is just a model, and depending on the industry these factors will have different levels of importance and qualities not mentioned may also be important. But the principle remains.

The first part of the book introduced some of these factors important to market entry. We discussed the importance of *jinmyaku* (networking; personal connections), and it is clear that *jinmyaku* lies behind and is important in supporting other qualities your product might have. Without *jinmyaku* it is possible to succeed, but it becomes much more difficult. 'Reliability and punctuality' are much more important in Japan than elsewhere, but are necessary in addition to whatever qualities your product has. The second part of the book develops and integrates these and other factors into the marketing process.

Nations apart

Over the centuries Westerners have introduced their cultures, religions and commercial goods into many countries, and in doing so have been able to colonize, dominate and extract the resources of those territories. Westerners have also used skill, good products and determination to establish at least a satisfactory level of trade with each target nation. Japanese, on the other hand, lacking resources, linguistic ability, knowledge of business protocol and confidence, have always fully appreciated that it would be difficult for them to market outside their homeland.

It came as a shock to Westerners, then, when Japan, which had been defeated in World War II and then helped back on its feet by the US, came to dominate certain industries and even to push Western companies out of such fields as textiles, steel and electronics. These had been important earners for Western workers. Furthermore, Japan then proved unaccommodating when Westerners wanted to enter the Japanese market. Japan had succeeded in the West, and it was felt unfair that Japan excluded the West from its burgeoning home market.

As Japan became a coveted market, stories of Western successes in Japan were offered as evidence that Westerners could sell there. These examples were only too happily heralded by the Ministry of International Trade and Industry which, while actually worried about the domination of its markets by Westerners, wanted to quell accusations of a restricted market. Western successes were also celebrated by enthusiastic and optimistic Western officials wanting to breed more success – it is in the interest of local governments worldwide to attract Japanese money into their areas.

This fuelled an 'emperor's new clothes' situation whereby many Western companies didn't want to admit that they couldn't penetrate or succeed in Japan. Many of the foreign companies already in Japan were doing poorly,[2] but, for many reasons, foreign business people in Japan tended to radiate success. It wasn't until the end of the 1980s that the difficulty of breaking into the Japanese market became widely known. As the dollar weakened against the yen, the feeling of helplessness grew. It became relatively more expensive for Westerners to invest in Japan, and they lost a sense of authority that they had once enjoyed in the market. This made it more difficult and frustrating, as they watched lucrative opportunities pass by.

The period signalled a shift in the approach Westerners took to the Japanese market. It invited questions about what the Japanese had been doing to succeed in Western markets, and what Westerners were doing wrong in Japan.

Old attitudes

A basic problem has been that the confident approach of many Western business people has worked against them. Confidence is not only a consequence of Western history; sales people in many cultures are conditioned to display confidence. They are expected to take an informed and often authoritative stance when selling. This becomes the stance that many revert to by default in negotiating, even with the Japanese. But this assertiveness has given many a false sense of propriety in Japan. Self-confidence is fine, but expressions of self-confidence can be interpreted as arrogance; by definition, it belittles others who don't share the speaker's good fortune. In Japan it's important to first consider the feelings of all others.

Being self- and success-focused has sometimes made Westerners unpopular negotiators. To many Westerners their own direct nature is normal, whereas the Japanese seem timid. But looked at from the Japanese perspective, Westerners seem blunt and pushy. Japanese are tolerant, but still can be offended by pushiness in business.

Arrogance can also indicate inflexibility. From a Japanese point of view, those sure of themselves and their products are less likely to be receptive to suggestions to change. While 'the customer (not the supplier) is always right', many foreign suppliers have been reluctant to adapt to customer needs to the degree expected in Japan.[3] To Japanese, who are used to looking out for, and conforming to, the needs of others, a forceful and determined stance quite rightly engenders suspicion.

'True grit'

An excellent illustration of 'the American negotiator', is made by John Graham and Sano Yoshihiro, who use the analogy of the John Wayne cowboy figure, riding into Japan, confident of winning sales single-handedly. They describe the American negotiating style as having its roots in this scenario. In America independence has been an important ingredient in survival. Going it alone has been an outgrowth of having to make it alone.[4] The reverse is true in Japan, where *interdependence* is important. Loners are distrusted, and only those willing to fit into a group will do well.

Japanese aren't good at demonstrating their displeasure toward 'persuasive' Western negotiating styles, at least not in terms that Westerners are used to. Japanese are averse to conflict and so rely on the complex system of indirect communication described in Chapter 6. A foreigner who thinks s/he is still on track, or can keep pushing because there hasn't yet been the level of resistance that usually signals rejection, may be failing to pick up the hint. Japanese may even cave in to pressure, and accept a product that is unwanted, and perhaps unsuitable. If this practice does work for a foreign company, then it should be considered only a temporary success, one that is unlikely to last.

It's better to abandon this approach and adapt to the manner of business that the Japanese counterpart is used to. When selling in Japan, it is considered appropriate that one appeal to the buyer. Doing so is not always the rule; elsewhere it is not uncommon to attempt to sell by pressuring or 'convincing' the buyer. The Japanese won't express dissatisfaction with this sales style, but they invariably aren't comfortable with it and where possible they'll avoid any further contact with such high-pressure sales people.[5]

By the beginning of the 1990s there were fewer of the John Wayne types in Japan. The high yen and tightening of the economy caused many would-be desperadoes to give up. Plus the reality had hit home to many that Japan would not be conquered by force alone.

Preparation

Westerners often assume that they will be able to defeat the opposition with raw skill – thinking that leads the same people to leave preparation until they get on the plane. Meanwhile the Japanese side, with its slow, methodical, group-orientated approach, wants to carefully prepare everything in advance. For important negotiations, Japanese companies with enough staff will have a cooperative, unified and well-informed force at the ready.

A loosely-structured approach to business can function well in the West – a good Western manager is expected to be able to improvise with fast decisions – but such looseness looks amateur in comparison to an organized Japanese group. In a negotiation the Japanese can then exploit this lack of preparation as a weakness. It will be in your interest to have information ready, because being unprepared when questioned won't strengthen their confidence in you and won't strengthen your position if you are hoping to negotiate a favourable deal. The contrast between Westerners and Japanese at the negotiating table is striking: the Japanese are known for having more staff, more intra-organizational coordination, and access to more answers.[6]

Westerners, often short of resources, have flown by the seat of their pants, with little tangible research and a loosely coordinated business strategy. Instead of research, they hope to rely on the sharp business sense and quick decision-making ability that got them their jobs in the first place. Japanese are insatiable information seekers and Japanese organizations tend to be backed with a relatively high number of white-collar staff, and so are able to put a lot of effort into collecting information. Or they use the services of a separate organization such as a *sōgō shōsha*, which handles negotiations and information. Information alone can paint a picture, and point the way for future plans. Lacking information, on the other hand, puts you on the defensive by having to follow up after the meeting, to find details they've asked for.

Westerners are normally under-represented at overseas negotiating tables, sending far fewer people on missions than Japanese do. This is because Westerners find it hard to form cooperative, interlocking work groups. They also decide that it's expensive sending a lot of people abroad. The result is that often one or two representatives get sent, and must do everything.[7] Realistically, preparation necessitates some form of division of labour. Budget-conscious Westerners, however, try to do everything themselves, meaning less important things may get left uncompleted. Important things include getting the aeroplane tickets, less important things include preparing detailed information. Budgetary constraints are a reality, but if possible it is useful to take at least one other person to share the workload, and to make observations that one person alone can't.

A second person may also be able to gain useful information from subordinate Japanese staff. Because a lot of business communication can't be exchanged in the formal context of a meeting, Japanese use after-hours get-togethers to get a feeling for what each side wants. There's nothing illicit about gathering information at this level. It's a functional part of Japanese business, and one you would do well to make use of by utilizing a lower-level team member.[8] Get your subordinate to ask some of the Japanese staff where a good pub is, and on an evening when you have another appointment, let them arrange to go to the pub together. The Japanese staff will see it as work, but will enjoy an evening out, chatting with a foreigner, and in addition to some relationship-building, your subordinate should be able to pick up some useful insights.

Smart data

Not only is it important to prepare technical information, but it is useful to find out anything you can about the other company, and, if possible, about the individuals you will be negotiating with. It shows you're taking them seriously and are genuinely interested if you can talk about the person's interests or the company's history with some knowledge. This may sound obvious, but few foreign companies really do their homework, and very few dig as deep as the Japanese do.

Personal information will obviously be difficult to get. There are two main Japanese *Who's Who*, called the *Zen Nippon Shinshiroku* and the *Jinji Kōshinroku*, containing information on top executives. These books are written in Japanese, and are available at the JETRO (Japan External Trade Organization) office in Toranomon, Tokyo. Check also to see if the company you are associated with is a member of the American Chamber of Commerce in Japan (ACCJ). Several Japanese companies are, and through the ACCJ you might be able to find out something about the management. If it was the Japanese firm that contacted you first, politely ask them the source they used to get your name – they'll be quite familiar and comfortable with this question – and, if possible, tap that source for information. If a third party contacted you on behalf of the Japanese firm, befriend that third party; if they're Japanese, they'll slip right into the role of supplying you with what you want; it's in their interests to help.

Of course, this is all time-consuming and depends on your resources and the size of your operation.

The second option is simply information about the company itself. Again, availability of information depends on the company's size. JETRO may be helpful here. So may the *Japan Company Handbook*. It's a two-volume data book, written in English, listing all publicly traded companies. Published four times a year, it gives an up-to-date thumbnail sketch of the main business and financial details of each. Also, there are volumes, available in English, of Japanese company histories.[9]

You can also buy information; one source is Teikoku Data Bank (TDB). TDB began in 1900 as a corporate credit research firm. It now maintains the largest corporate database in Japan, holding detailed corporate and personal information concerning over a million firms. It provides a type and level of company information that makes its service unique in the world.

Amongst the information collected by TDB are details about the company president, including his/her history, education, other business involvement, sports, hobbies, and date of birth. This, combined with other business information, constitutes not only excellent material to have when trying to market to a Japanese company, but also for other dealings with a firm. TDB also has information on the status of firms, including growth, creditworthiness and a firm's prospects. It gains accuracy through a 'visit-and-confirm' policy; TDB's information is based on first-hand interviews with company CEOs or senior accountants, and visits to the company premises to get a feeling for how physical aspects of the company match other information. From this and other peripheral information a profile and credit evaluation is constructed.

TDB also brings together industry sales and other corporate information to interpret the market and market trends. Their data is used by their clients for, amongst other things, strategic planning, M&As, marketing, including direct marketing, credit checks, and as a basis for other investment decisions.

On average, TDB makes about 5000 reports a day. These reports, which are available in English, might cover six or more pages depending on the type and depth of information requested, they are clearly laid out and are easy to read.

Patience is a virtue

When negotiating, instead of valuing quick debate, the Japanese typically take their time to discuss things and then reach a conclusion. What then, does a quick-witted, eloquent Western negotiator do when the other side is silent? Talk some more!? Japanese have no qualms about long pauses. Many Westerners, on the other hand, find silence uncomfortable and contribute by filling gaps in the conversation, sometimes with what amounts to business commitments or sometimes with irrelevant statements.

Another Western response is to lose patience. This results in foreigners pressuring the other side, or in intentional or unintentional displays of anxiety. If you hope to win concessions, impatience won't enhance your chances, since it is associated with a loss of the game in Japan. Further, when only one side does it, it adds up to showing one's cards to the other. It displays one's weakness, and the associated verbiage can display the limits of what one is prepared to concede, and the bounds of what one really wants. It will also surely make establishing a future warm relationship either very difficult or impossible. The matter has been summed up as: don't shout, don't point, don't get ahead of the interpreter, and don't walk around the room.[10]

When negotiating for concessions, some suggest it's a good idea also to remain vague about the time constraints of your trip. Knowing that Western companies often push their staff to not come home from a negotiation empty-handed, some Japanese companies are not beyond postponing a decision until their visitors are ready to leave.

After a meeting, the Japanese tend to take a long time to come to a decision. In order to check progress, if you or a member of your team speaks Japanese it is acceptable to contact the other side and politely ask how things are going. The easiest line is to say that you were asked a specific question by your supplier, so you are passing on the enquiry. Japanese people are basically friendly, and respond to genuine friendly approaches. The reality, though, is that few foreigners have the language capability to make a friendly enquiry. If you don't, inevitably it will come across as a rigid and cold request for information, and the answer will also come back cold and rigid, which is exactly what you don't want.

Protocol

Business meetings in larger companies in Japan are conducted formally. This is the type of formality that Westerners, especially Americans, often do their best to shake off in meetings at home. It's better not to succumb to the temptation of doing the same in Japan. Assuming that you are part of a negotiation team attending a meeting in Japan, there are some matters of form that it's useful to be aware of. Even if you aren't able to present yourself as the Japanese do in this situation, it's a good idea to compromise by excluding some typically Western characteristics.

When two Japanese people from different companies plan a meeting, in the course of their discussion they let each other know how many will attend, and the rank of each participant. It's understood that each company should provide a team to balance the other's in rank and numbers. It's not unlike Westerners balancing guests going to a dinner party. Japanese also see it as respectful to send a person of equal rank to their highest team member, even if that person's presence is only ceremonial. Foreigners will rarely be able to match them in numbers, and not all business trips will involve your senior executives, but at least be aware of what the Japanese are thinking.

On arrival at their company you will probably be escorted into a meeting room by a young woman referred to as an 'OL' (office lady). Once inside, you should remain standing and await further instruction. Since Japanese have a strong sense of hierarchy, seniors and guests are given priority. Guests always get the best seats, which are traditionally farthest from the door. This convention also allows the host's junior staff to run in and out of the room. When you enter a meeting room, you should take the side of the table away from the door. The most senior of your staff should take the central position, with key assistants on both sides. You will eventually have your senior counterpart opposite you, or at least in a convenient negotiating position near you. If you are on your own, and in a big room, again move towards a seat away from the door and await instructions. Eventually you will be invited to sit down somewhere where your counterpart(s) will sit near you.

Small talk

After your counterparts enter the room, they will approach you, and it's appropriate for you to meet them in order of rank: the senior member of your group leads the way, followed in order by others. Note that the senior person in a Western firm is not necessarily the oldest. Not so in Japan, where seniority runs strictly according to age. Yes, it is possible to run into a young president accompanied by older directors (especially in the newest high-tech fields, where thirty-something presidents are not unheard of), but it is still quite rare.

Since you must meet all their members, you will need a lot of *meishi* (business cards). The order in which you meet them also lets them know about the hierarchy of your group. Accordingly, if you are the top person, you should identify their senior, and direct your attention to this person, even if it seems that you are abandoning their subordinates. If it becomes necessary to pay more respect to one person than the others, it should be the senior – Japanese subordinates are at home with this.

Even in formal Japanese meetings one does not jump right into business. Initial discussion normally involves small talk about individuals, their responsibilities in the company, and other miscellany. A business meeting – whether the first or the twentieth – is part of an ongoing relationship, and must be treated with respect. The first meeting is an opportunity for the Japanese to find out about who they are dealing with. While you should initially present yourself in a formal manner, you need to be sincere, and express *who you are*. They want to get to know you and know that they can rely on you.

In a sense there is a contradiction here, since it requires that you retain your composure, but express something of yourself. For Westerners, being yourself may be a signal for formalities to end and everyone to relax and act casually. In Japan this is reserved until you get to the restaurant or pub; and in formal meetings it never happens.

High-level Japanese participants are often there only for ceremonial reasons, and it is appropriate that your head respond to any ceremonial activity. If it is formal enough for speeches to take place, your side should be able to respond with appropriate words. These should be of hope and support for the business, and preferably from someone equal in rank to their spokesperson. That might mean expressing a personal message of support from your president back home.

While styles of meetings differ, basically the rest of the meeting should flow on the basis of these and other factors that I discuss elsewhere.

The corollary of good preparation is keeping a record of what happened at the meeting. Having a good recall of the previous meeting's events is impressive and can show up the other side. However, since it is the Japanese who normally have a written record of events at the next meeting, it is normally foreigners who get shown up. It's useful therefore for you to keep records. Having notes of what was said would be ideal, but feeding your thoughts, based on any brief notes you have, into a tape recorder immediately after the meeting may be the most practical method, particularly when you are exhausted. This can be transcribed later.

Despite the formality, ultimately, what the Japanese care about is you. They understand that foreigners have different business customs, and won't assume that you will know all theirs. So if you have to make a choice rather than focus on business ritual, albeit while remaining relatively formal, it's better to demonstrate your personality, to be yourself. This doesn't mean that one should indulge in a lot of vigorous hand-shaking or back-slapping; that will likely have a negative effect. But the Japanese generally do relate well to a positive and cheerful personality. It's only when they have no other way of knowing you as a person that they must rely on your etiquette alone. Ultimately, they will be happier with someone whom they feel they know and can trust than with someone who is just formally correct.

What do the Japanese perceive as important in a seller?

Presentation

Presentation is important in Japan because that is the first means by which Japanese gauge how much trust can be placed in you. In any situation where we must form an opinion about a person, we rely on the clues and cues that the person generates – if the clues are not good, we won't rely on him or her. Since the Japanese put more trust in a relationship than Westerners, they have more at stake, and must rely more on such information. They must feel satisfied that those they deal with are capable of giving them the type of long-term and good service they are accustomed to.

Because of this, it's understandable that Japanese are wary of people whom they can't communicate with or find difficult to understand.

It's up to you to demonstrate that you understand how to act appropriately when dealing with them, so they will always be confident about you. In many ways they'd like nothing better than to get on with an interesting foreigner who knows how to fit in with them. You don't have to speak Japanese, like *sushi*, or enjoy sitting on the floor. Just be sincere, be pleasant, and be polite.

Image

The *meishi* (pronounced *may-she*) or business card has a special place in Japanese business. It is important for you to have one that is professionally made; it doesn't have to be fancy, but it must do more than just function, which is all it may be expected to do in other countries.

Standard boxes of 100 *meishi* are available in Japan from about ¥3000 ($23). Most stationery shops can arrange for them to be made; it takes about a week to do so. While it is common to have one side in English, the other in Japanese, arguably it's more expedient just to have them printed on one side, primarily in Japanese; that's all the Japanese will be interested in looking at anyway. If it's necessary for you to be contacted overseas, by mail, for example, your name should be written in both languages, your home (foreign) address just needs to be in English, with your Japanese address in Japanese; put one address on the left and one on the right. Having a card (only) in Japanese also gives the impression that you've got your feet firmly planted in Japan. It's better to then spend the money you've saved on printing your logo in colour.

In order to avoid mistakes with the language, unless you're handing the design over to a very professional Japanese printer, ask the opinions of a few different Japanese people about the phonetic spelling of your name, the best translation of your job title, and layout. You can't trust most Japanese-speaking foreigners to get these things right, and you should also cross-check Japanese opinions – since that's all they will be. It's easy to make fairly serious mistakes in your publicity material – these are quite common even amongst 'reputable' firms.

I once had the opportunity to introduce a very senior American executive from a leading US company to the president of a Japanese firm with which he hoped to do business. After he had finished his presentation and returned to his hotel I noticed the Japanese executives chuckling over the titles and translations used on his *meishi*. When I later asked the American where he'd obtained his business cards, he said his company had asked a Japanese housewife on their staff to translate them. Moral of the story: if you're going to follow protocol in Japan, make the effort to do it right.[11]

The standard (maximum) *meishi* size is 91 × 55 mm. Those made in Japan will be correct, but if you get them made overseas, check that they are no bigger than this since they will not fit into Japanese card books. In Japan these books, and everyone has some form of storing their *meishi*, function at least as a name and phone number reference – in part because telephone books are hardly ever used. Many Westerners throw business cards loosely in a desk drawer, but since *meishi* are a major part of Japanese business, it's better to buy a book and get into the system.

Apart from just being a physical means of communication and information storage, *meishi* in Japan are a subtle way of conveying the status or rank of a person, which is why they are given more status than if they were a simple information-bearing piece of card. Japanese can't make overt displays of their status – people are expected to act with humility, and ostentatiousness is not approved of. The *meishi*, then, functions as an acceptable means of conveying all the information one can't say about oneself. Further, the exchange involves more than pride. It's necessary that the information on a *meishi* be exchanged in order for two people to be able to talk to each other with the appropriate degree of respect.

When handling *meishi*, the intention is to bestow respect upon the other person. But since you are only using a piece of card, you are limited in what you can do physically to express this. It is customary when giving and receiving *meishi* to make it the focus of your attention and energies by holding it in both hands. When giving, hold the upper corners with both hands, with the print facing them, so they can read it. Lean forward in a slight bow while exchanging. If receiving theirs at the same time, take theirs in your right hand, then hold it in both.

When *giving* your *meishi*, behaving in this way shows your commitment, and when *receiving* another's *meishi*, it demonstrates your respect for that person.

Some say there is an art to handling *meishi*. Be that as it may, you will be able to do a very satisfactory job if you have the right *attitude*. If you understand that the *meishi* is an extension of the person whose name appears on it, you can start to appreciate the way to handle it and the way to deal with it.

After receiving a *meishi*, don't fondle it and bend the edges. After reading it, if in a meeting you may place it on the table in front of you; if there are several, place them in order to help you remember the names of those you are meeting. Then address those you speak or refer to in a meeting by their family name, *always* followed by *'san'* (Mr/Ms). Finally, place the *meishi* in your card wallet if you have one, and it's a good idea to get one – they are sold alongside wallets and purses in Japanese shops – otherwise, put it carefully in your wallet or purse, or top pocket. Treat it like the person's credit card.

It's not necessarily impolite to write on a *meishi*, though as a rule of thumb, don't do so until the person who gave it to you has gone. People may sometimes write on your *meishi*, but, consistent with respect, anything written on it should add value to it, such as adding more information about the giver. But the real point is, don't treat it like notepaper.

Skills needed by individuals in Japan

Language skills and negotiating

To overcome the difficulties the Japanese have faced when entering foreign markets, they have not only engaged in short-term, but also long-term preparation where possible. A Japanese company large enough to do so may, for instance, spend a lot of money on sending its staff to an English language school for a period of years. It may send selected staff to a good overseas university in order to learn business, or to groom staff to become future 'international' or overseas-branch executives.

A hundred years ago, when Mitsui Bussan was trying to develop its trading business in China, it stressed both language and cultural learning to such an extent that in China its staff were expected to wear pigtails and Chinese clothes, to work with Chinese merchants and stay with Chinese families. Bussan even promised incentives to those staff who married Chinese people.[12]

Unfortunately, Westerners from English-speaking nations have in general felt little need to develop abilities in other languages. After all, English is the *de facto* international language. This apparent advantage, though, is a disadvantage, not only in small business negotiations where no common language is available, but it is disadvantageous to have to rely on an interpretation. Language not only involves literal communication but is related to the importance of 'the social' which, again, is more closely related to business in Japan than in the West. It's much easier to trust someone whom you can understand clearly, and since trust is very important in Japanese business, foreign companies restricted to English are at a disadvantage. Perhaps most importantly, an understanding of their language allows an insight into the way the Japanese think.

The ability to operate in more than one language affords several advantages. Perhaps most strategic is the ability to control the release of information. By communicating in the language of your counterpart you also have available to you all the non-literal responses that are part of broader language expression, but cannot be conveyed through an interpretation. Essentially, a person capable in both languages knows everything that is going on, while others don't.

If you are functioning as an interpreter, you also have a brief period to qualify points with your own side while listening to or explaining information to them. You also have time to think before relaying information from either party.

Many Japanese business people have an understanding of English, but, rather than battle through negotiations themselves, many opt to use an interpreter for important meetings. This is partly because many Japanese lack confidence and are embarrassed about their English ability. It is also because, while the foreigner is responding to the interpretation of what has been said, the Japanese head, understanding English, can watch the foreigner's non-verbal responses, and therefore has double the time to formulate a reply.[13]

It is tempting to think that people who speak well are better informed or more knowledgeable than others, or at least will understand you the best. It is therefore tempting to make your case to their best English speaker, but instead, identify and address their senior person. If you have an interpreter, it is tempting to look at him/her, but resist this and look at your Japanese counterpart. It is more polite, more personal, and gives you access to verbal and non-verbal cues.

An additional problem for the foreigner is that during conversations conducted largely in Japanese the foreigner is left with an unnerving feeling of helplessness. The desire to escape this situation can sometimes result in not holding out for a better deal. You need to be aware of and make allowances for this.

Interpreters' abilities vary a lot, and you usually get what you pay for. Interpreters are ranked from AA down, and top (simultaneous) interpreters charge about ¥90,000 ($700) per person per day. For business interpreting, one of a lower rank would be quite sufficient. It is important to remember that interpreting is not just a translation of words, but involves an understanding of the culture and business you are involved with. Good interpreters will be able to tell you what the person is actually saying, whereas a literal translation is inadequate. By implication, interpreters need to be able to understand what your business needs are. There are many Japanese people with fairly good English ability, but unfortunately few of them can deal with subject areas they are unfamiliar with – Westerners are better at this but there are few who speak Japanese well. Of course there are good interpreters, but be aware of their limitations, especially non-professionals.

With this in mind, it's a good idea to meet the interpreter beforehand. Go over the material you want him/her to interpret. If you have written notes, make copies for the interpreter. If you will be using a number of technical terms or jargon, brief the interpreter beforehand. Don't think that you are 'doing their job for them'. Remember that helping the interpreter to understand what you want to communicate, before a meeting, is all for your benefit. One favour you can do the interpreter (and yourself) is to avoid telling jokes: they're hard to interpret and they don't travel well across cultures. By the way, the term 'translating' is used for written translation, 'interpreting' for verbal.

Supplying your own interpreter, rather than using theirs, has its advantages, and these are multiplied when your interpreter is also a member of your company and shares its interests and goals. This accounts for much of the power that Japanese companies normally have when negotiating in English.

The message is, whatever selling you do in Japan, you probably won't be able to survive with only an English understanding of events. The more language skills you have on your side, the better.

For Japanese business people, English is relatively easy to read; by contrast, the Japanese reading and writing systems are separate, and there are few Westerners who have systematically learned both – realistically, doing so requires a university-level intensity of study. And since learning written *kanji* (Chinese characters) requires a great deal of commitment and concentration, very few who've done so also have the resources left to be clever business operators. Some do, but the numbers are very small.

Most people in Japan who know English don't use it for business either, but because English is commonly studied there's a greater chance of a Japanese firm locating capable negotiators amongst its English-speaking staff.

The study of Japanese only became popular in the West in the 1980s, when Japan became a popular market to sell to. In addition to studies at school, crash courses in Japanese became popular amongst Western business people. Such study is rarely sufficient to conduct business. Often the most valuable result of studying Japanese was being able to proffer a few polite words to business contacts. But in many cases this allowed Westerners to be courteous in a courteous culture – Japanese people understand that foreigners find their language difficult, and they appreciate even a small effort.

Business education

There are other disadvantages for foreign companies marketing in Japan. Because foreign staff may not stay in the same company for long, it's not expedient for firms to sponsor staff on expeditions to Japan to learn Japanese business and the language. In too many cases, a foreign employee who gained such abilities would then quit and go looking for a new job and a higher salary.

With this option then unavailable to companies, managers who realize they need the Japanese language to increase their firm's chances of export success recruit Japanese-speaking graduates from university. They anticipate that these people will bridge the gap between the marketing expertise of the company and the Japanese buyer; but they can't.

What is needed are personnel sensitive to the wants of Japanese, able to interpret the quality they want, and evaluate the foreign products on offer. And they need personnel who know how to feel at ease with the Japanese. But individuals with these qualities are not in abundance. The increase in Japanese studies since the 1980s has resulted in the emergence of people with information but, typically, no knowledge of Japanese marketing. Having Japanese speakers in Japan isn't enough, it requires people with a sense of opportunism. Western firms need to have people competent in executing the business of the company who are also competent in dealing with the Japanese.

Japanese companies employ staff long-term; therefore they are more inclined to make an investment in their junior staff, whom they can count on in the future. Intertwined with this is another Japanese advantage: those staff members the company has invested in will primarily be members of the normal sales force. They will have the attitudes of sales people, not interpreters. When they go on a marketing mission they will be the ones who take their calculators, as they do when they negotiate at home, the difference being that when they go abroad they will also be using English. In other words, they are fully experienced and firmly rooted in the company as part of the normal business team, and then, secondly, they are English speakers.

Western studies in Japanese business suffer from two basic problems. Firstly, such studies are rare. Most scholars of Japan are dedicated to language, history or culture, and aren't acquainted with business. Business is often looked down on as being unacademic – and it is true, there is a genuine risk that the study of Japanese business at a university can be reduced to no more than a technical endeavour. Secondly, because Japanese business then becomes taught by business generalists – rather than people who have specialized in Japan – such studies at universities, by default, revert to Western models of business which often don't apply to Japan. As a brief summary of this problem, Western university-level study needs to educate students in Japanese business as a cultural, rather than just an economic phenomenon.

The European Delegation (the Delegation on behalf of the European Commission) seems to be having success in this area with its Executive Training Programme (ETP). The ETP is designed to build for European industry a core of business people competent to operate in Japanese business. The ETP is orientated toward young business people who take 18 months out of their working lives to first undertake 12 months of intensive Japanese language training in Japan, followed by six months working on location in Japanese companies. In order to be eligible, applicants must be EU citizens and must work for an export-orientated company, and there is particular emphasis on taking applicants from small and medium-sized companies. Participants are normally in their late 20s to early 30s. Selection is made by the European Commission in Brussels, and is based on a demonstration of business achievement by applicants, who also see Japan as important for their companies and themselves. Sponsoring (EU) companies are obliged to free their participants from company work during the period of study and companies are obliged to continue employing the participant afterwards. The bulk of the course expenses are paid by the European Commission; however, companies are responsible for covering air fares and, given the cost of stay in Japan, are expected to contribute to personal expenses of their employee while in Tokyo.

In the words of one participant, the second sent on the ETP by his company:

'The ETP is quite tough: you must go back to your school days, forgetting your previous work and studying a difficult language for long hours every day. But it works. After 18 months you can communicate. You can discuss business. And you discover that living and working in Japan is not so forbidding after all.

The programme is well organized. It gives you a smooth, gradual introduction to a country that must be absorbed step by step. The in-house training lets you experience the reality of a Japanese company, its mechanisms, and its unwritten rules.

Finally, let me suggest that you avoid considering the ETP as a master's degree in "Corporate Japan". Rather, think of it as what it has proved to be: a very useful tool for success in the Japanese market.'

Giuseppe Sceusi, Marposs K.K.

Notes

1 Kraar and Takikawa, 1994, p. 157.
2 Even the successful company IBM in the 1980s had a market share lower in Japan than in any other major market, bringing into question whether its position in Japan was actually the resounding triumph it had been heralded as (Prestowitz, 1989, p. 347).
3 A survey of foreign and Japanese firms found marked differences in perception between the two on a number of marketing factors. These included perception of the need to modify a product or service to suit the customer. Japanese take such adaptability for granted; foreigners not only don't do so, but tend to perceive that there is nothing wrong with what they are offering (see *Tokyo Business Today*, November 1994, pp. 20–23).
4 Graham and Sano, 1989, pp. 7–10.
5 Studies indicate that Americans who are considered better listeners and are orientated toward relationship building tend to be better at negotiating with Japanese (Graham and Sano, 1989, p. 37).
6 For excellent accounts of Japanese and American negotiations, see Graham and Sano (1989); Prestowitz, for government-level negotiations (1989); and Mark Zimmerman, former ACCJ president (1985, p. 100).
7 Research conducted by Rosalie Tung in 1984 found that most Japanese negotiating teams consisted of members numbering between four and seven. Most Western teams consisted of one person and an interpreter (cited in Zimmerman, 1985, p. 104. Tung's book is *Business Negotiations with the Japanese*, 1984).
8 See also Graham and Sano, 1989, pp. 165–66.

9 For instance, the *International Directory of Company Histories*, St James Press, Chicago, volumes from 1988.
10 Zimmerman, 1985, p. 31.
11 Since few foreign business people need only a box of *meishi*, contact one of the foreign service firms in Japan that can help you with these and other communications tools. See the Appendix for candidates.
12 Yoshihara, 1982, p. 232.
13 Graham and Sano, 1989, pp. 3 and 11.

Chapter 8

In the Japanese market

The mediator between Japan and abroad

An important role in trade is that of intermediary between the business needs of Japanese and foreign interests. There are variations on this role, depending on whether you are:

- working in the Japan office of a foreign company,
- representing the Japanese partner of a joint venture or subsidiary office, or
- an independent trader, sourcing from and communicating with home suppliers.

Typically, participants entering any of these relationships assume that each side will see the relationship's objectives rationally, so communication-based problems can be resolved. This is often not what happens; a *rational* response is relative to the values in your locality. Each side becomes baffled as to why the other is reacting as it is. Misunderstanding is rife. Being the meat in the sandwich in trade and negotiations can be a horrible, conflict-orientated experience, or a very strategic and vital position, depending on how you see and deal with it.

The independent importer of goods into Japan

Most of the foreign companies wanting to sell in Japan are small enterprises, and realistically they have no ability to market there. In many cases they make good products or components, and as a category these seedlings of companies have greater combined growth potential than large enterprises. For these producers, unable to market for themselves, and also for larger producers wanting to sell in Japan but not wanting to do it themselves, using a third party that specializes in Japan is a viable option. The following deals with that intermediary role.

Exporting to Japan is not a simple matter of freighting an existing range of goods to the customer. Since there are wide differences in interpretation of 'value' between Japanese and others, virtually all products need nurturing until adjustments are able to be incorporated into the product by the manufacturer. Very few products are Japan market-ready, so the needs of the Japanese must be fed from the Japanese buyer to the manufacturer in order to tailor the product to the market, and later to update models.

Accordingly, the best market research information is from the retailer, fed through a distributor and/or importer back to the manufacturer. It is best that that information come from someone sympathetic with, and able to communicate effectively between, the customer and the foreign manufacturer. The best candidates, if available, are foreign staff who are 'Japan-literate' and can communicate effectively back to their home country.

Japanese aren't particularly direct about problems, and foreign suppliers often get no feedback from their Japanese buyers. Some foreigners simply find that their products are no longer wanted, without sufficient explanation as to why. Staff of foreign companies who understand the culture should be able to interpret what the Japanese actually mean. Having done so, they will be more able to relay problems to the home country in order to have them addressed. Obviously this may mean the difference between a manufacturer's products being improved or being ignored.

This relationship between a foreign manufacturer and a Japan-based distributor becomes one of:

- Complaints, problems and other information fed back from Japan.
- This information feeds into the product upgrading process. Since suppliers don't know what the Japanese want in a product, they need this information in order to trigger them to make developments suitable for Japan.
- In the event of problems in the market, the Japan-based sales company needs to expedite an upgraded product to customers, delivering an apology along with a commitment for it not to happen again.

While there are many companies exporting a single product range to Japan, there aren't many 'successful' general traders that search for and take on any product that looks good. This raises the matter of the unified marketing of such products under the banner of a common and quality logo. The motivation for doing so is simple: Japanese buyers respect a known brand, in large part on the assumption that there is a consistency of quality attached to that brand. However, it is a difficult issue. Creating a brand out of disparate producers and maintaining quality is a challenge (though this is often done with discount products). There is a level of cooperation-under-pressure that foreigners aren't necessarily good at – supply companies would decide they didn't like something about the system and bail out, or try to go it alone, and the important unified image would break down.

On the Japan side, one other reason why it's difficult to market a range of goods is the need to have a broad and receptive *jinmyaku*. You might have established contacts in one business area, but few foreigners have a variety of Japanese people they can call on in different fields. Yet you need these people in Japan to ensure that the products you bring will at least get a good initial viewing, or, even better, an initial promotional push. Still, for a business that has good clout in Japan, that understands its market needs, and can also command respect amongst foreign suppliers, there is real potential for such a project.

The following is an example of a small Japanese trading firm, Fujita & Co. Ltd, that has helped different foreign businesses and products to enter or expand in Japan – though central to the firm's success is its founder, a playfully eccentric gent by the name of Fujita Den. If you're not familiar with the trader's name, you probably will be familiar with some of the companies associated with Fujita's business, some of them household names.

Fujita's firm initially exported electronics products from Japan and imported luxury goods, including fashion items, jewellery and golf clubs, early on winning the right to import Christian Dior and PGA golf goods. But he was only getting started.

While in Hawaii Mr Fujita noticed many Japanese eating hamburgers, and recognized that McDonald's outlets were doing a booming business. Through a mutual friend, Mr Fujita was introduced to an employee of McDonald's USA. McDonald's was looking for an individual rather than a large corporation to handle its product, and despite numerous applicants wanting to take advantage of a relaxation in Japan's rules on foreign business involvement, in 1971 an agreement was signed with Fujita that produced McDonald's Co. (Japan). The company was 50 per cent owned by McDonald's Corp. in the US, and 50 per cent was split between Fujita & Co. and a Japanese bakery called Daiichiya. McDonald's knew of Daiichiya through an existing supplier of theirs in the US, and, not confident that Mr Fujita had the business experience to handle the new food-based operation alone, McDonald's wanted to include Daiichiya. To the bakery's later regret, in the latter 1970s Daiichiya sold its 25 per cent stake to Fujita Trading, which now holds 50 per cent of a very successful organization.

One thing that was indeed amazing about the entry of McDonald's in Japan was the location of the first outlet. It wasn't only in the centre of Japan's most prestigious shopping area, it was in Japan's most prestigious store. Such a risky venture as McDonald's was considered then would, under normal circumstances, be given low priority by any sizeable Japanese organization; it would find its level in the hierarchy and, if it were capable, it would slowly work its way up. So the immediate question to those seeing a McDonald's in Ginza was, 'What's a fresh-off-the-boat foreign takeaway outlet doing in this prize spot?'

The twist is that Mr Fujita had a very close relationship with Okada Shigeru, who became president of Mitsukoshi in the early 1970s. Thus, Den Fujita was able to set up a McDonald's – the epitome of Western 'culture' – in a plum position, on the ground floor of Mitsukoshi – the epitome of Japanese status and sophistication. After Mr Okada was removed due to a scandal in 1984, McDonald's, by then having been determined a success, slipped a few doors down the street.

In 1991, through McDonald's Japan, Mr Fujita helped facilitate the entry of US retailer Toys 'R' Us into Japan, with McDonald's retaining a 20 per cent interest in Toys 'R' Us Japan Ltd. McDonald's Japan has taken advantage of the situation by putting a McDonald's outlet at many of the Toys 'R' Us sites – a rather strategic move on the part of both, particularly given the success in Japan of Toys 'R' Us. (A much more detailed description of the entry of Toys 'R' Us into Japan appears in Chapter 14.)

Similarly, further intending to strategically place its outlets, in 1997 McDonald's Japan became involved in another innovative tie-up. McDonald's joined with Mobil (Mobil Sekiyu), which was also going the extra mile to win customers under heavy gasoline price competition. In 1997 Sekiyu opened the first of an initial ten planned petrol stations, each to have an on-site McDonald's outlet. Customers can now drive through and get petrol and a hamburger at the same time.

By 1998 McDonald's Japan already claimed far more outlets than existed in any other country outside the US; at almost 2500, Japan has more than twice as many outlets as its closest rival, Canada.

Your supplier

A basic but important matter for those trading the products of others is who you will source from. Independent traders or trading companies may have some flexibility in who they will have supply their products or services. Different suppliers have different ways of doing business. A big problem is that some are fairly loose; the most common difficulty is being late in filling an order. This is something you can't afford to have happen when selling into Japan.

Nevertheless, once you've been through the process of securing a supplier, who then lets you down, it's tempting to be optimistic and hope that things will improve. The best thing to do is to back away from the situation before you become entangled any more than you have to in the other's incompetence. Basically, a supplier's old habits won't change quickly

– trying to get good performance out of suppliers who don't give it is an ongoing problem for those importing to Japan. The situation is not worth the loss to your credibility in Japan, the frustration, and the waste in trying to meet your commitments. While Westerners may have a degree of tolerance to delays, or will listen to the reasons for them, these generally don't cut any ice in Japan. There are normally other, more reliable suppliers who can give you what you want.

When I shipped vehicles to Japan in the 1980s I used a crating firm to pack them prior to delivery to the wharf. Inevitably the owner and I would discuss the shipping date, according to which he would schedule in his part of the process. It would then be common for me to turn up on the day of packing, or even after, to find my goods in their raw unpacked state, following which I would get an assurance that they had been busy and that 'leave it to him', he would see that they got on the ship. Luckily they always did, but obviously this policy leaves no time for anything else to go wrong and at least means a frenzied schedule. So, how do you get around it . . .? It was tempting to tell him the ship would leave two days earlier than it did, but one thing he could be relied on to know exactly was the shipping times. My problem was that there was no other company in the vicinity that did the same job, so he could stumble along with a monopoly in the business, with me in tow. This kind of situation is a recipe for disaster when dealing with Japan.

There is the criticism that Japanese are overly fussy about punctuality, but delays do cause clear practical problems for those downstream. Japanese supply chains are commonly geared to prompt delivery, and it is this prompt delivery that your Japanese customers are used to. If an overseas company can't respond quickly to customer supply needs, customers perceive it as a demerit, in broad quality terms. Illustrating this, a survey showed that more than nine out of ten Japanese buyers saw half a day to a week as the maximum acceptable delivery delay. In stark contrast were foreign suppliers, three-quarters of whom believed a two to four week delay was tolerable.[1]

Niichu vs. Simtek

Following is a frustrating if not a sad story for one Japanese import firm, Niichu Ltd. Niichu sources precision instruments from an American company, Simtek, that has proprietary technology in the manufacture of high-tech electronic equipment.

Niichu began operations in 1967, trading high-tech products, and grew over the next 30 years to become a main Japanese producer of equipment used in semiconductor and related manufacturing. By 1991 10 per cent of Niichu's supply came from US firms, including Simtek.

Simtek produced mass flow monitors protected by a patent, based on exclusive technology. Niichu had operated a branch near Simtek in the USA and the staff often visited Simtek. As Niichu was successful in the Japanese semiconductor market it was eventually agreed that it should become Simtek's exclusive distributor in Japan. The relationship developed relatively smoothly over the first several years, with some initial quality problems, but it was hoped that as time passed each of the two companies would develop a stronger understanding of what the other wanted. In particular, Niichu anticipated that Simtek would come to understand what was necessary in order to supply the Japanese market.

Initially, the main issues were the low quality of monitors and late delivery times. Another matter that became problematic was the turnover of personnel within top positions at Simtek, something which really began with the loss of Simtek's long-standing president. This ultimately affected Simtek's production ability. Its shortage of staff meant that Simtek tended to be even more behind schedule than it had been, and the lack of appropriate leadership affected decision making within the firm, which also affected production.

Niichu's R&D manager, Hashimoto Kenji, tells about one of the problems: 'Once the president of Simtek decided to visit Tokyo. He wanted to introduce their latest products and get orders from some of the leading Japanese companies. This was partly because he knew that Simtek had been losing market share worldwide, as competitors had been coming up with fundamentally new competitive technology.' Coming to Japan was essentially a positive move, as the Japanese value face-to-face contact. One day Mr Hashimoto introduced Simtek's president to Aqua Co. Ltd, one of Niichu's main Japanese customers and an existing user of Simtek equipment. Mr Hashimoto explains:

'As a direct result of his enthusiasm, because he promised to provide good service for Aqua, and because he promised to deliver a quality product within 90 days of receiving an order, Aqua's president placed an order on the spot.

'So, it put us in a very embarrassing position, then, when Simtek kept postponing the delivery date. Aqua lost respect for both Niichu and myself, and our sales to Aqua dropped drastically. And while this was going on, competitors spread rumours that Simtek had stopped updating their instruments because of poor research and poor engineering. Then some of the Japanese customers began to realize that Simtek's technology was gradually going downhill. . . . We finally received the product one year later.

'Once, we ordered mass flow monitors. These were based on an old type of technology that Simtek generally prefers not to use any more, but they accepted the order because their sales had been decreasing. But Simtek couldn't even supply us with these – and the president of Simtek wasn't even aware that the abilities of their engineers and researchers had dropped so drastically. Finally, after failing to receive the order we thought it was necessary, to preserve our reputation with our client, to buy a replacement, at our own expense, from a competitor of Simtek.'

It should be pointed out or reiterated here that the location of responsibility for problems is different in Japan than in the West. Whereas Westerners might explain to customers, 'It's not our fault, the problem is out of our control', those supplying customers in Japan are more likely to take responsibility for a problem that lies with an upstream manufacturer or distributor. It's not uncommon for an 'innocent' downstream party to do whatever it takes, which may mean spending a lot of money, to resolve a problem themselves, when it's impossible for those actually responsible to do so. Unfortunately, this can mean covering for the poor performance of a foreign producer. Indeed, it also means that if you're supplying product from abroad you are implicitly responsible for the quality of what you handle.

You can gain credibility by 'coming through' when a problem does crop up, or you can cause others to lose confidence in you by not doing so. When I imported textiles to Japan, my Japanese partner would go through the goods in detail, pulling out those items with flaws. At first I was surprised, but I learned that that's what you have to do. It stops bad quality going on to the next point in the system. Basically, within the Japanese system there's an *excess* of 'responsibility' – meaning quality is kept high and fewer problems do surface. Foreigners, however, typically don't demonstrate enough responsibility even within their own domains, resulting in lateness, and a poorer product.

On another occasion Niichu wanted a very sophisticated inspection system for its own use, and it placed an order with Simtek. 'Simtek promised to have the item ready for an acceptance test at our plant by the middle of December 1997. But Simtek informed us at the end of February [1998] that they couldn't complete the system by the end of the fiscal year.

They sent part of the equipment, but finally we had to turn down the order as our purchases are on an annual budget basis. At the end of March the budget for the year expired, meaning we had to forfeit any remainder, and there wasn't an allocation in the next year's budget. It's crazy, it meant a lose–lose situation for us and Simtek.' The latest development has been a very angry reply from Simtek, complaining bitterly that Niichu is unreasonable in refusing the order.

I know Mr Hashimoto personally, and this situation was driving him crazy – he simply didn't know what to do. As we'll see through other examples, unreliability amongst foreign firms is a common problem. Viewed from my perspective as a foreigner with trade experience now living in Japan, this amounts to 'criminal negligence'. The foreign firms are throwing away business, while at the same time creating (or reaffirming) the Japanese belief that foreign firms can't be trusted. Why does Niichu continue dealing with Simtek? 'Because of Simtek's patent which prevents the Japanese companies from producing it by themselves. . . . But, soon', says Mr Hashimoto, 'their patent expires . . . and then things will change.'

And what happens next is not hard to imagine. The Japanese are accused of duplicity, for ordering, then cancelling (on the 'weak pretext' of finance). Then they develop their own product on the basis of the original foreign technology, and are accused of taking the market away from the original foreign firm. But, in reality, both Niichu and Aqua would have been happy to have a stable and enduring relationship using Simtek, if it had remained a reliable supplier.

Leave it 'til tomorrow

Western workers often have a 'leave it 'til tomorrow' attitude. Ask Japanese office workers when they finish work, and they'll perhaps say 6.00pm. Qualify that by asking them when they *actually leave* work, and many would say between 7.30 and 10.00pm. Those who aren't just waiting around are tidying up the day's loose ends.

Westerners are less inclined to finish off work in their own time, but allow those loose ends to mount up, resulting in a build-up of delays. By Western standards Japanese offices are over-staffed, but this provides them with extra capacity. Consequently, while Westerners are consistently running just behind schedule, Japanese companies are usually on schedule. The results are that Japanese suppliers have satisfied not only Japanese customers, but satisfied and taken away markets from Western companies, successfully appealing also to Western buyers.

Even in doing research for this book the difference between foreign and Japanese punctuality was clear. Being prompt was, moreover, a phenomenon of the companies, not individuals. Japanese people working in the foreign firms I contacted were just as slow as foreigners – it's a function of the time and work pressure in foreign firms. On the other hand, Japanese companies typically respond to enquiries or requests within a few days. One company I contacted was Matsumoto Kiyoshi, a growing drug store chain – with perhaps its own twist: The firm was established by the unconventional mayor of Matsudo, who in local government was known for maintaining a 'do it now' philosophy. I sent a fax one Thursday evening to the company's promotions manager, Ōkubo Yukihiko, asking several quite specific questions. I guess the founder's policy is reflected in the response I received. It came just 24 hours later, but still, written on the bottom was an apology for taking so long to reply.

In the process of getting goods into Japan you are competing against the strong and proven performance of Japanese companies. With that and other handicaps you face in their market, you must present your service by taking the best advantage possible of those factors you do have some control over. As an independent exporter you might be in a position to choose your home suppliers considering punctuality and quality. And by also prioritizing punctuality in your own business, you can control such important factors as delivery time.

The new branch manager

Not only do Westerners who come to negotiate in Japan face problems, but so do foreign staff who come to work in a company. The attitude of some branch managers posted overseas is that they should tidy up the operation. They are the 'new broom about to sweep clean'. However, the Western management concepts they bring don't always fit into Japanese business. The 'right material' for Japan must be someone who already knows about Japan, or someone modest and prepared to learn – this not only reflects a universal rule, but Japanese in particular will appreciate these traits.

Foreign managerial policy may be at odds with the expectations and needs of Japanese staff, who are accustomed to operating in certain ways. Policy may also be at odds with the prevailing Japanese business environment. It's necessary, to some extent at least, to fit into established and accepted patterns of business behaviour – at least because many of these patterns have evolved for a reason. For instance, a 'new broom' policy of laying off the company's excess workers runs into conflict with broad Japanese business policy. Specifically, since most other Japanese companies are not accustomed to taking on mid-career employees, those made redundant are in a very difficult position finding good re-employment. As mentioned earlier, the fear of being laid off is one reason why many Japanese employees distrust working for a foreign company.

It is possible to successfully operate a company to a large extent on Western business principles. Many companies, especially those in the business centre of Tokyo, are in a Westernized environment. However, clashes of culture occur, and all companies, to varying degrees, must undertake compromises in their methods of management.

Head office knows best

Another problem that particularly affects Japan offices of foreign parent companies, and even of joint ventures, is that requests from Japan are given low priority or even ignored. Without an understanding of the Japanese environment, decision makers in foreign countries decide that they know what should be done – they know what is needed in Japan.

If a firm is going to enter the Japanese market, it needs to put in Japan a core group of Japan-literate people, and must make sure they have enough power that they are trusted and their decisions made to stick back home. There are sufficient peculiarities about the Japanese market that decisions will appear incomprehensible or irrational, but there needs to be a continuity of existing policies. It is fruitless to have the opinions and decisions of people on the ground in Japan undercut by someone in the head office who doesn't understand the reasons behind such decisions.

It's a problem sometimes compounded in cases where communicators are Japanese. As mentioned earlier, Japanese aren't accustomed to what Westerners consider clear and logical explanations, and therefore they don't produce a logical case for what they want.

The problem of communicating across cultures is not the central issue, however; the real issue is a lack of resources. Insufficient communication (or understanding at home) becomes a decisive factor when those back home can't see a good reason for allocating those resources. Western companies large and small have priorities; they must allocate time and finance where they think these are best deployed. Typically, the Japan office asks for something that taxes these resources, and in the absence of a persuasive case, or a powerful staff member making the request, business judgement back home prudently decides that Japan's demand isn't a priority.

Requests include those as basic as 'hurry up, we can't keep the customer waiting', though they may include such requests as money for a golf club membership. Clearly this might seem extravagant and unnecessary back home but the importance and usefulness of social relations makes 'entertainment' a necessary expense. There are a lot of unwilling golfers and alcohol drinkers in Japan who engage in these activities only to strengthen their personal ties.

Packaging and quality

The drain on resources is also one of the reasons why foreigners have problems producing quality products. Such demands can lead suppliers to ignore or cut corners on matters of detail that they don't see as important, but which in reality contribute to the quality of the product.

One of the reasons why detail is important is that many purchases in Japan are given as gifts. Before the recession hit in the 1990s, 40 per cent of the sales at Japan's four most prestigious department stores went to companies.[2] These, and the many items bought by individuals that ended up as gifts, contributed to the high general demand for quality goods in Japan. Particularly in the 1980s, gifts sent by companies were lavish. They had to be, since securing a good relationship was, and remains, a business investment. To present something cheap is to risk creating the impression that as giver you don't care enough about the relationship to pay a high enough price, or to put in the effort to secure a really good gift, or you don't have good judgement.

Thorough quality

To understand the effect of some gifts that have been given by foreigners to Japanese, imagine being presented with a woollen sweater with a small hole in the back. It would still be functional, but we would question the rationale of the giver. We wouldn't say anything to the giver, and neither do the Japanese when it happens to them. They make many allowances for foreigners, but the quality judgement of the giver would be questioned. Unfortunately, this type of situation occurs when foreigners give business gifts to Japanese, and it reflects a lack of perception of quality – the same judgement of quality that Japanese must rely on when they import foreign products.

I was asked to market in Japan a particular piece of golfing equipment. Since golf is not just a sport in Japan – more of a place to do business and maintain one's *jinmyaku* – capturing a luxury part of that market would mean generating a lot of money. I noticed a small manufacturing flaw in the product, but the maker told me that it couldn't be avoided, and from his point of view, that having been explained, business would go on as normal. But no amount of such explanation would placate Japanese customers – the product was immediately rejected by a Japanese business person on the same basis. I routinely ask my Western students to tell me what's wrong with this product, but virtually no one can identify the problem. When Westerners judge something visually, they focus on the functional symmetry or convenience of its features, but they must broaden their idea of quality to apply more to aesthetics. Sadly, the manufacturer had sold some of these to sales members of a top company in a leading New Zealand industry, which they had passed on to their Japanese buyers as gifts.

The matter of aesthetics is often described amongst foreigners as the strict demand Japanese have for quality presentation or 'packaging'. In the context of doing business in Japan, during the latter 1980s the importance of packaging attained mythical status amongst foreign manufacturers and would-be exporters. The matter is of course not really one of packaging, it is stress on 'thorough quality' – quality throughout an item. However, we lack the vocabulary to express what is really required by the Japanese, so we revert to the idea of it being the package or the presentation that's important.

It's useful to explain to suppliers the need for the product to be not only functional, but perfectly presented. By imagining his/her product as a gift, a supplier can gain an understanding of what is needed, and this can put a perplexed mind at ease. Allow the supplier to see the matter via a parallel example. For instance, if a person were handed a box of chocolates as a gift we would expect everything to be perfect, the design and materials, through to the actual contents. Imagine slicing the box, top down, through the centre, then looking at the cross-section, seeing the quality of each component material that has been used. The quality of the paper, the colour, design, the chocolate, right through to the nut or filling inside. Westerners often devote this sort of attention to boxes of chocolates, but are often less concerned about other 'practical' goods.

Exporters from abroad may walk into a Japanese department store and notice that their product would be much more price-competitive than the local product. But unless they understand the demand for 'frills' they are not going to make headway by supplying something that has function, but cuts corners on 'unnecessary' features.

It's often hard for Westerners to understand why Japanese are so particular about the quality and appearance of small adornments, or why they are interested in having designs or colourful logos on functional objects such as pens or stationery. One of the reasons is that many Westerners live on fairly large areas of land, with a garden, in a natural environment. For such people there is an abundance of visual and other stimulation just outside the window or door. However, many Japanese people live in highly concentrated, unnatural and virtually colourless city environments. For them it is rare to see the sun or a blue sky, and the air is commonly filled with a haze of silt. The insides of offices are normally grey, and houses are small, such that colourful ornaments, even a cartoon character logo on functional objects such as stationery items, can add some life. It is up to the mediator to understand and then explain this type of thing to suppliers.

The importance of effective communication cannot be over-emphasized. A mediator needs to become good at drawing out exactly what the Japanese person, or side, is trying to say. It is basic to the process of communication that someone interpreting in this way understand fully and logically not only what the problem is, but why the problem exists. Then that information needs to be passed on to the overseas supplier.

While such communication may seem a frustrating and time-consuming exercise, the amount of time and other cost spent on clear explanations is small if it enables the supplier at home to provide a product and service that suits the Japanese customer. This is especially true given the high costs of setting up an operation and considering that effective communication can ultimately mean the life or death of the project. If the supplier thinks that the Japanese requests are ridiculous, and that the Japanese are simply too fussy, the supplier will be left feeling there is no real reason to do what is being asked. Furthermore, manufacturers and other producers are normally *creators*. They are normally in a good position to improve, if not invent, in order to upgrade their product or system. Without an understanding of the consumer the supplier won't gain an understanding in principle of what Japan needs, and will be unable to come up with further innovations on his/her own.

Notes

1 *Tokyo Business Today*, November 1994, p. 22.
2 *The Economist*, 9 July 1994, p. 10. Also, MIPRO estimated the 1994 gift market to be worth around ¥10tn ($100bn), which was about 2.5 per cent of real GDP for 1994 (GDP at ¥422.083tn) (*Penetrating the Japanese Market*, MIPRO, 1995, p. 8; *Japan Almanac 1996*, p. 73).

Chapter 9

Small business

Under-publicized, under-recognized

Unfortunately, the possibility that foreigners could be operating 'small businesses' in Japan is often ignored by foreign organizations in Japan. As if in tune with their Japanese counterparts, foreign groups seem to think that the only business worth doing is big business. This is regrettable, because it means there is little advice for small operations. The reality is that small businesses play a significant part in all economies, and there is no reason why that reality should cease when we start dealing with Japan. Being in Japan doesn't mean that small foreign businesses can't perform a function – one thing they can do is represent the products of small firms back home – and it doesn't mean they can't succeed, but it can be much more difficult for them than for large businesses. Indeed, in this context there is a need for more, not less information and assistance from both official and unofficial bodies.

Nearly all material that is written in English about Japanese business is about large-scale business.[1] This is because books tend to be written, and stories told, about company successes. And foreign companies that have succeeded in Japan have tended to be large, or had large company backing. Promotional literature by JETRO (the trade promotion and 'PR' wing of MITI) has also focused on the small percentage of large business successes. To be fair, JETRO does devote a proportion of its literature to small firm market entry. However, the aim of much of JETRO (MITI's) literature has been to present a bright picture of foreign entry into Japan.[2]

Because they need to show and encourage strong trade at home, foreign local governments, too, concentrate on the companies that have made it in Japan. Yet, for the long-term benefit of their constituencies, they should devote much of their time to seeing where the problem lies with the small company failures.

The ACCJ (American Chamber of Commerce in Japan) does a lot for foreign business, but it, too, needs to examine whether its focus is not too narrow. The *ACCJ Journal* ran an article on small businesses operating in Japan, some of which were doing well. It included comments from business owners that they had had to learn everything for themselves as they'd got little or no official help from, amongst others, the ACCJ.[3] Basic ACCJ membership, at ¥100,000–¥150,000 ($770–$1150) a year, is a lot for a small business – and even ACCJ photocopying, at ¥100 per sheet, simply doesn't create a welcoming environment for small business operators. (Indeed, it is odd that the ACCJ, which has something of a monopoly on information, and which is leading the US charge to break down Japan's unfair trade practices, charges ten times the market rate for photocopying.) There are a lot of small foreign firms in Japan, or trying to enter Japan, that could benefit much more from the ACCJ's resources.

Unfortunately, promotion of the big business success scenario has left market entrants with an unrealistic account of dealing in Japan. While abroad I attended a government-run seminar, promoting entry into Japan, and while the audience consisted of Western small-business operators, the examples given were of that nation's top export categories. Of course, this was completely inappropriate. This sends examples of success into a camp where there is often none, and suggests methods of operating that are inappropriate. Because reports focus on large firm successes, the methods of market entry and other patterns of big business behaviour become the assumed norm. Available literature about doing business in Japan often discusses, as a matter of course, investment amounts which are beyond the finances of most companies. The sizes and style of meetings typified don't apply to the way most Japanese companies do business. Small company managers react in the same polite manner that Japanese culture dictates to all, but they are more casual and don't take part in the formal practices often described as characteristic of Japanese business. The manager of a small foreign company dealing with other small companies won't go to a conference room, and won't confront a Japanese team equipped with well-researched information about the foreigner's product and company.

It will probably also be impossible for the small foreign firm to obtain information about its Japanese counterparts. Yet literature often advises foreign business people to research Japanese companies, as the Japanese are known to research foreign firms and their management. It is sometimes suggested that such sources as the *Japan Company Handbook* be used. However, this book, for instance, only covers the 3000 companies listed on the first two sections of the Tokyo, Osaka and Nagoya stock exchanges.[4] Listings on these sections have traditionally been very difficult for companies to achieve. They have only been available to highly profitable and long-standing firms. Since there are millions of firms in Japan, the *Company Handbook* is clearly of limited use for small foreign businesses in finding comparable Japanese firms.

Perhaps most frustrating for foreigners is that, as mentioned earlier, they are told that in Japan they must have introductions in order to do business. Getting one contact can be difficult enough, but for the many foreign businesses wanting to trade within Japan, they need to deal with a number of Japanese firms. Since most foreigners don't know anyone in Japan, getting the required introductions can be impossible.

Despite the attention focused on large enterprises, most companies in Japan and elsewhere are small businesses. Many foreigners who want to do business in Japan operate small businesses. In the US, businesses with fewer than 100 employees account for about half of US employment, and over a third of US GDP.[5]

Small business is big business

In Japan too, most business is small or medium-sized:

- Over 98 per cent of Japanese firms are small or medium-sized enterprises (SMEs).[6]
- In wholesale and retail, over 80 per cent of workers are employed in SMEs.
- Over half of all manufacturing companies in Japan have fewer than ten employees.
- Retailers with fewer than 15 employees account for over half of Japan's retail sales.[7]

Small businesses, Japanese and foreign, tend to work well with other small businesses. One reason is that in Japan, where size is power, small firms aren't so attractive to large Japanese companies. And because small Japanese firms feel unable to command authority in a relationship with a large company, they may be happy to deal with a small foreign supplier. In doing so the Japanese side can benefit by being in a strong or equal relative position. They have more authority to negotiate terms of trade, including what is ordered, price and delivery details, as well as gain good, direct access to an international source.

Aside from the practical advantages of being able to control what they stock, there are human benefits. Dealing with a small foreign company can put some humanity back into business, and can bring some variety into the life and business of owners – the social lives of many Japanese small firm owners are closely associated with what happens in business. A feeling of independence and variety are, after all, amongst the reasons many small firm owners start, or stay in, their own business.

Small firms entering Japan

Small foreign businesses wanting to enter Japan have three immediate disadvantages. Most lack:

● contact with anyone they can do business with in Japan,
● knowledge of how to function in Japanese business, and
● the resources needed to focus on and represent themselves in the Japanese market.

In Chapter 7, I introduced the Delegation of the European Commission in Japan, an organization that is making progress, helping small firms in some of these areas. One of its projects is the *Gateway to Japan* export promotion campaign, which concentrates on ten specific sectors of European industry. Rudy Filon spent five years in Japan as the Commercial Attaché for the delegation, in charge of this and other business initiatives for Europe. He explains their difficulties and achievements in bringing small business operators into Japan.

'[Recently in *Gateway*] we brought over a number of people that are trying to sell marble and wood products etc. ... Some of them are rather culturally insensitive and believe that the whole world is just like Europe, and that ... Japan is no different. So, they slap the [Japanese] guy on the shoulder and they say, "hey! I can give you another 10% discount if you like, let's go for a drink" – I saw this from up close and I thought, "this is not going to work".

'The way we try to deal with this is that *Gateway* has a very strong educational component back in Europe. We try to educate the exporters before they come out. We explain some basic things about the need to have a *meishi* [business card], and the need to be properly prepared. Being properly dressed is another thing. You wouldn't believe how some people arrive here. It's simply because often they work in a factory. They may be the managing director, but they work in coveralls and they have their arms in grease, and suddenly they have to be in a business suit ... some of them don't even have a business suit. So it is that kind of cross-cultural education that we're trying to work on.

'...Sometimes you just close your eyes and pray that it will work out, but what we said from the very beginning is that it would be important to bring as many European companies as possible here to experience the reality, because ... at the end of the day we believe the only real way to experience it is by doing it. So on the trade missions we set them up with individual business people so that they can actually sit down with a potential Japanese client and see how it goes.'

And on business start-ups following the 18 months of the Executive Training Programme (ETP):

> 'We have never counted the ETPs who set up their own business in Japan after the course. Probably very few "go it on their own" after the ETP, though quite a number have set up a branch office for their sponsor. One ETP trainee set up his own business back in France after the course and, interestingly, sponsored another ETP – a woman – on a later course. One ETP decided to leave his company (which was owned by his family) and set up a consultancy in Milan which is quickly developing a reputation in Europe for helping companies that are getting into the Japanese market. Finally, I should not forget to mention the ETP who founded the first (and so far only) Portuguese trading company in Japan.'

One fact of life for small businesses in Japan is that they have to cope with their lot to a large extent alone, they can't rely on much support from other bodies. It's interesting, then; that the ETP graduates working in Japan make good use of each other. They've formed strong bonds with other ETP members while training and feel they can call them up with a particular problem, and in doing so they often find that others have had to cope with the same thing.

This raises a major issue for small firms, and a challenge for bodies overseeing them: how is it possible to create business advantage for small firms that are on the one hand highly motivated, but on the other are separated, diverse and lacking in basic resources? Take networking, for instance. While networking has, in this example, been effective, it has taken place on the back of a core programme. On its own, however, networking is often little more than a business cliché. To a large extent it should be up to central bodies (chambers of commerce, marketing boards) to generate creative mechanisms to either add value to such basic tools as networking or create other tangible opportunities for small (and large) businesses. Good overseeing bodies will provide a clearly structured and secure environment for small businesses to operate from.

Rudy, originally from The Netherlands, was just about to finish his term at the delegation when I spoke to him in 1998. Though he will work in a Japan-related capacity for the European Commission in Europe, the knowledge he had accumulated, and his interest in encouraging business in Japan, will clearly be missed in Tokyo.

Foreigners in 'small business in Japan'

JieStar

And now, let's meet some real people who have entered the Japanese market. The first example is an impressive one of market entry into Japan. It's hard for foreigners to set up, and in many ways it's particularly hard for women to operate in Japanese business. JieStar is an example of how both of these barriers can be successfully overcome.

JieStar is a small company that deals in catalogue and TV shopping. It is operated by Jie Wang, a 31-year-old Chinese woman who set up the company in 1995 after coming to Japan in 1990. As China began to move toward its version of liberal-socialism after 1978, it became easier for young people such as Jie to apply for visas to leave the country. This tied in with a 1984 Japanese plan to accept 100,000 young Asians, and with a relaxed Japanese immigration policy designed to cover the labour shortage Japan experienced during the bubble economy, in the latter 1980s. JieStar has two other staff members – both Japanese and both full-time – a male buyer, and a woman involved in sales and other work.

Appreciating the importance of the language, Jie's first two years were spent intensively studying Japanese, while working long hours part-time. She then got a job as a mediator for a Japanese company that wanted to expand business into China. But because of the Japanese economic slowdown after working there for just three years the company decided to abandon the Chinese market, and her job disappeared. She was then faced with the choice of getting a new job, moving to another division of the company, or going back to China, but, encouraged by her ex-boss, she chose to pursue her ambition of starting her own business.

Jie initially brokered small gift items, selling them on to a section of the government that sent them to favoured customers at gift-giving time. Following this, she started supplying TV shopping, having gained access to shopping programmes on two nationwide TV stations.

The question that should now arise in the minds of experienced Japan-watchers is how could a foreigner manage to gain such entry into Japanese business?

To understand this situation, it's useful to review how the system functions. Whereas in the West ascent to coveted business positions is gained through performance, quality and/or expertise of some sort, in Japan, while these are relevant factors, they don't stand alone. There are social factors that are equally important if one is to achieve a strong position in business. These social factors, difficult enough for Japanese to achieve, are usually inaccessible to foreigners simply because they don't know anybody influential. In Jie's case her ex-boss became the president of her new company, and while this was a nominal position, his name functioned as a good reference. He also provided her with (loaned) working capital, and, very importantly, he provided her with contacts to those he – as a successful business person – knew in positions of influence. Still, these factors, she insists, must be combined with having a 'good product'.

As an example of the value of *jinmyaku*, in order to sell gift items to the government, after approaching those people at the ground level in regional offices several times Jie realized that it was impossible to secure a contract this way. Through her former boss she was introduced to the (politically appointed) minister of the relevant ministry. 'Then everything became easy.' The minister contacted an official in the ministry, suggesting that they 'might like to buy the product' – a suggestion that in Japanese terminology is, in effect, an instruction. In a similar way, later business, too, became available via her ex-boss's *jinmyaku*.

To give an idea of the advantages of such contacts, I happen to know a retired official of the same ministry. He parachuted from the ministry as an *amakudari*, and landed a job in one of Japan's large stationery companies. His job was to do little else than to call his former subordinates or others in the ministry, suggesting that they might like to place an order for a product made by his host company. In other words, his host company's products competed on the same bureaucrat-mediated route as JieStar's products. For this they paid him a healthy annual salary, and after a seven-year stint at the post they provided him with ongoing pension payments. It's not difficult to imagine foreigners bringing into Japan products that are better or cheaper than those already on the market, expecting, logically, that theirs will surely be more popular. One can easily imagine their frustration at being unable to make a sale because the purchasing officer of a company or government department is on the receiving end of an obligatory buy arrangement with a government official who in turn has been asked to arrange the sale by a politician or other important contact. In this sense, JieStar was lucky.

In addition to specific *jinmyaku*-based introductions, in order to extend her business Jie also contacted people cold. She contacted mail-order catalogue publishers who might promote her product. She found companies in the phone book, rang and asked if they would be interested in a particular product and made an appointment with those who agreed to see her. If nothing else, this was a bridge-building exercise. She asked those who didn't want to see her product because 'it wouldn't be suitable' if she could contact them in the future, if she found something else that might suit them. 'They typically say yes, you can call again.' In other cases, those she did meet ultimately refused her product. But if she had come to know them well enough, she might ask them to introduce her to another dealer; in this way, contacts lead to contacts. In this context, it is an important part of her job, according to Jie, to 'show them my personality; it makes it hard for them to refuse'.

As mentioned earlier, because business in Japan is a social matter, and we interact with people best socially, there is a lot of value in polite, positive contact with potential business partners once we start to know them. Contact shows commitment and sincerity, and those we communicate with are left with a feeling that they have, to some extent, come to know us. It is common for Japanese suppliers to then take this a step further by giving a gift (*omiyage*) to further solidify the relationship. What this means is that there is a lot of emphasis on 'public relations', and perhaps the greatest difficulty this represents for the foreigner is that language skills are important – language needs to be at a certain level in order for communication to be warm and friendly.

Jie did say that in some ways she would have liked to have started the business on her own. But it would have been much more difficult for her to have made it alone. It is possible to make fairly small steps without good *jinmyaku*, but it's very difficult, or virtually impossible, to achieve significant business results without it. The concepts of 'independence and success' don't go well together in Japan; people progress best by cooperating with others.

One thing that is truly admirable, and perhaps amazing, given the problems that even those foreigners with strong backing face when operating in Japan, is that as a solo mother and foreigner, with no real family support, Jie has achieved what she has in Japan. The JieStar story continues when we look at TV shopping in Chapter 15 on non-store retailing.

Important assets in JieStar's case:

- language skills
- *jinmyaku*
- good social relations.

Fox Bagels

One of the better known small business successes in Japan is Fox Bagels, a story symbolic of what a young entrepreneur can do in Japan. Lyle Fox first came to Japan in 1979 for a brief period as a language student. Following that, he worked for three years full-time as a proof reader at one of the English-language newspapers, until 1982, when he formed Fox Bagels. Having some experience and interest in food, he hit upon the idea of making foreign cuisine to sell in Japan. He settled on bagels, and scraped together ¥2mn ($9000) from friends and family to rent factory space and buy equipment, which included an oven, a mixer and a freezer. He taught himself how to make bagels, and gradually established supply and sales links.

Foreigners liked the product, which they hadn't been able to get fresh in Japan. One central Tokyo shop with many foreign customers tried his bagels and proceeded to order 200 a day. While he did also have many Japanese customers in the beginning who had taken a liking to bagels while overseas, Japanese people who had never been to the US typically had no experience with the food. Tastes also differed in Japan. Japanese buyers had a preference for sweeter flavours, so Lyle adjusted and added products accordingly. He made his bagels a little smaller and softer, and in the early 1990s the company made a fundamental recipe change toward even lighter bagels. Lyle says, 'This alienated some of the company's original customers, but resulted in bagels that appealed to a much broader category of Japanese consumer.' By 1995 sales had reached 20,000 units a day.

In 1993 Lyle sold the business to Myōjō Foods, a large Japanese food company that specializes in making instant noodles, though he remained an adviser for two years. Fox Bagels continues to expand. It has added new services, which include immediate delivery, mail-order, and the supply of frozen dough to other bakeries. It also regularly adds new bagels to its range to maintain a fresh company and product image.

On starting a business in Japan, Lyle says:

'I tell people who ask: make sure you have total, absolute and unequivocal confidence and passion about the product or service you are offering. That's it: *confidence* and *passion*. These are contagious traits and will be picked up by customers and employees alike. Employees will respond with hard work and loyalty; customers will respond with a willingness to give you a shot. I believe that you create your own luck, or lack of it, much like karma.

'Consumer acceptance did take a long time for me though; it took years before the average Joe on the street started to learn of bagels. And the company didn't turn a profit for years. The business was able to survive only because I was more stubborn than lucky and absolutely refused to let it fail, and consequently was able to get things done by being creative and "pleasantly aggressive" as someone once commented.

'Life after Fox Bagels has been very good indeed. I've formed a company assisting foreign food companies interested in the Japanese market, both as a consultant and a rep. My clients are food manufacturers, restaurant companies and "niche" companies which own some special technology or patents and want to license these to a Japanese company. I have more offers for work than I can handle, so I'm very selective about the companies I take on. I also publish a monthly newsletter in Japanese about the latest news from the US food industry, called *Fox Foodservice USA*, which I sell to Japanese food companies. Since Japan looks to the West for new ideas, and since the West sees Japan as a land of tremendous opportunity, it works out quite well.'[8]

The product: cautions about entering the Japanese market

There are some basic questions about the product that small business entrepreneurs in many cases fail to ask before attempting to enter the Japanese market.

When choosing a product to export to Japan, ask:

- Is the product already in Japan?

  If **yes**, then

- Can your product compete with what is already available?

  If **no**, then why not?

  1 *Is your product simply not known to the market yet?*
  2 *Is your product not acceptable to Japanese people?*
  3 *Is there something about your product that has restricted it from the market?*

Can your product compete with what is already available?

Many people think that because an existing product is expensive it will be possible to import a competitor and undercut the existing price. The ACCJ Kansai branch says it is often disappointed by first-time callers: 'Most likely they've seen the price of M&Ms at the candy store and remember what those things cost back home. They think they can turn a quick and easy profit importing M&Ms into Japan.'[9]

The price at the candy store in Japan is a reflection of the dictates of the system. It is becoming possible to cut through the distribution system, thereby cutting intermediary costs and so the final price, but unless you know exactly what's happening, don't gamble on being able to short-cut the system in your industry.

How can your product compete?

In many cases, competing with an existing product means bettering it on **price, service** or **features**.

Price: (1) Don't assume that a better price will win you market share unless the product is sought after as a status item, or unless you have other insider advantages; a low price is, rather, a necessity. (2) A low export price doesn't necessarily mean a low retail price in Japan.

Service: A report on investment into Japan concluded that quality and service were prerequisites. Those foreign firms who saw them as options, albeit options that they had adopted as primary differentiating features, performed most poorly.[10]

Features: Constant product upgrading is the norm in Japan. If you want to sell M&Ms, to compete you actually need 'Super M&Ms' ... that aren't yet on the market.

How can you compete? You need all three of these on your side, plus a variety of other factors discussed in this book.

Restrictions on use

Your product might be acceptable to Japanese consumers but there might be restrictions against its importation or use. The government ministries still have tight controls in many areas. For instance, in cosmetics, rather than a list of harmful ingredients, the Ministry of Health and Welfare has a list of accepted products, so new or unlisted items must go through an expensive and time-consuming approval process. In order to set up in Japan it cost even The Body Shop, renowned for its use of natural products, a lot in time and money to seek approval for such cosmetic ingredients as watermelon, banana, blue corn, tea tree and parsley, which were not on the 'approved' list. Of those, banana and tea tree have now been accepted, but it is still unable to import about 10 per cent of its range – you can buy watermelon and parsley to eat, but not to smear on your body.[11]

Is your product simply not known to the market yet?

Having a product that is as yet unknown in Japan brings with it the uncertainty of whether it will be accepted at all. Take muesli and yoghurt, for instance – in Japan one of these made it, one didn't, but it would have been difficult to predict which. They came from Europe and Turkey respectively, and became popular in other nations, but neither muesli (which is typically seen as expensive bird food) nor other cereals caught on in Japan. On the other hand, yoghurt did succeed; Japanese consume nearly twice as much yoghurt *per capita* as the English and four times as much as the Americans.[12]

Fox Bagels is an example of a product that was unknown in the market; it had potential, and after a lot of time and effort it did penetrate the market. Body Shop products were also unknown in Japan, and since Japan isn't a conservation-orientated country, it wasn't known how The Body Shop would be received, but it and its products have become very successful. It started in 1990 with one shop. Between 1997 and 1998 alone it added 27 new shops, to reach a total of 120 shops by April 1998.

Some businesses make it in Japan and some businesses don't, and success is not always easy to predict. In spite of this uncertainty, there is one factor that keeps drawing people to do business there, and that is the potential gains 'if I do make it in Japan'.

Notes

1 The notable exceptions are Helene Thian's *Setting Up and Operating a Business in Japan*; Miyashita and Russell's attention to small Japanese firms in *Keiretsu*; and D. H. Whittaker's *Small Firms in the Japanese Economy.*

2 This is based on my discussions with a writer involved with JETRO (MITI) publications as well as my own observations. To qualify the relationship between MITI and JETRO, according to MITI, JETRO is independent of MITI. This depends on one's interpretation of *independent*. MITI provides JETRO's budget and *yoko suberi* (*amakudari*) officials to serve in JETRO. Nothing that closely related in Japan is *independent* of influence.

3 'The Small Foreign Entrepreneur in Japan', *The Journal*, November 1996, pp. 49–55. The article's author, Steve Porritt, told me that he set out to find solutions and services for small firms, but they insisted that there were none, though things have, he says, improved since then.

4 There are changes, but the First Section of the stock exchange has about 1360 companies. The Second Section has about 910, and there are about 770 firms traded over-the-counter (OTC).

5 *Business Week*, 30 September 1996, p. 117.

6 This is based on a 1972 law defining SMEs as having a maximum of 300 employees or ¥100mn, paid-in capital. However, in wholesaling it is a maximum of 100 employees or ¥30mn and in retailing and services of 50 employees or ¥10mn.

7 *Small Business in Japan*, MITI, 1991, p. 153; 1994, pp. 216–17; 1996, p. 263.

8 Interview with Lyle Fox, 1997.

9 'The Small Foreign Entrepreneur in Japan', *The Journal*, 1996, p. 55.

10 *Japan in Revolution, An Assessment of Investment Performance by Foreign Firms in Japan*, ACCJ, The Council of the European Business Community and A. T. Kearney, Inc., 1995, p. 19.

11 Interview with: The Body Shop, 1998.

12 *Imported Goods Data Book* (*Sōsetsu Yunyū Shokuhin Jiten*), Food Imports Research Association, 1996, p. 95, figures for 1993. N.B. 'drinking yoghurt' is very popular in Japan.

Chapter 10

Establishing a business in Japan

Setting up an office in Japan

This chapter gives an outline of some of the things that are important to know when setting up business in Japan.

Company formation

The main options for forming a company are outlined below:

Gōmei kaisha: partnership
Requires two or more partners. Has unlimited liability, meaning that in a liquidation partners have the responsibility of settling any debts that exceed company assets themselves. Articles of incorporation must be drafted and registered at the legal affairs bureau.

Gōshi kaisha: limited partnership
Two or more partners. Partners may include both those with unlimited and with limited liability. Articles of incorporation must be drafted and registered at the legal affairs bureau.

Yūgen gaisha: limited liability company
Requires two directors to establish a company, but one can be removed later on. Minimum paid-in capital: ¥3,000,000. Not for listing on stock market. Suits small and medium-sized companies.

Kabushiki kaisha: joint stock company
Requires three directors to establish a company. Minimum paid-in capital: ¥10,000,000 ($77,000). Can be listed on the stock market.

Rather than set up one of the company types above, or as an interim step to doing so, you can operate as a representative office of an overseas registered company. This is possible so long as technically you are only gathering information or conducting research, and not actually trading on-shore. For this there is no need to register, or obtain permits or approval, and there is no need to pay company tax. Activities such an office can undertake include advertising, supplying information, conducting marketing or other research – essentially, bringing in and spending money, but not making money.

Having the status of limited liability allows the owners of a company the privilege of restricting company debts to the assets of the company. The Japanese version of a limited liability company begins at the *yūgen gaisha* (YK); *yū-gen* literally means 'having a limit'. The limited liability concept also applies to the next level up of company, the *kabushiki kaisha* (KK). *Kabu* means share, and accordingly, for companies that meet the stiff criteria of doing so, a KK may be listed on the stock market. The *yūgen gaisha* form is best suited to small and medium-sized companies, while the *kabushiki kaisha* form tends to be adopted by larger companies.

The main advantage of being a KK rather than a YK is image. But there is much more hassle and expense involved in being a KK. The trick for foreign companies that don't want to register as a KK is to instead use the Western form 'Ltd' on their documentation. Ltd covers both YK and KK, but will likely be interpreted in Japan as a KK.

Office location

For many small companies, and some large companies, the business location isn't critical. While Tokyo and Osaka have obvious 'downtown' business districts crowded with famous corporations, even these areas are more diffuse than in other business capitals. And many big companies now prefer to locate their headquarters or operational offices away from the 'downtown' areas. Tokyo has countless, particularly small and medium-sized, companies scattered throughout the city, and even in 'residential' areas shutters along house-lined streets can open up to show a fully operational, compact manufacturing or wholesaling business.

This is not to say that there is no such thing as a 'classy' office location, only that your office may not need to be in one. To the Japanese, a good location means being where all the biggest and oldest companies are located. That doesn't suit a lot of businesses (high-tech firms, for instance), and it may not suit your firm either. This is also true if you import into Japan, since it's possible that your clients will never visit your office. Further, the physical place may not need to be as impressive as it appears on paper. Parts of an address can in some cases be left out, or added, so try to present your business in the best way possible. It's better to look like you rent the building rather than a small room in it.

Rents in Japan are not only high, but a system of deposits and advance payments makes them exorbitant. There is a two-month or upward – as office space increases in size and price – payment of a refundable bond called *hoshōkin* or *shikikin*, plus a non-refundable payment called *reikin*. For larger office space, these may be replaced with a 4–12-month refundable deposit. Thus when you rent a place – apartment or office – you'll have to provide, up-front, your current month's rent, plus at least four months' more. For a small apartment in Tokyo or Yokohama, which would suffice as a minimalist office, you may be paying $700 or more per month. This means when you start renting, you'll have to provide at least $3500 up-front, $1400 of which is non-refundable and considered an outright payment to the landlord, $1400 of which is a bond which is technically refundable when you leave unless there is damage, but is rarely refunded in full and often not returned at all. Since Japanese landlords don't use the concept of 'reasonable wear and tear' from which you are exempted payment, you are liable for practically any variation on the original condition of the building.

Further, after every two years for apartments and after three years for offices, there is normally a rent renewal fee to be paid. This may be equivalent to two months' rent or more.

Hired help

Approaching a Japanese company on your own with a business proposition is not impossible, but without good language skills and an introduction neither is it advisable. Japanese firms want to feel comfortable in their dealings with you. If an introduction is not practical, and your only option is 'cold-calling', try working with a Japanese person, who will at least chat and be able to present your case in a more natural, relaxed manner.

The clearest explanation Japanese business people will understand is one that comes from another Japanese person. Whether as a partner or employee, someone who can communicate in writing as well as verbally, and is conversant with your product and your goals, is extremely useful.

Due to the bias in Japan against women developing careers, there is often a greater possibility of finding competent women than men. A woman may also appreciate the opportunity. Since many women stop work after marriage, they may be available for long-term part-time help; this means your assistant can develop a greater feeling and depth of knowledge, and provide a sense of continuity, both of which are good for relations with your customers.

There are two problem areas. Firstly, in most business spheres in Japan women are not taken as seriously as men. Accordingly, while there are some successful women in business in Japan, the percentage is quite low.[1] However, women may do well in business if they are seen to be competent. Secondly, many foreigners are now marrying Japanese, who also become business partners. Doing business with your spouse appears a logical and attractive approach, but for various reasons it may prove to be otherwise.[2]

Notes

1 A low 8.5 per cent of Japan's upper administrative and managerial positions are filled by women. This compares with 41.5 per cent in the USA (*Japan Statistical Yearbook*; *Facts and Figures of Japan*, Foreign Press Centre, 1995, p. 55, data for 1994 and 1992 respectively).
2 For instance: (1) Foreigners expect to rely on their spouse to interpret the Japanese environment, but find that their structuring and explanation of information does not live up to what they expect. (2) Relying on the same source of income can be unreasonably tough during the long climb into the Japanese market.

Chapter 11

In the market

Approaching large buyers

By the end of the 1980s Japan had become the ultimate target market for the world's manufacturers. Specifically, Japan's large department stores,[1] and especially those in Tokyo, became a thoroughfare for salespeople from around the world. However, most of them were nowhere near successful. All else aside, realistically, a retailer only has shelf space for a certain number of brands. So the first problem is that too many things were being forced into the same market. Second, large retailers were also offered many versions of the same product; they'd often *seen the product before* – sometimes exactly the same one, and this was particularly a problem amongst Japan's large department stores.

Indeed, one of the first points of contact for foreigners approaching the retail market in Japan is the department store; it's the obvious place through which to sell a product. Foreigners on a marketing junket are apt to find expensive products similar to theirs in a very large Japanese store and think, logically, that they could supply their own cheaper. They reason that they could supply product direct to the retailer, bypassing expensive distribution links – an opportunity clearly too good for either party to pass up. This sort of deal is possible, but for the most part it's unlikely. Typically, such attempts lead to rejection – often the foreigner cannot understand why.

In many cases, large retailers would shock exporters by telling them to present their ideas to one of the store's wholesalers or suppliers. This may appear to be an unreasonable response to the foreigner's perfectly rational proposal, but it is, instead, economically expedient. Such factors as time to devote to an individual enterprise mean such a project is better handled by a wholesaler, who is equipped to deal with individual exporters. Large stores don't want to expend energy initiating foreigners into the art of producing goods fit for Japan; they'll let a supplier do that. In such a high-volume business it's expedient to specialize in one task. Even if yours is 'too good an idea to pass up', it's still a good idea for a large store to let a wholesaler handle it.

Furthermore, while department stores started out handling their own merchandise, today they rent much of their floor space to independent businesses. The manager of one large department store I dealt with said it was embarrassing that they only owned 5 per cent of the goods in their store. This is possible in part because department stores are located on choice land; many of the newer department stores were created by railway companies in station buildings to attract passengers. A by-product was that people congregated around these areas, which eventually became prime locations. Older department stores had simply grown in prime areas. As land prices rose, both found themselves in a good position to capitalize on the increased value, collecting rents from others who would take the business risks.

Performing as a supplier

Not only is it difficult to get the opportunity to supply a large retailer, but, once in, it is difficult to stay there. If you are able to get product in, either directly to the store or via a wholesaler, then it is necessary to perform in accordance with the expectations of others involved. These requirements include such things as adjusting your deliveries to accommodate Japan's lack of storage space, providing in-store demonstrations or free samples, supplying in-store staff, upgrading your products and introducing new products.

Amongst those 'insiders' already supplying a retailer, there is tremendous competition. There is much more in-store involvement of suppliers at large and also small retail stores in Japan than the West. Suppliers see it as in their interest to present the product in the best possible way, and that means supplying resources, including staff. From the retailer's point of view, so long as a product is sold it doesn't matter whose product it is, so it's up to the supplier to push the sales as well.

Price busters

After the 1980s' bubble burst, sales at department stores dropped, making it more difficult to sell to them – 1992 signalled the first year-on-year decline in department store sales extending for more than two straight years. Meanwhile, sales at other chain stores continued to increase. Many consumers became cost-conscious and shifted to buying from discount retailers.

The problem of selling to discount stores is the importance they place on low price. They tend to either import from Asia or other low-cost sources, or at least bypass foreign intermediary sales people and find their own direct supply. This makes it difficult to market to them. It's expensive and difficult for manufacturers or producers to come to Japan and promote their own goods. And there is little incentive for an intermediary marketer or agent to promote goods to a cost-conscious buyer who prefers direct access to the foreign producer anyway.

The upshot is that the chance of a successful one-hit sale to a large outlet is low; a slow climb into the market is more realistic. As a result, many people have hit Japan anticipating a few one-off expenses, only to find that if they are successful it has required much more time, effort and budget than originally anticipated.

Sales to industry

Suppliers face slightly different requirements when marketing to industry as opposed to selling to consumers. However, the general points about struggling to become a supplier, and fighting to stay one, remain. In fact, some suppliers feel they must go to even greater lengths to strengthen and maintain ties with corporate buyers.

Pharmaceuticals

Medicine provides an interesting example. Doctors have the power to channel a lot of money from the public, government or hospitals to medical supply companies. For this reason they need to be buttered up, and the butter is applied in a uniquely Japanese style. This situation has meant that suppliers have resorted to 'extra-business' pleasantries to win favour. One pharmaceutical salesperson said to me, 'I can't remember how many doctors' wives I've taken shopping. . . . I used to take the son of one, who had a chronic ear problem, to a specialist each week. And at New Year [the rough equivalent of Christmas in the West] at 11.30pm I'd visit the homes of three doctors and take them gifts. .... In the West, Santa Claus, in Japan, pharmaceutical suppliers. . .'.

A pharmaceutical R&D worker from a different firm said 'there's a ranking. . ., going shopping is not as bad as some of the other things, like taking the dog for a walk, washing the doctor's car, or cleaning the bathroom and toilet'. (He makes a convincing scrubbing motion.) 'I did that sort of thing for two years as part of "learning the ropes" in the company. And, in the case of a woman doctor, if the salesman is young and nice looking, he might offer sex.'

And, incidentally, while these people were Japanese, their companies were not, they were large foreign drug firms in Japan. One problem with foreign firms is that the overseas head office doesn't have an appreciation of investing in 'entertainment' to get business results. The simplest form of gift is the monetary kickback – an immediate refund on the sale that goes to the doctor. But 'this happens much more in Japanese companies; foreign companies like ours have a tougher time because head office would never authorize that kind of expense. They would never understand a request for cash to be given to a doctor.' Also, 'In dealing with public hospitals, where the doctors are civil servants, especially nowadays the rules against bribery are strict, so pharmaceutical suppliers have to take special care. We would never give a cash refund to them directly – but we do have certain techniques. For example. . ., we would ask the doctor to write a report and then offer a compensation payment, and then submit the report. But . . . the report might only take five minutes. One took thirty seconds [he indicates a very small piece of paper]. So I would end up writing the real report myself.'

The ultimate goal of all of this is to present yourself as a friend or companion of the doctor, rather than someone with a 'cold' business association. Then, just as you do things for the doctor, the doctor will happily do things for you – buy your product. '. . .And part of developing a strong social relationship is taking them to play golf, to a restaurant, or taking them on a trip abroad. Personal relationships are very important.' In reference to the scandal that erupted around the top banks and the Ministry of Finance (MOF) in early 1998, part of which involved bank staff winning the favour of MOF bureaucrats by taking them to *'no-pants shabu shabu'* – eateries where the waitresses don't wear any underpants – the R&D worker says: 'It's a very good way to strengthen human relations. Doing something illegal or illegitimate together is very effective in building bonds between people. . . . It's a secret that remains between the two of you.'

Not only is it normal for suppliers to give doctors either money or other gifts, but it is not uncommon for patients to do the same, with amounts in both cases ranging into hundreds of dollars, depending on the capacity and needs of the giver and the reputation of the doctor. Patients see it as a type of assurance that they'll get the best service if they, via a gift, remain on good terms with the doctor. As for pharmaceutical firms, they are moving away from these practices, but traditions and doctors' expectations are not easily changed.

Purchasing power

The same applies on a slightly different scale in the case of suppliers of medical equipment. Doctors or university professors who have discretion over purchasing are rewarded in the kindest way for having the sense to choose one company's product over another.

Unfortunately for outsiders, supply channels to powerful customers tend to already be set. The stakes are so high that suppliers make sure that they remain suppliers by providing good service and incentives to their buyers.

For those wanting to achieve a position as a supplier to large or valuable customers, important factors include:

- a long history of service, and/or
- an introduction from a strong mutual associate, and/or
- for large companies, the employment of an *amakudari* ex-bureaucrat.

Ex-bureaucrat support was important in the early 1980s for pharmaceutical firms struggling to develop and switch to AIDS-safe blood products. With five ex-Ministry of Health and Welfare bureaucrats in senior executive positions, and another ex-bureaucrat, Dr Abe Takeshi, on its payroll, one company, Green Cross, which was lagging behind others in heat-treated blood-product research, was given time to catch up. The ludicrousness of this matter highlights well the advantages available to privileged insider-firms in Japan: as a result of this favouritism, the continued sale of unsafe blood products was actively encouraged. Consequently, thousands of haemophiliacs and other patients who were allowed to receive existing blood products were infected with the HIV virus. This illustrates the official or quasi-official support given to insiders in Japan, at the expense of outsiders and sometimes the public.

It's not easy to gain the coveted position of being an insider. There are anecdotes about people who eventually leave a stack of their business cards with the secretary of a potential client – each card representing a failed attempt to meet the person required, and, by implication, demonstrating the seller's perseverance. While in the West this would indicate that the salesperson didn't know when to take a hint and stop calling, in Japan it indicates commitment.

Obligations in the market

After-sales service and 'service'

Once your product has been accepted for sale on the Japanese market, it needs continued *value added* in order to maintain competitiveness. Your product needs not only ongoing additions in features, it also needs product support. You need to become a service provider.

As it is used in the Japanese language, the word *service* has lost much of its English meaning. It is often used to apply to a free gift supplied with the purchase, or an input of labour, such as fitting or installation. If you go to a bank and open an account, the bank may give you a gift such as a piggy-bank, a toy, or other novelty, probably along with a packet of tissues tastefully bearing their name. If you were to say, 'What is this?' they would reply, 'Service'.

Alternately, very small, traditional shops are good examples of service providers, since with a low turnover, and spare time, they can – or must – provide 'free' inputs of labour in order to differentiate themselves from larger stores. Offering installation with the purchase of electrical goods is an example.

Since there's no such thing as a free lunch, the cost of the service is built into the price. In economic terms, the existence of both service and after-sales service is possible because the consumer accepts paying a high price for goods. The comparative absence of these services in the West exists in part because Westerners tend to want goods at as low a price as possible, after which there is no financial room for the supplier to offer anything else.

When times are good, charging more to provide extra services works well, but in hard times, the perceived value of money, and the desire to keep it, increases. Accordingly, along with the economic downturn in Japan, no-frills and cash-and-carry outlets increased.

Budget-minded Western consumers have more often than Japanese weighed up the value of their labour against the savings from buying no-frills goods. They've decided that they can either do without the free gifts, or, with a little bit of effort, can provide any necessary extra labour input, such as assembly, or registration or follow-up service, themselves – cash being perceived in many cases as having a higher value than their own time and labour. Certain products in the West, though, such as computers and vehicles, often do have a warranty or tutorial allowance built into the cost. This is because if faced with problems with these products, most consumers, Japanese or Western, don't have the means to cope by themselves.

Regardless of fluctuations in the economy, after-sales service and service are an accepted part of business and are important to many Japanese consumers. Survey findings have shown that, given two equivalent products, a quarter of Japanese shoppers would avoid buying the foreign one. Alternately, only 1 per cent of shoppers would actively favour an imported item (this doesn't support the oft-held view that Japanese shoppers are crazy about foreign goods). The main reason given by those Japanese shoppers not choosing imports is problems with after-sales service.[2] Basically, Japanese don't want the hassle or risk of having something go wrong with their purchase.

There are three reasons why the system of service in Japan is viable:

- Retailers purchase gifts or labour at wholesale rates, which they then offer as service.
- Japanese consumers often want start-up and back-up assistance (service).
- Japanese aren't accustomed to handling assembly difficulties.

My local bicycle shop in Tokyo will paint a new owner's name, address and phone number on a bike purchased there, and arrange for it to be registered with the police. These are things that would be very difficult for a customer to do, but are easy for them. To physically get anywhere in Tokyo is time-consuming, and, with an unfamiliar registration process added to this, the cost of doing it oneself is high. Many foreigners accustomed to doing such things themselves give up after living in Japan because they realize that the time and effort involved are not worth it.

The latter of the above three reasons why providing service is sound practice relate to the character of the Japanese. Faced with foreign technology, the Japanese consumer can be fairly much at sea regarding use and operation.

An example is provided by the *nouveau riche*, who constituted a prominent consumer group until the bubble burst in the early 1990s. For this group in particular, certain things Western were novel and trendy, even if some held a somewhat traditional or non-wealth-orientated status in the West. Such things included purchase and appreciation of classic cars, classic musical instruments, antique furniture, paintings, jewellery, and wine. However, many such things were so new to all Japanese that they didn't know how to 'consume' or care for them. In these cases additional items included with the purchase – detailed instructions, and after-care or after-service – became important.

In the West, many consumers of these goods have a history of personal knowledge, and involvement with these items. A wine connoisseur doesn't need to get a free corkscrew and a book about wine, and a Jaguar enthusiast doesn't need a spare parts kit. For the Japanese, however, recreational leisure appeared as a new phenomenon.[3] Many who became involved in such activities had little idea of what to do. They needed (what they call) accessories, and start-up assistance. A good shop was one that could supply what they required to 'paddle their canoe'.

Indeed, virtually all canoe and kayak shops have or are associated with schools, and in the early 1990s there was a boom which filled these schools with novice customers. Customers were typically given package deals to learn, as well as have all their equipment supplied by the shop. All their needs were met with one-stop shopping.

A Westerner who believes s/he is helping by giving the customer a cheaper deal rather than being helpful may be considered to be supplying a cheap and inadequate product by Japanese standards.

I was told by the foreign manufacturer of an electric bathroom fitting who wanted to export to Japan that the company doesn't supply wall screws since different types of screw are required depending on the type of surface the product is to be attached to; it's better for customers to get them separately depending on the surface they have. This is completely opposite to the response made by Japanese suppliers in that type of situation. In such an event, Japanese supply multiple sets of different screw types. It's easier for customers to pay an extra ¥50 (50c) and throw away the unneeded ones than spend time going to a hardware shop to get the correct screws.

Do-it-yourself (DIY)

The third reason why it makes sense to provide service is that Japanese customers tend not to be so resourceful in *ad hoc* problem solving. Many Westerners avoid paying for a service by doing the job themselves, but many Japanese consumers lack the resources in not only hardware but also the ideas to do so.

This is something that foreigners living in Japan face on a daily basis. The following is a fairly typical example. I wanted to buy an electric adaptor (100V $\rightarrow$ 6V transformer) so I went to the local electronics retailer – a fairly large store. I knew the adaptor needed to produce 6V, and I knew that polarity was important (on some adaptors the centre output pole is positive, on some negative). The store attendant asked me what the product was and who the maker was. If they have this information, they can then locate or order one which they know will be correct. But I know this can take a long time and an original product might be twice the price of a substitute. Yet to talk to them about the voltage, etc. falls on quite deaf ears – a rhetoric that's almost surely followed by, 'Oh, yes . . . well, anyway, what is the product and who's the maker?' So, while we both have the same basic goal, we have completely conflicting approaches. Westerners are more used to thinking, 'Create something new out of what you have available'. By contrast, the Japanese are used to relying on an existing formula, and Japanese customers are of course also accustomed to this. What this means is that:

> DIY isn't accompanied by the same creative approach that it is in the West.

In the early 1990s do-it-yourself or DIY became popular, particularly amongst young people in Japan. This was partly the result of a desire to save cost, but at least when it began, before the downturn in the economy, the DIY trend reflected a bid to actually be different, to be somewhat creative. Since the concept involves a degree of personal input, customers could get some variety in, for instance, the furniture and household accessories they bought.

Do-it-yourself in the West normally involves buying from a shop which sells sheets of uncut timber, various bathroom pipes and fittings, or electrical parts – the stress being on cutting cost, and hoping you do the job properly, that is, not to botch it up and have to get a plumber or a builder in anyway. Though there are hardware shops throughout Japan, those which are involved in the DIY trend tend to stock pre-cut and measured items. Though pieces of various materials are sold individually, they tend to be cut to a certain variety of suitable lengths, many of which don't need further cutting and are easy to put together, but allow for a modicum of imagination.

Kit-sets

DIY products other than these are essentially 'take home and slot together'. For anyone who has sweated over assembly instructions and many inadequately described similar-looking parts, belonging to what was a perfectly functioning whole in the shop, you may have no fear in Japan. Kit-sets, since that's what much of the DIY concept in Japan adds up to, are very simple. This is because they have to be very simple. And rightly so.

A foreign engineer who produced a canoe in semi-kit-set form, imported to Japan by us, once told me that he normally saw assembly as a type of challenge. This was in response to me suggesting that I thought it was important to have very clear instructions. Manufacturers need to appreciate that most people want to take their new product home, plug it in and use it.

Part of supplying quality to Japan (or anywhere) is providing a trouble-free product for the customer. In the case of these items, if a Japanese customer couldn't fit them together easily, s/he would just think they weren't very good. Indeed, being unable to use them easily would be the result of an inability of the foreign supplier to empathize with the needs of Japanese buyers, who aren't very good at doing these things themselves.

Implicit guarantee

Generally speaking, if supplying Japan you should be prepared to be more responsive to problems, complaints and returns than would be normal in a Western country. Even when there's no specified product guarantee, there has commonly been an implicit guarantee, or the expectation that the supplier will deal with any problems the customer may have. This does depend on the type of product and where it was purchased. It especially applies when buying a well-known brand, from a well-reputed store, or from a small local dealer who has to ensure continued patronage.

What is considered an acceptable complaint or demand for service will vary. It is a matter of convention and common understanding, and, as in the West, there are grey areas where what is acceptable is defined or redefined between customer and supplier.

At the legal end is the Product Liability Law. Perhaps ironically, thinking of the consideration given to the Japanese customer under normal circumstances, Japan had lagged behind all other industrialized nations in offering and clearly defining legal protection for the consumer. Instead, legal responsibility to prove fault weighed upon the consumer, not the supplier. After having debated the issue for 20 years, on 1 July 1995 the law was changed to put more power in the hands of the consumer. Now suppliers are responsible for compensation when a defective product causes damage to life, body or property – a defective product is one which fails to safeguard against such damage under foreseeable use.

Consumer-friendly

In addition to responding to problems, as a supplier in Japan you should be prepared to go to greater lengths than you would at home in supplying *extra-contractual* customer support. One reason is that Japanese see a quality product as one that suits the customer. A foreign maker may not see anything wrong with the product – if it doesn't vary from its design, it has fulfilled quality requirements. Then it's up to the customer to decide whether it is suitable.

But most consumers in Japan don't have the investigative resources to carry out a pre-purchase analysis of a product. They expect to take it home and have it work perfectly. Not only won't they be happy if they get it home and it doesn't do what they expect, but they may return the product, and will never buy the same brand again.

Electronic products are a good example. Answer machines, video players and even telephones, nowadays, are sophisticated technological devices. Many Westerners feel that they are somehow incompetent if they can't operate such devices. Japanese people can't operate many of those features either, but when they find it hard to operate necessary functions they simply write off the machine as unsuitable and buy from a different maker next time. The reason is not important; the point is that clearly the product is not as good as a competitor's which doesn't fail.

Of course, there are examples in the West of after-sales supplier responsibility. But often, particularly in the US, the motivation is legal requirements that force suppliers to take responsibility. Moreover, consumers in the West are still blamed when they can't operate complex products. It is still common to hear: 'you can't blame the computer – it's a machine – the user hasn't operated it properly'. The responsibility in the West is still placed on the user for not being smart enough to use the product. This doesn't work in Japan. Japanese makers bend over backwards to cater to the consumer's needs. This concern for the consumer is what drives Japanese firms to make products 'user-friendly'.

There is little pretension amongst Japanese buyers to be product-literate; instead, greater emphasis is on the supplier to make sure buyers can use their products. Japanese makers even make otherwise boring instruction manuals easy to read by putting in cute cartoon pictures of the product with happy or sad faces to indicate what the user should or shouldn't do with the item. In short, the supplier takes the responsibility for product usability, not the consumer.

Technology for the consumer

Westerners tend to develop products or services that appear good from a production or technology-only standpoint, without focusing on the consumer. Video technology is an example; as mentioned earlier, it was invented in the US but was only used professionally until Sony began a development process that by 1995 had put consumer video players in three-quarters of Japanese homes. Ingenuity is only the start of the process – one that culminates in the satisfaction and ongoing patronage of the consumer.

Camera users had complained that auto-focus cameras produced blurred shots of moving targets. Manufacturers and retailers were selling what was, from a technological point of view, auto-focus, but was actually of limited use. Minolta 'redefined' auto-focus; it got hold of the same type of tracking technology available in US defence weapons systems and put it into one of its cameras so the camera could 'predict' the trajectory, and therefore take clearer shots of moving objects.[4] Instead of letting the existing technology define what is suitable for the consumer, the Japanese spin the idea around, letting consumer needs define what the technology should be.

Table 11.1 Not invented here: products developed in the US but commercialized by the Japanese – meaning a loss of export share to Japan by the early 1990s[5]

Product	Developer and date developed
Television	RCA, 1939
Transistor	Bell Labs, 1940s
Video tape recorder	Ampex Corp., 1956
Micro-circuitry	Texas Instruments, 1959

Damage and subsequent repair to the first Sony Walkmans were, in about two-thirds of cases, predictably the result of them being dropped. It would be easy to see this as simply the fault of the customer, but, seeing it as a design matter, Sony redesigned the case so it would be less likely to be dropped and, if so, less likely to be damaged. While this was successful, as Walkmans increasingly accompanied physical activity, the incidence of damage continued to increase. Sony responded with another redesign, using automotive body technology to make the units more damage-resistant.[6]

That Japanese manufacturers take responsibility to provide implicit guarantees and improve the suitability of products has had important implications for business. It's more cost-effective for a manufacturer to remove the weak points from a product than to have thousands of customers cope with them, leading to repairs and returns. Both Japan and the West have fostered their respective systems. Japan's manufacturers have shouldered the burden of looking after the customer in this way. In the West, the *customers* have had to be aware. When the two business cultures have met, it has been the Japanese system that has appealed to Western consumers. Western makers trying to satisfy Japanese customers have then had to go back to the drawing board to redesign and upgrade their products in order to achieve the performance that Japanese, and now Western, buyers have come to expect.

Buyer power

Returned goods

With the exception of a consignment sale agreement, or of legal requirements to stand behind their products, Western companies often distance themselves from ownership and from any obligation once the product is out of their hands. As discussed, enduring, trust relationships in the Japanese trading environment make this less of an issue.

One of the manifestations of this interplay in Japan is that unsold goods can often be returned from the retailer, through the wholesaler, and back to the manufacturer. Depending on those involved, this can be interpreted as healthy cooperation, or the domination of suppliers by retailers. At least, in economic terms it functions to keep difficult-to-sell goods off the shelves, and in the Japanese market, where turnover can be very high for a popular product, it is in the interests of those upstream to keep popular goods on the shelves.

Insufficient storage space in both large and small stores in Japan encourages the returns system. Clearance sales – as Westerners know them – to purge redundant stock haven't been common in Japan – though they became more accepted amid the 1990s recession.

Therefore, if not removed, poorly selling stock would clog the shelves and inhibit the sale of other products.

In traditional buying situations, where the retailer was small and had little capital, the wholesaler acted as financier. Wholesalers were not only in a better position to provide finance, but better positioned than small shops to absorb the effects of short-term sales irregularities. Part of financing involved taking responsibility for, and ownership of, the goods.

This situation still exists. Furthermore, since the retailer is not putting up cash, it has lower overheads in terms of risk and capital, and so doesn't need such a high margin on the sale. The wholesaler who is providing the service is entitled to a higher commission for doing so. This fits in with the general tenor of specialization, and a fair share of the pie for all, that exists in Japan.

One thing that appeals to many Japanese is Western antique jewellery, which led me into this business in the 1980s. The one-off nature of this market means items are bought *ad hoc* and then sold normally through small antique shops. In supplying antique jewellery to Japanese retailers, I was involved in three types of sales system.

First, there is the straightforward sale. Second, since this particular market is subject to changes in taste, some retailers want to reduce the risk of holding potentially unsaleable items. Since the retail position – where the product meets the Japanese customer – is a very strategic point, it is in the supplier's interest to work with these needs of the retailer, in this case by accepting returns of unsold stock. This is, however, predicated on the supplier's access to other avenues to dispose of returned goods without losing (too much) money. It is a matter of economics – the gains from selling to the retailers must be sufficiently in excess of any losses resulting from having to take back merchandise.

An important factor that differentiates Japan from Western countries in many of its markets is that a downstream buyer – in this case a retailer – is normally seen to be in a strong position. Therefore suppliers work hard to ensure both a high turnover at the retail level and to provide additional care and service for the buyer so that their position as suppliers is maintained. This means a lot of effort, even after the sale.

The third practice is the commission sale. Retailers wanting no risk may accept goods on the basis of payment if and when the goods sell. After the bubble burst, luxury spending in particular plummeted, and this practice became more popular. In the antique jewellery market, some retailers prefer a mixture of these three purchase systems. Some may be willing to buy some items outright, but only accept others if they can be returned.

Different economic and logistical demands are placed on the supplier and the retailer by different products. For this reason, the nature of the system of returning goods – in their entirety, for repair or upgrade or exchange, or for full or partial refund – depends on the particular industry. It of course depends on economics – nobody expects you to run at a loss. It's up to you to enter into a supply arrangement in a spirit of cooperation, and respond to the Japanese expectations of your after-sales role, mindful of your own economic needs.

Reliability of the supplier

If you are supplying a product to Japanese buyers, it is of course important to present yourself as a reliable supplier of quality products. Japanese let down by imported goods tend to respond that that's what you can expect, 'foreigners don't understand'. Any love relationship Japanese once had with anything exotic has been tempered. You have no room to manoeuvre, no room for error. You must be ready to jump, to replace goods perceived as not being good enough, and perhaps to change existing stock for a newer, more saleable model, possibly at your own expense. To not do so is simply to be uncompetitive. Virtually all of the foreign products sold in Japan will have been through this grist mill.

A small European company, working through the European Delegation, was successful in exporting marble to a Japanese company. But the owner got a phone call at 2.00 in the morning from Japan saying that the quality of a shipment that had arrived was inadequate. That the owner got on the plane to Japan to try to sort out the matter reassured the Japanese customers that they were dealing with someone they could trust, and proved to make their business relationship stronger. In this case the product, which varied slightly in colour from that originally agreed upon, did not have to be replaced, although having to do so is not uncommon in this type of situation.

The effort that you invest in Japan may even seem to fellow foreigners to be excessive, but that's the price suppliers pay for the privilege of remaining competitive in a potentially rewarding market.

Notes

1 Japan's major department stores include: Takashimaya, Mitsukoshi, Seibu, Daimaru, Marui, Isetan, Matsuzakaya, Hankyū, Tōkyū, Kintetsu and Sogō, with top sales figures roughly in that order. Japan's so-called large supermarkets, which carry a diverse range of goods – specifically Daiei, Itō-Yōkadō, Jusco, Mycal and Seiyū – all have sales (again in order) greater than even Takashimaya.

2 Most shoppers (72 per cent) were not discriminatory about the country of origin of goods. Other problems with imports, in order of frequency cited, were: uncertainty about safety; inferior quality/performance; wrong size; labelled in a foreign language; problems with durability. The survey is conducted randomly throughout Japan every two years. In 1994 n = 1502 effective responses (*The 6th Survey on Consumers' Awareness*, MIPRO, 1994, p. 11; *Penetrating the Japanese Market*, MIPRO, 1995, p. 6).

3 After becoming a rich nation, pressure from foreign nations for Japan to reduce work hours and increase its consumption triggered cuts in official work time, and encouraged a drive for Japan to import – that is, to reduce work output and to increase personal consumption. Examples of the effort made by government included PM Nakasone (1982–87) asking Japanese people to buy $100 worth of foreign goods, and PM Miyazawa (1991–93), who claimed he wanted to make Japan a lifestyle super-power. Surveys show leisure to be of increasing importance; between 1975 and 1994 the number of people seeing leisure as their top priority had more than doubled, to reach 35.3 per cent. Dining out, domestic travel/outings, driving, and then *karaoke* continue to rank as the top four Japanese leisure activities (*Japan Almanac*, 1996, p. 262).

4 Ohmae, 1990, pp. 256–57.

5 *Economic Survey of Japan 1991–1992*, Economic Planning Agency White Paper, 1992, p. 223.

6 Johansson and Nonaka, 1996, pp. 27–28.

Chapter 12

Marketing mechanisms

This chapter will deal with communicating the marketing message in Japan: from the consumer to the marketer in the form of research-based information, and from the marketer or manufacturer in the form of advertising and other promotion.

Many of the marketing mechanisms used in Japan are also common to other countries, though some of these have been interpreted and are used in Japan in a different way, and some are unique to Japan. These marketing tools may be divided into two forms:

- *Third party* research and promotional mechanisms involve activities handled by independent publishers or other firms. These include advertisements in newspapers, magazines, radio, TV and other electronic media.
- *In-house* mechanisms involve research or promotional activities and material that is generated and issued by the selling company. They include catalogues, flyers and other mail-outs. They also include such other forms of 'self-promotion' as articles written about a company, self-promotion on the Net, dispersion of *meishi* (business cards), New Year cards and the promotion of one's self or company at a PR level.

The use of these in Japan will be examined throughout the following chapters.

Marketing research

Marketing research[1] as a strategy for marketing didn't get under way in Japan until after World War II. Now, in terms of global money spent on marketing research, Japan's expenditure is equal to the UK's. Both spend 9 per cent of the world total; this is slightly less than Germany at 11 per cent, and more than France at 8 per cent. The US spends 36 per cent, and the European Union (including Germany and the UK) spends about 46 per cent.[2]

In fact, Japan's 9 per cent is rather low, considering that research in Japan is more expensive than in any other country. On average, it is about twice the cost of research in Western Europe, and 18 per cent higher than in the US.[3] It would therefore be expected that Japan spend much more on research than individual European nations. Further, comparing Japan's marketing research with advertising expenditure, Japan's 9 per cent of the world total on research compares poorly with its 16 per cent of world expenditure on advertising.

Indeed, Western marketing research came relatively late to Japan, and it is still treated with some apprehension. The idea of incorporating Western methods of research into marketing grew in the 1950s, and coincided with Japan's post-World War II growth. The line of attack amongst Japanese firms had been to keep throwing improved goods at the customer – and they were good at this. The Western approach had instead been to first find out what consumers wanted (i.e. through market research), then build products accordingly.[4]

Specific factors began to emerge that influenced the use of research in Japan. Consumers began to want more variety in the products they bought, and the flow into Japan of foreign culture meant a shorter product life-span and turn-around of fashion trends. In an increasingly competitive market, research was used in order to compete by helping to understand the wants of the consumer.

Of the Japanese marketing research that did take on a Western appearance, early research involved the collection of quantitative data. As a systematized and routine process it was, and remains, well suited to the organizational style of lower-rank employees in a Japanese company. Influenced by Western techniques, in the mid-1960s marketing research in Japan began a shift to qualitative research. From a statistical orientation it shifted to concern itself more with consumer motivational factors. Research firms accordingly began to shift from simple problem identification through data, to provide information and ways to solve problems. Marketing research companies in some quarters became expected to understand and interpret information about the market in order to provide proactive assistance for product planning.

Yet, despite the money that is spent in Japan on research, in many cases these concepts about research are based on traditional methods of interacting with the market. Many Japanese companies disregard Western marketing research, or they see its importance as overstated. And many who do use marketing research don't use it to make policy decisions, but to trigger more legwork in the market.[5]

While this may appear conservative, it is not without its advantages. Many Japanese managers believe they should remain in close contact with lower levels of their business. It is in part a reflection of the humble stance evident in other areas of business in Japan. There is a strong notion that it's improper that those at the top remain distinct from others. Managers should mix with others, and in doing so they will understand the market better. That Westerners need to do market research, in the view of many Japanese, indicates that Western management is aloof of the market. The Japanese response when they don't know what is happening with sales in their industry is to go out to the wholesale or retail level and find out.

One Japanese president of Toyota's sales subsidiary in the US, for instance, would visit every Toyota dealer there at least once a year. In doing so he found that five or six complaints out of ten could be attributed to misunderstandings, two or three could be solved on the spot, and just one or two needed extra work.[6]

The Japanese are fastidious information collectors, and by having a large body of staff to collate information – part of the 'excessive' workforce often criticized by Western managers – it is possible to create an accurate picture of the movement of products in the market. Often Japanese suppliers deploy staff either formally or informally to monitor activities at the retail level. As part of their training prior to being posted overseas, two junior staff I knew, of the Japanese agent for Bic, were sent to convenience stores around Tokyo for a period of months just to observe and gather information on product sales.

Such contact with the market as is illustrated by these examples provides a core of qualitative (and some quantitative) information useful for planning.

Western companies often don't have the staff to collect data and monitor the market, plus the cut-and-dried relationship that often exists between Western sellers and buyers means that once a sale is made each party keeps out of the other's domain.

Western forms of marketing analysis, however, are increasingly used by upcoming Japanese managers, many of whom have formally studied research techniques that were unavailable to their predecessors. Still, it would clearly be a mistake to equate modern market analysis with a superior methodology. In many cases where the Japanese have employed them, Western techniques have been used to supplement their own successful strategy.

Data collection

Japan shares with Western nations many methods of data collection, though there are some differences. One is the relatively low use of telephone surveys. In the US 45 per cent of *ad hoc* research money is spent on data collected over the phone, but in Japan it is only 8 per cent. This accompanies a general lack of trust within Japan of phone survey reliability. In part this is because of a lack of reliable databases. Expenditure on phone surveys in the UK and other European countries ranges between 20 and 30 per cent of their total.[7]

In the mid-1990s pre-recorded/automated telephone surveys began to appear in Japan. These were faster and cheaper than conventional phone research and it appeared that these advantages would result in an increase in the popularity of phone research. However, within a year or two they had disappeared. Low cost may have made them attractive to research firms, but the Japanese public simply didn't respond well to them.[8]

A relatively high one-fifth of Japan's *ad hoc* research expenditure goes into mail surveys. Expenditure on mail research by other nations is in single digits, with the exception of the US, at 14 per cent. Due to increases in mail-order material turning up in mailboxes, the response rate to surveys has decreased in Japan, meaning it has become more expensive to generate the same amount of data.

In both Japan and in other countries face-to-face interviews conducted at home have been the most common method of sourcing *ad hoc* data, accounting for over a third of the data collected. That is, with the exception of the US, in which home interviews account for about a tenth of the data collected. But changing Japanese attitudes toward privacy, and increased restrictions by local governments on access to information on residents – a traditional database – has made selection of samples difficult. Further, changing Japanese lifestyle patterns mean that people are less often at home. In 1986 two-thirds of Japan's *ad hoc* research data was collected through in-home and office surveys; by 1994 the rate had dropped to just over one third.[9]

Trade-level research

When, in 1986, Japan Market Resource Network (JMRN) was established, it introduced to the foreign entrant another means of understanding the market. JMRN first analyses data from secondary sources, including magazines, newspapers, trade journals and industry reports. This data is then supplemented by interviewing industry participants and observers in order to provide a well-rounded view of the overall market. JMRN specializes in providing information on consumer lifestyle products and services, including food, credit, healthcare and leisure. Its customers include firms involved in market entry, as well as established firms that want to monitor or expand in the Japanese market.[10]

In the words of JMRN president, Debbie Howard:

'Anyone who has read a translation of a Japanese-language report (or even just a newspaper article) might have noticed that those materials often lack the details that Western marketing professionals expect. But we provide those details. And we provide an understanding of the Japanese market from an industry marketing viewpoint – rather than a consumer research viewpoint – based on Western marketing standards.

'. . . A new market entrant needs to understand such basics for its product or products as market definition, size and growth rate, consumer and industry trends; it needs to understand major domestic and foreign players, market shares, pricing, and distribution alternatives. Also, for companies already marketing products in Japan, the same sort of research may be required when the environment shifts, such as when the economic bubble burst in the early '90s.'

Another useful contact is Trans-Pacific Productions, a Tokyo-based firm that provides a wide variety of services for foreign companies operating in Japan. TPPro is run by a couple of bilingual Americans with both foreign and Japanese staff. It designs and produces everything from company brochures, corporate logos and magazine advertising to bilingual Internet web-sites.

Co-founder and vice-president Jeff Klein comments,

'Localizing your company's image isn't just a matter of translating your old ads or brochures into Japanese. To win in this market you need to have the very best corporate communications tools you can get. And that means designing with Japanese customers in mind. All too often Western execs say, "Just take this ad we've been using in the States and put it into Japanese." Sometimes that works, but usually not. You have to think like the market thinks, appeal to your customers on their own terms, not try to educate them about Western ideas. And you still need to do it all on a reasonable budget. Our usual advice is to start with the best of your existing materials, and then build on them so that they have even greater appeal to Japanese clients.'

Klein summarizes the business this way: 'We create corporate communications tools that can enhance any company's image, and we advise our clients about which tools to develop and how best to employ them. In Japan, the consulting work is just as important as the creative, maybe more so.'[11]

On-line research

Developments in electronic media have opened new possibilities for getting information from the market. In 1998 NTT Data Corp., a subsidiary of NTT, Japan's largest and originally state-operated telephone service, developed an on-line data collection system to gather information on consumer food purchasing and usage. NTT Data, working with 35 other companies, including Japan's condiments giant, Kikkōman, put PCs in the homes of hundreds of families who type in purchase information as well as information on how they use ingredients in meals. Existing point-of-sale systems provided data on what left the store, giving information on which products did or didn't sell, but by tapping into food preparation and cooking habits within the home the firms involved believed they could also develop new products suited to the tastes of the consumer.

BMW Japan is an innovative company which, in the 1980s, worked its way up from nothing to develop a strong brand image that made BMW one of Japan's top selling imported cars. BMW has also made good use of information technology. In late 1997 BMW began an interactive web-site so it could gain regular Japanese consumer feedback, which would help it guide product development and advertising. And in order to streamline its activities, in 1988 it established an intranet system linking its dealers in order to allow them real-time access to promotional and other company information.

Advertising

A: *'Say, can't you give me a better price on this car?'*
B: *'Let me ask you this: do you use your seat belts when you drive?'*
A: *'What? Well, um, not really. . .'*
B: *'Okay, let's take them out. I'll cut the price by that amount!'*
A: *'Whaaaaut . . . ?'*

Voice-over: *Feel unsure when you don't have them?*
If so, be sure you use them properly. Seat belts by Takata.

Japanese radio advert for Takata seat belts[12]

As Japan's expenditure on research is low, so is its spending on advertising. Japan's ad expenditure doubled through the bubble expansion, from 1986–89. As a proportion of GNP it reached a peak of 1.3 per cent, which it held from 1988–91, before dropping away. But this figure was still low. It was almost half of the US ratio, which stood at 2.4 per cent of its 1989 GNP.[13]

Nevertheless, the Japanese advertising business and Japan's ad companies are anything but small; as we'll see soon, Japan's number one ad agency is the largest in the world. Also (due primarily to business related to the auto and information industries), in 1997, right in the middle of a recessionary economy, ad agency billings grew by 3.5 per cent over the preceding year, exceeding the previous peak, which was in 1991.

Ad agencies in Japan

Japanese advertising agencies evolved as space brokers. They originally specialized in a particular medium, within which they bought up advertising space and sold it. The close interpersonal relations that predominate in Japanese business helped strong ties develop between certain advertising agencies and corresponding media. Clients (that is, advertisers) continued to patronize certain ad agencies, even after the agencies gained ready access to all the various media.

This situation also suited the media companies. It was advantageous for them to have a guaranteed sale for their space. The best customers of the media were large ad agencies – heavy users who could afford to invest in forward purchases of bulk media space. These good customers became privileged customers and the big ad agencies got bigger.

While Japanese ad agencies took the role of brokering space or time, the clients themselves undertook much of the task of developing the marketing plan in-house. Japanese advertising involves a mix whereby the creative ad work is shared between ad agencies, the client and possibly a 'production' firm(s) which compete to handle design, copy, PR work and planning. This differs from the system prevalent in the West in which an ad agency handles all promotion.[14]

To those foreign firms entering Japan, the difference between the two systems had implications for both client confidentiality and the type of ads that were produced. Foreign companies have traditionally expected to readily share important data with their agency, combining their own and the ad agency's marketing information in order that the agency could produce a quality campaign. Foreign companies have therefore been reluctant to use the same ad agency as their competitors, fearing that competitors would gain access to their ideas and other information. Since Japanese advertisers have developed ad campaigns in-house, there has been less risk of ad agencies leaking information – in many cases agencies haven't done enough to be a business risk; that is why Dentsū, for instance, maintains it can successfully 'compartmentalize' client information.

Also, unaccustomed to organizing the ad campaign themselves, foreign firms needing to use several media have expected but been unable to gain a coordinated campaign strategy from Japanese ad agencies. Because of the limited role undertaken by Japanese agencies, some foreigners have interpreted them as incompetent. One commentator notes a client as saying '. . .I asked for an agency presentation. What I got was a courtesy call from ten people and a bowl of fruit.'[15] For Japanese ad agencies, used to providing only a space-broking function, the rest may be pleasantries associated with maintaining a good *jinmyaku*.

Foreign advertisers have, understandably, preferred to use Japan-based foreign rather than Japanese ad agencies. The primary reason for this choice, though, is language.[16] Discussing an intangible product such as advertising is difficult when working with someone you can't easily communicate with. Communication is easier with someone who shares your culture and language.

Change is happening. Japanese ad agencies are getting better at servicing foreign companies, and some Japanese clients have started to have their campaigns handled by one agency.

In a historic move, in 1992 Nissan broke with convention and decided to give the responsibility for all of its advertising to one agency, Hakuhōdō. Nissan claims this meant more efficient ad spending and a more coordinated campaign. Still, while ad agencies have been willing to take full control of their clients' accounts, on the whole clients have remained reluctant to sever ties with existing agencies. Well. . ., why *don't* more advertisers do what Nissan did? In part it's a matter of 'keeping in good' with others in the industry, if not because of an economic benefit down the line, because 'it's good to keep on good terms with the others'.

Dentsū, Inc.

Dentsū is the world's biggest advertising agency. However, in the mid-1980s a number of mergers and acquisitions resulted in various international groupings of agencies, which meant that in 1985 it was toppled by Young & Rubicam as the biggest advertising organization – as such, by 1996 it ranked fourth. In Japan Dentsū has over 20 per cent of the advertising market and is twice the size of Japan's second biggest agency, Hakuhōdō.

Table 12.1 Major advertising industry participant rankings

Advertisers/clients (top advertising spenders)	Advertising agencies market share (%)		Media
Toyota Motors	Dentsū	21.8	TV
Kaō Soap	Hakuhōdō	11.5	Newspapers
Nissan Motors	Tōkyū	3.2	Magazines
Matsushita Electric Industrial	Asatsu	3.1	Radio
Mitsubishi Motors	Daikō	2.8	Other media

Client rankings for 1995; agency rankings for 1996 (*Japan 1998 Marketing and Advertising Yearbook*, Dentsū; *The Nikkei Weekly*, 4 August 1997, p. 7).

Hakuhōdō is, in turn, over three times as large as each of Japan's third, fourth and fifth largest advertising firms, Tōkyū, Daiko and Asatsu (see Table 12.1). The strongest foreign advertising agency in Japan, ranked tenth in sales, is McCann-Erickson, a 100 per cent foreign-owned business after the dissolution of a joint venture it entered into with Hakuhōdō in 1960. At ¥72bn ($766mn) McCann-Erickson's 1995 sales equalled a paltry 6 per cent of Dentsū's.

Dentsū's power has grown from a combination of legitimate and illegitimate factors. It is common knowledge that it has abused the privilege of being Japan's top ad agency, and has created a reputation for illicit tactics. By pressuring the media it has controlled the release of news damaging to itself and its clients.[17] It is known to threaten to spread scandal unless it gains access to advertisers' accounts. And are foreigners exempt from these activities? In negotiations with a division president of American Express, Dentsū made the blatant threat that if American Express didn't use them, Dentsū would ensure that their firm failed in Japan.[18]

Advertising media

The media that attracts the greatest amount of Japanese advertising expenditure is TV at 33 per cent, then newspapers at 22 per cent and magazines at 7 per cent.[19]

Television

Japan's public sector TV is represented exclusively by NHK (Japan Broadcasting Corp.), the world's largest public broadcasting company. NHK has two conventional ground-based channels – one devoted to education – and is considered similar to Britain's BBC. Funded by fees collected from TV owners, it broadcasts no advertisements. It stands out in Japanese TV as having shows considered to represent culture, art and serious programming.

Private TV broadcasting in Japan was originally funded mainly by newspapers. Now terrestrial broadcasting is dominated by five newspaper-related, Tokyo-based stations. Consistent with Japanese business practice, these have developed strong intra-industry *keiretsu* structures of local stations that exchange services, including programming.[20] In 1995 there were 120 commercial TV companies operating terrestrial broadcasts, most associated with the five major stations. Not surprisingly, these five stations are also linked to Japan's major advertising agencies (see Table 12.2).

With satellite broadcasting, pressure grew for new TV services. In June 1996, News Corp. (owned by Australian media mogul Rupert Murdoch), and the Japanese software firm

Table 12.2 Links in the Japanese media

TV station	Newspaper	Advertising agency
Tokyo Broadcasting System (TBS)	Mainichi	Mainichi Advertising
Nippon Television Network (NTV)	Yomiuri	Yomiuri Agency
Fuji Television Network	Sankei	Fuji Sankei Ad Work
Asahi National Broadcasting	Asahi	Asahi Advertising
Television Tokyo	Nihon Keizai	Nihon Keizai Advertising

Softbank Corp., operated by Son Masayoshi, entered into a joint venture which bought into TV Asahi – the first major advance of foreign management into a Japanese network. It was a preparatory move on Murdoch's part to enter the conservative Japanese television arena. He planned to launch a digital satellite that within two years would provide at least 100 channels. The joint venture bought all of Ōbunsha Media Co. for ¥41.7bn ($383mn), providing it with the 21.4 per cent of TV Asahi shares held by Ōbunsha. Japan, like other countries, has been protective of its information media, but the purchase didn't infringe on Japan's (maximum 20 per cent) limit on foreign equity since only half the venture was foreign-owned.

While the Japanese public had been exposed to frequent market liberalization commitments, the announcement that the purchase was welcomed by the Minister of Posts and Telecommunications was surprising, as this time it was about a deal that was actually going through, and so came across as a genuine expression of reform. But all this was undone in March 1997, when Murdoch and Son sold their shares to TV Asahi's affiliate, Asahi Shimbun Publishing Co. What had happened was that initially Ōbunsha had offered the shares to Asahi Shimbun, but negotiations had broken down over price. Then Ōbunsha announced its sale to Murdoch–Son. This set off alarm bells within some areas of government, and in both Asahi Shimbun and TV Asahi, all afraid of the instability and lack of control brought about by heavy foreign involvement.

Asahi Shimbun rallied its *keiretsu* members, who pooled their shares in order to weaken Murdoch–Son's relative position, and it asked Murdoch–Son to sign an agreement saying that they wouldn't buy any more shares nor interfere in management. For their part, Murdoch–Son were dependent on TV Asahi to supply them with programmes and, using inability to secure programming as a reason, the Ministry of Posts and Telecommunications turned down some of their licence applications. Murdoch and Son decided to pursue their media ambitions in Japan by maintaining a slightly greater distance from, but by keeping positive relations with, Asahi, and re-sold their shares for the original purchase price. This example summarizes much about the traditional character of business in Japan, and shows that 'Japan Incorporated' is still alive and kicking as we move into the twenty-first century.

But things were changing, albeit in some areas more than others. As mentioned above, foreign stockholding in broadcasting firms had been limited to a maximum of 20 per cent. When Hitachi Ltd, which is 25 per cent foreign-owned, wanted to launch its own satellite TV network, HK Channel, providing special interest programmes dealing with such topics as education and medicine, it initially faced the same restriction. However, fortunately for Hitachi its plans coincided with the Posts and Telecommunications Ministry's relaxing of the foreign ownership rules. The Ministry redefined its terminology, now referring to such satellite operations as 'communication' rather than broadcasts, thereby allowing Hitachi to bypass the restriction and begin 'communications' in April 1998. Utilizing its existing skills as an electronics maker, Hitachi began working with Intel to produce innovative computer-based multimedia equipment – contributing to the move of the computer into the living room. Hitachi contributed to the HK Channel satellite project by providing ground-based operations equipment and in-home decoding hardware, while the project uses an existing satellite to relay between the two.

As seen on TV

Japanese TV commercials are normally short, only 15 seconds, leaving little time for much product information. TV advertising in Japan became very expensive, and since many of Japan's TV programmes are relatively slow-moving in-studio panel-discussion or quiz shows, advertisements are often designed to contrast by being punchy, active and delivering a quick message.[21]

Advertising on commercial Japanese TV is divided into *sponsored time* and *spot* advertising. Spot commercial rates have ranged up to ¥1mn ($8000) for a 15-second slot on the larger Tokyo-based stations. Time advertisers sponsor a programme, throughout which their commercials are aired, meaning the same commercial may appear with the same programme each week. In this way viewers may be linked to the product through a programme that draws a particular audience, rather than through a particular time slot.

Japanese programmes end with the sponsors' commercials, plus additional spot ads, before a switch to ads for the next programme. For longer programmes the sponsorship is divided, meaning the programme is punctuated with a break announcing a change of sponsors for the second half.

As mentioned earlier, Japanese are highly brand-conscious. The Japanese public equate brand names with quality, and, unlike contemporary advertising in the West, Japanese brands and corporate identities are still almost synonymous. It is a rare TV spot that does not prominently feature the company name – the ultimate guarantee of quality. Foreign companies in Japan that are experienced at creating 'brand equities', too, tend to follow the Japanese lead. For example, Pampers are made by P&G – and the name of the manufacturer is slipped in as a postscript at the end of the commercial.

There is a popular idea that the Japanese respond well to 'mood' advertising while Westerners respond to logic-based advertising. It is said that Japanese don't want to be bombarded with logic; they don't like strong arguments which pressure them to buy, or which compare and criticize competitor brands, and it is believed better to seduce them through imagery. It is true that Japanese advertising is not aggressive, and those accustomed to hard-sell promotion should avoid it, and though comparative advertising has appeared it is also deemed unsuitable. There are, however, clear examples of both image and logic-based ads in both Japanese and Western environments.

As just mentioned, the limits on screen-time due to cost boost the 'image' content of TV ads. Analyst Brian Moeran did a lengthy study of a Japanese ad agency in which he covered a promotional campaign for contact lenses. During extrapolated negotiations over the content of a TV ad, a push by the maker to include technical information about the lenses was ultimately overridden. Essentially, there wasn't enough time to fill the ad with too much detail. Instead, an image ad was opted for, in which a well-known personality was used to simply draw the attention of viewers to the product.

In Japan as elsewhere, the pull, in advertising, of a famous figure, whether there be any relation between that person and the product or not, is alive and well. There *was* a relation when 'Ringo Starr' advertised a brand of apple juice by the same name – *ringo* means apple in Japanese.

Moeran says, 'The [maker, NFC...] proceeded to enter deep and troubled waters by querying the use of images in advertising generally. Needless to say, this led to a fruitless argument over the rationality of persuasive strategies in advertising, with NFC calling for more logical propositions and cause–effect body copy, while the Agency's creative team counter-argued that advertising was neither rational nor logical, and that the strength of "soft hard" thus lay in its *not* being explained.'[22]

Other factors, however, influence Japanese advertising such that the imagery–logic dichotomy is not a reliable rule of thumb. Relevant factors include the type of product and whether it has any new or distinctive strengths.

Where there are identifiable merits, the same rationality in both Japan and in the West dictates that advertisements point these out. Where there are no relative merits, an advertisement has to deliver something else to the potential customer. Cigarette advertising is a good example; in both cultures 'atmosphere' or location are used to create a positive image.

Many of the Japanese are 'land-locked' in an urban jungle – almost half (44 per cent) live in the very built-up areas around the three cities, Tokyo, Osaka and Nagoya, and so tend to respond well to natural imagery and open scenery. In the process of trying to provide some competitive edge, especially in the bubble era, many companies produced very expensive 'on-location' advertisements in a variety of exotic sites. A lot of money was spent – in some cases 'money was no object' – on filming or photographing very short scenes in very far off places, with very non-Japanese looking models. During the cost-cutting recession of the 1990s advertising underwent a shift as many ads moved away from idyllic imagery and spoke to the real person in the street. They dealt with real people (and sometimes some famous people) dealing with a real family budget.[23]

Natural imagery is still a medium to catch the interest of most Japanese, and it may be one factor that foreign promoters – with access to breathtaking natural scenery from home – can use to tempt Japanese consumers.

TV ratings

In October 1994 the ratings firm Nielsen (Japan) caused a stir when it introduced a new TV ratings system called the Advanced People Meter (APM). The existing system for gauging viewer preferences used data fed from 775 Japanese households. But it was limited in that it aggregated 'household' member viewing. Extra information gathered through diaries also lacked accuracy because these relied on viewer memory and were only filled in two weeks in four.

Nielsen in the US had come up with a device called the People Meter to automate ratings work, improving ease of use, speed and amount of data collected, as well as accuracy. In Japan they went one step further, with what they called the Advanced People Meter. Nielsen's system incorporates a unit placed on the TV. Viewers push buttons on a modified remote control, and this tells Nielsen who is watching what programmes, allowing age and gender information to be monitored. One might think such an innovation would be welcomed, after all, it leads to more accurate data, but there was strong reaction against it.

One of three groups opposing the system was Japan's other ratings firm, Video Research (VR). Although Nielsen is the world's biggest ratings firm and was the first to set up in Japan, VR rose to become Japan's main ratings provider, holding 97 per cent of the market by the late 1990s. It was able to do this because it was supported by vested interests within the TV industry, as well as by its main clients, who also happened to be the other two parties that came out against the system: Dentsū and Hakuhōdō.

In the West one might expect that a ratings agency should be independent in order to provide objective, accurate data, but VR is not. It was created by Dentsū in 1962, the year after Nielsen initiated TV ratings in Japan. Its shares are held by other major advertising firms, including Dentsū (37 per cent) and Hakuhōdō (6 per cent) and by Japan's major TV stations – TBS, Nippon TV and Fuji TV, each with 6 per cent – and other TV stations. Dentsū and the TV stations also supply VR with executives and a president. Upshot: It's too easy for firms that make money out of 'the public's' evaluation of TV content (TV stations) or firms financially connected to those making that money (Dentsū, etc.) to create the results they want if they have exclusive control over the research data. And indeed Dentsū has been known to influence the interpretation of data.[24]

According to one industry insider:

'Most people in the industry are suspicious of Video Research. It's very easy for Video Research to change their data. It's very easy. And there are some rumours in the Kansai [Osaka–Kōbe–Kyōto] area. In one case there was a very, very famous production house for the TV industry which had a very close relationship with Dentsū. This company's top management talked with the top management of Dentsū about changing the data – TV data. And finally they did. But no one could prove it because actually in the Kansai area, Video Research is now the only research company – a few years ago Nielsen also collected that kind of data in the Kansai area. In Kantō [the Greater Tokyo area] if people are suspicious of Video Research's information it's easy to use Nielsen's data in order to check, but not in the Kansai.'

It was the TV stations that objected most to the technology. This was because of the strong relations they had with their existing, stable suppliers of programmes and advertising. They didn't want the inevitable disruption accompanying the revelation of who was (or was not) watching the endless line-up of repetitious game/humour shows that almost dominate Japan's commercial TV. One reason for the predominance of these shows is that the ratings system averaged viewer tastes. Unable to differentiate age and sex preferences, programming and advertising has been based on a common denominator, which is 'family entertainment'. In a typically Japanese response, one reason the TV industry gave for resisting Nielsen's improved technology was that channelling programmes to specific age/sex audiences would 'destroy TV's role in keeping families together'.

Nielsen and the advertisers – supporting the new technology – began extended negotiations in 1994 with the stations, ad agencies and VR in order to reach a consensus. Why the need for a consensus? After all, Nielsen's system was up and running. Indeed, in the West there would be no need – this is a Japanese response. It's considered appropriate for all involved to have a chance to have their needs met, which may mean the dominant party compromising its plan – it's not unlike the way a family might settle such an issue. Also, in a more practical sense, they needed to appease all parties because, for instance, following the introduction of Nielsen's machine, its customers (the TV stations) slashed their purchases of Nielsen's data. There is a need for harmony.

But despite the conclusion of the talks in 1996, whereby an agreement was reached that the new technology be accepted, the TV stations were not happy. The real problem in this case was that the matter didn't lend itself to a compromise.

As an example of the problem encountered by the stations, see Figure 12.1. The top line of the graph shows aggregate *household* viewing of the women's marathon for 1994. At that point, cosmetics giant Shiseidō had sponsored this event on Asahi TV for 15 years. In 1994 Nielsen's APM provided the data represented by the lower three lines. These show three age categories of women viewers. The upper represents a strong viewing audience of women over 50. The second line shows women of 35–49, but the high-spending category is represented by the few viewers at the bottom (18–34 years), which was also the audience Shiseidō's advertising had targeted for the last 15 years. Asahi TV's initial reaction was that the data shouldn't be released. Though this data had been around since 1994, it was only available for general inspection from June 1996, when the parties produced their final report on the technology that generated the data.

Rather than pull its advertising, Shiseidō changed the product range it promoted to better suit the older audience.

Video Research did soon bring out its own version of an automated meter, but Nielsen believes it has the jump on VR and can keep ahead in technology updates. Furthermore, Japanese companies, and ad agencies with them, are internationalizing. Dentsū won't have the same advantages internationally that it has domestically: it won't be able to rely on the support of a network of those in the industry linked or subordinate to it. And Nielsen, as a data provider, will become more attractive to those Japanese companies

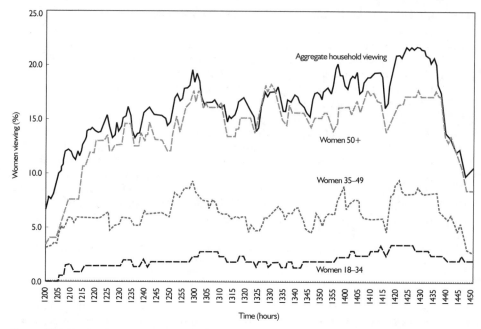

Figure 12.1 Viewing figures for the annual women's marathon

expanding overseas, since Nielsen will be able to offer a more thorough international service than the Dentsū–VR model. This, believes Nielsen, will help it win back its market share in Japan as Japanese companies begin to look for service providers with international reach.[25]

Newspapers

Japan is often described as a homogeneous society, with homogeneous views. Japan's mass media, including its newspapers, helps to reinforce this.

All five major Japanese daily newspapers are nationals. Japan's *per capita* readership is 578 copies per 1000 people, meaning just over one paper is shared between every two people. Of larger nations, Japan's readership is second only to the former East Germany, at 585. The former USSR follows Japan, with 15 per cent less readership; the US is well back, with fewer than half Japan's readership.[26]

Japan's population believes that it is relatively classless,[27] and because it doesn't harbour a strong plurality of values, the same papers are acceptable to and are bought by virtually the whole population. The same messages reach virtually everybody. For better or worse, this leads to an incestuousness of ideas.[28]

Japan's total newspaper circulation is the largest in the world. This is in part due to the system of home delivery which, ensuring consistent deliveries, accounts for 93 per cent of sales. If placed one on top of another, all the newspapers printed in one day in Japan would be ten times the height of Mt Fuji.[29]

Japan's two top newspapers each have a daily circulation higher than any other in the world, and only Germany's *Bild* prevents Japan claiming the top three positions (see Table 12.3).[30]

Table 12.3 Daily newspaper circulation (millions)

Japanese		Foreign	
Yomiuri Shimbun	(10.0)	*Bild* (Germany)	(5.6)
Asahi Shimbun	(8.3)	*The Daily Mirror* (UK)	(2.6)
Mainichi Shimbun	(4.0)	*USA Today*	(1.5)
		The New York Times	(1.1)

Japanese figures include the morning editions only

There are two other national dailies, the *Nihon Keizai Shimbun* and the *Sankei Shimbun*. The *Nihon Keizai Shimbun* (circulation 2.9 million) is a daily targeted at business people.

The *Nihon Keizai Shimbun*'s English counterpart, *The Nikkei Weekly*, is suited to English-speaking business people. There are also four daily English newspapers: *The Japan Times*; *The Daily Yomiuri*; *Mainichi Daily News*; and *Asahi Evening News*. A full-page ad in the English dailies costs between ¥2,100,000 and ¥2,400,000 ($16,000 and 19,000); *The Japan Times* is the most expensive, while a full page in *The Nikkei Weekly* costs around ¥780,000 ($6000).[31]

Magazine advertising

Over the years, as a proportion of all advertising expenditure, that committed to Japanese newspaper and radio advertising has consistently dropped. By the mid-1990s the share for newspapers had dropped to almost half of its 1960 figure. And while TV has been relatively steady, hovering at about a third of all ad spending, the share absorbed by magazines has gradually increased.[32]

Japanese magazines serve as an excellent vehicle for communion on hobbies and interests. Despite Japan's cultural isolation and homogeneity, Japanese people undertake a diverse range of sometimes quite specific activities. Indeed, from a promotional viewpoint Japan has the world's best combination of a highly concentrated, literate population with a high disposable income, many of whom pursue very specific interests. Those whole-heartedly committed to such interests are referred to as *mānia* – derived from the English word *maniac* – meaning they are crazy about their sport or hobby, and many of Japan's magazines are targeted to such readerships.

In 1995 about 200 new magazines were introduced, and though the life of magazines is often short, it was a 30 per cent increase on new issues launched the previous year. Notable amongst the new start-ups were computing magazines; in 1995 these accounted for about 15 per cent of new titles.

Women's magazines are excellent conduits through which to directly influence fashion, or to otherwise reach an audience, through advertising. In many ways fashion in Japan is less left up to the individual and is dictated by external factors such as brand name, popularity abroad, and exposure through various media. Accordingly, women's magazines featuring 'international' fashion are orientated to the passive consumption of global trends and issues rather than reader interest in them.[33] In other words, Japanese – in this case, women – are vulnerable to product publicity. In August 1988 the magazine *Hanako* ran a feature on where to get the best value Chanel cosmetics, as a result of which Hong Kong stores were stripped of their stock in days. The same magazine a year later ran an article on slick British restaurants, which caused a flow of magazine-bearing Japanese women, dubbed 'Hanakos' (after the name of the magazine) by London waiters.[34]

The costs of a full inside page advertisement in a magazine ranges up to ¥800,000 ($6200) for a weekly or a women's weekly magazine; up to ¥740,000 ($5700) for a monthly; and up to ¥1,180,000 ($9000) for a women's monthly.[35]

In addition to magazines, there are industry-specific trade newspapers and journals. These have a smaller circulation but are targeted to specific industry participants. Advertising rates for these publications are normally much lower than for magazines. These publications are normally not handled by an advertising agency; many are published by small firms that produce one publication and would deal directly, and often gladly, with the advertiser. As is the case in other areas of Japanese business, it is often easier to strike up a good relationship with a small company than a large one. These small publishing firms may be difficult to locate, but are likely to be easy and more pleasant to work with in the long term.

Whether you're involved in small or big business, you can gain effective free advertising by having articles about your product or service printed in magazines related to your industry. Depending on the industry, editors may be willing to insert a story and photos if you can come up with something that is interesting. In many cases a foreign product is either unique or there is something unusual about its background, and it is stories detailing this type of information that will catch readers' attention. This can then build interest in a product.

Getting friendly with reporters or editors is relatively easy – at least if compared to the time and the effort needed to establish business links with those in client companies in Japan. Therefore, cultivating your friendship with these people may give you good value for money.

If possible, it's better to provide a story to a reporter or editor with at least the details already written in Japanese, since it is unlikely that reporters will have good English communication skills, and they are often pressed for time. However, if what you have is interesting, you may be able to strike some sort of compromise.

Multimedia

Multimedia is an area which involves and therefore brings together otherwise disparate industrial sectors, including broadcasting, telecommunications, advertising and software development. Seeing imminent growth, Japanese investors from this variety of fields began to get involved in on-line media. In 1988 Nifty Serve, which became a long-standing top Internet service provider, began a computer shopping service, with orders placed either by phone or via the computer. By 1994 6 per cent of Japanese companies involved in direct marketing had used the Internet to accept orders.[36]

Nifty Serve is a product of Nifty Corp., which is in turn backed by the *sōgō shōsha* Nisshō Iwai and the electronics firm Fujitsū. Another large company to invest in media services was the newspaper company Asahi – involved with *Asahi Net* and *People*, both are Japanese on-line servers. Even the ad agency Hakuhōdō became involved in the production of game machine software on CD. Games software started to include advertising in order to defray the costs of development. By mid-1995 Hakuhōdō had produced three game CDs, and, while these contained no advertising, Hakuhōdō planned to get into the games market, anticipating the lucrative advertising business that would piggy-back on the CDs.[37] In the mid-1990s Dentsū began planning a combined news–shopping format, to be accessible through an on-line service. Other ad agencies began pursuing variations of the same course by combining advertising and shopping services.

Personal computers

PCs are not as common amongst Japanese as amongst those in other industrialized countries. In 1994, *per capita* ownership put Japan seventh internationally, with Americans topping the list by far.[38] While the PC diffusion rate (household ownership) in Japan reached 25 per cent in 1998, by 1995 the US rate had already reached 40 per cent.[39] This slow take-off is in part but not completely due to language problems. Because Japan traditionally hasn't relied on the alphabetic language system, people have been less familiar with typewriters. Japan did, however, launch early on into laptop-style Chinese *kanji*-character word processors, which substituted to a large extent for PCs. Still, it's notable, for instance, that Hitachi, though not one of the top PC makers, had been a top computer manufacturer for many years, but only began using computers itself in 1993.

Amongst Japan's small and medium-sized businesses, by 1997 under a third were not yet computerized and a fifth were just starting to become involved with computers. The other half considered themselves to be 'efficiency building' or better. Of that half, 5 per cent were at a level of strategic use.[40]

It's understandable that small companies should be at various stages of computer usage, but Japan's government and other large bureaucracies, renowned for having desk-high mountains of paper cluttering the floors of their offices, took until the mid-1990s to wean themselves off documentation and begin to install computers. There is a sort of technological quirk to all this: despite the nation's well-known prowess at manufacturing technology, and the abundance of consumer electronics goods spilling out of stores, as late as the mid-1990s such organizations were still conveying the essential information of the nation on black dial-telephones, or running copies of documents between departments or ministries via armies of young employees drafted as gophers.

The Internet

Internet use was slower to take root in Japan than elsewhere, partly because it is an English language-based system, partly also because it's based around computer use. However, the Internet quickly grew in popularity in Japan. In 1994, in total number of Internet hosts, Japan ranked sixth in the world, but it took it just two years to reach second place, behind the US.[41]

Internet user characteristics are similar in Japan to those in other countries. Initially most Japanese Internet users were in their early 20s, with usage progressively dropping away into the 30s age group. Over time, however, the spread became flatter, as a wider range of people got to know the Net. Engineers initially comprised the single largest category of Net user, with students also becoming prime users, but their predominance diminished as others, including sales and other business people, began to use the Net. The prime locations from which Internet access was gained were the office and school; however, home users had increased their relative share to almost 60 per cent by 1998.

Once on the Internet, Japanese users are hooked. By 1998, 80 per cent of Internet users connected to the Net five or more days a week, with very few connecting less than once or twice a week.[42]

Meeting the Japanese consumer on the Web

Japan's main Net shoppers have been technical users – with computer-related hardware and software merchants making relatively strong sales. However, innovative uses have been made of the Net as a marketing tool.

Nissan, in a sense, took the Net to the customer. In addition to selling new models of existing vehicles over the Net, in 1998 Nissan began providing free three-year Internet server subscriptions to customers who bought selected Nissan models, with plans to eventually extend the service to all of its customers. At a cost to Nissan of about $100 annually per customer to provide the Internet service, Nissan sees the system as far more cost-effective than conventional promotion and sales. In Japan a lot of car sales are made by personal visits to existing customers. This means not only repeated communication with the customer, but a lot of footwork, with the dealer calling on the customer perhaps several times in the course of a sale. Neither is the concept of indirect purchases of cars alien to Japanese buyers, who are accustomed to ordering vehicles by using a brochure, without actually seeing their car until delivery. Nissan also sees the Internet as useful for sending customers inspection reminders as well as promotional information by e-mail. Maintaining positive contact with customers, as a form of after-sales service, is very important in Japan, where securing customer loyalty means repeat orders in future. The Internet and related services have also provided opportunities for foreigners as a means of advertising or of selling – in cars, the American company Auto-By-Tel, for instance, has also entered Japan, retailing cars over the Net.

The Net of course opens up other opportunities for foreigners, but establishing a presence on the Net in Japan requires specialist assistance. CyberSpace Japan (CSJ) and LINC Media are Net service providers who will, amongst other things, set up a Japanese language home page and links to that page for foreign firms. According to Hosoe Harumi of CyberSpace Japan, it's important to communicate with Japanese clients in Japanese in order to convey quickly at least the main features, if not the specifics, of your service. And once the home page has been established, it's important to keep updating it.[43]

LINC Media was created by Terrie Lloyd as LINC Japan Ltd in 1983, an advertising and publishing company. One of its initial projects was *Computing Japan*, still the only English-language computer magazine dealing with the Japanese market, which by 1996 was reaching over 60,000 readers in the Asian–Pacific region.

'LINC's second major track, systems integration', says Terrie, 'became a company called LINC Computer which we established in 1990 – it grew at an average 90 per cent a year for six years. The company eventually became large enough that we sold it to the American computer services giant EDS, for a seven-figure sum, equal to 40 times its share value.'

The remaining wing of the business, LINC Media, continues to publish, as well as offer, Internet systems integration and design services. On establishing a web-site, an executive of LINC says:

'The biggest challenge we face in creating a web-site is a lack of understanding of what it takes to get a site up. This is regardless of whether the client is Japanese or foreign.

'The best reason for having a web-site developed for the Japanese market is that a company can gather valuable marketing data without having to be on the ground in Japan. Cost is a factor; while it will cost a start-up business, maybe, $1 million to get off the ground in Japan, a reasonable web-site starts at $10,000. As an example of what a web-site can do: surfboards are much cheaper in Australia than Japan, but Japanese surfers want shorter boards that are more suited to the size of the waves in Japan. If a surfboard manufacturer has a site up in Japanese, they are able to start a dialogue with potential clients on what type of boards the Japanese are looking for. Of course this type of research depends on whether the manufacturer has in-house Japanese skills or good mechanical translation software.

'Foreign companies continually make the mistake of marketing to the Japanese in English and then wonder why they are getting a poor response. In fact companies still set up in Japan, and start off by sending their brochures and promotional material in English to Japanese clients. This is both a waste of time and money. The Japanese are very sensitive and consider themselves to be different or special in their demands and tastes. To succeed in this market companies must address this and develop web-sites and other promotional materials in Japanese. Japanese are looking for foreign products on-line and will buy on-line if catered to in the fashion they need: IN JAPANESE.'[44]

Trade fairs

Back down to earth: trade fairs are also useful meeting grounds, but, consistent with the importance of long-term relationships in Japanese business, they normally do not provide the on-the-spot deals that Westerners sometimes expect. A first-time trade fair in Japan for a new export company is at best a PR exercise. It provides an opportunity for buyers to start to gain trust in you and to get to know your product. After seeing your company at a show and perhaps in a magazine, they will start to see you as a serious market entrant. Ultimately, when they meet you in their office, rightly or wrongly they'll give you and your product more credit on the basis of familiarity.

There are between 400 and 500 trade fairs and exhibitions in Japan each year, about a third of them are in Tokyo. Most are held when Japan's new products are released, in autumn and spring. More visitors will attend at that time since the weather is relatively comfortable. The best source of trade fair information is JETRO. They have lists of fairs, and should be able to provide you with lists of Japanese firms in your industry that you can contact.

Prior to participating in a trade fair it is a good idea to make written invitations to companies you think may be potential customers. Tell them that you are attending the fair, and that you would like to see them there. In this introduction you disclose a piece of your company's personality as well. The letter should not be abrupt, but should express a formal yet personal desire to have the company attend. Any such letter should of course have a slightly humble tone, rather than display the confidence often involved in marketing in the West. Express deference rather than dominance.

Specific points about participating in trade fairs in Japan:

- Japanese promoters at trade fairs often stand back and wait for customers. This is common in Japanese retailing; however, the trade fair is perhaps the one opportunity in which it's acceptable to be proactive and solicit passers-by. This, though, should of course be done in a polite manner and not aggressively.
- The major error made by foreign participants in trade fairs in Japan is lack of advance preparation.
- Prepare catalogues, other information, and, if possible, samples. Japanese expect more of these than are given at Western trade fairs (see Appendix for companies that can help with this).

Setting up and operating a display is normally more difficult than people expect, even in their own local area. The problems are compounded when the physical distances and cultural differences of trying to set one up overseas, especially in Japan, are added.

In Japan there's no way to hasten things. Since there are so many people, in many situations you just have to wait your turn. Neither transportation of goods nor people can be speeded up simply because you're in a hurry and any delay will, instead, be accentuated by the fact that you are in a foreign and unfamiliar environment. Make sure you allow a lot of extra time for things to go wrong, and allow for setting up to take much longer than expected.

Notes

1 Marketing research covers a broader range of activities than market research.
2 ESOMAR, Market Research Industry Trend Report, data for 1996.
3 In *The Nikkei Weekly*, 22 April 1996, pp. 18–20.

4 Robert Wilk, managing director of Marplan Japan, 1987, in *Taking on Japan*, Look Japan, 1987, p. 13; my interview with Chris Fay of McCann-Erickson, Japan, 11 June 1996.

5 See, for instance, Johansson, K. and Nonaka, I., in Durlabhji and Marks, 1993, p. 293.

6 Johansson, K. and Nonaka, I., in Durlabhji and Marks, 1993, pp. 291–92.

7 Japan Marketing Research Association.

8 This is the view of the Japan Marketing Research Association, interview, 1998.

9 Japan Market Research Association statistics, 1998; *The Nikkei Weekly*, 22 April 1996, pp. 18–20.

10 Reports available from JMRN range from regular monthly monitoring reports, starting at ¥450,000 ($3460), to complete market overviews, which include both analysis of secondary research and industry interviews, at about ¥1,700,000 ($13,000). A typical market overview is approximately 60 pages in length, and includes individual interview summaries.

11 See the Appendix for details of TPPro.

12 Source: *Japan 1998 Marketing and Advertising Yearbook*, Dentsū.

13 *US and Japan in Figures II*, JETRO, 1992, p. 102; *US and Japan in Figures IV*, JETRO, 1995, p. 86.

14 Particular thanks to Ōshima Miyuki for information on this topic. Miyuki is a freelance advertising producer; her details appear in the Appendix.

15 Huddleston, 1990, p. 173.

16 Huddleston, 1990, p. 169.

17 See, for instance, van Wolferen, 1993, p. 234.

18 Huddleston, 1990, p. 171.

19 *Japan 1998 Marketing and Advertising Yearbook*, Dentsū, p. 97, figures for 1996.

20 Ohsono, 1995, pp. 205–07.

21 My interview with Chris Fay of McCann-Erickson, Japan, June 1996; Moeran (1996, see p. 235) does a convincing job of demonstrating some of these points in his thorough case study of the ad business.

22 Moeran, 1996, p. 149 (italics his).

23 *Japan 1996 Marketing and Advertising Yearbook*, Dentsū, p. 201.

24 See, for instance, van Wolferen, 1993, pp. 233–34 and 505.

25 I'm grateful to Saitō Mikio of Nielsen for much of the information on this topic.

26 *Japan's Mass Media*, Foreign Press Centre, 1994, pp. 15–19.

27 Surveys are produced occasionally that show that Japanese overwhelmingly see themselves as 'middle class'.

28 Japanese people may say, for instance, that the *Asahi* newspaper is strongly left-wing. From a Western point of view, it might be best described as simply being slightly provocative.

29 *Japan 1991 Marketing and Advertising Yearbook*, Dentsū, pp. 90–91.

30 *Japan Almanac*, 1998, p. 265; *Facts and Figures of Japan*, Foreign Press Centre, 1995, p. 95.

31 *Japan 1996 Marketing and Advertising Yearbook*, Dentsū.

32 *Japan's Mass Media*, Foreign Press Centre, 1994, pp. 24–25.

33 See *The Nikkei Weekly*, 3 June 1996, p. 1.

34 *Far Eastern Economic Review*, 5 May 1994, p. 63.

35 *Japan 1996 Marketing and Advertising Yearbook*, Dentsū.

36 *Direct Marketing in Japan*, JADMA, 1996, p. 22.

37 *Tokyo Business Today*, July 1995, pp. 10–11.

38 Japan was behind the US, New Zealand, France, Singapore, the UK and Germany, in that order (*Japan 1997*, Keizai Kōhō Centre, 1997, p. 35).

39 *Japan 1999*, Keizai Kōhō Centre, 1999, p. 102; *Japan 1996 Marketing and Advertising Yearbook*, Dentsū, p. 134.

40 *Small Business in Japan*, MITI, 1997, p. 176.

41 *Japan* [various years], Keizai Kōhō Centre.

42 CyberSpace Japan Inc. supplies data on the Net and can be accessed on home page: www.cjs.co.jp.

43 Interview with Hosoe Harumi of CyberSpace Japan, 1998.

44 Interview with Terrie Lloyd and Simon Laight of LINC Media, 1998.

Chapter 13

Marketing – the Japanese way

As indicated above, marketing and marketing research in Japan are a mixture of both Western and Japanese business approaches – in reality, it is impossible to pull these apart. Furthermore, as Japanese marketing and management students go through programmes that are more and more Western in nature, the edges will be further blurred.

There are, however, concepts and ways of interacting with the market that are essentially Japanese – as fundamental as shaking hands and saying '. . . but, call me Jack' is to many foreigners. Because these are basic to Japanese business people, they are important marketing tools and they should be understood by foreigners entering the Japanese market.

A few points of culture

That a lot of Japanese business is dependent, not on the forcefulness of the individual, but on how much favour s/he can engender, is reflected in a lot of the business practices identified as typically or exclusively Japanese.

Yoroshiku

The word *yoroshiku* is quite common in Japanese. It is used often in business, and carries the connotation of 'please take care of me', or 'look after my interests'. It connotes the speaker putting him/herself at the mercy of the other; it is a fundamental Japanese concept which, naturally, also has a real place in Japanese business. Outside of business, *yoroshiku* is simply considered one of many Japanese greetings, though even there it carries the legacy or essence of this meaning.

Yoroshiku is normally first used when handing over a *meishi* (business card), which is done when meeting someone for the first time. It is also used throughout a business relationship, particularly at the end of visits and phone calls, as a way of saying something more than just 'goodbye'. And when you have a difficult request to make (asking for a higher or lower price, better delivery date, etc.), it always makes the task easier to finish with *yoroshiku* (or the more proper *yoroshiku o-nay-gai-she-mas*), to soften the blow of your request while at the same time implying 'please do your best (to help me out on this matter)'. In short, *yoroshiku* is one word that every business person working in Japan should know and use.

Nenga-jō or New Year cards

It is appropriate for businesses and individuals to send New Year cards. In Japan this traditionally means a card with the insignia of the particular animal being celebrated that year – New Year is, after all, a celebration of the Chinese calendar, in which there is a cycle of 12 animals. Some smaller businesses vary the theme by sending cards that are personalized with a colour photo of some aspect of their business. Such cards double as advertising and are interesting for the recipient. And at a personal level, families take pride in sending cards with photos of the family or children.

The cost of printing a photograph is not so high, even in small quantities. Even small photo shops are set up to provide a service whereby a customer can bring in a negative or print, and have printed as many as are needed, with whatever message is required on the card. Or it's possible to hand over the task of design, printing and mail-out of these cards to a specialist firm – a good idea for busy foreign companies.

The Post Office does its bit by selling a variety of suitable cards which are pre-stamped. Unlike other *nenga-jō*, these cards each have a number printed on them and after New Year numbers are drawn, lottery-style, and printed in the newspapers. Thus, people who have received such cards can check the paper to see if they've won a prize. How popular are these cards? For New Year 1995, the Post Office alone sold 3.7 billion cards!

Not unlike Christmas cards in the West, it is bad form to send a customer a New Year card one year, but not send one the next. This is unless, of course, business has ceased and is not likely to start up again. If there is any possibility that you may wish to have business contact with that person in future, it is a good idea to keep sending cards. Even more so than with Christmas cards, you're knitting a strong relationship with people. A person who receives a card thinks that you are considering him or her. The feeling is stronger if you continue doing so through low or inactive periods in business; the relationship will be stronger when things finally pick up.

Omiyage

The practice of giving *omiyage* dates to olden times, when people brought back mementoes from famous and distant shrines in order to share their blessing with others. Without the spiritual aspect, and in a much more commercial form, the practice remains.

Overseas gift shops have this custom to thank for a large proportion of their sales. Virtually no Japanese person would return from abroad without a stock of gifts. It is a matter of courtesy to give a gift to those with whom one is closely associated.

The practice is also carried out within business. If you work for a company, you'll notice that people who have been on even short trips will bring back a gift of, normally, some food – since this is the easiest commodity to share amongst fellow workers. Different areas of Japan still have their own particular food products, and these are often purchased as *omiyage*. *Shinkansen* (bullet train) stations have shops full of pre-wrapped boxes of such food, since modern travellers often need a gift on the run. *Omiyage* are not only available there, but prepared *omiyage* gift boxes are even sold on the *shinkansen*.

For foreign business people in Japan the practice is equally valid. After living, working, or negotiating business in Japan, should you return to your home country, before coming back to Japan, buy a small stock of *omiyage* for those you have close contact with, and some to keep for emergencies. Such things as beef jerky or even wine are useful; something most people can consume, that is light, that keeps well, and, if possible, is characteristic of your home area. When visiting a valued business associate from another company after returning from such a trip, it is customary to give *omiyage* at the time of meeting, by saying, '*omiyage des*'. Further, when receiving a gift, it's inappropriate to unwrap it in front of the giver, unless the giver suggests you do so.

The problem for many foreigners is that because it is an informal practice *omiyage* are slipped in around other, more structured aspects of business, meaning that it may go unnoticed or seem unimportant. Don't be misled. Not giving *omiyage* will be overlooked by the Japanese you deal with, but only because you are a foreigner. If you want to succeed in Japan, don't rely on a 'dumb foreigner' image – buy *omiyage*, send *nenga-jō*, and play the game like the locals do.

Ochūgen and oseibo

Mid-year (*chūgen*) and end-of-year (*seibo*) gifts are given to thank individuals and businesses for their support during the last half year. It is not essential for a newly-established business to become involved with these gifts straight away, and, for a foreign business, arguably not at all. Still, the rule about 'when in Rome' applies; if possible, your company should do so, and it doesn't cost much.

At gift-giving times, supermarkets and department stores are heavily stocked with packaged gift boxes of assorted fruit, of prestigious-looking canned foods, and gift boxes of assorted beer. Similar to the handling of New Year cards (above), department stores provide a service at these times whereby they will handle the whole process of wrapping and delivery; all a firm need do is supply them with a customer list.

Popular gift items include tea, dried seaweed, alcoholic drinks, canned fruit, fruit juice, other foods and soap. Soap has an interesting history as possibly the item most gifted. The stocks of soap that families received commonly reached a point where it became a burden. And since about 75–80 per cent of soap bought in the mid-1980s was for use as gifts, over two-thirds of Japanese families didn't need to buy soap for themselves.[1] That so many products are given as gifts is just one more reason why makers need to offer good quality and presentation.

The gift coupon is very popular; over the last 20 years its sales have grown faster than any other gift. It has the advantage for recipients of allowing them to freely spend the amount specified, at a particular store. It does, however, have the drawback for the giver of specifying the monetary amount that is being given, implying the value the giver places on the relationship.

Since Japanese like to give unique gifts, there is a potentially good market for foreign gift items. But one would have to be very astute in order to supply appropriate products and to get them onto the market at the right time. The right time for *ochūgen* giving is technically 1–15 July, and the *oseibo* season is through December. Goods are not necessarily bought on practical grounds (practical in a Western sense), such as price or function. They are bought for their universal appeal; soap and beer, for instance, can be consumed by most people. As gifts they are also bought for their novel and aesthetic qualities.

Lack of knowledge of what are appropriate gifts, and of current tastes, makes it difficult for outside suppliers to service this market. That sales are over in a very brief period means there is no opportunity to test the market, and very specific planning is required in order to arrange for a short run to arrive in the market on time. Furthermore, there is no real buffer to absorb excess or late stock; there is no provision for continuing sales – not until the next gift season. There are good potential sales at the time, but there are risks for an exporter.

Price and the market

Rebates

Rebates are a refund given by suppliers to motivate downstream distributors or retailers to sell more. They can be calculated in various ways and given in such forms as a percentage of the sales amount or a progressive percentage on sales, as a refund for volume sales, an allowance for advertising, and/or payments of gratitude at year end.

In addition to rebates, a new supplier to the market may have to give an incentive to distributors or retailers to start dealing with its product. It may have to discount an initial supply or provide some free product. This, in a sense, offsets the risk a buyer faces in handling a product that may result in additional hassles or costs, or which may simply not sell.

Where large and relatively powerful suppliers are involved, in many cases the rebate system becomes a patronizing relationship whereby the supplier administers control over the prices and the activities of those who dispense its product.[2] Rebates not only act as an incentive but also make downstream firms dependent on, and therefore conform with, the guidance of their suppliers. It's the private sector version of 'Japan Incorporated'.

Supporters of traditional Japanese business practice would claim that this is positive in that this guidance has a stabilizing effect on the market. With the guiding hand of a large supplier – such as Matsushita – in the background, everyone is sure of reasonable sales and a reasonable profit and no one goes broke through excessive (cut-throat) competition.[3] This suits government and responsible private sector firms.

A negative view of such control is that it takes the freedom out of the market. Specifically, it encourages downstream firms to favour business with their traditional suppliers, who provide rebates and other benefits. Accordingly, long-standing suppliers can exert pressure over their dependencies to spurn the business of competitor suppliers.

This was the claim made by Eastman Kodak Co. about Fuji Photo Film Co. Ltd in May 1995. Kodak filed a petition under Section 301 of the 1974 US Trade Act against Fuji for its marketing activities. In Japan rebating itself is not prohibited, but it becomes an anti-trust concern when it results in restricting others from the market.

Fuji claimed that the photographic film and paper market was open and that foreign suppliers had not done all they could to compete. Kodak maintained that by offering 'kickbacks' to retailers for meeting quantitative sales targets, Fuji effectively controlled retailers in the industry. An executive of one large retail chain said that in order to get a rebate from Fuji they had to achieve not only sales, but had to sell the right balance of products.[4]

The matter was difficult for Kodak to prove. Kodak film had generally been readily available in stores, with the exception of rural outlets too small to stock more than one brand, and national railway kiosks, which ran a policy of stocking the national label.[5] Further, many retailers said Kodak just didn't sell well because customers preferred Fuji. Fuji's claim of Kodak's lack of effort was backed by retailers, who noted that Fuji sales people provided excellent retail-level service and marketing, while Kodak 'takes a month off at the busiest time of the year'.[6]

Part of the problem is that Kodak and other Western firms often see moving into Japan as a rational financial investment. But the relationship between such companies as Fuji and its customer firms approaches social involvement. In such cases there is continued contact and attention given by the manufacturer, who may give retailers in-store support, including assistance with layout and displays. They may also assist with other problems by extending credit and otherwise making sure retailers don't go broke. In the broader context, these are extensions of the concept of 'rebate' – a payback to retailers for good work – or put another way, the rebate is one direct financial expression of assistance.

Precisely one of the problems for Westerners is proving that a 'kickback' exists. Japanese companies pull the lining from their pockets and show only a few small financial rebates, and some additional in-store help. These things don't easily lend themselves to claims made in terms of the limited concept of anti-trust. The problem for outsiders to the system is that this combination of assistance to retailers over a long period of years wins for manufacturers the cooperation and loyalty of the retailers.

After considerable analysis of the matter, the US side came to the conclusion on 14 June 1996, a year after the 301 petition, that Japan's acts regarding photographic products were, they said, 'unreasonable, [they are] a burden and restrict US commerce'.[7]

The matter was also reviewed by the World Trade Organization (WTO), and in 1997 it released a preliminary report that came out in favour of Fuji. Their conclusion was based on a lack of evidence to support Kodak's claim of a blocked market. It is, of course, not surprising that the WTO found no 'evidence'; the matter is one of private negotiations and favours that take place amongst close business associates who are more like friends in the way they behave than 'calculating' business people. It took Kodak many years of being in Japan to understand this for itself, and others in Japan take for granted, and chuckle about, the goings on that the WTO could find no evidence of. The real issue is not whether the activities that Fuji came to represent exist or not; the issue is, should Japanese business conform to Western free market ideology? And that is a complex, many-sided question.

Amongst business people in Japan, opinions about whether rebates are beneficial or not vary. The recession had a strong impact on Japanese businesses and brought some of those opinions to the surface. By 1995, while support for rebating remained amongst many Japanese wholesalers and retailers (notably small and medium-sized retailers) by a small margin, overall opinion favoured simplification or abolition of the system.[8]

The store rep

The functional aspects of the manufacturer's representative are:

- to establish and reiterate positive *jinmyaku* relations with the retailer,
- to conduct in-the-field market research,
- to keep an account of the turnover of goods,
- to assist with in-store layout, e.g. placement of new products and displays.

Japanese think it is important to have someone representing the manufacturer out in the field, to sound out complaints and problems, to keep an eye on market changes by seeing what's being bought, or by chatting to downstream proprietors. From these people a lot of useful information can be gained about market trends and problems. This type of friendly, field interaction is also valuable PR. In some cases this may mean the manufacturer must bypass the wholesaler to visit its retailers. In the West these activities are not expected and some may not be accepted, but they have an important function in keeping informal information links operating through the Japanese supply chain.

Pricing structure

Many goods in Japan have a set retail price before they leave the factory door. Often you'll find the price of goods printed on the packet. This practice has decreased since the economic bubble burst, in part because retailers were forced to drop prices in order to sell. Traditionally, though, pricing hasn't been at the discretion of the retailer.

The practice reflects the control producers have had over the product. In a negative sense, it restricts the freedom of downstream firms to cut price and attract spending. In a positive sense, it results in business stability. Price cutting means that suppliers and other retailers are vulnerable to a drop in what is a fair return for their contribution.[9]

Typical examples of the Japanese pricing system in operation appear within vertical distribution *keiretsu*. The manufacturer can set the price, and sell through its distribution structure, aware of what those at each stage will make. This structure has survived because many of the retail outlets have been small. Their size has made them dependent on a system in which, by setting a relatively high retail price, the manufacturer can profit well. The manufacturer can then judiciously reallocate that profit in the form of rebates or other forms of gratitude. In this situation the company is a responsible parent-like benefactor who knows best, overseeing the system, making sure it functions well for all those involved.

In relative terms, a free market has no control mechanism and therefore risks instability and the failure of those involved. A big risk for a stable system is a foreign party coming into the market, undercutting the price and pulling buyers and income away from reliable businesses. Destruction of existing firms causes trauma to employees and to related businesses. (You can see why 'foreigners' are not welcome within the system.)

While many Japanese businesses have supported the system, others haven't. By the mid-1990s, a slight majority of retailers were in favour of an open pricing system. The strongest supporters of the system were large retailers. Among wholesalers, a slightly greater number wanted to retain the set price system.[10] But those objecting to set prices had been reluctant to break ranks by either discounting or taking on cheaper products, at least because even large retailers had on occasion been refused the opportunity to sell if they did discount.

Shiseidō

In April 1990 Japan's top cosmetics maker, Shiseidō Co., stopped supplying products to Fujiki Honten Ltd, a Shiseidō customer of almost 30 years. Shiseidō claimed Fujiki had broken a contract that specified that its cosmetics had to be sold face-to-face in order to provide counselling for the buyers. It is commonly understood that this contract is a convenience that ensures the goods won't be discounted.

What ensued was a volley of Fair Trade Commission (FTC)[11] and court action with appeals and rescinded decisions, which lasted until the end of 1995.

Fujiki took the matter to the FTC in 1991. The Commission ruled against Fujiki, saying that there was insufficient proof that Shiseidō had violated the Antimonopoly Law. In October Fujiki filed suit in the district court. Shiseidō defended itself, saying that consultation was needed to guard customers against adverse skin reactions. Fujiki responded that cosmetics products already needed approval from the Ministry of Health and Welfare before being sold, and argued that, 'If they are so dangerous, why is Shiseidō marketing them?'[12]

In July 1993 another long-standing Shiseidō customer, a chain store called Kawachiya, filed a complaint with the FTC against Shiseidō and two other giant firms, Kanebō Ltd and Kaō Corp., for blocking Kawachiya's discount sales. This led to an FTC raid on Shiseidō later that month.

On 25 September 1993 a cosmetics association and 85 member stores filed a counter-complaint with the FTC over Kawachiya that was perhaps odd by Western, or at least free market standards: they claimed that at 25–30 per cent below recommended retail, Kawachiya was causing a drop in their sales by selling at unfair prices.[13] Their claim provides eloquent testimony to the belief that the Japanese system entitles established firms to more than just a chance to compete.

The matter continued, and on 21 June 1995 the FTC ordered Shiseidō to stop pressuring retailers not to discount. Shiseidō at first informed the FTC that it would not conform to the decision. But in early October the company agreed to the FTC's terms.

In the 18 months to the end of 1995 cosmetics underwent a real drop in price of 10 per cent, and in the six months to September 1995 Shiseidō's profits dropped 6.2 per cent over the same period a year before.[14] Shiseidō shifted its strategy to differentiating its products. In 1996 it announced the release of an upmarket line called Benefique, which would only be available in specialist stores.

The manufacturers vs. discounters battle goes back at least to the 1960s. The electronics behemoth Matsushita had refused to allow a supermarket chain called Daiei to sell its (National/Panasonic brand) goods because Daiei wanted to discount them. The battle became a personal issue between the two founders, Matsushita Kōnosuke, who was convinced that discounting was bad for the public and bad for businesses, and Nakauchi Isao, founder of Daiei, who thought the consumer deserved a break, and believed that could also be good for business.

For many years Matsushita had been supplying a retail chain called Chūjitsuya, but when Daiei bought the chain, it put Matsushita on the spot. Ultimately, the world's largest consumer electronics company gave in and agreed to supply what was now a Daiei group member, knowing full well that this would mean discounting of Matsushita products.[15]

A family affair

Manufacturers haven't necessarily wanted to control prices just for profit, but for the benefit of their industry. Just as Western business people believe that the superiority of the free market system is a universal constant, Japanese are convinced that mutual support and social responsibility – not complete freedom – is the most natural approach to business. Perhaps the most outspoken proponent of this was Matsushita Kōnosuke himself. Matsushita, and dozens of other business leaders after him, have assumed a parent-like role in guiding their industries – in parallel with, and in much the same spirit as, the bureaucracy has done to business overall.

This shouldn't be interpreted as a bid just to gain power; in many ways it's altruistic. 'Parental' industry leaders are looking after the welfare of the responsible and reliable firms for which they feel responsible. They are keeping the business environment stable for the benefit of its participants.

The protected and closed nature of Japanese business has contributed to the phenomenon of local prices of Japanese goods being higher than their price abroad. This has led to the grey market phenomenon, in which genuine goods are imported to compete with exactly the same but higher priced products sold locally. It is not illegal, but traditionalists do not sanction the (grey market) activity. It has been difficult for retailers to engage in this practice because of their dependence on, and their reluctance to offend, the manufacturer – though some would have liked to.

Yodobashi Camera, a major electronics discounter, was large enough to challenge Fuji Photo Film. It imported authentic Fuji film from Korea and resold it cheaply in Japan. Fuji's response was to change the name on the film sold in Korea to Lotte. Yodobashi continued the practice by putting a sign by the film saying that it was still genuine Fuji film – just in a different box.[16]

Setting the price

The above portrayal of the market is one in which large suppliers have authority, power and control. It may seem as if the Japanese market is completely static. But in fact there is a great deal of competition within the system. Large as well as small manufacturers in Japan are subject to strong pressure from competitors. Retail prices are traditionally set by manufacturers, who are indeed aware of prices set by their competitors.[17] Such a system of pre-calculating the price is also often the means by which foreign market entrants are expected to establish their prices.

Basic price-setting, common in the West, is called 'cost plus'. In this system, the retail price is the simple sum total of factor costs. It's so logical that it's difficult to imagine any alternative, and many people haven't. Under a structure in which cost plus dominates, it becomes easy for manufacturers to justify price increases as resulting from increases in factor costs. The problem for Western business is that this doesn't work in an international market, where overseas rivals do not face the same factor cost increases. Local increases in such input costs as labour or materials may have no effect on competitor prices. Thus, the traditional justification for mutual price hikes disappears. Manufacturers in many cases are competing on just one thing, the retail price. Manufacturers can accept or reject the mission of trying to reduce costs to achieve, or better, that retail price.

The Japanese system turns the Western retail price structure upside-down. Instead of upstream suppliers passing on their costs downstream, downstream sellers pass the pressure of the market upstream, forcing suppliers to reduce costs in order to survive.

Japanese sellers normally calculate what the market can bear, that is, the end, retail price, then calculate the next step back, which is a fixed wholesale price. In 1991 Daiei took the system a step further by setting the retail price at the point where real (strong) demand would occur, not where competitor prices were. They found out, for instance, that consumers would drink 100 per cent orange juice every day if it were the same price as milk, and that is the price at which they targeted their product. Today, orange juice in Japan is still about the same price as milk.[18]

The normal mark-up depends on the function of the intermediary and the type of product – product categories normally have their own mark-up structure. For example, see Table 13.1. If a golf ball were retailed at ¥100, the retailer would have bought it for ¥70, representing a 30 per cent profit on the sales price. The wholesaler would have bought it from the importer (or manufacturer) for ¥60, meaning a profit for the wholesaler of ¥10.[19]

Table 13.1 Profit margins in the distribution of a golf ball

Importer selling price	Wholesaler selling price	Retail selling price
¥60	¥70	¥100

This set percentage can be discounted when selling to, for instance, a big retailer with power. Such stores may have a policy of buying at lower than the standard percentage – this is an expression of their power in the market. The savings this company makes by demanding to pay less then comes to it as bonus profit. As a result of buying more cheaply, those larger shops that offer special deals or discounts are in a better position to cut prices on old models without losing money. They can off-load their old stock in order to upgrade without suffering the same losses that would be faced by a smaller outlet.

The phenomenon is another factor that reinforces Japan's dual economic structure. Large businesses gain greater profit than small, and so become even larger. Small proprietor-operated shops are, by contrast, in many cases scraping out a living selling goods at the set rates, and sometimes slightly discounted rates, earning a minimal profit from a minimum of sales.

Your money and the tegata

An important feature in the Japanese billing system is the long time lag between receipt of goods and payment. The payment for many goods sold to small dealers can be effected in around a month, depending on the store policy, but other businesses insist on operating a delayed payment system. Some buyers will issue the seller with a promissory note – the *tegata* – as a commitment to pay at a set future date. Depending on the industry, this involves a delay of normally between two and four months but sometimes up to six months after the transaction. In some cases sellers wishing to cash in early may be able to do so through a bank; however, there is an interest premium for the privilege of having the money before it is due. Essentially, such a delayed payment system means that for most businesses there is an extra cost, equivalent to the interest value of borrowing that money for the *tegata* period.

The system does two things. On the one hand, it reflects the power of the buyer, when it is the stronger party. It allows larger companies, which are often in a position to demand long *tegata* periods, the opportunity to strengthen their financial position with a reserve of free credit which is supplied by smaller operators. On the other hand, the system has evolved – often by inserting an intermediary to perform a financing function – to allow buyers with little cash flow to stock more goods than would otherwise be possible.

As a foreigner buying abroad and selling in Japan, you may be a loser in the payment system. As a seller in Japan, you may be subject to a long wait for your money under the *tegata* system. Since it is unlikely that you can impose this system on your home suppliers, you may have to be prepared to absorb the shortfall in the supply of credit. But, like other Japanese intermediaries, you might charge for taking on the additional function of supplying credit.

Sole agencies – a frequent request

It is not uncommon for a Japanese buyer to ask to be a sole agent for the goods an exporter wants sold in Japan. The request is that all exports should go through only that importer or distributor. It is a natural request, since for the importer it reduces the likelihood of competition from others also wanting to sell your product in Japan. A sole agent could generally expect that any money it commits to advertising will be exclusively for its own benefit. The agent would also undertake responsibilities, including dealing with repairs and returns of the product.

There are, however, problems for the exporter. Though many Japanese wholesalers and retailers are large by Western standards, many don't operate nationally but cover or dominate a particular region of Japan. If you're lucky enough to have a product that can sell well, it won't be wise to restrict yourself to an agent that has only limited coverage. Also, granting a sole agency may be devoid of meaning unless the company can come up with sales results to back up the advantage. Therefore, it may be pointless agreeing to a sole agency relationship, at least at an early stage.

Furthermore, an overseas supplier granting sole agency is at the mercy of that agent to do its best to sell the product. It may be tempting for an agent to relax its promotional push once it has sole sales rights, confident that it won't face competition. For this reason it might be necessary to build into a contract with an agent that, in return for rights over a territory, the agent will guarantee to devote a certain amount of floor/shelf space or sales staff as well as funding to the promotion of your product.

Another problem is that operating a sole agency is a breach of the law if it prevents others from competing in the market. The case of Porsche provides an interesting example.

Porsche

Porsche cars had been sold in Japan through a sole agent, a small family company called MIZWA Motor Corporation, which had imported and distributed the cars since the 1950s. By the mid-1990s MIZWA sold through 30 dealers; 22 were independent and eight comprised a subsidiary of MIZWA, called MIZWA Motor Sales.

Sales of imported cars rose only very gradually until the mid-1980s when, with the wealth that accompanied the high yen and the bubble, imports started to soar. Car imports quadrupled in the 30 years until 1985, but they more than quadrupled again in just the five years between 1985 and 1990. Understandably, sales fell when the economic bubble collapsed. What bothered Porsche was that while other foreign car sales quickly recovered, some reaching new heights in the three years to 1995, sales of Porsche cars remained flat, meaning that it was rapidly losing market share.

MIZWA Motor Corp. had undergone changes, including the handing on of its family management to the next generation. At the same time, Porsche had been pursuing a global policy of taking direct control of Porsche marketing. As a result, in accordance with the terms of their contract, Porsche informed MIZWA that it was giving two years' notice of termination of their long-standing relationship. Porsche did, however, invite MIZWA to continue as a Porsche dealership.

According to one insider, Porsche bent over backwards to accommodate MIZWA. 'Porsche offered to buy back the cars and parts that remained in stock as of December 1997, and was willing for them to stay in business, retaining the majority of their retail outlets, and Porsche was willing to take over a significant number of their staff.'

MIZWA were in a strategic position as their eight affiliated dealers were well located, and controlled 50 per cent of the Porsche sales in Japan. MIZWA signed a memorandum agreeing to the 'smooth' transfer of the business but otherwise continued doing business as usual. However, when the two-year deadline approached and Porsche pressed the issue, they responded by suing Porsche on the basis that the termination contravened the spirit of the relationship, and that Porsche should have given more notice, considering their years of association.

MIZWA had for many years depended to a large extent on distributing this famous brand. Still, in addition to the 2000-odd Porsches MIZWA imported annually, it had also acted as the agent for SAAB, handling about 1000 cars per year. However, shortly after Porsche gave notice of termination, General Motors, a 50 per cent shareholder of SAAB, terminated its importer contract with MIZWA with just a three-month grace period, and transferred the rights to a much larger importer, Yanase.

Should MIZWA lose Porsche's business, it might be ruined. This might seem a flimsy defence, but it is the type of reasoning that lies at the heart of Japanese business, and has a powerful influence on Japanese law. According to the Commercial Code, in cases where a business agreement is terminated after an 'agent' has invested heavily in promotion, appropriate compensation must be paid.

And indeed, in this case a lot of money was discussed, but a compromise couldn't be reached. While there's no official figure on the matter, it's believed that MIZWA demanded from Porsche roughly 40 times the average annual profit it had derived from its Porsche business, whereas Porsche offered something close to ten times. This figure, and the inability to reconcile the very large gap, helps explain why, when I visited the Porsche Japan office atop the plush ARCO Tower in Meguro, Tokyo, it had just been outfitted with a plethora of security features; business in Japan isn't normally so challenging.

European law weighs even heavier than Japanese law in favour of 'good faith', so this put MIZWA on a relatively good footing when it decided to take the matter to court, which by law had to be in the manufacturer's domicile area; in this case Stuttgart, Germany.

By coincidence, the FTC had begun investigating MIZWA for monopolistic activities regarding Porsche sales. Japan's FTC, though relatively weak, does occasionally step in where free trade is under threat. Free trade here means that, in the name of competition and prices to benefit the consumer, anyone should be allowed to sell your product in any market. In light of this issue, under general antimonopoly provisions, the policy of Porsche (and other manufacturers) worldwide is to offer an agent primary responsibility for a territory, with a guarantee that Porsche will not make the same arrangement with anyone else. Thus, dealers are given some security, but parallel imports are not blocked.

Indeed, parallel imports – or the grey market – in cars does exist in Japan. The level of grey market imports increases with the exclusivity of the vehicle and the price difference between Japan and abroad. In Japan 50 per cent of Ferraris come through means other than the primary agent; 20 per cent of Porsches, about 10 per cent of Mercedes, 5 per cent of BMWs and about 2 per cent of Volkswagens and Audis come through alternative routes.

But the crux of the matter was that MIZWA, as a Porsche agent and representative, was obliged to provide service for Porsche cars regardless of how they got into Japan. Still, given its position as 'sole agent' and the expenditure it puts into promoting and providing service facilities, such an agent may not want to provide after-service for grey market products. What offended the FTC was that MIZWA made this blatant by shunning customers who had bought Porsches through other routes.

It's generally believed on the Porsche side that a disgruntled grey-market dealer, who felt damaged by MIZWA, informed the FTC. But, under the general climate of discontent, MIZWA believed (as it still does) that it was Porsche that had tipped off the FTC. In November 1997, after six months of investigation, the FTC ruled that MIZWA's activities conflicted with Japan's Antimonopoly Law, and reprimanded MIZWA accordingly. MIZWA disputed the claim, and decided to take the case to the Tokyo High Court.

Meanwhile, MIZWA lost its case in Stuttgart. Based on similar cases from the auto industry, the court noted that, even where there had been a long business relationship, a two-year grace period after notification was deemed sufficient. When Porsche's lawyers asked why, two years earlier, MIZWA had accepted the termination without challenging it, and had even signed a memo of agreement, company representatives answered that they had not really taken the agreement seriously. This brought a rebuke from Porsche's lawyers, who claimed breach of trust: what are they doing in business with Porsche's products if they don't take such a matter seriously?

This raises the issue of the Japanese handling of contracts. Japanese firms do use contracts in certain (especially international) transactions, but this is a relatively recent phenomenon. Japanese companies are not accustomed to it and are often not good at it. According to Porsche, MIZWA believed that it was in a strong position and thought that Porsche wouldn't really take control of sales in Japan. It would have been a mammoth task for Porsche to duplicate the sales channels that MIZWA already had, particularly given that MIZWA directly controlled the strongest Porsche outlets – if it came to a showdown, Porsche would immediately lose at least 50 per cent of its Japan sales.

MIZWA therefore didn't take the matter seriously, and assigned a low degree of importance to the contract, which they saw as just a written declaration of Porsche's 'plan' to go it alone. 'But', says one manager from Porsche Japan, 'Japan is Porsche's second largest market next to the US, consuming 10 per cent of Porsche's production. Japan was too important for Porsche not to address the matter of poor sales. We naturally didn't want to lose any of the dealers; but by late 1997 we were reconciled to the idea that we would not have MIZWA's eight affiliated outlets when we started importing on our own on 1 January 1998.'

As it turned out, in 1998 MIZWA came to the table and struck a deal with Porsche. In this MIZWA agreed that Porsche would operate as importer, and MIZWA would waive further legal action over the matter. MIZWA received a compromise financial settlement, significantly below their initial request, and through 1998 MIZWA would close about half of its dealerships, while continuing to operate the other half.

Notes

1 Michael Schofield, then Chair of Nippon Lever, estimated that 75–80 per cent of toilet soap in Japan was gifted (*Taking on Japan*, Look Japan, 1987, p. 31; March 1990, p. 100).
2 See Manifold, in Czinkota and Kotabe, 1993, pp. 49–51.
3 Matsushita is a good example of such traditional forms of business. The company not only engaged in such practices, but Matsushita himself was a proponent of traditional stable business policy.
4 *Tokyo Business Today*, October 1995, pp. 36–37.
5 Ex-Kodak Japan head Albert Sieg, in *Tokyo Business Today*, November 1995, p. 37.
6 *Tokyo Business Today*, October 1995, p. 37.
7 NHK TV News, 14 June 1996.
8 *Small Business in Japan*, MITI, 1995, p. 65.
9 To most Westerners, 'stability' as a reason for price maintenance cuts no ice – stability has no overwhelming appeal, unless you're in a boat. Both business people and customers are part of the drama called free-market capitalism, and there will always be winners and losers. Those who end up as losers were obviously not good enough to succeed. But the Japanese economy, which, within living memory of many, was decimated, has grown and stayed strong in large part by emphasizing stability over competition. In the past 50 years, most Japanese (at least those in authority) have felt that it's better to have everybody do reasonably well. This attitude has kept reliable business people in their jobs for a long time. One problem is that the Japanese haven't been very good at explaining this 'social contract' to foreigners.
10 *Small Business in Japan*, MITI, 1995, p. 65.
11 The FTC is a body set up in the post-World War II Occupation period to keep a check on cartels and other monopolistic activities.
12 *The Nikkei Weekly*, 4 October 1993, p. 10.
13 *The Japan Times*, 28 September 1993, p. 2.
14 *The Economist*, 4 November 1995, p. 73.
15 *The Changing Face of Japanese Retail*, JETRO, 1995, p. 19.
16 *Tokyo Business Today*, November 1995, p. 37.
17 Suzuki, T., in Czinkota and Kotabe, 1993, p. 224.
18 *Tradescope*, JETRO, April 1994, p. 4.
19 Adapted from a JETRO survey on profit margins, in *Sales Promotion in the Japanese Market*, JETRO, 1983, p. 6.

Chapter 14

The distribution system

Japan's distribution system has been controversial largely because it has been seen as a block to foreign goods entering Japan, and for this reason it was brought up at the 1989 Structural Impediments Initiative (SII) talks as a non-tariff barrier. Still, assuming the SII and later objectives have been to 'reform' the system, since the system is based on social relations its features are very difficult to legislate away. Also, its social base provides benefits for Japanese business and society.

Its controversial characteristics include many small family-run stores, a multi-layered system of distributors, and close-knit trading relationships which have kept foreigners out.

History and determinants of the distribution system

Guilds or craft associations called *za*, which were most active from the fourteenth century, controlled business activity within goods and service markets. And not too different from the present day, guild member interests and privileges, including their trade monopoly, were supported by the *za*'s patrons – at that time Buddhist temples, Shintō shrines and the aristocracy – who were given an honorarium for doing so. Businesses had money and could boost the income of those in power, who gave them support. Nowadays it's politicians and ex-bureaucrats who protect and benefit from the contributions of business.

Protection and exclusive membership meant that competition was restricted. The *daimyō* (local lords) began to do away with the *za* in the mid-sixteenth century, in order to increase the flow of goods and local wealth. Their policy, called *raku-za* and *raku-ichi*, meaning open guilds and free markets, was supported by two of Japan's famous unifiers, Oda Nobunaga, and later Toyotomi Hideyoshi, who extended the policy to the whole country. Hideyoshi's efforts didn't last long – in the place of *za* arose *kabunakama*. *Kabu* today means share (or stock), and each member had a share in the guild. Realizing that these groups had a stabilizing effect on business, the Tokugawa government (1603–1868) sanctioned the system.

By 1842, when inflation had become rampant, the distribution *kabunakama* (suspected to be the cause) were again abolished, but they had actually become weak and had lost pricing control. In 1851 they were again reinstated. Finally, they were eliminated after the 1868 Meiji Restoration. The point of introducing this history is this: whether they're called industrial associations (cartels), *zaibatsu*, *keiretsu*, or are less well-defined groups, they continue. And as long as Japan remains a self-determined economy, the likelihood is not high that after hundreds of years the spirit of business grouping will end in the near future because of, amongst other things, foreign pressure.

Japan's trade and distribution system retains a localized, segmented character. Historically, this was influenced by factors including:

- the restrictions the Tokugawa shōgunate placed on travel from one's own domain,
- the tendency of local trade associations to stick together, at times in opposition to central government efforts to break their monopolies,
- local restrictions and regulations which further reiterated the domain-centred system.

The tributary pattern that resulted had its corollary in the cities of Osaka and Edo (Tokyo), from which goods were distributed nationally. The local structures were homogenous and the system was never streamlined, so the same pattern of trading activity remained.

Not only historical but physical factors influence Japan's trading pattern. In sparsely populated environments in Western countries, with low turnover and few retail outlets to service, it is cost-effective to use one distributor. Further, where turnover is low, people are prepared to take on extra functions which they can perform in down-time in order to save or earn extra money: in a small town the butcher kills, cures and delivers. However, where turnover is high, it's more efficient to specialize. In a populated area, with many outlets to service, even sections of the delivery route may be divided up.

Japan's small wholesalers and retailers

The feature of Japan's distribution system which is most often discussed among Western business people is the multi-level *tonya*, or wholesalers, that handle a large percentage of all merchandise before it ever reaches Japan's many small retailers.

- There are about the same number of retailers and wholesalers in both the US and Japan. But since Japan's population is half that of the US, there are more of these service operations per Japanese customer.
- Total dollar sales going through US wholesalers has been about equal to US retail sales, but total sales of Japanese wholesalers has been about four times Japanese retail sales. This reflects Japan's higher level of multiple wholesaling activity.
- In short, the US has been able to generate more retail sales from a smaller amount of business activity than Japan.[1]

In Japan there are many small retail outlets, often run by a husband and wife who handle low volumes of merchandise and operate with low economies of scale. The average retail shop has one-third of the number of staff that US retailers have, and about 50 per cent of Japanese stores are run by one or two people. These shops – affectionately, 'mom and pop' stores – are, however, decreasing with dispatch, and are being replaced by larger retailers.

Japan's distribution system is often accused of being inefficient. It is not the distribution system but the proliferation of these small stores that has been costly. The Japanese actually have a rather efficient distribution structure to cope with this situation. It is also worth noting that, were the distribution structure not fragmented in order to reach the many small, out-of-the-way retailers, it would be up to manufacturers to service those retailers, which would mean a complex in-house system. Furthermore, small independent wholesalers not only have agility, enabling them to better cope with the many small-lot orders of these retailers, but will strive to use their resources efficiently.

The large number of small shops in Japan means there are not only many deliveries, but, since the stocking capacity of small stores is low, supplies need to be frequent. What's more, frequent deliveries are also needed by big stores in Japan, which are also cramped

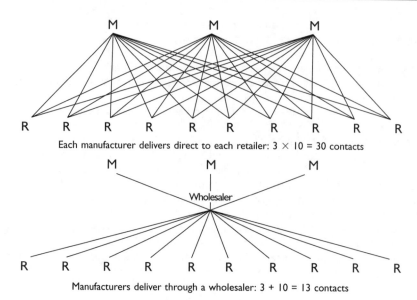

Figure 14.1 Efficient distribution. Source: adapted from Czinkota and Woronoff, 1993

for space. The image foreigners might have of a large department store is that it will naturally have ample warehousing, but in Japan, where land is scarce, a department store might have just a small storage room on each floor, insufficient to hold enough stock to replenish normal turnover.

Under the circumstances, the distribution system handles the situation efficiently. Looking at it schematically (see Figure 14.1), if every manufacturer had to service every shop it would require a high number of contacts, and each delivery would contain only a few goods, delivered over a long distance. In Japan goods are sent to local wholesalers, who stock goods, consolidate them with other goods, and deliver them to outlets within their locale.

The existence of bigger shops in wider areas of land in the West has meant that the roads are easier to negotiate and orders are needed less frequently. A large truck from the manufacturer can, in many cases, still make deliveries in lots suitable for those retailers. In Japanese cities there have been too many small shops hidden in narrow streets for this to be practical.

Large-Scale Retail Store Law (Dai-Ten Hō or 'Big Store Law')[2]

Protection of business is the rationale behind laws, including the Big Store Law. It was designed to keep small business people – very important members of the community – in employment.

The Large-Scale Retail Store Law, or *Dai-Ten Hō*, dates back to conflicts between large and small retailers in the 1920s. At this time small retailers grew in number but faced tough times in the economically unstable, and, for many, very tough period between the two World Wars. Department stores were also growing and operated more efficiently, and in doing so engendered the ire of the small retailers. The government was initially reluctant to intervene, but ultimately responded to public attention and pressure over the matter, and in 1938 the Department Store Law was introduced to protect small retailers.[3] After World War II, the Occupation scrapped the Department Store Law, but it was reinstated in 1956.

1974 Supermarkets, discount shops and other chain stores that also impacted on existing small businesses but were outside the law had emerged, and so the Large-Scale Retail Store Law of 1974 was introduced. It involved a system of reporting store proposal details, including floor space, opening, operating and closing times, which were subject to revision and adjustment as authorities saw appropriate.

1979 The law required a permit from MITI for the construction of stores with floor space of over 1500m^2 (3000m^2 in Japan's 13 largest cities). Store operators skirted the regulations by opening several small stores in the one building. In order to address this type of problem, in 1979 the *Dai-Ten Hō* was strengthened. It divided stores into two sizes, the original Class I (above), and Class II, which applied to stores of between 500 and 1500m^2 (1500 and 3000m^2).

Class I applicants had to present a detailed business proposal to the prefectural government, and then to the local Business Regulation Council (*Shōgyō Chōsei Kyōgi Kai* or *Shō Chō Kyō*), which was under the Chamber of Commerce. Following this a subcommittee prepared a report which went to MITI. Class II stores went through the same procedure, but instead of going to MITI, the report went to the prefectural governor.

The process and the law were typically complex and vague, allowing MITI to regulate the allocation of store permits.

- The process was so slow that this itself acted as a barrier. Theoretically, applications were to be processed in under two years, but in reality they commonly took between seven and ten years. Almost a third of the applicants withdrew within the first year after applying. This time frame, and the cost in unfamiliar territory, in practice counted foreigners out.
- MITI could stall applications simply by boycotting their acceptance. This is not an uncommon back-up tool for the bureaucracy where more formal regulations are unavailable.
- Store proposals and plans were subject to negotiation. Local Business Councils – comprised of local businesses, academics, consumers, existing large stores and others – could negotiate the same, now redundant details of the 1974 law, requiring compromises on floor space, opening and closing times, and the number of holidays per year. Fewer operating hours would benefit smaller stores, which gained trade while large stores were closed.

To foreigners and other applicants, it all looked like noisome and inefficient bureaucratic red tape, or simply prejudice against foreigners. However, it was a quasi-official method of regulating the number of large stores which were displacing small shops, done largely at the discretion and judgement of MITI. Its discretionary aspect was based on the idea that the law *per se* was too rigid to respond to both changing circumstances and to regional differences to be truly effective. The notion that the law should be flexible and interpreted is not uncommon in Japan.

In the late 1980s the *Dai-Ten Hō* came under strong attack from abroad. It was raised at the SII talks as a clear impediment to foreign access to Japan. Consequently, MITI made efforts at appeasement, but (naturally) didn't want to relinquish control. Defenders of the law argued that:

- While the regulated system appeared less efficient, the small shops, and the distribution system which served those shops, promoted full employment.
- Travelling to a supermarket for bulk buys would not suit elderly people used to piecemeal local shopping. Nor should the community sacrifice the social relations built up around local shopping.

There were also politics at stake. Politicians who were backed by those involved in the small business sector couldn't afford to alienate their supporters.

1992 As part of the concessions made in 1990 at the SII talks, as of 1992 the *Dai-Ten Hō* would be relaxed. Japan would gradually reduce the power of small shop owners to block the construction of larger stores.

From 31 January 1992 *Dai-Ten Hō* permit approval time was shortened to a maximum of one year. Instead of having to close for four days each month, the restriction was changed to a compulsory 44 days closure each year. Instead of closing at 6pm, large stores were able to stay open until 7pm. Also, under the 1992 changes special provision was made to allow retailers selling imports to operate store areas of up to 1000m^2 without the normal restrictions.

1994 In May 1994 further concessions were made. Lengthy procedures were removed for store applications of up to 1000m^2, the number of compulsory holidays was halved, from 44 to 24 days per year, and stores could remain open until 8pm. Stores had been disadvantaged by not being able to stay open to catch the after-work traffic. When allowed to trade in the evening, many shifted their opening time from 10am to 11am; before 11am only a small 3–5 per cent of the day's business occurs.[4]

In the context of targeting deregulation, according to Daiei's founder, Nakauchi Isao, assuming one got *Dai-Ten Hō* approval to set up, one still needed to submit 200 written applications to gain 42 licences, covered by 19 different laws. The cost of dealing with the bureaucratic processes to set up just one supermarket, Nakauchi estimated, was around ¥160mn ($1.2mn).[5] In 1993 Nakauchi told PM Hosokawa – himself intent on deregulation – that if the regulations required to open a large-scale store were removed, prices could be reduced by 0.3 per cent. He maintained that the removal of regulations meant savings to the customer, which would put spending power back in their pockets, thereby increasing demand.[6]

When Daiei imported Brazilian orange juice after the 1992 import liberalization of citrus, demand was so high that Daiei found it was making too much profit and so reduced the price, ultimately by 20 per cent to ¥158 per litre.[7] Through Daiei's direct import and distribution system it imported New Zealand (NZ) ice cream. Previously 500ml of luxury brand ice cream had sold for about ¥800 ($8), but Daiei introduced a 2-litre pack – four times the volume – for just ¥598, much lower than even the 500ml price; and both were produced by the same NZ company.[8]

The changing face of Japanese retail

The displacement of traditional shopping structures is not new, and not exclusive to Japan. The same thing happened decades before in Western nations when supermarkets became popular and took customers away from grocery shop owners, who objected. The results of that are now history. Structures within Japan have made its system much more stubborn, but changes in Japanese work patterns, advances in computing technology, and changes in the *Dai-Ten Hō* have all contributed to changes in traditional Japanese retailing.

The increasing number of working women meant the practice of a housewife grocery shopping every day at a range of small stores had been decreasing. While never financially expedient, it fitted in with a broader lifestyle, including eating raw fish, which must be consumed while fresh, and it gave women the opportunity to get out of the house. Habits are, however, slow to change; in the mid-1990s, while 40 per cent of women in their 20s bought from convenience stores, under 10 per cent of women in their 50s and 60s did.[9]

Before computers were readily available, logistics and accounting were far more laborious, and it was rational to have an intermediary in the distribution channel who ordered, consolidated and controlled supplies, and perhaps also financed the stock while it was in the system. It became harder to justify having an intermediary when the logistics and accounting functions could be handled by the house computer. The increased availability of computer-based stock control coincided with pressure to economize in the early 1990s, and some firms consolidated their operations. They did this either by combining existing wholesalers, by joining manufacturers and wholesaler(s) or retailers absorbed wholesaler(s) or all three combined.

In 1993, convenience store operator 7-Eleven responded to high distribution costs by teaming up with 80 of its confectionery makers to establish Japan's first nationwide, jointly owned, delivery system. Distribution was put in the hands of just two wholesalers and four delivery operators. Goods from participating producers were consolidated by the delivery firms and dispatched to the thousands of 7-Elevens that dot Japan. Once introduced, the system also more than halved the average delivery time, from over eight days to four. In the early 1980s, 7-Eleven Japan had also become the world's first store to use POS (point-of-sale) for merchandising, improving its ability to efficiently control inventory. A new distribution system was emerging to match that part of Japanese retail that was changing. 7-Eleven now offers, along with other convenience stores in Japan, such additional customer services as receiving bill payments for utilities, and functions as a parcel delivery collection point.

7-Eleven is an interesting parable about the potential of the Japanese market. The company was originally owned by the US firm, Southland Corporation. In 1973 Southland franchised the 7-Eleven format to a major supermarket company, Itō-Yōkadō, which opened the first store in Japan in 1974. Southland got into over $3bn of debt, forcing it into bankruptcy in 1990. By then, Itō-Yōkadō's subsidiary, 7-Eleven Japan, had become successful enough that, in 1991, Itō-Yōkadō negotiated the purchase of 70 per cent of the US company (it now owns 64 per cent), for $430mn. 7-Eleven was an early innovator that challenged conventional wisdom about what foreign business could do in Japan and went on to become Japan's biggest convenience chain. It is now Japan's top food retailer and is amongst Japan's top 15 income-earning companies. In 1996 its sales exceeded that of its parent, Itō-Yōkadō, making it Japan's second biggest retailer, after Daiei.

As early as 1988 Daiei, too, began to gradually take over its supply channels which had been handled by wholesalers.[10] Small and widely scattered retailers had been unable to consolidate deliveries, but as a single large-scale operation Daiei could.

On the heels of the changes to the *Dai-Ten Hō* came an increase in large-store applications. By 1996 the number of applications for stores of over $500m^2$ had quadrupled over the 1980s' average, to 2206. In the 1990s Japan experienced a mall development boom. Whereas large stores were traditionally located near downtown train stations, during the 1990s more than four out of five shopping centres were targeted for rural and suburban areas.[11]

One town involved in the boom was Shimoda, in Aomori prefecture, at the top of Japan's main island, Honshū. Its residents had previously done 90 per cent of their shopping out of town. Shimoda's acquisition of a mall reversed the practice; 70 per cent of the mall's ¥16bn ($155mn) income for fiscal year 1995 flowed from neighbouring towns – which began complaining. The mall created 1100 new jobs for Shimoda residents (equivalent to 10 per cent of its population) and the mall's land tax contribution provided 15 per cent of the town's 1995 fiscal year tax revenue.[12]

Toys 'R' Us

In December 1991 Toys 'R' Us, the world's biggest toy store chain, entered the Japanese market, and in its opening week 100,000 customers passed through its doors. Its entry rode on the back of attempts by the US administration under President Bush to prise open the Japanese retail market by striking at the *Dai-Ten Hō*. Illustrating its significance, President Bush was even in Japan to open the second Toys 'R' Us outlet in Nara in 1992.

Toys 'R' Us came to be seen as a test case, and it did successfully enter and challenge established Japanese toy wholesaler–retailers in price, variety and patronage. Its presence came as part of a double blow to local toy suppliers, who were hit soon after by the recession. In 1991, the year Toys 'R' Us entered Japan, seven Japanese toy retailers went bankrupt; in just the first ten months of 1996 there were 15 toy retailer bankruptcies.

Toys 'R' Us 'bought direct' from manufacturers, and was thereby able to save the consumer about 20–30 per cent of the manufacturer's recommended retail price. On imports, it could slice off up to 50 per cent of the shelf price. By 1994 other Japanese stores had no choice but to bypass their wholesalers and establish direct links with toy manufacturers. Furthermore, a 1994 FTC survey found that the number of toy retailers adhering to the traditional maker-set retail prices had dropped in the previous five years from around 70 per cent to 29 per cent. The large makers could no longer control the retail prices of their goods. They had been able to do this in part because the *Dai-Ten Hō* had kept out large unruly dealers who may have wanted to rock the system – which is just what Toys 'R' Us did. By the end of 1994 even traditional stalwarts of propriety, the department stores, began offering hefty discounts, initiated by some Osaka department stores that began slashing up to 30 per cent off store prices.

Whereas traditional Japanese toy stores have been small one or two-person operations, Toys 'R' Us established shops in wide open suburban areas where it could build large stores with plenty of parking. By 1994 Toys 'R' Us had 16 outlets, by 1996, 36, and it expected to have 100 stores by the year 2000.

One of the challenges undertaken by Toys 'R' Us was against Akachan Honpo, an Osaka baby-products wholesaler. Large Japanese wholesalers are not allowed to operate as retailers, and according to Akachan Honpo it, too, would deal only with registered dealers. However, it operated a scheme whereby individuals paying a yearly fee of ¥2000 ($20) could become registered member retailers and buy direct from the wholesaler. As a wholesaler, Akachan Honpo was not affected by the *Dai-Ten Hō*, but Toys 'R' Us complained that since it was actually acting as a retailer the law not only applied, but Akachan Honpo was breaching the law by being open every day of the year; a retail operation had to have the mandatory 24 days' holiday, as Toys 'R' Us had been doing. Despite prior government 'administrative guidance' – advice a number of years before from MITI that Akachan Honpo should desist its retail activities – it didn't, and MITI hadn't pressured it to. This was in part because to operate as a retailer would have required it to stop trading for months while the application was processed. But when Toys 'R' Us complained, something had to be done lest there be further complaints from the US government. In early 1996 MITI ordered Akachan Honpo to do something about its retail activities, to which Akachan Honpo responded that it would apply to operate as a retail store in conformity with the *Dai-Ten Hō*. However, in order to avoid damage to the company MITI did allow it to remain open over the application period.

Selling in the distribution system

Higher-priced market

Many foreign business people have noted that the prices of foreign goods available in the Japanese market are higher than in their home country and accuse Japan's distribution system of being biased against foreign goods. The distribution portion of the market may inflate the price of goods, but it does so without respect to their origin. Basically, Japanese people have paid high prices for everything.

It is true that at times when the yen has strengthened, importers have not always passed on the exchange benefits to the consumer, and this has made foreign goods more expensive, or has taken away the price advantage they may have had. It's quite easy not to drop one's price when the exchange rate changes – that is, if there is no other competition in the market.

The question, then, is why hasn't there been more competition in the second biggest market in the world? If there had been competition, merchants would have had to drop their prices. The answer is related to the oligopolistic control wholesalers and manufacturers have had through distribution, and to official government influence. This control has kept outsiders – both foreign and Japanese – out.

The other reason for the higher prices of some imports is that during the bubble expansion, and to a lesser extent after it, consumers paid to buy status. Despite the best efforts of foreigners to keep prices down to achieve entry into the Japanese market, once their product was accepted by a Japanese firm, those firms sometimes jacked-up the price in order to sell the good as a status item. Otherwise, the retail price of goods is a function of the factor costs that accrue as they pass through the system.

Distributing in Japan

Marketing through a trading company (sōgō shōsha)

When the Japanese wanted to export products after the country opened up more than 100 years ago, lacking foreign language skills, knowledge of foreign culture and business protocol, they developed *sōgō shōsha* (general traders) to handle their trade. And in the 1950s, while the economy was recovering after World War II, those small manufacturers still without any avenue to export were linked by MITI to *sōgō shōsha*.[13] Japan's smaller companies became an important income earner and greatly contributed to the nation's growth. Even now, smaller manufacturers of 100 or fewer employees account for a third of Japan's ex-factory manufacturing output.[14] And much of the penetration of Japan's smaller companies into overseas markets can be attributed to the assistance given by the *sōgō shōsha*.[15]

For some time now, the situation has been reversed. Westerners have been trying to enter and sell in Japan, and Japan's cultural, linguistic and business systems have been problematic. Small foreign producers lack presence in Japan and also, importantly, their products lack brand recognition.

Some exporters have been fortunate enough to sell through a large Japanese *sōgō shōsha*. Having goods go through a *sōgō shōsha* avails you of a number of benefits. There is the possibility of having your purchases financed, or at least having a quick enough turn-around time – between buying, then selling to the *shōsha* – that extended finance isn't an issue. It is also possible that you would be virtually left out of the transaction, since there may be no role for you when dealing with such an omnipotent organization. Instead ,you could be in receipt of a commission for the purchase of the goods. And that's a nice position to be in; it frees you up for other things.

I knew of a small foreign partnership with good enough contacts inside Marubeni (one of the big *shōsha*) that they got a product imported through Marubeni, and sold through Seibu Seed, a trendy retail wing of the very large Seibu department store. They negotiated an annual commission for themselves, and Marubeni handled the whole trade. They were indeed very lucky; for most 'mortal' foreigners, this type of deal is one chance in a few hundred. It was so rare a possibility that because they couldn't repeat the process, that is, generate continued business, they had no other trade and so eventually stopped marketing to Japan.

It's common for a foreign manufacturer to have a product that hasn't yet seen the light of day in Japan, but which is keenly awaiting someone to try to sell it there. The problem is getting such an organization as a *shōsha* to throw its weight behind the product. From the point of view of the *sōgō shōsha*, it is far easier to sell an item that comes from an already well-known stable than an unknown. This is applicable regardless of the recognition a product may have 'at home'. It's easy for those at home to think they have a product right for Japan, and in their own territory theirs may be by far the dominant brand.

But many foreigners find they must start marketing their product as a new brand when they enter Japan. In many cases the reason is the sheer number of suppliers that want to enter Japan – it can be stifling. I was once looking for a brand of swimwear I knew had been imported into Japan. I went into the swimwear section of a major Tokyo department store and found the swimwear rack. I saw some famous brands, but not the one I wanted. Then there was another rack, so I continued looking, at the end of that was another long row, and looking further I realized that two-thirds of the floor was full of 'unique' swimwear – at which point I gave up.

Generally, that much variety doesn't make it onto Japanese shelves, simply because store buyers intervene, limiting the number of brands they handle to either their long-term suppliers, or to what they interpret to be a remarkably different product.

It's clearly difficult for a producer to supply a product that does stand out in an environment that is already full of original goods, and where designs are restricted. Naturally, the differentiating characteristics become brand and price. Yet even price – unless it's very low – isn't necessarily an advantage where the brand, and by implication the quality, are unknown.

There is criticism that the *sōgō shōsha* take an excessive cut for their mediator services. However, these firms, which have spent years carving out a position in the Japanese economy – and generally operate on very thin margins – feel they have a right to a high premium for placing the product of an unknown firm through their hard-won, comprehensive trading network.

Marketing power is in the hands of distributors

True to its reputation, distribution in Japan is difficult, yet distribution is the heart of marketing. With the notable exception of industries in which powerful manufacturers or big retailers dominate marketing, distributors have extreme discretionary power over which products will be promoted.

In many industries there is a bottleneck in the system which is due to a type of oligopoly of distributors. Passage is normally based on quality, traditional supply, and favouritism. Control of distribution by Japanese companies has thereby contributed to the limited flow of imports through the Japanese supply chain.

Even if your product is fortunate enough to be accepted by a distributor, unless it is well known or otherwise very desirable, it will join others, with no special status or promotional push. You are essentially dealing with people who are too busy to be sympathetic to your cause. It's easy for a distributor not to push a product, particularly if it doesn't get a good initial response. Western quality is now often treated with some apprehension, at least in the case of goods that are not known or recognized.

For those who would like to 'sell direct', getting to Japanese retailers is a major difficulty. It not only involves barriers of language, protocol and custom, but those of general costs, including transporting people and products. All of these factors make distribution difficult and have led Japanese, as well as foreigners supplying Japan, to try to work through existing distributors. The problem with distributors is that they have a strong incentive to refuse: because distribution is expensive, those with an adequate range see no point in taking on another product. While a retailer can to some extent benefit from the additional variety of taking different products from a distributor, it's a nuisance for a distribution firm to handle a variety of suppliers. There's an incentive to keep trading only those few products that are guaranteed to sell well.

Although it is difficult, it is certainly not impossible for a foreign manufacturer who has market-savvy staff to enter the distribution part of the supply chain, or for a Japan-literate foreign trading operation to represent other, non-Japan-literate foreign suppliers in the distribution chain.

The infamous tight buyer–seller relationships that exist in the depths of the Japanese distribution channel are more of a bind for Japanese than foreign companies. Ironically, Japanese companies are often locked into structured trading relationships. An attractive foreign supplier offering a product not strictly available through a local distributor doesn't technically compete with them. Japanese retailers happy with a foreign supplier may deal direct.

In the 1920s the original Matsushita firm (maker of National/Panasonic brand goods) started selling electric bicycle lamps – to replace the candles used at the time. Since distributors didn't have faith in the product, Mr Matsushita felt he had to bypass them. Although his company was really too small to provide service to the retailers, he tried to promote the lamps directly to shops.[16] His success is now the stuff of legend, and Matsushita's company today controls about a third of Japan's smaller electronics retailers.[17]

The quality barrier

Matters relating to image can also let a product down. For instance, regardless of actual quality, a fashion item from Australia or the US won't compare well with products from such nations as France or Italy, or even Japan; national image stereotyping is accentuated in status-orientated Japan.

Compounding this status disadvantage is the actual quality of the goods. Most foreign-made goods that go into Japan need upgrading in order to sell. They need upgrading in terms of either finish, consistency of quality, or added features, since while the manufacturing will is often there, the needs of the consumer aren't known. This is not only a matter of suitability to the market, but of quality. Many products, though saleable in their home markets, are seen to have tangible quality problems. This may appear to be a strong attack on foreign goods, but it is unfortunately true.

Just as a small example, I have a souvenir pen from my home country. It's designed so that the nib emerges as the top half of the barrel is twisted. But after starting to write, the barrel rotates back and the nib retracts. It is not a cheap pen – it has the national logo and is sold as a tourist gift. But cheap or expensive, since there's not much demand for an auto-retract function on pens, it's poor quality. It's not a trite question to ask: is there any point in a company making such a pen?

I've had ties, on which the 'keeper' (the cloth loop on the back of the tie), which may proudly claim to be 'Made in Italy' or elsewhere, comes adrift at the stitching. There are not many parts of a tie to target for improvement. It therefore leaves one with the impression that product improvement was not part of the manufacturing process – if it were, the makers of those ties would have focused on that weak point long ago. Textile manufacturers should be aware that stitching is a perennial problem associated with textiles brought into Japan.

According to Zenith, a mid-sized Japanese company that manufactures nylon active wear, it buys 70 per cent of its textiles domestically and 30 per cent from Europe and Thailand. The Asian materials are the lowest in quality, but are the cheapest. In quality of design the European supplies are best, but practical quality matters 'appear beyond their sphere of importance', according to a Japanese executive. It's not uncommon for Zenith to face quality problems with goods received from Europe. For instance, they unroll a bolt of European material to find that the pattern lags at the edges, which means the edges have to be cut and thrown away. Imports fail on other criteria; for instance, they fail to meet the minimum standards of waterproofing. Japanese supplies, too, sometimes fail, but imported products pose much more of a gamble. It's a matter of 'what will happen next' – late delivery, or a product fault. . .? Furthermore, and most importantly, Japanese firms will react quickly and work intently to resolve a problem and get replacement product to the customer. For Japanese firms that import, this kind of situation is very common – which is why in this firm's case only 30 per cent of its supplies come from abroad.

Yanase, Japan's largest importer of foreign cars, has a side business repairing those cars – not after they are sold, but as the vehicles enter Japan before they even reach the market. And according to an executive at Yanase, their American cars have far more problems than their German cars, although American quality did improve through the 1990s.

Foreign car makers have altered their approach to the market and many chose to enter distribution directly. Chrysler chose to create its own marketing channel and became the first of the old 'big three' auto makers to gain direct and complete control over its Japanese distribution and retail activity by buying into car dealer Seibu Motor Sales Co. in 1995. BMW was the first foreign car company to set up a 100 per cent foreign-owned subsidiary in Japan. It began by selling through an agent, Balcom Japan, but in 1981 it took over Balcom's business. From a marketing point of view, BMW is interesting in that then, instead of developing and selling through existing generic car dealers, it established exclusive BMW dealerships. It advertised for and chose people it considered had good potential as dealers, without focusing on their automotive experience. And it succeeded. By taking this approach it gained more contact, and enhanced its image with its customers, presenting an exclusive image that helped make foreign cars a symbol of status in Japan.

At the end of 1992 Volkswagen (VW) was dumped by Yanase because VW's policy of being marketed as a 'people's car' conflicted with Yanase's upscale image. VW expanded its own network of franchises and improved its sales to become, in 1994, the top-selling foreign auto maker in Japan. Japanese distributors are often tied to the needs of other suppliers, or have preconceived marketing strategies detached from the plans of their foreign suppliers. In this case Yanase preferred to profit from high price rather than volume, and so wanted to limit sales volume and sell VW as a luxury car. VW wanted volume, and they got it.

Marketing to specific regions

These are examples of big firms, but small foreign suppliers dealing in smaller volumes can also take advantage of Japanese distribution channels, but it becomes very taxing. For instance, Japanese industrial buyers expect suppliers to have a lot of service staff. According to one commentator, in order to have any effect marketing pharmaceuticals, you need a sales force of more than 1000 field staff.[18] Localized marketing, however, can result in the penetration of a manageable geographical area. It's still costly, and requires the skills discussed earlier, but can be developed from a smaller business base.

There are other specific advantages in operating locally. High advertising costs make it financially prohibitive to engage in nationwide marketing. The high population density throughout most of populated Japan makes mobility of goods and people difficult. Furthermore, in Japan it's desirable to maintain close contact with clients – Japanese business people prefer a person-to-person approach. These factors support the idea of localized marketing. The dense population then becomes a benefit – relatively small areas constitute rich markets, which are relatively easy to target for sales promotion. Localized, targeted advertising, through local newspapers and TV stations, is normally cheaper and can still reach a large audience.

It's interesting to note, and it may be a vital concern for your company, that many foreign companies enter Japan expecting to soon move to nationwide operation. Yet survey data on foreign companies shows that few actually achieve this goal: 50 per cent of foreign companies that had been in Japan for over 30 years operated nationally, and fewer than 20 per cent of those that had been in Japan for between ten and 20 years did.

Still, this doesn't mean they have failed; of those firms that had not reached national level, 60 per cent expected to meet or exceed their corporate objectives.[19] The upshot is that new entrant firms should either be prepared to allow a longer time frame before reaching nationwide distribution, or perhaps set their sights on operating at a regional level and bear in mind that strategically, operating locally is not a bad thing, as regions can constitute a loyal and healthy market.

We don't want any more accounts

One problem faced in the course of distributing in Japan is coming up against buyers who decline business on the basis that they have a sufficient number of existing accounts. For them to buy your goods, they say, would require them to go through the process of opening another account for your company. Although this might seem odd at first, there are reasons. Long-term participants in the market are naturally wary of new, fly-by-night entrants. Also, Japanese distributors may have many companies knocking at their door – yours may be just one. If they were to take on everything that looked good and was inexpensive, they would simply be expending time on a plethora of firms and products when it would be far better to try to develop trust among a relatively small number of suppliers.

Handling small unknown companies generates paperwork and risk. Once business begins, Japanese firms like to drop their guard, put trust in the other firm, and get on with business. Thus, they have to spend a lot more time going through the process of getting to know a new company first. Also, in a market that is brand-loyal more than it is bargain-conscious, it is important for a merchant's customers that the new supplier remain in the market. Regular customers, if satisfied with a product, expect to be able to return to a shop in order to buy it again, or have it serviced.

Foreigners sometimes complain that their competitively priced goods aren't even given a chance in Japan. They conclude, therefore, that it is due to prejudice. But to reiterate the point, while price is important, it's not important to the exclusion of other factors, including a long-term relationship. Japanese companies consider it more expedient to deal with trusted suppliers and existing products. They prefer a consistent supply, without payment or delivery hassles. In economic terms, delinquent payments, changes of supplier – in other words, inconsistency – comes at a cost. Japanese have considered it better to pay a bit more for an existing supply than face such costs and take on additional risk.

The relationship between Japanese auto firms and their parts suppliers provides a good example. Auto firms claim that they judge the suitability of their suppliers on, amongst other things, the stability of the management, previous performance, and reliability, because consistency of supply is vitally important once the production schedule is decided upon.[20] Long-standing suppliers obviously have an advantage in this since they will engender greater confidence in their buyers; new foreign firms are simply an unknown quantity. If a Japanese firm already has a sufficient number of suppliers, and unless you have something very unique to offer, it's not in their interests to go to the effort of taking you on.

Conclusion

It may be a bit of an understatement to say that the distribution sector is challenging. It's a tiresome system, and it's one in which the doors to entry are not left open. But it is possible to create links with the many friendly and cooperative business operators – this is especially so of Japan's small and medium-sized businesses – the key being the approach you take. If you work smart, you can not only get a foot in the door, but actually make the Japanese distribution system work for you.

Notes

1 *US & Japan III*, JETRO, 1994, pp. 80–81.
2 In full, *Daikibo Kouri Tenpo Hō*; abbreviated, *Dai-ten hō* or Big Store Law.
3 *Dai-Ten Hō* references include: *The Changing Face of Japanese Retail*, JETRO, 1995, pp. 12–15; *Japan's Distribution Channels*, JETRO, 1995, p. 16; Itō and Maruyama, in Krugman, 1991, pp. 158–59; Suzuki, Y., in Czinkota and Kotabe, 1993, pp. 163–70; Hsu, 1994, pp. 220–21.
4 *The Changing Face of Japanese Retail*, JETRO, 1995, p. 14.
5 *Tokyo Business Today*, December 1993, p. 9; also November 1993, p. 22; October 1994, pp. 4–9.
6 Johnson does note that Nakauchi didn't want to do away with the *Dai-Ten Hō* altogether (1995, p. 84).
7 *Tokyo Business Today*, October 1994, p. 7.
8 Lady Borden's 'secret recipe', and Daiei's modified recipe, sold under its Savings brand, were both produced simultaneously by Tip Top, in Auckland, New Zealand.
9 *Nikkei Ryūtsu Shimbun* survey, in *The Changing Face of Japanese Retail*, JETRO, 1995, p. 31.
10 March 1990, p. 112.
11 *The Nikkei Weekly*, 9 September 1996, pp. 1 and 23.
12 *The Nikkei Weekly*, 9 September 1996, pp. 1 and 23.
13 Miyashita and Russell, 1994, p. 37; Johnson, 1982, p. 206.
14 These businesses also accounted for a third of the value added. Output is measured in yen. Calculated from *Small Business in Japan*, MITI, 1994, pp. 218–19.
15 See Yoshihara, who notes the importance of the *sōgō shōsha* to small businesses. Also, that the SMEs were not only important to Japan's post-World War II economy, but that they were of much greater importance than SMEs in the US (1982, pp. 212–17).
16 Koren, 1990, p. 150.

17 Matsushita's businesses evolved to dominate a strong vertical *keiretsu*. In 1982, of over 71,000 Japanese electronics retailers, two-thirds were under the top five makers, Matsushita, Tōshiba, Hitachi, Sony and Sanyō, and half of those were under the single control of Matsushita (Miyashita and Russell, 1994, p. 124).

18 Ohmae, 1990, p. 156.

19 *Japan in Revolution, An Assessment of Investment Performance by Foreign Firms in Japan*, ACCJ, The Council of the European Business Community and A. T. Kearney, Inc., 1995, p. 13. Sample: US and EU firms, n = 127 (which is a 21 per cent response rate).

20 Auto makers select suppliers on the basis of quality, cost, capability of development and of delivery, management stability, previous performance and trust (FTC 'Survey of Transactions between Firms and Auto Parts', *FTC/Japan Views*, No. 17, February 1994, pp. 56–57).

Chapter 15

Direct marketing – non-store retailing

While there are many difficulties associated with the Japanese distribution system, it has proved extremely effective for some Western companies. But many firms coming into Japan either don't have the knowledge, the time or the resources to begin developing relationships with Japanese distributors. For those who want to appeal to Japanese consumers quickly, efficiently and economically, there is another option: go direct.

Direct marketing (DM) involves promoting a product direct to the buyer, bypassing a retail point of sale. It includes door-to-door selling, television and telephone sales, direct mail and catalogues, and the other sales promotion methods shown in Table 15.1. It also includes the emerging forms of selling via electronic media. This new media adds convenience to non-store marketing and shopping and is expected to experience continued strong growth.

While Japan has a history of non-store retailing, it has been late to adopt some of the now popular forms of direct marketing, and is behind other nations in non-store sales. Whereas in the US and Germany by the mid-1990s mail-order shopping accounted for 4–5 per cent of all retailing, in Japan it only accounted for about 1.5 per cent.[1] However, Japan's market is quickly growing.

For foreigners wanting to sell in Japan, direct marketing has several advantages. Advances in communications technology are making distance less of an obstacle to international selling. And marketing direct to consumers and supplying goods by mail avoids many of the non-tariff barriers associated with conventional trade with Japan. Further, more and more Japanese consumers want novel products, and through direct marketing and mail-order selling many foreign suppliers will win the chance to put their products on the Japanese market.

The distinction between direct marketing and direct mail should be clarified. At times the two are discussed as though they were the same thing. This is largely because mail – the world's third largest promotional medium next to newspapers and TV – is often the primary medium used in direct marketing. But mail is simply one form (employed to convey promotional material) used in direct marketing. Confusion is only compounded when some publications use the abbreviation DM to refer to *direct marketing* and others to *direct mail*. Here – and in accordance with Japan Direct Marketing Association (JADMA) usage – DM refers to *direct marketing*. One practical reason for this is that direct mail is becoming dated both as a term and as a system as it becomes eclipsed by other methods of promotion, such as electronic media.

There is also a definitional problem with the use of mail-order (MO). Years ago, order forms were sent by mail and goods were received by mail, so 'mail-order' was a good general description. But nowadays mail is simply one of several means of transfer. This raises the question, do orders by telephone, the Internet, and TV shopping qualify as 'mail-order'? As it is defined here, and by Japan's Ministry of International Trade and Industry,

Table 15.1 Direct marketing. Adapted from JETRO, *Mail Order Market*, 1995

	Means of contact	Point of sale	Media	Sales promotion method	Means of purchase
Store marketing	Store	Store	Store	Retail store	
Direct marketing (DM)	Face-to-face	Visit buyer's home	Door-to-door sales, sales with catalogues, taking orders		Face-to-face
		Buyer's home	Organized network	Co-op, joint purchase	
		Buyer's home	Home party	Home party, door-to-door	
		Workplace	Visit workplace	Sales at workplace, organized channels	
		Hotel, etc.	Temporary space	Exhibition sales, mobile shop, dispatched sales staff	
	Telephone	Telephone	Telephone	Telemarketing	Mail order
	Non-face-to-face	Buyer's home	Newspaper/magazine ads	Direct mail	
			Leaflets/fliers	Direct mail	
			Mail targeting specific customers	Direct mail	
			Catalogues	Catalogue shopping	
			Television/radio	TV/radio shopping	
			Multimedia	Electronic shopping	
	Vending machines	Machines	Vending machines	Vending machines	Electronic

yes, they do. Here, mail-order refers to those types of non-store purchase where delivery to the buyer is 'by mail'. (Still, this too is becoming a misnomer; as we'll soon see, nowadays most goods are sent by means other than postal delivery.)

The forms of purchase included in 'mail-order' are clearly shown in the shaded area in Table 15.1. Table 15.1 also shows the relationship between direct marketing and mail-order: DM refers to the means of marketing, mail-order refers to the means of product delivery.[2]

Japan's non-store experience

When Japan began to become a wealthy participant in the world market, the Western concept of DM was considered one possible idea to be exported from the West. It was another form of marketing which was succeeding in the West, and Japan, a new and buoyant market, was an obvious new port of call for those wishing to expand their business.

However, there was also a belief that DM wouldn't work in Japan.[3] This belief had its roots in the idea that the risk-averse Japanese would be reluctant to make purchases where the vendor wasn't visible or of fixed abode. In addition, Japanese shopping was structured around small community stores. This way of shopping had been cited as traditional and immutable, and it was believed that it would block other forms of buying.

True, Japanese do share a degree of apprehension about non-store purchases, and this has slowed the progress of direct marketers. Suspicion of non-store sales, including door-to-door selling, was eased in Japan with the introduction in 1976 and the revisions in 1984 and 1988 of the Door-to-Door Sales and Other Sales Law. This legislation aimed to curb exploitation through exaggerated claims (false advertising) and the intimidation of buyers. It also allowed a cooling-off period of seven days after the day of purchase, in which goods could be returned without penalty. In general, the view that there is Japan-specific cultural resistance to direct marketing is largely unfounded.

Door-to-door

Various types of direct marketing have long histories in Japan. In pre-war Tokyo, people would do much of their shopping from the house. Grocers would phone to ask if customers needed to make orders, and greengrocers, butchers and *tōfu* sellers called on homes to take orders.[4] Though much of the home delivery service has declined, some of these non-store services remain, and they fall into three categories. There are those who deliver in response to an order, e.g. a telephone order. Examples include picking up and returning laundry, and delivering beer, *sushi* and other Japanese takeaway foods such as noodles – empty noodle bowls are left by customers on their doorstep and are collected afterwards.

There are merchants who circulate through the neighbourhood. These include *tōfu* sellers who deliver by bicycle, cooked potato sellers and cooked octopus sellers who pull carts equipped with an open fire and grill. Some modern merchants use a light truck with an open stove on the back. Even around modern Tokyo these traders are still visible.

The third category are those who go door-knocking. Apart from regular callers, Japan also has a long history of cold door-to-door selling. Nomura Tokushichi II, of the famous house that produced Nomura Securities, pioneered Japanese retail stockbrokerage at the end of the nineteenth century by riding around Osaka on a bicycle. After World War II, Nomura staff continued the practice of knocking on doors, trying to convince housewives and shopkeepers to invest their money in stocks.[5] It is quite common for business people to engage in door-to-door selling. Newspaper subscriptions in particular are solicited in this way. Banks go door-to-door trying to enlist customers or extend existing business. Car dealers make about half of their sales door-to-door.[6] They go around streets, check the age of vehicles, and if the expensive government-authorized certificate of inspection (*shaken*) is near due they will approach the owner with the offer of a new car. A popular example of door-to-door sales is of yoghurt, normally peddled by women who travel by bicycle.

Modern forms of direct marketing have continued where traditional forms have left off. The home party approach to direct selling, involving a gathering of 'friends' who have a party based around a product range as supplied by the sales person, has grown. Examples of companies involved in this are Tupperware and Amway. Amway is doing well in Japan. Of foreign affiliated companies (Amway Japan is 91.5 per cent non-Japanese owned), Amway moved from tenth highest income earner in 1989 to reach second highest, next to Coca-Cola (Japan), in 1994. It also made Amway 76th income earner amongst all Japanese companies at that time.[7]

Mail-order

Of all sales that result from direct marketing, purchases using MO delivery account for over a third.[8]

Sowing seeds

MO in Japan is assumed to have started with the sale of seeds through an agricultural magazine in November 1876. From the middle of the 1890s, department stores, newspapers, other publishers, and other merchants provided MO services. Both those offering MO as a secondary or supplementary business and specialist MO houses grew. In 1943, during World War II, while there were materials shortages and rationing, these operations ceased trading, and after the war, faced with a continued shortage of goods, the businesses struggled. In the 1960s the market picked up again and expanded along with the burgeoning economy.[9]

During the 1970s the MO market entered a period of strong growth. But MO was still hampered by inadequate means of exchanging both goods and money. Traditional delivery services were poor – delivery took a long time, was unreliable, and resulted in unacceptable damage and loss. While this was often the fault of the mail system, it reflected on, and was at the expense of, the MO industry.[10]

The situation started to change in January 1976, when Yamato Transport Co. Ltd began its *Takkyūbin* service, providing to-door delivery of small parcels. Speedy delivery was assisted by the consolidation of Japan's highway network. Now, parcels couriered from Tokyo to anywhere in Japan's main island, Honshū, or to Shikoku, can be delivered overnight; those to Hokkaidō or Kyūshū take two days. From the mid-1970s until the mid-1980s Post Office small parcel deliveries went into decline, and private delivery companies experienced exceptional, virtually continuous growth. The MO business, too, continued to grow, with strong sales expansion only affected slightly by the 1990s recession. Overall, the development of the delivery and MO services assisted each other.[11]

By the mid-1990s home delivery services accounted for over two-thirds of merchandise deliveries, while the postal service only accounted for about one tenth, and MO in-house systems accounted for slightly more than a tenth.[12]

In the mid-1980s the Japanese MO business entered a growth phase. Sales doubled from ¥1mn to ¥2mn, in the period between 1986 and 1994.[13] Other changes came with advances in electronic media. Computerization made information processing and stock control accurate and efficient, making it more cost-effective for those in the industry, and making it easier for newcomers to enter. This enhanced competition and allowed the industry to raise its profile and its sales.

Communication, however, is still limited; as a 'delivery' system it lacks convenient, instant exchange of cash, goods and information. There is a delay in communication between buyer and seller that is absent in face-to-face sales. Mail-order houses have tried to make it easier for the buyer by, for instance, providing postage-paid reply or free-dial services. Telephone – the easiest form of communication – is responsible for over half of the orders placed for MO goods.[14] These media are, however, still a long way from providing the confidence available in a face-to-face sale.

Payment systems

As of 1996 Japanese firms had begun experimental testing of electronic money systems, with authorization for use expected before the year 2000 – clearly offering good potential for making MO payments. Still, most Japanese people have been conservative bankers. They bypassed the use of the personal cheque, with some people moving from cash transactions and turning to credit cards as a higher class form of payment. By 1996 credit card payments were worth 6 per cent of the value of Japan's total retail sales – representing a total 1 per cent increase over the previous two years.

However, even with the existing and ready availability of other forms of payment, the primary method of paying for domestic (dispatched within Japan) MO supplies remains the postal transfer – requiring the buyer to go to the Post Office and deposit the payment, which is then credited to the MO firm. This method is used in almost 40 per cent of sales. The next most common method is cash on delivery, accounting for payments in a third of sales. One problem with cash on delivery is that people feel they have to be at home to receive the goods. Around a tenth of payments are by bank transfer. In historical terms, these are crude forms of payment. They didn't pose the same problems in a more traditional Japan in which the wife didn't work and could more easily go to the Post Office or receive deliveries, but this way of life is changing.

Payment by credit card accounts for just 15 per cent of domestic MO sales.[15] One reason for low card use is a reluctance to pay in advance of getting the goods: the future will bring swifter forms of payment, but the focus shouldn't be on urgency of payment, rather on systems to maintain consumer confidence. What is needed overall is technology that will lessen the distance between the buyer and the seller, making it feel easier and safer for customers to purchase by mail. For instance, Mitsui Bussan was one of the first to offer a CD-ROM – called Curio City. It provided a virtual 'stroll' through a shopping mall, allowing buyers to drop into specific shops and view products at a click of the mouse. Continued developments in technology will take home shopping beyond catalogues, give the buyers more contact with the products, and make shopping more realistic and enjoyable.

Perception of mail-order

Problems with MO can be divided into those that affect the customer and those that affect the seller. One problem for buyers is that the product doesn't always match up with customer expectations. Either it just isn't suitable, or sizes of, for example, clothing, shoes or bedding don't fit well. Buyers also like to touch and see the products they buy, and some buyers want the excitement of actually going out shopping.[16]

Experiencing the system

There is also a perception problem. The most striking perception amongst people who haven't used MO is that it is unreliable. Alternatively, favourable perceptions held by those who have used MO include: that it is easy, convenient, fun, and that it is very reliable.[17]

The positive perception may in part be because buyers tend to justify their purchases, and non-buyers also justify their behaviour. Nevertheless, for those selling by MO the fact remains that there will be more reluctance to buy amongst those who haven't bought by mail before.

Furthermore, repeat usage is common. According to survey results, of those who bought by MO in a single year only one fifth bought only once. Almost 60 per cent bought by mail between two and four times, and another fifth bought more than five times.[18]

This reflects the general point that once a person is familiar with a system it takes much less energy to repeat the process. For people who have gone through the steps involved in ordering goods, doing it again is easy. A marketing tool which could persuade individuals to make that first purchase would therefore be very profitable.

Overall, MO in Japan has developed a positive image, or at least its image has improved. Responsible management, voluntary development of efficient returns systems – domestic returns were about 3.2 per cent in 1996 – and help lines have given confidence to MO users.[19] Still, there are problems in this respect. By mid-1998 the number of MO companies on the Internet had doubled over the previous year to 8400, and there had, understandably, been an increase in the number of complaints from people who hadn't received what they'd ordered or paid for. In response to this, and the fact that only about 10 per cent already did so, as of 1 June 1988 all domestic MO companies were required by law to supply a contact number and the name of a contact person on their home page to field enquiries.

For MO merchants in Japan, the perennial and dominant problem is developing and stocking unique, original merchandise. This was by far the issue most often cited by Japanese MO companies as important. While this is a nuisance for Japanese MO firms who need novel goods, it is a good omen for foreign suppliers, who have greatest access to products that are unavailable in Japan.

Other problems frequently cited by merchants include the compilation and maintenance of customer lists, and the high cost of both advertising and postage in Japan.[20] It is quite acceptable in Japan to pass on the cost of postage to the buyer as an additional charge.[21]

Many MO products are imported by DM companies before being on-sold to customers. In research on these imports, the problem cited by the greatest number of DM companies was merchandise quality. The second most often cited problem was punctuality. These two stood head and shoulders above other problems – including number three, which was exchange rate fluctuations.[22] Further, these two problems are exactly the same as those noted in purchases of foreign goods in other areas of Japanese business. It should be a message to foreign exporters and export advisers who deal with Japan to monitor quality and punctuality.

Individual importers

The problems experienced by MO firms that import their goods differ from those felt by individuals who import goods direct by international MO. Two problems cited by over a third of individual users were higher than expected shipping and customs charges, and, again, that receiving the goods took longer than expected – i.e. punctuality.

About a quarter of international MO users were dissatisfied with product size or specification, the wrong goods were sent by the MO company, or the products didn't match their expectations. Problems cited by fewer than 15 per cent of international MO users included merchandise not turning up or merchandise arriving damaged. Less commonly cited problems included a variety of accounting errors.[23] Many of the problems involve errors that should be readily managed with modern accounting and stocking technology.

What are the three things Japanese customers want most of foreign MO companies?

1 A list of exact shipping charges to Japan
2 A catalogue in the Japanese language
3 A clear and understandable size conversion chart.[24]

Japan uses the metric system, and sellers should supply measurements (if not products) that conform to that system. Clothing sizes S, M, L and LL are at best indications, and seldom match Japanese body sizes. It's less troublesome for the supplier to provide universal measurements than for customers to gamble on getting the right product size.

When ordering from overseas, Japanese are also troubled by having to complain or otherwise communicate with suppliers who don't speak Japanese. There are services available to cope with the problem. A subsidiary of the Japanese phone company KDD, called KDD Teleserve, provides an ¥800 ($6) per minute interpreting service to assist with such problems. At least one up-market women's magazine has offered an English writing course to help housewives communicate with MO firms by letter. But these are not exactly solutions if the things a buyer expects from MO include low price and convenience.

Many Japanese people can write English better than they can speak it, and this, coupled with the quick-response capabilities of on-line communication – increasingly used to order goods – will also ease trouble-shooting – that is, assuming foreign firms can respond quickly, and be sensitive to the indirect way Japanese communicate. Those foreign MO companies who seriously intend moving into Japan would boost customer confidence more by providing a trouble-shooting office in Japan.

Sales

Buyers

1 Most MO buyers are women. Overall, 45 per cent of women, vs. 20 per cent of men have used MO.
2 Most women buyers are in their 30s, then 20s. About 70 per cent of women in these age groups have bought by MO. Buyers tail off on either side of that age group.
3 The main buyers are housewives, the second most frequent user category is part-time workers, third is full-time workers.[25]

Women are normally the family shoppers in Japan. Since Japanese women traditionally control the family finances, they are an influential spending group. In addition, as more Japanese women enter the workforce, as a group they have less time to shop, and they have more disposable income, both of which impact on their use of non-store shopping. Japanese housewives are also – depending on their husband's income – quite 'competent' luxury shoppers, and, even with spending reduced relative to that in the 'brand label' years of the 1980s, many of these women want to maintain a certain lifestyle, and many are willing to buy fashion goods at the lower prices available through MO.

From a marketing point of view, it is worth remembering that most Japanese see themselves as belonging to the same (middle) social class. And, as mentioned earlier, much of their buying involves the 'consumption' of dominant fashion – few Japanese want to really stand out, even in fashion.[26] For those supplying fashion goods, this means a large, homogeneous customer base, which makes marketing easier. Differences in buyer preferences within the same age group won't depend on fashion as much as spending power.

Many Japanese people who use MO want to get something that is unavailable in the shops. While one of the reasons they want to shop by mail, is to save money, they normally also want something of good quality and something that has unique features.

There are also practical reasons for shopping by mail and these will become much more important as the population ages. While there is some reluctance amongst today's older generation to shop by mail, as Japan's now young population of MO-literate buyers ages, and the MO system matures, it will be easy for the elderly to use mail in order to fulfil their shopping needs. MO will, in particular, allow them to continue to shop as their own mobility decreases.

Business buyers

When thinking about MO, we tend to overlook an important category of buyer: businesses. It is very much in the interests of businesses to have inexpensive, reliable and high-quality supplies; in many cases supplies sourced by mail from overseas should be able to meet that demand. I've been involved in supplying McIntosh-built Manx Norton motorbike parts to Japan. Ken McIntosh is the world's only supplier of all this bike's parts made to 100 per cent original specifications, and these have been sold to dealers who, once they knew of a good supply, were happy to order by mail. Our first means of promotion and contact with Japanese buyers was via articles in a specialist magazine.

McIntosh is also one of the small handful of people I've known who, from the outset, had a level of quality that meant his goods needed no improvement in order to enter Japan. Instead, his quality level even impressed Japanese people in his line of business. But from a marketing point of view, his quality goods are stuck at the bottom of the Pacific amid a relatively small market. Internationally, his buyers are low in concentration, well-dispersed specialists. A MO system is the best means of disseminating his products overseas.

Computer-related goods are also suitable for sale to businesses by mail. As the field is innovating rapidly, computing magazines are a good avenue for buyers to find information about new products and to then order by mail. Relatively small purchases can be made, and an efficient supplier should be able to land goods in Japan quickly. Making small *ad hoc* purchases may be useful for buyers, either to test the market, or because in a quickly changing field products can soon become obsolete.[27]

Price ranges of mail-order purchases

Research has revealed that almost one-quarter of domestic MO purchases were for goods of between ¥10,000 and ¥15,000 ($80–$120). Purchase categories at either side of these figures, that is, cheaper purchases of between ¥5000 and ¥10,000 ($40–$80), and also more expensive purchases of between ¥15,000 and ¥20,000 ($120–$160), each accounted for about 15 per cent of MO sales.

As for international MO purchases, the average value was higher. Almost 60 per cent of orders involved transactions of between ¥10,000 and ¥30,000 ($80–$240); 14 per cent of

Table 15.2 Popular products – Sales by JADMA direct marketing firms[a] (weighted average[b])

Product	Sales (%)
Apparel and bedding	39.2
Furniture, appliances and household goods	19.8
Correspondence courses	14.2
Dress ornaments and precious metals	7.7
Health, beauty and pharmaceutical supplies and equipment	5.5
Food – general and health	4.4
Hobbies and toys – cameras, DIY, sports, motorbikes	2.9
Art and music – CDs, tapes, art supplies	2.1
Books and stationery	0.9
Insurance, financial and travel services	1.9
Others	1.4
Total	100

Source: JADMA (Japan Direct Marketing Association), *Direct Marketing in Japan*, 1996, p. 30; figures for 1994.
[a] JADMA members account for 90.5 per cent of sales from direct marketing.
[b] To get a more accurate picture of average sales, JADMA compensates for small companies selling high percentages of certain products by multiplying the proportion of sales for each company by its total sales.

purchases were for less, that is, ¥5000–¥10,000; 15 per cent of purchases were for between ¥30,000 and ¥40,000. Few orders were for very expensive items. It should be noted that these international figures included postage and tariff amounts.

Compare these prices with the price of goods sold on Television Tokyo's late-night shopping programme. One mid-1996 show offered two different types of women's necklaces, a portable electronic word processor, a video camera, an air filter, a multi-purpose cleaner, and a dietary supplement. Though these may seem standard products, most had features new to the market – a prerequisite of MO goods in general. Both electronic products were produced by famous Japanese makers. Prices ranged from ¥12,800–¥128,000 (about $120–$1200). The average price was ¥54,370 ($500). In some cases cheaper versions were also on offer – the prices cited here represent the higher-priced options.

Two things can be expected to happen regarding the value of MO goods in future. The volume of purchases, as well as the purchase price of more expensive goods such as those sold on late-night TV, can be expected to increase. Also, as MO becomes more common and accessible, an increase in lower-priced sales can also be expected. In other words, an increase across the board can be expected.

International mail-order purchases

Buying from overseas by MO grew in the mid-1980s in the period referred to as *endaka*, that is, the period after the 1985 Plaza Accord when the value of the yen was raised and foreign products became cheaper in Japan. In the 1990s the growth trend continued. Overseas goods became even less expensive and as more Japanese experienced foreign countries, Japanese tastes broadened.

'Art for art's sake' represented one aspect of Japanese spending during the bubble years with, in many cases, 'spending for spending's sake' influencing purchases. But while in the 1990s shoppers still wanted fashion, they were more discerning about their spending.

Compared with sales from domestic MO companies, a relatively small number of Japanese people have ordered from abroad. Still, international MO buying has expanded considerably. By 1993 the number of international MO buyers had reached 7 per cent of the population; by 1996 the figure had more than doubled, to 15 per cent.[28] Also, in contrast with domestic purchases, almost nine out of ten international buyers pay by credit card, but note that this is still a low aggregate figure of credit card use.[29]

As an indication of how successful a foreign company can be at direct selling in Japan, consider US outdoor goods supplier L. L. Bean: in 1995, Bean's products accounted for 60 per cent of the international parcel mail that came into Japan. L. L. Bean sends on average about 3000 parcels a day to customers in this country.[30] By any yardstick, that is a dramatic mail-order success story.

Some Japanese opt to buy overseas goods through an agent. Agents stock a variety of foreign catalogues and take orders. They profit by obtaining a rebate from the supplier and/or, in a few cases, by selling catalogues to consumers.

Of the reasons given for buying from overseas, again, buyers wanted products at lower prices, and products unavailable at home. About a third of those who bought from overseas also wanted something other people didn't have.[31]

Type of promotional media used

Once again, let's look at the division of in-house media and media handled by a third party.

In-house: The major share (something under three-quarters) of MO advertising expenditure is devoted to in-house promotional media, which fall into two dominant categories:

● catalogues (about two-thirds)
● leaflets (a bit under a third).

Third party: Just over a quarter of MO advertising expenditure is spent on, and MO sales result from, third party promotional media. Of this:

● newspaper advertising accounts for about 30 per cent of spending
● magazine advertising accounts for just over a quarter
● TV-based promotion accounts for another quarter.[32]

Looking at the consumption of MO promotional media, the most popular category is domestic catalogues. Survey data found that 44 per cent of MO shopping is done through catalogues. Over half of all women MO shoppers used catalogues, and of those, two-thirds of women in their 20s and 30s did. Clearly, the catalogue is the most useful method of making contact with young female MO buyers. Magazine ads were responsible for 16 per cent, and inserts in newspapers for another 16 per cent of MO purchases made by women.

Another popular approach to direct sales is TV shopping, as we shall see in a moment. This is the case in particular amongst older women. Almost 40 per cent of women shopping by MO in their 50s bought through TV. There is much less of a spread between types of DM promotion used by male shoppers. A quarter of men use catalogues; this is followed by TV, then other print media.[33]

Entering the mail-order market

Though there are other forms of non-store selling, MO is the method that best lends itself to use by foreigners. One of the biggest incentives for being involved in MO in Japan is that it bypasses very difficult areas of Japanese business. It avoids the distribution system and many of the other formalities involved in bringing products into Japan. Furthermore, the MO business is free of entry restrictions, both for those operating within Japan and those supplying direct from abroad.[34]

There are, however, certain considerations. Mail-order imports are still subject to import tax. Overseas JETRO offices normally have a copy of Japan's customs tariff schedule – written in both Japanese and English.

Goods are subject to the scrutiny of specific product laws. These include, for instance, the Food Sanitation Law, Household Goods Quality Labelling Law, Pharmaceuticals Law and Product Liability Law. Sales are also subject to the Door-to-Door Law mentioned above, which stipulates that advertisements have to mention price, delivery charges, payment method, and delivery time.[35] It is also obligatory for merchants who have received payment in advance to notify customers of the 'agreement' unless the product itself is dispatched within a week after the order has been received.

What service will you provide?

Depending on the nature of your business and your product you might wish to:

1 provide an MO service to Japan for the goods of other producers
2 start a comprehensive database to market your own products by mail
3 offer an MO parts or accessories supply service in addition to your main export.

In the first two cases you will need comprehensive customer lists. Unfortunately, useful lists are not as readily available in Japan as they are in the West. Many lists in Japan are not regularly updated and many are incomplete. Many also lack extra sociographic detail useful from a marketing point of view. A typical Japanese list will give the name of the household head and the address, while some do and some don't provide the phone number. Whereas in the West it is common to exchange lists, most MO companies in Japan see lists as confidential, further limiting the exchange of usable information. Lists are also expensive, costing from ¥30–¥200 per name, depending on the quality. Comparable lists in the US are only 10c–20c per name. Options therefore include using incomplete lists, with the hope of securing a good list source, or going through the slow process of compiling a list yourself.[36] The DM company Franklin Mint is one that built its customer database in Japan initially by gaining contact through replies to other forms of advertising. Having made that first contact, it began to build a profile of each customer.[37]

For those in the latter category (3), the best place to start looking for customers might be JETRO or one of the other government-related bodies charged with the mission of promoting imports. JETRO specializes in dealing with businesses that want to trade with foreign companies but is also a good place to start if you need to look for other business categories. It can supply lists of these companies free of charge.

TV shopping

TV shopping was introduced in Japan in the early 1970s. By the mid-1990s TV shopping accounted for about a fifth of Japanese non-store purchases.[38] In 1994 the trading company Mitsui Bussan stumbled onto a gold mine when it joined forces with the US company National Media to become involved in TV shopping. The venture began early morning shopping on Television Tokyo, Channel 12. They expected to get a few dozen calls but got 100,000 – the telephone circuits couldn't handle the rush of orders. By 1996 the show had annual sales of over ¥10bn ($93mn), almost a fifth of which was profit. Goods were being shipped to 100,000 people a day.[39] Clearly, interactive television will expand the convenience and use of this means of marketing.

JieStar and TV shopping

In Chapter 9 we looked at JieStar, a firm involved in supplying products for TV shopping. Now let's look at the company's business activities in a bit more detail.

On one of the TV channels for which JieStar supplies goods there are two shopping programmes, which we will now look at in some depth. One shopping spot airs on Saturday morning, and the other every weekday morning. Each shopping programme is on for just ten minutes each day, during which two or three products are on offer.

The audiences differ at these two times. On Saturday morning the target is young couples in their 20s–30s, while on weekday mornings it is women aged between 25 and 60. Understandably, the programmes and the products must appeal to and attract their respective category of viewers, and this viewing audience contrasts with those viewing shopping programmes on other TV stations.

One shopping programme on another channel, for instance, targets the 45+ age group. Japan has many wealthy retired people who live off investments and a pension. Many of those in this group literally have more time and money than they know what to do with, and may spend it on expensive beauty products, jewellery, expensive fashion items and health equipment. By way of example, massaging and massage equipment are common in Japan, and in the late 1990s a fad developed for electric rotating-drum foot/neck massagers, many of which were sold on TV and through catalogues, a phenomenon which also helped revive the depressed appliance market.

Three or four months in advance of airing, meetings are convened between the TV station and the product suppliers in order to plan for the coming month's shopping. First, the TV station holds a briefing amongst its suppliers. An overview of the market is given – economic events, vacations and also the weather can affect buying behaviour, so these are outlined. Based partly on this, an image or product concept is proposed. Summer foods, clothing or seasonal furnishings are examples of seasonal products.

There has been a general shift in TV shopping toward building a theme so as to make it an attractive experience rather than simply a source of cheap goods. This channel's audience and programming are 'lifestyle' orientated. Still, the channel would like an even closer fit between shopping and the programmes that appear before it in order to create an atmosphere that would, in a sense, take viewers shopping at the place they've just seen on TV. In reality, however, doing so is difficult. In this context, though, the station does plan to feature particular countries or regions, sourcing the products for a specific series of shows from that particular location.

The suppliers, of which JieStar is one, are given a chart (see Table 15.3) representing the *TV station's* target product balance. Since different suppliers have different special-ities – some may specialize in food, others may handle jewellery – the show can achieve a good overall product mix. In this example, over the one-month period of weekday morning shows (with two or three products on each show) the station will deal with 53 different products. As an example, see the left column: at a quarter (25 per cent) of the total (or 12 items), jewellery represents the largest single category. Of those 12, nine will

Table 15.3 Example of a TV station's target product mix for a one-month period

Product category	Jewellery	Clothing	Food	Household goods	Bedding	Furniture and health equipment	Total
%	25%	20%	10%	←	45%	→	100%
Number of items	12	10	6	←	25	→	53
Price category ¥			(Number of items per price category)				
Up to ¥5000 ($40)							
¥5–10,000 ($40–80)			6	←	6	→	
¥10–30,000 ($80–240)	9	6		←	16	→	
¥30–50,000 ($240–400)	3	4		←	3	→	
¥50–70,000 ($400–560)							

Note: each figure in 'Number of items' in the top section is broken down into price categories in the lower section.

be sold for between ¥10,000 and 30,000 ($80–$240), and three will be sold for ¥30,000–50,000.

Three or four weeks after the briefing, over a three-day period, suppliers meet and present their products to the station. Evaluating the products are a specialist for the product category, the programme producer and other relevant participants (another channel uses a panel of 15–20 consumer–housewives among others). Suppliers may propose any number of products. JieStar is a small company; typically it might submit ten and expect, on average, two or three to be accepted. Some of the other suppliers include department stores – bigger firms that would expect to get a greater number of products on TV.

Flow of products for TV shopping

Examples: (1) exclusive; (2) inclusive of independent TV programme maker

1 Importer/manufacturer → JieStar → TV station → Consumer

2 Importer/manufacturer → Product supplier → Sponsor → TV station → Consumer

The suppliers of goods for the TV programme naturally need profit, but there are different systems of getting it. While in some cases the TV stations are the programme makers (see Example 1 above), as in the case of all JieStar's sales, in other cases the TV stations sell TV time to separate companies, a 'sponsor', which creates the programme. The sponsor then recoups that outlay by charging a flat fee to suppliers to have their products aired. In some cases the fees are very high, at about ¥3,000,000–¥4,000,000 ($23,000–$30,000). In this way the risk is passed on to the product supplier – if there are no product sales, the supplier is out of pocket. That JieStar deals direct with the TV stations is, in Jie's opinion, a better system. Regarding the cut for the stations, one channel takes around 30 per cent of the selling price and charges an additional flat fee of about \$2000–\$3000. This channel charges different amounts depending on the customer (it can cut deals depending, normally, on size and status). The other station JieStar deals with takes a 50 per cent cut of the sales figure but has no flat fee.

The supply

An interesting aspect of TV shopping, at least as it exists in this form, is that it is a 'small lot' business. Products are bought and sold in quantities of 300 or 400 on a one-off basis, with no guarantee of repeat business. So what is in it for the manufacturer? The answer depends to some extent on the product, as well as the other activities of the manufacturer. For suppliers established in Japan, TV shopping is just one sales avenue, one that provides free advertising for the other sales routes. TV shopping is useful for foreign suppliers considering entry into Japan, as it provides manufacturers with product feedback as well as selling experience – and it's a good product test for possible entry. And for all this a manufacturer can make a quick sale, with products that do sell well earning the chance to appear again.

There are also advantages to the importer of these one-off purchases. The quality and reliability problems already mentioned regarding foreign goods mean a headache for the importer and/or seller in Japan. A one-off purchase can lessen this problem since such small initial quantities can be monitored; furthermore, a supplier is normally putting his/her best foot forward for a first order, again ensuring quality. On the other hand, the inevitable bugs aren't out of the system yet, which means importers have to be vigilant.

A by-product of the import business is getting stuck with product that doesn't sell. TV sales of locally-made products can be ordered direct from the manufacturer to be sent on to the customer, but products made abroad need to be imported and stocked beforehand. Part of JieStar's job has been to off-load what doesn't sell. It's difficult to find retailers to take that sort of *ad hoc* stock. As we noted earlier, Japanese retailers have emerged from a culture of stable purchasing. The kind of opportunistic buying represented by cash and carry outlets is rare, and when it has happened it has been a reflection of tight economic circumstances. Jie has instead sold her excess by recommending that business people buy those goods to give as *omiyage* gifts – remembering that part of the *omiyage* concept is to supply something not otherwise readily available. In the process of doing business she has asked some of those she has met if she can sell these goods to their staff. Jie enjoys golf, and met one of these business contacts while playing. This reiterates the importance of the Japanese language. In addition, Jie says about her contacts: it is a matter of numbers. Few contacts will bear fruit, but one has to keep meeting more people to increase the number of successes.

Jie is moving away from importing, preferring to buy from existing import firms which will take the associated risks, including handling excess product. That means she is slotting into a particular role in the supply chain; specifically, she is focusing on selecting good products and then introducing them to people who interface directly with the public. It's worth noting again here that many foreign firms see it as more expedient for their company to take on such related activities themselves – to 'cut out the middle person'. Japanese firms often find it is better to work within an existing distribution system than to try to control everything. Indeed, in Jie's case she is sensible to focus now on a limited role, though she says she doesn't know what role(s) she will undertake in future.

Conclusion

However you choose to approach it, the direct marketing strategy can be a cost-effective end run around the complexities of the Japanese distribution system. If your firm has products that can be sold on TV, represented in a catalogue, or explained through brochures sent directly to housewives, DM might be the best solution to capturing a piece of the Japanese market.

Notes

1 Nomiyama Kaoru, executive director of JADMA, in *Look Japan*, June 1996, p. 16.
2 Instead of 'mail-order' JADMA uses 'direct marketing', but restricts its usage to the (shaded) category defined in Table 15.1 as mail-order.
3 For instance, Huddleston (1990, pp. 156–57) notes that American Express was told it would need door-to-door sales people, it wouldn't sell by direct mail – while both are direct marketing, a conservativeness persists. Another commentator notes that guests who are unknown aren't so welcome at Japanese homes. Actually sales people at the door are common, but visitors inside are not.
4 Fields, 1988, p. 172.
5 Alletzhauser, 1990, p. 37.
6 Figures available for cars sold door-to-door are 1988: 52.5 per cent, 1991: 43.7 per cent (*Japan's Distribution Channels*, JETRO, 1995, pp. 44–46).
7 *Tokyo Business Today*, 'TBT 300', 1995, pp. 28–32.
8 *Mail Order Market*, JETRO, 1995, p. 2.
9 *Mail Order Market*, JETRO, 1990 and 1995.
10 Komori, 1995, pp. 59–60.
11 Ohsono, 1995, pp. 95–96; *Japan Almanac*, 1994, p. 176; 1996, p. 177.
12 *Direct Marketing in Japan*, JADMA, 1996, p. 44.
13 *Mail Order Market*, JETRO, 1990, p. 2; Komori, 1995, p. 32; *The Nikkei Weekly*, 24 July 1995, p. 18.
14 *Direct Marketing in Japan*, JADMA, 1996, p. 41.
15 *Direct Marketing in Japan*, JADMA, 1996, p. 45.
16 See Dodwell, *Direct Marketing in Japan*, 1990, p. 11.
17 In Komori, 1995, p. 58.
18 In Komori, 1995, p. 44.
19 *Look Japan*, June 1996, p. 16.
20 *Direct Marketing in Japan*, JADMA, 1996, p. 50.
21 See Komori (1995, pp. 78–80) for a breakdown. According to her, 85 per cent of mail-order houses charge customers the postage or carrier fee.
22 *Direct Marketing in Japan*, JADMA, 1996, p. 38.
23 *Overseas Mail Order Shopping*, MIPRO, 1996, p. 23.
24 *Overseas Mail Order Shopping*, MIPRO, 1996, p. 25.
25 Komori, 1995, p. 43; JADMA Survey on Direct Marketing Usage, 1997, p. 7.
26 In 1988 87 per cent of Japanese people said they try to look like everyone else. Hakuhōdō, in Eastwood, 1989, p. 212.
27 See also Komori (1995, pp. 179–82) on this.
28 MIPRO.
29 *Overseas Mail Order Shopping*, MIPRO, 1996, p. 13.
30 'Mail-order boom takes off among Japanese consumers', *Asahi Evening News*, 6 July 1995; *Overseas Mail Order Shopping*, MIPRO, 1996, p. 4.

31 *Overseas Mail Order Shopping*, MIPRO, 1996, p. 8.
32 *Direct Marketing in Japan*, JADMA, 1996, p. 8; Komori, 1995, pp. 70–71.
33 JADMA Survey on Direct Marketing Usage, 1997, pp. 9–10.
34 Nomiyama Kaoru, executive director of JADMA, in *Look Japan*, June 1996, p. 16.
35 See *Mail Order Market*, JETRO, 1990, p. 23.
36 For a comprehensive look at direct marketing in Japan, see Komori Keiko's book by that name. She recommends her company, Telemarketing Japan, as one possible source of a database for new entrants (1995, pp. 97–99 and 149–50).
37 Michael Golding, President of Franklin Mint, Japan, 1987, in *Taking on Japan*, Look Japan, 1987, p. 41.
38 JADMA Survey on Direct Marketing Usage, 1997, pp. 9–10.
39 *Tokyo Business Today*, January 1996, pp. 22–23; 'Home Shopping Goes Through the Roof; Marketers Taken by Surprise', *Mainichi Daily News*, 27 December 1994.

Chapter 16

Signs of hope: openings in the Japanese market

For all the negative comments made over the years about the difficulty of breaking into the Japanese market, there has probably never been a better time than right now. In the following pages, I will present just a few examples of foreign firms that have done well because they have approached this market intelligently, and also give a few hints as to possible areas for future growth.

Companies

Understanding brand value

In good times Japanese consumers have been averse to price slashing and 'sales' (though under certain circumstances discounting has been accepted). One reason for the resistance to sales is that customers interpret a price cut to mean that the product is having trouble selling, which could mean problems.

Accordingly, as this indicates, there is a place for top-line, high-price products, and in the bubble era in particular there was a high demand for goods in this category. In the recession people became more price-conscious and started to look seriously at the products themselves, rather than at the brands. But some makers tried to hold onto the status image, and some succeeded.

Louis Vuitton began as a modest luggage-maker in France, and the company remained a modest French company until it could no longer resist the pressure of demand for its products from Japanese tourists. In the late 1970s, securing the wisdom of Japanese management, it began to make moves to market in Japan. Louis Vuitton began to sell through either its own retail outlets or license the sale of its products to top department stores.

Like other businesses in Japan, department stores have seasonal sales (note that these are not clearance sales of the type more common elsewhere). At such times the stores issue a tasteful catalogue of the goods that will be able to be purchased at a lower price over the sales period. However, Louis Vuitton Japan had a strict policy on the matter; despite encouragement from the department stores on the basis that it would stimulate sales, Louis Vuitton management didn't want its products to be in any such campaign, or in any other way discounted. Vuitton believed that their products had high status and a quality image, and that the company could retain that image and maintain its customers by maintaining a 'respectable' price.

The phenomenon of a high-class image and prices to match was common enough in the period of the economic bubble, but the taste test for Vuitton and other companies was how such a policy would hold up when the recession came. In Vuitton's case, in

1993, at the trough of Japan's business downturn, Vuitton's sales increased by 20 per cent for the first time. In 1996 Mitsukoshi sales of Vuitton products jumped 53 per cent over 1995.[1]

Vuitton products were perceived by the Japanese to be of exceptionally high quality and therefore deserving of their high price tags, and so they maintained healthy sales in the depressed Japanese market. But Vuitton wasn't the only 'brand' success in Japan. Even in the mid-1990s Japan accounted for two-thirds of the brand label sales in the world, and accordingly other luxury brands also entered the Japanese market or strengthened their position in it around that time.

In Ginza

One of Vuitton's exclusive shops is located in Ginza, *the* central Tokyo shopping area, renowned for its quaint art emporiums, 'galleries', expensive boutiques and nightclubs. At the centre of Ginza is the large Chōu Dōri, or 'Ginza Street' as it likes to be known. On one side of Chūo Dōri are the major department stores, Matsuzakaya, Mitsukoshi and Matsuya – the '3 Ms' of Ginza. However, it's not on this busy, vibrant street that the 'class' stores of Ginza reside, but toward the Matsuzakaya end, opposite the department stores, in the three or four streets behind the other side of Chūo Dōri. During the 1990s this small block with a Japanese flavour saw an influx of exclusive foreign brand stores. While Louis Vuitton had been an early entrant to the area, setting up in 1981, many more 'brand' manufacturers decided that, even in the recessionary period, there was demand for high-status quality goods, and established their own stores there. As Ginza sports the highest priced land in Japan, doing so is no mean feat. Land in this area can cost ¥16mn ($120,000) per square metre; a shop of 600 m^2 can cost around ¥10bn ($77mn). Still, by the end of the 1990s over a dozen top foreign labels were represented in just this small block, many in under a half-minute stroll from each other.

Namiki Dōri (Tree-lined Avenue), central to the block, comprises the single street in Japan with more foreign stores on it than any other. The stores in Namiki Dōri alone include Louis Vuitton, Chanel, Cartier and Gucci, with the most recent, Christian Dior, having opened in 1998. Mont Blanc has a small shop displaying pens at $1500 each. Bvlgari, in terms of location, is the exception: it is positioned back around the corner on Chūo Dōri, amongst heavy foot traffic and 'sales' that are decidedly absent just a few streets away. Still, in this more 'commercial' site Bvlgari showcases watches at about ¥2.5mn ($19,000) a timepiece.

If there's a conclusion to be drawn, it is this:

● Though it is said that Japanese shoppers have become accustomed to discount buying, quality suppliers positioned in Japan – even in a downturn – can expect business to be as strong as ever, or stronger when the Japanese economy is even moderately healthy.

Kicking around Tokyo

Now, a world away from the glamour of Ginza to a more down-to-earth category of fashion: sportswear. In the mid-1990s there was a sports shoe boom, and on the crest of the wave was Nike; in addition to Nike shoes, Japanese teenagers could be seen with Nike shirts, headbands and other paraphernalia.

According to Nike:

'After the bubble economy collapsed, young consumers went after more casual, economical fashions. At about the same time American rap culture and Afro-American culture came into Japan, and became a big influence. Young rap fashion, with baggy pants *et cetera*, became a status symbol for the young kids and that is how this boom was started. Some of the street fashion magazines worked with parallel import shops to promote old model shoes at very high prices and that drove the Nike boom. Our sales increased as a result of this boom but we didn't create the boom intentionally and we were trying to slow it down to maintain secure and stable growth.'[2]

It is interesting that before the boom, in 1993 Nike had begun an approach to marketing that appeared to provide an effective way for the company to maintain a strong brand image. Retailers were required to pay in cash at the time of delivery, they had to make six-month advance orders with no supplementary orders thereafter, and Nike allowed no returns of stock. Nike also became selective about the retailers it sold to, and maintained a policy of not allowing stores to discount, at least on new models.

That, anyway, was how the retailers saw it. It was an interpretation that led them to complain to the Fair Trade Commission (FTC), and led to a subsequent FTC investigation which focused on Nike's policies of restricting retail prices and blocking parallel imports.

I phoned Nike, interested in how they maintained their image (brand, not corporate!). Interestingly, although I asked for the marketing department I was assured that I wanted to speak to the public relations department. But the PR department said: 'We don't really have time to deal with the public'. I told them that I was researching a book on foreign business in Japan. They told me that they didn't really have time to speak to the press, or academia. . .

Eventually I did get my information: I asked about the six-month ordering and cash payment policies. Nike replied, 'Our intention is to plan ahead and manufacture the product efficiently to provide consumers with a great product at a very competitive price.'

When I had asked if Nike had a 'no-discount' policy, they answered with a curt 'No'. (Still, six months later, in July 1998 Nike announced that it would comply with an FTC demand that it stop pressuring retailers not to discount.)

Unfortunately for the sports shoe industry, the boom proved short-lived, and by late 1997 many retailers were hard pressed to sell their inventory. In this situation, not being able to reduce prices was a noose around the necks of retailers. But the dam broke, and by early 1998 it was all over bar the discounting. Despite Nike's desire for rationality in the market, faddishness had prevailed. The situation is explained well by Tadano Kōichi, chief editor of youth magazine *Boon*. 'The trendoids who gather in Tokyo's fashionable Harajuku district mostly stopped wearing sneakers last year. Guys sensitive to cutting-edge trends rapidly moved on once anybody and everybody was outfitted with what were once "the most" in brands of sneakers.'[3]

Just jeans (. . .mum, I've been shopping)

Harajuku is well known in Japan for its swarms of 'trendoids' willing to spend large sums on whatever is in fashion this week. In Harajuku there is a shop paradoxically called 'Fake α', a clothing shop in which run-of-the-mill-jeans on the shelf are on sale for a few hundred dollars. At the top of the range Fake α's most expensive item is for sale at ¥3mn ($23,000) – a pair of the much sought-after Levi Strauss 501 jeans.

Levi Strauss jeans became strong sellers in the Japanese market, but their marketing efforts were, initially, surprisingly weak. The company entered Japan in 1971 as a small branch of its Hong Kong-based Far East division. It had poor sales and no brand recognition. Partly responsible for its problems was that Levi's strength in the West gave the head office in the US a feeling of confidence about how to run the operation in Japan. For example, whereas many businesses in Japan operate on a three-month *tegata* (bill payment) system, the head office expected that the Japanese office should insist on payment within 20 days, and, like Nike, that it refuse to accept returns. But these rules went against normal business practice in Japan, where Levi's was, anyway, in no position to dictate terms. Furthermore, while people looked to the West for fashion, Levi's status as an authentic piece of American culture was undercut with the 'Made in Hong Kong' label the jeans carried.

A shift to control by local management in Japan, however, reorientated the operation. One thing Levi Strauss Japan then did was undertake an ad campaign based on still shots of American folk heroes including John Wayne and Marilyn Monroe wearing jeans. The campaign struck a chord in the Japanese for this type of Western nostalgia. And the person who stood out by far in popularity in the campaign was not the higher profile Monroe or John Wayne, but James Dean. He brought with him an image of rebellion that Japanese youth could, or wanted to, identify with. The promotion ignited popularity in Levi Strauss jeans, sales of which peaked in 1993 just as other firms were hit by Japan's economic woes.

Jeans had been popular in Japan for some time, and then, just as the wind was dropping out of the sails of the jeans boom, Levi's broke away from standard US designs and produced fashion jeans conceived of and designed in Japan. These became so popular as to then inspire a similar trend in the US.

Then 'classic' Levi jeans became popular. This was partly due to the concept of 'originality' that influences purchases in product categories anywhere – a phenomenon to which the Japanese are by no means an exception. Part of it was also in the lay of the denim used in the old jeans. This was different enough in character from the modern product that it was able to be distinguished by 'experts', and also appreciated by buyers. That the 'real' jeans had something extra inspired the company to bring back into operation the old equipment used to produce the original fabric. The jeans, once made, were then exported from the US to Japan, where they were sold for about twice the price of a conventional pair.

One problem Levi Strauss Japan faces is that it, like Nike, is subject to the whims of fashion. Though this is not unique to Japan, the peaks and troughs can be particularly strong and sudden in Japan. For this Levi introduced a system to centralize point-of-sale information, via 'Levi Link' computer, allowing real-time information on product sales to be gathered in order to adjust production. Levi Strauss does face one other problem, and that is that while it has to some extent diversified, the 'magic' of its image remains related almost exclusively to the conventional jeans market.[4]

Creating brand identity

Korean firms face the problem in Japan that their products have a low-price, low-quality image. This was the case with the Korean electronics maker Samsung. It had produced TVs, video players and other products, but like other Korean firms, including Korean car makers, the company had failed to get a foothold in the Japanese market.

Japanese are cautious about buying foreign goods where quality is at issue – particularly where there are good Japanese alternatives – and those made in Asia rank low on the list. Korea, the only Asian nation listed of 11 countries exporting cars to Japan, does rank lowest. Korea had total car exports in 1996 of over one million vehicles. Still, according to the Japan Automobile Importers Association, in 1997 Korea's market share was the only one on that list to rank behind the 'others' category, with just 105 cars having entered Japan. According to Hyundai, it's still researching the market but hasn't begun sales in Japan yet.[5] This is despite Hyundai's approximate 50 per cent production share of Korea's million-plus auto exports; a more than reasonable production level amongst car-producing nations. When I asked a Japanese executive at a leading car import firm why Korean cars hadn't made a dent in Japan, he phrased it this way: 'Japanese like quality'.

Japanese people intuitively feel some justification in the 'policy'. In the 1980s Hyundai's Pony, at only $4000, became a novelty in the US, but it was plagued with quality problems – just what the Japanese want to steer clear of, at any price. When my own Korean-made video player broke down I took it to the local electronic repair shop – one of very few general repair shops around Tokyo. The owner took one look and said, 'It's not Japanese. . ., I only repair Japanese products'.

A Japanese person would say it's clearly much better to get a (reliable) Japanese product from the start; it probably wouldn't have broken down in the first place, and if something were to go wrong it would be able to be fixed. In defence of the small repair shop, it's probably a hassle to deal with a foreign parts supply, whereas it's much easier to source Japanese parts, which are better represented in the market. While there are valid concerns – Japanese products are still better quality than Korean – it is to some degree a self-fulfilling prophecy; don't service them and they remain a bad purchase. The real issue is that Japanese are still unwilling to take the same degree of 'risk' that foreigners are by buying a cheaper, unknown product. Foreigners think, it's cheap; therefore I already have a, say, 20 per cent cost advantage, if something does go wrong I can pay to have it fixed and I'll still probably be ahead; Japanese people don't think like that.

When, in May 1997, Samsung announced that it would start marketing personal computers in Japan, it took a different approach. It aimed to supply a high-price, high-quality product, even at a time when tight Japanese budgets meant lower priced PCs were favoured. Samsung was actually already a front runner in semiconductors, LCDs and other electronic products. It hoped to, then, counter the low-quality stereotype, creating for itself an image as a high-performance information technology supplier. In order to establish itself in Japan, in 1994 it bought 50.7 per cent of Lux, a high-performance Japanese electronics maker, and in 1995 it bought 42 per cent of Japan's Union Optical. Also in 1995 it spent a huge ¥1bn ($10mn) to co-sponsor the Volleyball World Cup, held in Japan, and it has supported other activities, intending to create a strong, positive profile.

Markets with enormous potential

Women

And now a category, not of product, but of consumer. The stereotype of Japanese women portrays them as petite, compliant and docile. While there's a degree of truth to this, the portrayal conceals other important characteristics. In Japan's large southern island, Kyūshū, it's said that women still walk a few paces behind their husbands, but in the internationalized metropolis, Tokyo, this tradition, and much of the thinking associated with it, has vanished.

Japanese schools place great importance on mathematics. And at school women are normally taught home accounting, and, as adults, many still keep all shopping receipts, and tally them at the end of the month as part of household budgeting. Curious, perhaps. More interesting is that it's common for women in Japan, when they get married, to set up a bank account and have the husband's salary direct credited into it. Thereafter the wife controls all the finances and typically gives her husband pocket money. I knew a Japanese man who came to Tokyo from out of town for three months on business. His wife confiscated his credit card for the duration, but continued his pocket money. It's not uncommon for a husband to ask the company for any extra payments to be given to him in cash, in order to bypass the wife.

As an extension of the woman's accounting skills it's very common, where a husband runs a small business, for the wife to go to the company and do the accounts once a month, before continuing on with her family responsibilities.

Women also, at varying points in their lives, have a lot of spare time and can concentrate on such things as the investment of their money. I know three women, unrelated to each other, who all surreptitiously invest money in the stock market – their husbands know, but don't really approve, and the wives simply avoid bringing the matter up. This isn't an addiction but a judicious investment; they're interested in the stock market. I talk to another, retired friend about the stock market sometimes, and when we get into details he professes ignorance and claims that his wife does the actual investing and is really the expert. Stockbroking firms for many years have employed women to peddle their products to those many housewife buyers who feel more at home and less threatened by another woman than they might a man.[6]

What this means is that many Japanese women are sharp; they are the real financial decision makers in the family, and they are, in many cases, proudly prudent about how they spend or invest that money. Having said that, given access to money they can 'spend up large' on luxury or luxurious necessities. A friend talking about a gradual decline in the amount of time Japanese men put in at the office said that men don't do as much overtime nowadays because Japanese wives have bought everything they need.

One particularly interesting spending group is young unmarried women. They often have a good income but don't feel the need to save. In the bubble era, before the economic downturn, as a group they spent freely on trend and fashion goods. By 1996, after the economy had shown signs of revival, they too were showing signs of revamping those buying patterns. Research in 1996 showed that the 'pocket-spending money' of working women between 27 and 35 was on average ¥94,000 ($875) a month – twice as much as their male counterparts.[7] Many young women nowadays have a temporary job, and since they have few overheads – many live at home – they spend their income on fashion, a hobby, or they travel abroad for short stays, or they quit and have a longer holiday before returning and getting another job.

One retail category that has successfully netted young, and some quite young, women is 'drug stores'. Characteristic of drug stores in Japan is that they have traditionally handled few prescription drugs, as these have been sold directly to patients by hospitals and clinics. Drug stores have instead generated profit from the sale of 'health and beauty products'. They have also traditionally been 'mom and pop' operations. However, a trend that emerged in the 1990s was for larger chains to enter or expand and, in the process, invigorate the drug store market.

Compared to the traditional small drug stores, the new versions are large, bright and open. In fact a move from the dusty-shelved, one-person, bell-on-the-door little shop was a marketing event waiting to happen. The modern layout facilitates window shopping, and provides an attractive environment, the result of which is that it draws in more customers. And once in, shoppers have freedom to browse and try on products, including cosmetics. By 1997, according to one survey, a quarter of Japanese women in their teens, 20s and 30s visited a drug store more than once a week, and two-thirds visited more than once every fortnight.[8]

Matsumoto Kiyoshi is one such chain retailer. Assisted by trendy 'young image' ads that it put on TV, it became a popular place to shop. Prices are low, and some of them very low. Many products are advertised at half the standard price, and many others are less. One product – a fish extract assumed good for brain development (DHA) – that normally retails for ¥16,000 ($120), at ¥3380 is almost a fifth of the price. But many of the products are already lower price range goods, selling at around ¥300–¥800 ($2.30–$6.20).

Young women spend an average ¥900–¥1000 ($7–$8) buying beauty and healthcare necessities each time they make a purchase. And at such shops one could find oneself in a long queue of people at the till waiting to spend that ¥1000. According to Ōkubo Yukihiko, promotions manager of Matsumoto Kiyoshi, between 5pm and 7pm is their busiest time of the day, and Sundays and holidays are their busiest days.[9] At its peak, sometimes there'd be an ongoing queue at the tills of 15–20 people spilling out of a Matsumoto Kiyoshi store.

Silver savers

Japan has a large and fairly wealthy greying population. The portion of that population aged 65 years and over is increasing at the fastest rate in the world. This is in part because Japanese people have the greatest longevity in the world – 65 is still fairly young in Japan – and because the birth rate has declined. A birth rate of 2.1 (children per woman) is necessary to maintain the population; Japan's hit 1.39 in 1997, with no indication of improvement.

A large elderly population, a portion of which are well off, implies two markets. On the one hand, there's a growing healthcare market. And on the other, there's the luxury market. We will look at these two markets and the Japanese health market in general.

Luxury spenders

Japan has a lot of elderly people who have good spending power and a lot of time on their hands. According to government survey information, 'elderly households' have both greater assets and more income than 'standard' households. During a six-month period in 1997, while overall household spending dropped by 0.5 per cent over the same period in the previous year, for households with a working head 60 years old or over, spending instead increased by 1.8 per cent.[10] But relative to their assets, the elderly are still holding onto their money. It's been estimated that if Japanese people spend 10 per cent of the savings they have earmarked for their retirement Japan would experience a ¥60tn ($460mn) increase in consumption.[11] Compare this with the government's March 1998 ¥10tn economic stimulus package designed to boost the flagging economy.

That the elderly have held onto their money is in part due to a feeling that they must save for security in their retirement, and also because there are too few attractive entertainment services or products to spend their money on. Japanese firms could be doing much more to come up with innovative goods and services to tap this market – which in some ways represents 'cash looking for something to be spent on'. An Economic Planning Agency survey found, for instance, that brand consciousness amongst people from around 50 years old increases sharply on some products. These include cosmetics bought by women, and women's cosmetics and clothes bought by men.[12] Medical professionals have been benefiting from this spending category. One retired man I know, on his dentist's advice, goes to the dentist once a week for a check-up.

A healthy market

Every home in Japan has a thermometer and a cupboard stuffed with unused drugs, and it's quipped that you can go to hospital and be put on an IV drip for the flu. There is a particular preoccupation amongst the Japanese with healthcare. The young and the elderly are especially targeted as beneficiaries of Japan's excessive medical service. There's a particular paranoia regarding children; a moderately high thermometer reading, regardless of the child's condition, can determine a visit to the doctor and at least, a take-home set of drugs.

Japan's total medical expenditure, at 7.2 per cent of GDP, is not high by international standards. However, there are areas of high spending. Expenditure on drugs in Japan accounts for 30 per cent of total health spending; this compares with the US (11 per cent), France (20 per cent) and Germany (17 per cent).[13] And in total Japan is responsible for about 20 per cent of the world's drug consumption. This is a result of over-prescription and the public's blind acceptance of doctors' advice; since it's normally unacceptable to question a doctor, even to ask what the medicine is for, most people don't. (There has been some reaction against this in recent years.) It is commonly known that doctors (hospitals), who traditionally both prescribe and sell drugs routinely over-prescribe in order to capitalize on the profit. Doctors see it as others see side-stepping the tax system, as an acceptable or even natural means of rounding out their income.[14]

While there are not a lot of doctors *per capita*, in relation to other nations there are a lot of hospital beds. Japan has over twice as many beds as the average of all the other nations listed (Table 16.1). More impressive is the average hospital stay in Japan, which is between three and four times the average of the other nations listed.

This has been good news for medical-related businesses, and is responsible for the high representation of Japan's top pharmaceutical firms amongst Japan's high income-earning companies. It also accounts for the high representation of foreign affiliated pharmaceutical

Table 16.1 Healthcare – an international comparison

	Doctors per 1000 pop.	Hospital beds per 1000 pop.	Average length of hospital stay (days)
Australia	2.2[d]	8.9[b]	14.0[a]
Belgium	3.7[a]	7.6[a]	12.0
Canada	2.2	5.4[a]	12.6[c]
Finland	2.8	9.3	11.8
France	2.9	8.9	11.2
Germany	3.4	9.7	14.2
Italy	1.7[c]	6.5[a]	10.8[a]
Japan	**1.9**	**16.2[a]**	**45.5**
Netherlands	2.5[e]	11.3	32.8
Spain	4.1[b]	4.0[a]	11.5[b]
Sweden	3.1	6.5[a]	7.8
United Kingdom	1.6[a]	4.9[a]	10.2[b]
United States	2.6[a]	4.1	8.0

Figures for 1995 except for: [a]1994, [b]1993, [c]1992, [d]1991, [e]1990.
OECD Health Data statistics, 1997, OECD. Source: Keizai Kōhō Centre

companies amongst top-earning foreign firms – there have been five such firms amongst the top 25 foreign companies in Japan.

The bad news, in a sense, is that Japan's average had been higher. The 45.5 days' hospital stay in 1995 represented a decrease from 54.2 days in 1985. Further decreasing dependence on state care, in September 1997 the government reduced its contribution to the very generous state health insurance system which, for many patients, meant they had to pay a 20 per cent share of the medical cost rather than the previous 10 per cent. This still might not seem a lot, but it meant paying twice the previous amount to see the doctor.

Especially before the increase, retired people were said to make regular visits to the clinic/hospital not because they were sick but just to chat to their friends who were doing the same thing. For the elderly with nothing to do, going to the doctor became a leisure activity, and one available at reasonable cost, but one that was costly for the state that dished out money to the doctors, and drug firms that supplied them. Two months after the increase, in November 1997, a significant number of medical institutions had experienced a decrease in outpatient attendance, particularly amongst the elderly,[15] though after the initial shock of the fee hike, patronage to some degree recovered.

Another area of high spending is medical equipment. Expensive business relations that fend off competition in the equipment procurement market fuel the nation's medical costs. A 1996 JETRO survey on medical equipment found that it was expensive in Japan, with examples of medical equipment all about three or more times higher in Japan than elsewhere. Two years later, a Health and Welfare Ministry report on medical insurance and equipment determined that the distribution system and 'unclear business practices' (which means procurement over-spending to benefit friendly suppliers) were responsible. In 1997 Japan's Fair Trade Commission, having conducted its own study, said it would ask the Ministry and companies involved to amend the pricing.[16] Indeed, the situation will probably have to change, at least because it is becoming increasingly difficult for the government to find the budget to maintain the outlay. Greater emphasis on cost saving will almost certainly benefit those foreign suppliers that are already price-competitive, assuming they have the quality and service to match.

Elderly care

The greying population also means an expanding market for healthcare services and equipment for the elderly. Currently the number of bedridden elderly is assumed by the Ministry of Health and Welfare to be around 2.5 million people. By 2025 this number will have doubled to over 5 million, causing a huge expansion of related product and service markets. For instance, given the number of bedridden, there is a need for better bathroom lifts. Current models are awkward to operate, are far too bulky, or they are too expensive – figuring out how to serve this market can open opportunities for imaginative foreigners. Using water as ballast, for instance, may overcome the bulk problem – in a bathroom it is readily available and also disposable. 'Compact and storable' is also an important or necessary feature of very many products in Japan, where homes are small and there isn't the culture of rolling up the sleeves and doing some heavy lifting.

Foreigners are better at developing computer software than the Japanese. But Japanese make good use of their software in applications. MITI, universities and other institutions are now working on the creation of caring-robots. Much more human-like than previous forms, it's expected that they will be able to do much of the manual work for elderly people living alone. Foreigners long ago gave away their advantage in robotics to the Japanese, but they should be able to be competitive in equipment, or simply programs that utilize their advantage in software.

It is notable that the market in healthcare equipment remains dry and colourless. Not only the wealthy, but other elderly will want to spend their money on something that looks classy and perhaps is fashionable. Take, by way of example, children's stationery and clothing. Much in Japan is nowadays branded, is adorned with a cartoon character logo, or has a character built into the product, but still costs little or no more than plain product. This makes it more colourful and appealing to children. 'White goods' have for years in Japan been sold in a variety of pastels – they look better. There's no reason why wheelchairs and walking aids have to be either silver or grey. Still, it's not just a matter of colouring, but of moving away from the clinical image, to products that are more appealing. The trend in hearing aids, for instance, is toward discreet inner ear types; compact and attractive electric wheelchairs will replace traditional types. Making products more appealing or even fashionable won't, however, justify high prices, but good products at a reasonable price may win you market share.

More research is being done on Japan's elderly-care market, and more specific information for prospective exporters is available, on comparative prices, import trends and demand, with JETRO currently the best immediate source of that information. Plus, JETRO and others hold regular trade fairs on healthcare-related products and services – again, information on these is available from JETRO.

Despite the potential of the healthcare market, for exporters, barriers and other problems still exist, and accordingly the skills mentioned above as being important still apply. Furthermore, product adaptation is likely to be necessary for the Japanese market because of physiological differences, and because the elderly, at least in Japan, are a consumer group like other Japanese consumer groups, many of whom are wealthy and discerning about what they use.

Notes

1 Kishi and Russell, 1996, pp. 51ff; *The Nikkei Weekly*, 28 October 1996, p. 10.
2 Correspondence with Nike (Japan), 1998.
3 Thanks to Kotani Yōji, of the Nikkei, for giving me information about Nike, as well as getting the retailers' views on this topic, and for his articles in *The Nikkei Weekly* on the subject (1 December 1997, p. 6; quote from 23 March 1998, p. 19).
4 *Gaishi*, Vol. 8, 1997, pp. 22–29. For the full story behind Levi Strauss Japan, see Kishi and Russell, 1996.
5 Communication with Hyundai, 1998.
6 Alletzhauser says that although it wouldn't exactly advertise the fact, Nomura employs almost as many sales women as men (1990, p. 188).
7 Nikkei Research Institute of Industry and Markets, in *The Nikkei Weekly*, 13 May 1996, pp. 1 and 23.
8 Survey by Nikkei Research Institute of Industry and Markets, in *The Nikkei Weekly*, 8 September 1997, p. 8.
9 Interview with Ōkubo Yukihiko of Matsumoto Kiyoshi.
10 White Paper on National Lifestyle, Economic Planning Agency, 1996, p. 62; Calculation by Japan Research Institute, in *The Nikkei Weekly*, 8 December 1997, p. 2.
11 Wada Hideki, in *Views From Japan*, Foreign Press Centre, March 1998, p. 4.
12 National Survey on Lifestyle Preferences, Economic Planning Agency, 1995, p. 78.
13 White Paper on National Lifestyle, Economic Planning Agency, 1996, p. 52.
14 Since my wife is a (Japanese) dentist, who's worked for other private surgeries, I've seen this from both sides.
15 Nikkei survey, in *The Nikkei Weekly*, 3 November 1997, p. 2.
16 *The Survey on Actual Conditions Regarding Access to Japan, Medical Equipment*, JETRO, June 1996, pp. II, 8 and 9; *The Nikkei Weekly*, 25 August 1997, p. 3.

Conclusion

There's an ongoing debate about whether or not Japan is unique. It is, however, a tautological question: each country is unique to the extent that it differs from any other. What Japan does have is quite a unique background, one that continues to feed into the mixture that goes to make up what Japan is today. We can see strong elements of that background in contemporary Japanese business, albeit that some of those elements are fading under the pressure of other contemporary influences. The result has been a particular, very productive version of a capitalist economy. What's more, it has been an economy that has regularly pulled something out of the bag, and it's generally believed that this is unlikely to stop, at least in the near future.

This context constitutes an extremely good base – one of the best in the world – in which to expand business. This is especially so given that the Japanese market is becoming increasingly open to foreign enterprise. Finance is a good example. The picking up by Merrill Lynch of a large part of the retail side of big four brokerage Yamaichi in 1998, and the 25 per cent purchase of another of Japan's big four brokers, Nikkō Securities, by Travelers Group Inc. of the US, were ground-breaking examples of foreign penetration into Japan's (lucrative) financial arena. Ford's move to managerial control of Mazda, and GE Capital's purchase in early 1999 of Japan Leasing, with other large foreign investments also in progress started to make the world of business a smaller place. In the 1980s Westerners had lamented the buying up of their assets by the Japanese – but now Japanese business has become much more available to foreigners.

Key features of success

For you as a businessperson, the question is beyond whether Japan is unique or not. The matter is simply that there are business activities in Japan that are not familiar to foreigners, and you need to understand or at least be aware of these. This book has covered a broad range of those that are important to marketing.

First, it should be clear by now that success in Japan requires more than just the product; it's a package deal involving a range of assets that you bring into the market.

Jinmyaku

For those entering Japan, the most basic thing to remember is that Japanese business is fundamentally social. Social or cultural aspects are often seen by Westerners as an appendage to the main field of business activity. However, the social domain is the base supporting, and is interwoven with, economic and other aspects of business in Japan. Understanding its social features is basic to understanding Japanese business, and especially to understanding problems Westerners have with it. This stands in contrast to the Western context, where business and social life are often sharply separated. The Japanese case is best exemplified in the importance of *jinmyaku* (personal networks), and that Japanese people devote so much of their social life to establishing a good *jinmyaku*.

What this means is that you have to become involved in the social aspects of business in Japan. Devote time and budget to gifts for your clients and associates, to activities such as golf and after-hours entertainment, and to joining business associations. Become 'in the club', and you'll benefit from those you know at a social level. Connect with people who are well connected. This is a win–win game for all those involved – as the Japanese well know.

Japan takes time

You need to anticipate a long start-up and a long-term presence. Consultant Ohmae Kenichi explains to foreign CEOs: 'It took you fifty years to get where you are in the US, and fifteen years to explore the ground in Europe; so why do you expect to get things up and running in Japan in anything less than ten or fifteen years?'[1] But people do.

Japan takes longer; people in Japan want to know that they are dealing with someone reliable; that they can expect a consistency of product and that you will still be in the market in years to come. Foreigners are surprised when Japanese turn down an 'offer too good to refuse': even in the face of a great product, the fast-buck business deals that occur elsewhere seldom happen in Japan. The Japanese will also turn down business with you because they have already got other suppliers who have proved themselves and they want to preserve those valuable relationships. This is understandable. Your task is to work your way into that kind of trusted position, which of course takes time.

Meet the Japanese on their terms

You are not alone in your battle to win useful business relationships. Alongside you are many other Japanese companies also trying to gain insider status. You need to now use your foreigner status to best advantage. In the past some foreigners have bludgeoned their way into Japanese business, but this engenders resentment and any informal business channels will be shut off. Most Japanese people can, however, find foreigners interesting and will look for any novel business opportunities they bring. In other areas too, avoid imposing preconceived ideas of what is appropriate business – onto employees, onto consumers, or across the negotiating table. This is not to say your organization should 'become Japanese': there needs to be a well-informed balance between employing your own methods and doing as the Japanese do. Indeed, as a foreigner you can bring in methods and ideas to differentiate your product or service, and to enhance your business operation. But you need to understand the environment first. There's been a lot of damage done by home-office directives forced on Japan, and by itinerant managers fresh to Japan, insensitive to the local environment. On the other hand, a lot of gains have been made by combining the best of Japanese and foreign employment and operations systems, where the mix has been made mindful of the existing Japanese business context.

You can learn a lot from the Japanese

The Japanese have been successful marketers around the world, and not surprisingly there are many aspects of Japanese business that you will need to emulate just to compete. Some of the following recommendations are fundamental to Japanese business.

- **When meeting Japanese contacts. . . .** In part because Japanese firms typically have a lot of staff they can prepare thoroughly for negotiations; don't be unprepared when you meet with them.

  Take an interest in your client or partner company, as they take an interest in yours. Find out a bit about the company, and the president, if possible. It leaves a good impression if you show an interest in your associates.
- **Quality** The biggest problem faced by virtually all foreigners trying to enter Japan is 'quality'. When you enter the market, remember that quality is one of the keys to success; you have to live and breathe quality. Quality includes improvement; you must keep upgrading your products just in order to remain competitive.
- **Be adaptive** Tailor your goods to the Japanese market, as the Japanese research and tailor their goods to yours.

What about Japan's future?

The general opinion is that Japan will recover from the problems that it experienced following the collapse of the 'bubble' and, somewhat reorientated, it will continue as a 'diligent' and prosperous economy. But it won't be without problems.

Work ethic

Increasingly, Japan's younger generation lacks the spirit of determination possessed by their post-World War II seniors; indeed, many of these seniors are lamenting the decadence of Japanese society. Still, even before World War II, amid some decadence Japan managed to be very productive. The next generation might work smarter; Japan has a high GDP as a nation because everybody pitches in, but other developed nations rank higher on per worker output.[2] And the Japanese have spent a lot of time at work. In one case in court in 1998, a 33-year-old employee who died from over-work had clocked up an average of 300 hours overtime a month (that's 75 hours a week; over 12 extra hours a day). But fewer young Japanese people are now willing to spend a lot of extra time in the office. They are learning, to a large extent from the West, to work more 'efficiently'. Indeed, the degree to which attitudes about work affect future output will be closely related to the degree of Westernization. One result will be that Japan will act more like and will accordingly face many of the same problems as those now experienced by Western countries.

The knowledge market

Another problem Japan faces – its most serious economic problem – is the greying population. This will steal the nation's workforce, depriving it of income while burdening the social welfare system. The best thing it can do to compensate is move toward high-return, knowledge-related production, which places less emphasis on young, physical labour. But Japan's educational strengths don't lend themselves to knowledge production. Japan's balance of trade in services is indicative of its problems. Computer software trade, for instance, runs at about (imports) 19:1 (exports).[3] Historically, this is an anomaly given that Japan typically identifies important industries and moves to dominate them. Japan continues to generate a trade surplus in manufacturing but it runs an ongoing deficit in knowledge and services.[4]

While certain categories of knowledge or software production (particularly animations) have been very successful, where Japan's dominant category of big business enterprise controls production, output is lacklustre. This is an institutionalized problem in Japan, rooted in education and the orientation of the big business workforce.

Compounding this, Japan lacks the ability to effectively mobilize its less shackled, more creative small business sector. This means a very big gap in Japan's 'creative' market.

Still, there are a growing number of 'creative' workers, increasingly motivated to work for innovative companies. What better place for a foreign company to operate than the fertile Japanese business context, with a good market and diligent workers? The finance arena is the latest successful example; where foreign companies have brought skills into a nation starved of competitive services. The field of communications technology, too, is throwing up opportunities within the Japanese market, unable to be filled by Japanese firms. There are many cases where foreign ideas – formalized as 'software' or not – have been readily absorbed by Japanese clients unable to produce the same results themselves.

Japan's economy has been locked behind administrative barriers, but, prompted by recession, these are being forcibly peeled away, creating a much more available and accessible market for the twenty-first century.

Notes

1 Ohmae, 1990, p. 127.
2 When ranking GDP per person *employed*, Japan ranks last of ten advanced nations (*Nippon*, JETRO, 1997, p. 127, figures for 1993).
3 Figures for 1994, industry survey, in *The Japan Times*, 2 November 1995, p. 9. In 1997 the Science and Technology Agency expressed concern at Japan's growing software royalty payments abroad; these typically indicate the strength/weakness of an industry (in *The Nikkei Weekly*, 14 April 1997, p. 3).
4 See Melville, I., 'Japanese Education, Creativity and Work', *Sophia Economic Review*, Vol. 43, No. 1, December 1997, for a development of this theme.

Appendix

Following is a selection of organizations and useful contacts in Japan.

Phone and faxing

Japan's country code is +81.
Local phone numbers are normally listed with the area code as a prefix. For example, Tokyo's area code is (03); an international call made to a Tokyo number would therefore begin +81 3.

Organizations in Japan

American Chamber of Commerce in Japan
The ACCJ can provide informed opinion, and they provide many services to their members. They help fund and publish surveys of the market, they put on seminars, and this all helps provide a clear voice to promote market opening.

5th Floor, Bridgestone Toranomon Building
3-25-2 Toranomon, Minato-ku, Tokyo 105
Phone (03) 3433-5381   E-mail info@accj.or.jp
Fax   (03) 3436-1446   Home page www.accj.or.jp

European Commission
Delegation of the European Commission in Japan
Europa House
9–15 Sanban-cho, Chiyoda-ku, Tokyo 102-0075
Phone (03) 3239-0533   Fax (03) 3261-5194
E-mail Deljapan@deljpn.cec.eu.int

European Commission
Directorate General for External Economic Relations
Phone 32 2 299-00-23   Fax 32 2 299-10-33
The Executive Training Programme (ETP) in Europe is:
E-mail Direction-F@dg1.cec.be

Japan Marketing Association (Nihon Marketing Kyōkai)

The Japan Marketing Association is a non-profit organization under MITI. It gets its funding through member subscriptions and seminar fees. It has a membership of about 750 – mostly large companies – from various areas of the economy, and some of these are foreign affiliates. The association holds seminars/courses, and produces regular publications and reports; however, all of these are in Japanese. It does host some international conferences presented in both English and Japanese. About a quarter of the staff of 20 speak English.

The seminars and courses offered by the association cover basic-level and advanced-level marketing. The topics are interesting, covering a range of marketing areas, including Japanese marketing and distribution; creating sales channels; marketing strategy, analysis and marketing theory; product concept, product and brand life-cycle, and brand strategy; communication theory and mix, and advertising; customer servicing; and others. While unavailable to non-Japanese speakers, they would be useful for Japanese staff of foreign firms – remember, too, that Japanese universities don't teach specific skills; this is up to the employer. Seminars and courses are available to non-members, but at a higher fee.

Annual membership fees are ¥200,000 ($2000). Most of their activities are quite expensive, with programmes at upward of $1000 – clearly aimed at larger firms.

3rd Floor, Wako Bldg.
4-8-5 Roppongi, Minato-ku, Tokyo 106
Phone (03) 3403-5101   Fax (03) 3403-5106
E-mail jma03@jma-jp.org   Home page www.jma-jp.org

Japan Marketing Research Association

Has breakdown data on research expenditure and forms of marketing research. They have all of their information on their home page, which appears in Japanese and in English.

Phone (03) 3813-3577 (Japanese language only)
Home page www.mictokyo.co.jp/jmra/

JETRO (Japan External Trade Organization; Nihon Bōeki Shin-kōkai)

JETRO has a certain body of documented information, most of which is introductory market material. Their staff, while helpful at supplying these materials, are not good at providing 'informed opinion'. Neither are their staff necessarily familiar with the range of what they do have. In terms of content, JETRO has a history of presenting the face that is good for Japan to present, and this is reflected in the style of their information. This makes their information and service useful up to a point.

JETRO has a library on the sixth floor of the Kyodo News Building. On the same floor is JETRO's 'International Lounge', where the various free publications and loan videos are available.

Library and International Lounge
6th Floor, JETRO/Kyodo News Building
2-2-5 Toranomon, Minato-ku, Tokyo 105
Phone (03) 3587-1143

MIPRO (Manufactured Imports Promotion Organization)

6th Floor, World Import Mart Bldg.
3-1-3 Higashi-Ikebukuro
Toshima-ku, Tokyo 170
Phone (03) 3988-2791   Fax (03) 3988-1629

Useful contacts in Japan

Advertising

Ōshima Miyuki

Ōshima Miyuki is a freelance advertising producer who speaks very good English and knows her way around the ad business. She coordinates advertising in Japan and would be an asset to foreign firms wanting to advertise in the Japanese market.

Phone (03) 5560-0568   Fax (03) 3541-7074

Business Consulting

Japan Consulting Group (JCG)

JCG is the only consultancy known to be dedicated exclusively to helping firms enter or expand in Japan. JCG prides itself on its experience, depth of knowledge, and extensive network of personal contacts. The firm has two main functions: consulting and research. Both are designed to offer strategic advice to help clients with critical market decision-making.

E-mail simon@japanconsulting.com

Corporate Communications

Trans-Pacific Productions (TPPro)

TPPro is a 100% foreign-owned and managed firm that provides the combined services of an advertising agency and corporate communications specialist. They can produce first-rate Japanese language materials of any kind. TPPro has a long list of well-known clients and can also help smaller firms devise promotional strategies tailored to their needs and budgets.

Phone (03) 3414-0311   E-mail marketj@tppro.com
Fax   (03) 3414-0351

Head-hunters

East West
E-mail eastwest@ewc.co.jp   Home page www.ewc.co.jp

Mail-order

JieStar
E-mail Jiestar@ro.bekkoame.or.jp

Market research

JMRN (Japan Marketing Resource Network)
Phone (03) 5721-5990   E-mail jmrn@gol.com
Fax   (03) 5721-5993

Teikoku Databank, Ltd
2-5-20 Minami Aoyama, Minato-ku, Tokyo 107
Phone (03) 3404-4311   Home page www.teikoku.com
Fax   (03) 3404-4339   E-mail   teikoku@tdb.co.jp

For more information, see TDB's home page. You can communicate with TDB and order their services, if in English, in Japan, best by fax or e-mail. Or communicate with their sales office in New York:

Teikoku Databank America, Inc.
1120 Avenue of the Americas, 4th Floor, New York, NY 10036
Phone 212-626-6871   Fax 212-626-6872

Multimedia

CyberSpace Japan Inc.
E-mail csj@csj.co.jp   Home page www.cjs.co.jp

LINC Media
Phone (03) 3499-2399   Home page www.lincmedia.co.jp
Fax   (03) 3499-2199

Computing Japan
Home page www.cjmag.co.jp

General Directory

The Japan Times
Classifieds e-mail jtsales@japantimes.co.jp
Home page   www.japantimes.co.jp

The Nikkei Weekly
Home page www.nikkei.co.jp/enews/TNW/page/index.html

Tokyo Stock Exchange
Home page www.tse.or.jp/eindex.html

Ian Melville
E-mail MktEntry@venture.co.jp

References

Abegglen, J. (1994) *Sea Change*, Free Press, New York.
Abegglen, J. and Stalk, G. (1985) *Kaisha*, Tuttle (1987 edition), Tokyo.
Alletzhauser, A. (1990) *The House of Nomura*, Bloomsbury, London.
Beasley, W.G. (1990) *The Rise of Modern Japan*, Tuttle, Tokyo.
Benedict, R. (1946) *The Chrysanthemum and the Sword*, Tuttle (1954 edition), Tokyo.
Bisson, T.A. (1954) *Zaibatsu Dissolution*, Greenwood Press, Connecticut.
Clark, R. (1979) *The Japanese Company*, Tuttle (1987 edition), Tokyo.
Czinkota, M.R. and Kotabe, M. (eds) (1993) *The Japanese Distribution System*, Probus, Chicago.
Czinkota, M.R. and Woronoff, J. (1991) *Unlocking Japan's Markets*, Tuttle (1993 edition), Tokyo.
Dodwell (1990) *Direct Marketing in Japan*, Dodwell, Japan.
Doi, Takeo (1971) *The Anatomy of Dependence*, Kōdansha (translation 1973; 1981 edition), Tokyo.
Durlabhji, S. and Marks, N. (1993) *Japanese Business, Cultural Perspectives*, Suny, USA.
Eastwood, J. (1989) *100 percent Japanese*, The Japan Times, Japan.
Fields, G. (1988) *The Japanese Market Culture*, The Japan Times, Japan.
Graham, John L. and Sano, Y. (1989) *Smart Bargaining*, Harper Business (revised edition), USA.
Halloran, R. (1969) *Japan, Images and Realities*, Tuttle (1970 edition), Tokyo.
Hamada, T. (1991) *American Enterprises in Japan*, State University of New York Press, Albany.
Hasegawa, K. (1986) *Japanese Style Management*, Kōdansha International, New York.
Hsu, R. (1994) *The MIT Encyclopedia of the Japanese Economy*, The MIT Press, Massachusetts.
Huddleston, J. (1990) *Gaijin Kaisha*, Tuttle (1991 edition), Tokyo.
Iacocca, L. (1984) *Iacocca, An Autobiography*, Bantam Books, USA.
Imai, M. (1986) *Kaizen*, McGraw-Hill (1991 edition), Singapore.
Ishihara, S. (1991) *The Japan That Can Say No*, Simon & Schuster, New York.
Ishizumi, K. (1988) *Acquiring Japanese Companies*, The Japan Times, Tokyo.
Itō, T. (1992) *The Japanese Economy*, The MIT Press, Massachusetts.
Johansson, J. and Nonaka, I. (1996) *Relentless*, Harper Business, New York.
Johnson, Chalmers (1982) *MITI and the Japanese Miracle*, Tuttle (1986 edition), Tokyo.
Kang, T.W. (1990) *Gaishi*, Tuttle (1991 edition), Tokyo.
Kanō, Y., Noguchi, Y., Saitō, S. and Shimada, H. (1993) *The Japanese Economy in the 1990s, Problems and Prognoses*, Foreign Press Centre, Tokyo.
Kishi, N. and Russell, D. (1996) *Successful Gaijin in Japan*, NTC Business Books, Illinois.
Komiya, R. (1990) *The Japanese Economy*, University of Tokyo Press, Tokyo.

Komori, K. (1995) *Direct Marketing in Japan*, The Japan Times, Tokyo.

Koren, L. (1990) *Success Stories*, The Japan Times, Tokyo.

Kraar, L. and Takikawa, S. (1994) *Japanese Maverick*, John Wiley and Sons, New York.

Krugman, P. (ed) (1991) *Trade With Japan*, University of Chicago Press, Chicago.

Look Japan (1987) *Taking on Japan*, Look Japan Ltd, Singapore.

March, R. (1990) *The Honourable Customer*, Longman, Australia.

March, R. (1988) *The Japanese Negotiator*, Kōdansha, Japan.

Melville, I. (1997) Japanese Education, Creativity and Work, *Sophia Economic Review*, Vol. 43, No. 1, December.

Miyamoto, M. (1994) *Straightjacket Society*, Juliet Winters Carpenter and Kōdansha, Japan.

Miyashita, K. and Russell, D. (1994) *Keiretsu*, McGraw-Hill, USA.

Moeran, B. (1996) *A Japanese Advertising Agency*, University of Hawaii Press, Honolulu.

Morikawa, H. (1992) *Zaibatsu*, University of Tokyo Press, Japan.

Morita, Akio (1986) *Made in Japan*, Fontana (1988 edition), London.

Murphy, R.T. (1996) *The Weight of the Yen*, W.W. Norton & Co., New York.

Nakamura, T. (1981) *The Postwar Japanese Economy*, University of Tokyo Press, Tokyo.

Nakamura, T. (1994) *Lectures on Modern Japanese Economic History*, LTCB International Library Foundation, Tokyo.

Nakane, C. (1970) *Japanese Society*, Tuttle (1984 edition), Tokyo.

Nakane, C. and Ōishi, S. (1990) *Tokugawa Japan*, University of Tokyo Press, Tokyo.

Nonaka, I. and Takeuchi, H. (1995) *The Knowledge-Creating Company*, Oxford University Press, Oxford.

Odaka, K. (1984) *Japanese Management: A Forward Looking Analysis*, Asian Productivity Organization (translated 1986), Tokyo.

Ohmae, Kenichi (1991) *The Borderless World*, Fontana, London.

Ohsono, T. (1995) *Charting Japanese Industry*, Cassell, London.

Okimoto, D. (1989) *Between MITI and the Market*, Stanford University Press, California.

Ozaki, R. (1991) *Human Capitalism*, Kōdansha, USA.

Ozawa, I. (1994) *Blueprint for a Modern Japan*, Kōdansha (1995 edition), Japan.

Prestowitz, Clyde V. (1989) *Trading Places*, Basic Books (revised edition), USA.

Rafferty, K. (1995) *Inside Japan's Power Houses*, Weidenfeld & Nicolson, London.

Roberts, John G. (1973) *Mitsui*, Weatherbill (1989 edition), Tokyo.

Sakiya, T. (1982) *Honda Motor*, Kōdansha (1987 edition), Tokyo.

Schonberger, R.J. (1982) *Japanese Manufacturing Techniques*, Free Press, New York.

Suzuki, T. (1973) *Words in Context*, Kōdansha (translation 1978; 1984 edition), Tokyo.

Tamaki, N. (1995) *Japanese Banking*, Cambridge University Press, Cambridge, UK.

Thian, Helene (1988) *Setting Up and Operating a Business in Japan*, Tuttle, Tokyo.

Tsurumi, Y. (1978) *Japanese Business*, Praeger, USA.

Uchino, T. (1978) *Japan's Postwar Economy*, Kōdansha (translation 1983), Japan.

Van Wolferen, K. (1993) *The Enigma of Japanese Power*, Tuttle (revised edition), Tokyo.

Viner, A. (1987) *Inside Japan's Financial Markets*, The Japan Times, Japan.

Whittaker, D.H. (1997) *Small Firms in the Japanese Economy*, Cambridge University Press, Cambridge.

Wood, Christopher (1992) *The Bubble Economy*, Tuttle (1993 edition), Tokyo.

Yoshihara, K. (1982) *Sōgō Shōsha*, Oxford University Press, Tokyo.

Yoshino, M.Y. and Lifson, T.B. (1986) *The Invisible Link*, The MIT Press, Cambridge, Massachusetts.

Young, A. (1979) *The Sōgō Shōsha*, Tuttle (1982 edition), Tokyo.

Ziemba, W. and Schwartz, S. (1992) *Invest Japan*, Probus Publishing Co., USA.

Zimmerman, M. (1985) *How to do Business with the Japanese*, Tuttle (1987 edition), Tokyo.

Regular publications

Nippon, JETRO Business Facts & Figures, JETRO
Japan Almanac, Asahi Shimbun Publishing Company, Japan
Japan Economic Data Book, JETRO (1991)
Japan Statistical Yearbook
Statistical Handbook of Japan, Management and Coordination Agency
Japan Marketing and Advertising Yearbook, Dentsū
Japan Company Handbook, Tōyō Keizai

Special publications

Attributes of Success of American Companies in Japan
    Japan–US Business Council and US–Japan Business Council, published by American Chamber of Commerce in Japan (1997)
Japan in Revolution, An Assessment of Investment Performance by Foreign Firms in Japan
    Joint study by the American Chamber of Commerce in Japan, the Council of the European Business Community, and A.T. Kearney, Inc. (1995)
Survey Report on Foreign Affiliated Companies LBS, Tokyo (1997)
    LBS Co. Ltd, IBM Japan HQ Building, 3-2-12 Roppongi, Minato-ku, Tokyo 106

Magazines and journals

Gaishi, published by LBS Co. Ltd (IBM Japan Headquarters Building, Tokyo)
FTC/Japan Views, published by the Fair Trade Commission of Japan
Industrial Groupings in Japan, published by Dodwell
The Journal, published by the American Chamber of Commerce in Japan
Look Japan, published by Look Japan Ltd
Nippon, BBC TV series (1990)
Tokyo Business Today, published until 1995 by Tōyō Keizai
Tradescope, published by MITI

Index